Anonymus

Military Commission to Europe in 1855 and 1856.

Report of Major Alfred Mordecai, of the Ordnance Department

Anonymus

Military Commission to Europe in 1855 and 1856.
Report of Major Alfred Mordecai, of the Ordnance Department

ISBN/EAN: 9783743335479

Manufactured in Europe, USA, Canada, Australia, Japa

Cover: Foto ©ninafisch / pixelio.de

Manufactured and distributed by brebook publishing software
(www.brebook.com)

Anonymus

Military Commission to Europe in 1855 and 1856.

36TH CONGRESS, } HOUSE OF REPRESENTATIVES. { Ex. Doc.
2d Session.

MILITARY COMMISSION TO EUROPE,

IN

1855 AND 1856.

REPORT OF MAJOR ALFRED MORDECAI,

OF THE

ORDNANCE DEPARTMENT.

WASHINGTON:
GEORGE W. BOWMAN, PRINTER.
1861.

IN THE HOUSE OF REPRESENTATIVES OF THE UNITED STATES,
March 2, 1861.

Resolved, That there be printed, for the use of the members of the House of Representatives, twenty thousand copies of each of the Reports of Major A. Mordecai, of Ordnance, and Major Richard Delafield, of the Corps of Engineers, two of the commissioners appointed by the War Department in 1855 to visit Europe for the purpose of obtaining information with regard to the military service in general, and especially the practical working of the changes which have been introduced of late years into the military systems of the principal nations of Europe.

JOHN W. FORNEY,
Clerk.

INDEX.

	Page.
Letter to the Secretary of War	1
List of Books, Drawings, &c., obtained by the Commission—	
English books	5
French books	5
German books—Prussia	8
Austria	9
Russian books	10
Maps	10
Engravings and drawings	11
Specimens of arms and equipments	11
PART I. MILITARY ORGANIZATION—	
Russia	13
Bureaus of War Department	13
The active army	15
The reserve	17
Garrison troops	18
Irregular troops	18
The militia	19
Recruiting	20
Appointment and promotion of officers	21
Retirement from service	22
Prussia	23
Organization of the army	23
Government of the army	24
The Ministry of War	24
The General War Department	24
The Department of Military Administration	24
Military grades	25
The Infantry	26
The Cavalry	27
The Artillery	28
Battery equipped for the field	29
Engineers	29
General Staff	30
The train	31
Special corps	31
Establishments for military instruction	31
Formation of army corps	31
Force of the war establishment	32
Recruiting	33
Appointment and promotion of officers	33
Discharge and retirement from service	35
Department of Supplies and Disbursements	36
Courts-martial	37
Courts of honor	39
Rewards	41

INDEX.

	Page
MILITARY ORGANIZATION—(Continued.)	
Austria	41
Bureaus of War Department	42
Military grades	43
Appointment of officers	44
Military education	44
France	46
Strength of the army	46
Divisions of the War Ministry	46
Military grades	47
Special Staffs	48
Artillery establishments	48
Appointment and promotion of officers	49
Military schools	49
Recruiting	50
Retirement from service	50
Pensions	50
Furloughs	51
Military districts	52
Administration of justice	52
Courts-martial	52
Courts of appeal	53
Courts of inquiry	53
General remarks	54
Great Britain	55
Strength of the army	55
Cavalry	55
Infantry	55
Artillery	56
Militia force	56
Recruiting	56
PART II. ORDNANCE AT THE SIEGE OF SEBASTOPOL	61
French mortars	62
Navy guns	62
British batteries	62
French reserve depot of ordnance	63
Official return of guns burst in the English trenches before Sebastopol	65
Official return of mortars burst and rendered unserviceable at the bombardment of Sweaborg	65, 67
PART III. REPORT OF THE FRENCH MINISTER OF WAR TO THE EMPEROR ON THE ADMINISTRATIVE ARRANGEMENTS FOR THE WAR IN THE EAST	69
First part—Personnel—Movement of troops—	
Number sent out	69
Losses sustained by the army	69
Number returned	70
Recapitulation	70
Second Part—Matériel—Ordnance and ordnance stores—	
Siege park	74
Field artillery	75
Field park	76
Ammunition	76
Engineer materials	78
Subsistence, fuel, and forage	80
Clothing and equipment	81
Camp equipage	82
Harness	82
Supplies for hospital service	83
Military trains	85
Civil rights, justice, &c	86
Service of the military chest and mails	86
Telegraphic service	87
Printing	87
Third Part—Transportation by sea—	
Number of vessels employed	87
Recapitulation—men, horses, and stores, sent out and returned	89

	Page
PART IV. ARSENALS OF CONSTRUCTION—	
Russia	89
Prussia	91
Austria	94
Belgium	98
France	101
England	102
PART V. RIFLED CANNON	109
Practice with Cavalli's breech-loading rifled cannon	110
The Lancaster gun	110
The Whitworth gun	111
Experiments with Whitworth's gun	113
Krupp's cast-steel gun	114
PART VI. CANNON OF LARGE CALIBER	117
Great gun of the Kremlin	117
Belgian "Monster Mortar"	117
Horsfall & Co.'s 13-inch wrought-iron gun	118
PART VII. GARRISON ARTILLERY—	
Russia	121
Wrought-iron gun carriages	122
Pointing guns in open batteries	123
Prussia	124
Garrison carriages	124
Experiments on pressure of fired gunpowder	124
Electro-magnetic apparatus for measuring the velocity of projectiles	125
Austria	126
France	126
Cast-iron gun carriages	127
PART VIII. FIELD ARTILLERY	129
Russia	129
Prussia	131
Austria	132
Artillery Riding School	134
Regimental Artillery School	134
Central Direction of Artillery	135
France	135
Personnel of French artillery	136
England	138
Weekly return of reserve ammunition	139
PART IX. NEW SYSTEMS OF FIELD ARTILLERY	141
The Napoleon gun-howitzer	141
Description of 12-pounder howitzer guns	142
Austrian field carriages	143
Gun cotton in the Austrian service	143
Simplification of the Prussian system	143
Saxony light 12-pounder gun	143
Russian new light 12-pounder gun	144
Russian plate-iron gun carriage	144
Great Britain	145
PART X. SHRAPNELL SHELLS OR SPHERICAL CASE SHOT	147
England	147
Captain Boxer's new diaphragm shrapnel shell	147
Fuze for mortar shells	148
France	149
Spherical case shot for the Napoleon gun	149
Belgium	149
Colonel Bormann's fuze for spherical case	149
Prussia	150
Russia	150
Austria	150
Colonel Bowman's spherical case for mortars	151
PART XI. FUZES FOR COMMON SHELLS	153
England	153
France	153

INDEX

	Page
FUZES FOR COMMON SHELLS—(Continued.)	
Captain Splingard's new fuze	154
PART XII. SMALL ARMS—	
Russia	157
Russian musket	157
Swords and sabers	158
Prussia	158
New percussion musket	158
Wall piece (defensions gewehr)	159
Needle gun (zundnadel gewehr)	159
The rifle	160
Cavalry fire-arms	160
Side arms	160
Austria	160
New arms for infantry and riflemen	161
Rifle-pistol	161
Cavalry saber	162
Artillery saber	162
France	162
Carabine à tige	162
Breech-loading rifle-carbine for the Cent Gardes	163
Great Britain	164
Brunswick rifle	164
Enfield musket	164
Deane & Adams's revolver	165, 197
Miscellaneous	165
Report of trial of Swiss rifle	166
Tabular statement of shots	168
Rifled small arms in use in the armies of different countries	170, 171
General remarks on rifled small arms	172
Patch around the ball	172
Loading at the breech	172
Expanding the ball by the rammer	173
Expanding the ball by powder and conical plug	173
Caliber of small arms	174
Weight of infantry soldier's fire-arms	175
English plan of measuring distances	175
TRANSLATION OF "SCHÖN ON RIFLED INFANTRY ARMS"	177
Preface	179
Explanation of Plates	181
Contents	183
A glance at the chief defects of the smooth and grooved arms	185
Use of grooves in Germany	186
On the charge	187
Number and depths of grooves	188
The system of Delvigne	189
The system of Pontcharra	189
The Delvigne-Pontcharra system	190
The Delvigne-Pontcharra system as altered by Baron Augustin	190
Consol or percussion primer lock	191
The oval rifle	191
English two-grooved rifle	192
The breech-loading system	192
The needle gun	193
Loading the needle gun	194
Advantages of the needle gun	195
The Norwegian breech-loading rifle	196
Lieutenant Von Frilitzen's breech-loading rifle	196
Table of deviations, in feet, of the Swedish breech-loading rifle	197
Do. do. Norwegian breech-loading rifle	197
Do. do. Swedish tige rifle	197
The revolver pistol	197
The system of Wild	198
The system of Thouvenin	198

	Page.
SCHÖN ON RIFLED INFANTRY ARMS—(Continued.)	
Advantages of Thouvenin's system	201
Defects of Thouvenin's system	202
Prussian tige rifle	203
Bavarian tige rifles	204
Saxony Jäger rifles	204
Hanoverian seven-grooved rifle-musket	205
Hanoverian eight-grooved rifle	206
Oldenburg tige rifle	206
Russian Jäger rifle	208
The system of Minié	208
Advantages of the Minié system	209
Disadvantages of the Minié system	210
Commission at Enfield, England	211
The Swiss system	216
The system of Wilkinson	218
The system of Lancaster	219
Conclusion	220
Table of the twist of rifle grooves	223
Table of elevations of various rifles for different distances	227
Experiments in Switzerland	229
Experiments made at the National Armory, in Belgium, to compare the fusil de munition, the carabine à tige, and the fusil Minié	232

REPORT.

WATERVLIET ARSENAL,
March 30, 1858.

SIR: I have the honor to present herewith a report of notes and observations on certain military subjects, made during my visit to Europe, as a member of a military commission sent out in April, 1855, under the orders of the Hon. Jefferson Davis, your immediate predecessor in the War Department.

The special reports of the commission, from time to time, show the course pursued in our journey, and the causes which prevented us from proceeding, as we wished to do, directly to the seat of war in the East. Those reports also show the courteous reception which we met with in most of the countries that we visited, and the facilities extended to us for accomplishing the object of our mission.

I regret that untoward circumstances prevented us from reaching the Crimea during the progress of active operations at Sebastopol, and that our observations of the conduct of that remarkable siege were limited to the results which were apparent a month after the evacuation of the place by the Russians. My own opportunities of information were further diminished by a serious illness, which kept me confined to camp during the latter part of our stay in the Crimea.

I fear that my report will be found very imperfect, but I am unwilling to defer the presentation of it any longer for the purpose of making it more full. With regard to the delay which has already occurred in this respect, I think it but just to say that, during the greater part of the time which has elapsed since our return from Europe, I have been much occupied with other duties—having been at first assigned to special duty in the War Office, and then to the command of this, the principal arsenal of construction.

The small portions of this report which embrace some of the topics of Captain McClellan's report, were prepared before the publication of the latter.

Respectfully submitted by your obedient servant,

A. MORDECAI,
Major of Ordnance.

Hon. JOHN B. FLOYD,
Secretary of War.

1 M

CONTENTS.

List of Books, Drawings, &c., obtained by the Commission in Europe.

Part I.—Military Organization:
    Russia.   Austria.
    Prussia.   France.
                            Great Britain.

Part II.—Ordnance at the Siege of Sebastopol.

Part III.—Report of the French Minister of War on the operations in the East.

Part IV.—Arsenals of Construction and Manufacturing Establishments:
    Russia.   Belgium.
    Prussia.   France.
    Austria.   England.

Part V.—Rifle Cannon.

Part VI.—Cannon of large caliber.

Part VII.—Garrison Artillery:
    Russia.   Austria.
    Prussia.   France.

Part VIII.—Field Artillery:
    Russia.   Austria.
    Prussia.   France.
                            England.

Part IX.—New Systems of Field Artillery:
    France.   Saxony.
    Austria.   Russia.
    Prussia.   United States.

Part X.—Spherical Case Shot and Fuzes:
    England.   Prussia.
    France.   Russia.
    Belgium.   Austria.

Part XI.—Fuzes for common Shells.

Part XII.—Small Arms:
    Russia.   France.
    Prussia.   England.
    Austria.   Miscellaneous.
                            General remarks.

Translation of "Schön on Rifle Arms."

LIST OF BOOKS, DRAWINGS, ETC.

OBTAINED BY THE COMMISSION IN EUROPE.

English Books.

Douglass on Naval Gunnery	1 volume.
Edinburgh Review, April, 1855	1
Queen's Regulations for the Army, and Addenda	2 volumes.
Fergusson's Fortification	1 vol. and atlas.
Cavalry Outpost Duty	1 volume.
Cavalry Regulations	1
Nolan's History and Tactics of Cavalry	1
Nolan's Cavalry Remount Horses	1
Quartermaster General's Instructions	1
Thackeray's Manual of Rifle Firing	1
Instructions for Musketry Firing	1
Platoon Exercise for Musket and Rifle	1
Pendergrast's Law for Officers of the Army	1
Memoir on Crimean Expedition, (translated from French)	1
The Malakoff, Inkerman, and Kilburn	1
Army List, 1856	1
Navy List, 1856	1
Reports of Sebastopol Committee of House of Commons	6 parts.
Report on the Army in the Crimea, and Appendix	2
Report on the Capitulation of Kars	1 volume.
Commissary General Filder's Letter	1
Letters of Lords Cardigan and Lucan	1
Report on Sandhurst Military School	1
Report of Small Arms Committee, and Index	2 parts.
Report of Commission on Manufacture of Ordnance on the Continent of Europe—Procured by Hon. Mr. Morrell	1 volume.
Report of Commission on Machinery in the United States—Presented by Hon. Mr. Morrell	1
Russell's Letters from the Crimea	1
Napoleon's New System of Field Artillery	1
Shirley on Transport of Cavalry	1
Cavalry Sword Exercise	1
General Orders of the Army in the East	2
Straith's Fortification	2 vol. and atlas
Specification of a Fort on the Isle of Wight	
Report on Barrack Accommodation	1 volume.
Report on the Paris Exposition of Industry	1
Duckett's Military Dictionary, (German and English)	1
Pamphlet on Ambulances	1
Guide Book of Germany	1
Guide Book of Russia	1
Guide Book of Greece and Turkey	1
Guide Book of Northern Italy	1
Guide Book of France	1

French Books.

Ordonnance de Cavalerie	3 volumes.
Service Intérieur des Troupes à Cheval	1 volume.

C   LIST OF BOOKS, DRAWINGS, ETC.

Siège de Bomarsund	1 volume
Louis Napoléon—Manuel d'Artillerie	1
Vauchelle—Cours d'Administration	3 volumes.
Ordonnance sur le Service en Campagne	1 volume.
Instruction sur le tir du Fusil de la Garde Impériale	1
Bégin—Etudes sur le Service de Santé	1
Maillot et Puel—Aide-Mémoire Medico-legal de l'Officier de Santé	1
Des Plaies d'Armes à Feu	1
Boudin—Opérations Medicales de Recrutement	1
Saurel—Chirurgie Navale	1
Roubaud—Sur les Hôpitaux	1
Papillon—De la Ventilation Appliquée à l'Hygiène Militaire	1
Boudin—Etudes sur le Chauffage, &c., des Édifices Publics	1
Annuaire Militaire, 1855	1
Système d'Ambulances	1
Boudin—Ventilation des Hôpitaux	1
Verdu—Mines de Guerre	1
Projet de tir des Carabines d'Infanterie	1
Instruction sur le tir des Chasseurs à Pied	1
Ordonnance sur le Service des Places	1
Ordonnance sur le Service Intérieur	1
Essais sur la Fortification Moderne	1 vol. and atlas.
Instruction sur le tir d'Artillerie	1 volume.
Instructions et Circulaires sur le Service des Subsistances	1
Mangin, Mémoire sur la Fortification Polygonale	1
Rapport sur l'École Polytechnique	1
Journal Militaire Officiel—Années 1851, 1852, 1853, 1854, 1855	9 volumes.
Maurice de Sellon—Etudes sur les Forteresses de Mayence et Ulm	1 vol. and atlas.
Défense Nationale de l'Angleterre	1 volume.
Ponts de Chevalets	1
Notice sur les Fusées	1
Examen du Système de Cavalli	1 vol. and atlas.
Mémoire sur Rastadt	1 vol. and atlas.
Mémorial de l'Engénieur	
Mémorial de l'Officier du Génie—Tomes 12, 13, 14, 15, 16, et Table de Matières	6 volumes.
Baucher—Oeuvres Completes, Equitation, &c	1 volume.
Curmleu—Science Hippique	1
D'Aldéguier—Tactique de Cavalerie	1
Lamoricière—Rapport sur les Haras	1
Carrière—Force Militaire de l'Autriche	1
Guillot—Legislation et Administration Militaires	1
Paixhans—Constitution Militaire de la France	1
Duparcq—Etudes sur la Prusse	1
Ronet Villaumez—Batailles de Terre and de Mer	1
Robert—Sièges Remarquables	1
Duparcq—Armées des Puissances engagées dans la question de l'Orient	1
Laisné—Aide-Mémoire du Génie	1
Mémorial d'Artillerie—Tomes 5, 6, 7, et atlas	4 volumes.
Louis Napoléon—Etudes sur l'Artillerie	2
Programme de l'Enseignement pour l'École Polytechnique	1 volume.
Emy—Affuts de Mortiers, &c.—Lithographic	1
Bouches à Feu en bronze, do	1
Règlement sur les Manœuvres d'Artillerie, 1847	1
Mémorial de l'Officier d'Infanterie et de Cavalerie	1
Bibliothèque du Sous Officier	1
De Rouvre—Aide-Mémoire d'Etat Major	1
Haillot—Equipages de Ponts	1 vol. and atlas.
Birago do	1 volume.
Cavalli do	1
Andréossy—Opérations des Pontonniers Français	1
Manuel Réglementaire de l'École d'Etat Major	1
D'Arenberg—Défense des Places	1
Zacconi—Fortification	1 vol. and atlas.

LIST OF BOOKS, DRAWINGS, ETC.

Grivet—La Marine Dans l'Attaque des Places	1 volume.
Naves—Application de l'Électricité à la Mesure de la Vitesse des Projectiles	1
Expériences de Bapaume—Mines, &c.	1
Zoller—Eprouvette Portative	1 volume.
Martin de Brettes—Projet de Chronographe	1
Lay Fay—Aide-Mémoire de l'Artillerie Navale	1
Mangeot—Traité de Fusil de Chasse	1
Chertier—Feux d'Artifices	1
Documents Relatifs au Coton Détonant	1
Remond—Armes à Feu Portatives	1
Anquetil—Pistolets Tournans	1
Cours Abrégé d'Artifices	1 vol. and misc.
Bormann—Sur les Shrapnels	1 volume.
Delobel—Revue de Technologie Militaire	2 volumes.
Decker—Expériences sur les Shrapnels	1 volume.
De Masses—Mémoire sur les Cuivres, &c.	1
Expériences d'Artillerie, faites à L'Orient	1
Marion—Recueil des Bouches à feu les plus remarquables—125 planches et texte.	
Bismark—Tactique de Cavalerie	1
Emploi de la Cavalerie à la Guerre	1
Saint Ange—Cours d'Hippologie	2 volumes.
Cardini—Dictionnaire d'Hippiatrique	2
Musset—Commentaires sur l'Equitation	1 volume
Guérin—Ecole de Cavalerie au Manège	1
A'Aure—Cours d'Equitation Militaire	1
Livret du Soldat d'Infanterie, de Chasseurs à Pied, de Cavalerie, d'Artillerie	4 volumes.
D'Arboval—Dictionnaire de Médecine et de Chirurgie Vétérinaires	6 vols. and atlas
Instruction en Natation	1 volume.
Escrime à la Baionnette	1
Pavé—Cours à Vincennes	1
Haxthausen—Etudes sur la Russie, (translated from the German)	3 volumes
Force Militaire de la Russie, (translated from the German)	1 volume.
Paskiewitch—Prise de Varsovie	1
Telinkoffski—Fortification permanente, (translated from the Russian)	1 vol. and atlas
Berg—Dessin Géometrique	2 volumes
Zastrow—Mémoire sur la Fortification, traduit par De Sellon	1 volume.
Deuxième Mémoire sur l'Expédition en Crimée	1
Martin des Brettes—Etudes sur les Appareils Electro-Magnétiques	1
Artifices Eclairantes	
Fenton—La Russie en Asie Mineure	1 vol. and atlas.
Manuel du Commis au Vivres	1 volume.
Gillon—Cours sur les Armes Portatives	1
Instruction sur le Matériel de l'Artillerie Belge	1
Reglement sur les Exercices de l'Artillerie Belge	1
Thierry—Mémoire sur le Chevalet Belge	1
Dessins du Matériel de l'Artillerie Belge—Presented by the Minister of War.	
Memoria Sobre la Fabrica de Armas, Liége, (in Spanish)	1
Memorial de Ingenieros, (Spanish—from 1846 to 1855.)	
Le Blanc—Atlas Vétérinaire	1
Boulay et Raynal—Dictionnaire Vétérinaire	1
Cours de Maréchalerie	1
Dilwart—Médecine Vétérinaire	1
Jacquinot de Presle—Cours d'Art Militaire	1
Block—Dictionnaire de l'Administration	10 parts.
Mémoires sur l'Hygiéne Vétérinaire	6 volumes.
Emy—Fabrication des Armes Portatives, lithog.	1 volume.
Préaux—Manuel de l'Artificier	1
Rellencourtre—Tir à Ricochet, lithog.	1
Artifices de Guerre de la Marine, lithog.	2 volumes.
Poncelet—Cours de Mécanique Appliquée, lithog.	1 volume.
Jourjon—Cours d'Art Militaire, (fortification,) lithog.	1
Ardant—Cours de Constructions, lithog.	1
Calmes—Sur les Chaux et Mortiers, lithog.	1

Cours de l'École Polytechnique, lithog., viz:
- Cours de Physique.. 2 volumes.
- Sommaire des Cours de Physique................................ 1 volume.
- Cours d'Astronomie et de Géodésie............................. 1
- Cours d'Art Militaire.. 1
- Cours de Mécanique et de Machines........................... 1
- Cours de Topographie... 1

Mémoire sur le Tir Convergent des Vaisseaux................... 1
Chevét—Système de Musique Vocale................................ 1
Nouvelles Annales de Constructions, 1855, 1856............... 24 numbers.
Cours de Gymnastique... 1 vol. and atlas.
Cours de Commandes.. 1 volume.

German Books.

PRUSSIA.

Kameke—Description and Drawings of the Prussian Artillery............ Text and plates.
　　Description and Drawings of the New Field Artillery of 1842........ 1 vol. and plates.
Hoffman—Course of Instruction for Officers, on Ordnance and Small Arms...... 1 volume.
Djobeck—Engineers' Aide-Mémoire.................................... 1
San Roberto—On Manufacture of Gunpowder, (translated from the Italian)...... 1
Wittich's Fortification.. 1
Schwinck's Fortification... 1
Prussian Army List... 1
Prussian articles of War, (in French).................................. 1
Regulations for the Government of Hospitals................... 1
Handbook for Hospital Assistants...................................... 1
Schilfer—Circulars of the Surgeon General...................... 2 volumes.
Bernhard—Medical Service in the Field........................... 1 volume.
Grafe—Artillery Horse Equipments.................................... 1
Handbook of Cavalry Field Service.................................... 1
Mirus—Aide-Mémoire for Cavalry...................................... 1
Doschbeck—Field Pocket-book... 1
Regulations for the Clothing of the Troops....................... 1
Infantry Tactics... 1
Cavalry Tactics... 1
Fleck—Punishments by Courts-Martial............................. 1
Friccius—Military Laws from 1835 to 1850...................... 1
Busch and Hoffman—Pyrotechny...................................... 1
Seidler—On Equitation... 1
　　On Breaking Bad Horses... 1
Kameke—On Percussion Arms.. 1
Klake—Explanation of Articles of War............................. 1
　　On Military Punishment... 1
Herstatt—Cavalry Catechism... 1
Direction for Saddling and Packing................................... 1
Instruction for Light Cavalry... 1
Exercises with Pistol and Carbine..................................... 1
Squadron Drill.. 1
Cavalry Commands.. 1
Schimmel—Cavalry Percussion Arms............................... 1
　　Compendium for Officers in the Field......................... 1
Wittich—Instructions for the March................................. 1
　　Military Vade Mecum... 1
　　Tactics of Light Percussion Arms................................ 1
Schön—Infantry Rifle Arms.. 1
Hirtenfeld—Handbook of European Armies..................... 1
Official Regulations and Instructions on Schools, Repairs of Arms, &c...... 11 parts.
Oenshausen—Guide for Rider and Horse.......................... 1 volume.
Hertwig—Care of the Horse.. 1
　　Veterinary Surgery.. 1
　　Veterinary Medicine... 1
Büer—Studies in Masonry.. 1

LIST OF BOOKS, DRAWINGS, ETC.

Kalkstein—The Prussian Army, (organization, &c.)	1 volume.
Koltschmidt—German and English Dictionary	2 volumes.
Schweinitz—Expedition to Bomarsund	1 volume.
Bergman—Cavalry Tactics	1
Rustorf—Theory of Fire-arms	1
Rüstow—On Missile Arms	1
Fenex—Treatise on Engineering	1
Oelze—Manual of Artillery	1
Danmeyer—Officer's Aide-Mémoire	1
Regulation for Cavalry Maneuvers	1
Toubert—Tactics of Field Artillery	1
Zastrow—Permanent Fortification	1
Witzleben—Army and Infantry Service	1
De Vignau—Modifications Required in Field Artillery	1
Handbook for Engineer Service	1 vol. and atlas.
Förster—Light Infantry Service	1 volume.
Defenses of Dantzic, (translated from the Spanish)	1
Description of wrought-iron Gun Carriages—Presented by the Minister of War	1
Programme and Regulations of the Engineer and Artillery School at Berlin	1
Regulations of the Division School	1

AUSTRIA.

Regulations for Infantry Exercises	1 volume.
Regulations for Infantry Service	1
Regulations for Pioneer Drill	1
Regulations for Pioneer Instruction	1
Regulations for Instruction of Engineer Troops	1
Regulations for Exercises of Engineer Troops	1
Regulations for Rifle Drill	1
Regulations for Rifle Service	1
Regulations for Cavalry Exercises	1
Regulations for Cavalry Instructions	1
Smola—Handbook for Artillery Officers	1
Dwyer—Field Pocket Book	1
Wasserthal—Pioneer Service	1
Hausknecht—Guide for Marine Artillery	1
Hirago—On Military Bridges	1
Streffleur—On the Arms of the Austrian Army	1
Instructions for Infantry of the Line	1
Evolutions of Infantry of the Line	1
Evolutions of Cavalry	1
Hauser—Fortifications	1 vol. and atlas
Treatise on Military Mines	1
Káuegh—On Pressure of Earth	1 volume.
Wurmb—Military Constructions	1
Streffleur—Military Instructions, &c	5 parts.
Dub—Military Organization	1 volume.
Sindier—View of the New System of Military Schools	1
New Austrian Rifled Arms	1
Stromeyer—Military Medical Practice	2 volumes.
Isfordink—Military Medical Police	9 parts.
Aust—Military Hospitals	1 volume.
Kraus—Military Medical Service	1
Hofsinger—Cavalry Service	3 volumes.
Nedozy—On Equitation	2
Roll—On Internal Diseases of the Horse	1 volume.
Laws Relating to Military Punishments	1
Weiss—Course of Constructions	2 vols. and atlas.
Becker—Roads and Railways	1 vol. and atlas.
On Constructions	1
Ghega—Description and Views of the Semmering Railroad	1 volume.
On Railways	1 vol. and atlas.
Kühne—Military Surveying	1 volume.
Scheda—Topography	1 vol. and plates

Moering—Notes on the United States	1 volume.
Instructions for Triangulation—Present from the Geographical Institute	1
Triangulation of the Papal States, do do	1
Instructions for Drawing, do do	1
Schematismus, or Austrian Army List for 1855	1
Provisional Instruction for the Exercise of Garrison Guns	1
Organization of the Austrian Artillery	1
Sind—Veterinary Art	1
Hünersdorff—On Training Horses	1
Haumeister—On the Points of a Horse	1
Gunther—Homœopathic Treatment of Animals	1
Course of the Josephinum, or Army Medical College	1
Organization of Military Hospitals	1
Fortification for Infantry Officers	1 vol. and plates.

Russian Books.

Russian and English Dictionary	1 volume.
Russian and English Grammar	1
Engineer Journal—1827 to 1855	74 numbers.
Bezact's Course of Artillery	1 volume.
Resvoy's Notes on Artillery, with plates	3 parts.
Teliakofsky—Fortification	3
Cavalry Tactics	6
Infantry Tactics	6
Skirmish Drill	1 volume.
Instructions for Markers and Guides	1
Foot Artillery Drill	1
Engineer's and Sapper's Manual	1
Instructions for Sappers and Pioneers	1 vol. and atlas.
Civil Engineer's and Architect's Manual	1 volume.
Usoff—Military Topography	1
Constantinoff—Improvement of Small Arms	1
On Metal Fuzes	1
Laws for Field and Company Officers	1
Military Organization and Ordinances, Official—Presented by the War Department	11 parts.
Programmes of Military Schools, do do	35
Regulations of Military Asylum	1 volume.

Maps.

Jarvis's Map of the Crimea	10 sheets.
Map of Turkey and the Seat of War	6

2 Maps of the Environs of Sebastopol.
Carte de Sebastopol, &c.
Captain Spratt's Map of the Defences and Attack of Sebastopol.
Carte de la Crimée.
Maps of the Black Sea, with description, (in Italian.)
Carte du Departement de la Seine.
Plan of Cherburg.
Plan of Lyons.
Plan of Toulon.
Plan of Strasburg.
Plan of Belfort.
Plan of Mayence.
Plan of Coblentz.
Plan of Posen.
Plan of Venice.
Plan of Verona.
Plan of Mantua.
Plan of St. Petersburg.
Plan of Cronstadt.
Map of Russia, showing the distribution of troops.
Map of Russia, showing post routes, &c.
Map of Central Europe.

LIST OF BOOKS, DRAWINGS, ETC.

Engravings and Drawings.

Photographs of Sebastopol	31 sheets.
Plan of the Arsenal at Vienna	1 sheet.
Bird's-eye view of the Arsenal at Vienna	1
Bird's-eye view of the Arsenal at Verona	1
Photographs of the Arsenal at Verona, presented by Mr. Sicandsberg, architect	27 sheets.
Views of the Semmering Railroad	20
Surveys and drawings from the Geographical Institute, Vienna	17
Specimens of printing from nature, (Naturselbstdruck)—Presented by Mr. Auer, director of the Imperial printing office, Vienna	1 volume.
View of the Cadet School at Heinburg	1 sheet.
Bird's-eye view of the new Artillery and Engineer School at Wiener Neustadt	1
Austrian Ordnance and Artillery	15 sheets.
Austrian Ambulances	4
Drawings of Barracks at Vienna	7
Drawings made by pupils of Austrian Schools, viz:	
Engineer Academy	24
Artillery Academy	10
Cadet's School, Hainburg	10
Military Academy, Wiener Neustadt	43
Artillery School Company, Vienna	47
Flotilla School	7
Marine Academy	16
Plates of Prussian wrought-iron Gun Carriages, Ambulances, Provision Wagons, &c.	34
Saxon Artillery, Ambulances, &c.	14
Uniforms of Prussian Army	6
Cannon Foundery at Spandau	14
Barracks of Berlin	9
Drawings made by pupils of Prussian Military Schools, viz:	
Provincial Military Schools	15
Cadet Corps, Berlin	20
Artillery and Engineer School	18
Drawings of Russian wrought-iron Gun Carriage	4
Uniforms of Russian Army	10
Drawings of the Arsenal, the Military Hospital, and the Military Asylum, at St. Petersburg—Presented by the Minister of War.	
Drawings made by pupils at Russian Schools, viz:	
Engineer School, at St. Petersburg	11
First Corps of Cadets, at St. Petersburg	56
Mechanic's Institute, Moscow	121
Plates of Ordnance, &c., relative to the Cannon Foundery at Liége, (from Colonel Frédérix)	20
Plates of French Barracks and Stables.	
Plates of English Ambulances	2

Specimens of Arms and Equipments.

AUSTRIAN: 2 Rifled Muskets and appendages—Presented by the government.
    2 Rifles, do. do.
    3 Cavalry Sabres, do. do.
    1 box Small Arm Cartridges do. do.
    1 Officer's Undress Cap, do. do.

PRUSSIAN: 1 Cavalry Saddle and equipment.
    1 Infantry Knapsack and Canteen and Belt.
    1 Officer's Knapsack.
    1 pair Cartridge Boxes and Waist belt.
    1 pair Medicine Boxes on Waist Belt.

RUSSIAN: 1 Cavalry Belt.
    1 Cossack Cap.
    2 pair Pantaloons, 2 Uniform Coats, 2 Stocks, 2 Great Coats, specimens of clothing—Presented by the Minister of War.

BELGIAN: 1 Rifle Musket and appendages.
         1 Rifle, with Sword-bayonet.
         1 Adams & Deane's Revolver.
         1 Norwegian Breech-loading Rifle.
FRENCH: 1 Uniform Cap of Chasseurs à Pied.
        Specimens of AUZOUX's preparations of Anatomy of the Horse, viz:
           Set of models of the teeth, at various ages.
           Model of the leg and foot.
           Model of the hoof.
ENGLISH: Camp Equipage, purchased for use in the Crimea.

PART I.

MILITARY ORGANIZATION.

RUSSIA.

In this great military empire the Emperor is not only, as chief of the State, the fountain of military honor and authority, but he exercises the active functions of Commander-in-Chief of the army; much of his time and personal attention are given to the details of its administration and discipline, and on the occasions of reviews and field exercises he often takes command of the troops in person and conducts the maneuvers. In the exercise of these functions he is assisted by a very numerous personal staff, composed of the Minister of War, a chief of the staff, high officers of the different arms and departments of service, aides-de-camp-general, and orderly officers. These constitute a staff of more than a hundred and fifty officers, of whom, however, only a small number are employed at one time about the person of the Emperor. Many of these appointments of aides-de-camp-general are only marks of distinction conferred on meritorious officers.

War Department.—The department of the Minister of War includes:
1. The Bureau of the Minister.
2. The General Staff and Topographical Bureau.
3. The Bureau of Inspections.
4. The Bureau of Artillery.
5. The Engineer Bureau.
6. The Bureau of Clothing and Equipments.
7. The Bureau of Subsistence.
8. The Medical Bureau.
9. The Judge-Advocate's Bureau.
10. The Bureau of Military Colonies.

Besides these administrative bureaus, there are many permanent boards or committees of the War Department, such as:

The Council of War, charged with the consideration of questions of military legislation and administration.

The Committees of Boards of Instruction: Of Infantry; of Cavalry; of Improvements of Arms; of Medical Affairs; of Military Ecclesiastical Affairs; of Military Asylums; of Publications; of the Administration of Justice. These committees are composed of from ten to twenty-five officers, each under the presidency of a general, and they are charged with the consideration of questions submitted to them relative to their respective departments, and with examining new inventions and propositions for changes, and also with suggesting improvements in arms, equipments, &c., in the several branches of service.

The Minister of War is always an officer of the army, and the chiefs of bureaus are selected for those positions at the pleasure of the Emperor, according to their special capacities, without reference to rank. The bureau of the minister has charge of the general correspondence; the commissioning and registry of officers; the archives; military publications, &c. No general army register is printed, because owing to the great force of the army, the immense territory over which it is dispersed, and the peculiar system of promotion, no register would be sufficiently correct for use at the time of its publication. The whole number of officers in actual service is about 20,000.

The archives of the War Department are deposited in a large fire-proof room or building, which forms a part of the palace of the general staff, in St. Petersburg. They are placed on iron shelves, so classified and arranged that any document may be readily referred to. When this building becomes too much encumbered, the oldest documents are sent to a depot in Moscow, and after about sixty years the useless ones are burnt.

The bureau of the General Staff, at the head of which is an officer styled Quartermaster General, is divided into two principal sections, one of which is charged with what relates to the distribution and movements of troops; the other is the topographical section. The general staff corps is formed by selection of officers who have served not less than two years with their regiments in the active army, and are not above the grade of captain. They are employed at the general headquarters of the army, or on the staff of a separate army, or of an army corps under a general officer as chief of the staff. The promotions are made separately in this corps to the grade of colonel.

The Topographical Corps consists of more than 100 officers, including several generals, and 400 men formed into companies of topographers, who are engaged in the general survey of the empire, or attached to army corps. The topographical depot in St. Petersburg directs the geodetic and topographical operations in the field, and executes all those relating to the preparation, engraving, and printing of maps, and the collection and preservation of military topographical information relating to Russia or to foreign countries.

The mechanical operations, including the drawing of maps, are performed entirely by soldiers, and form a topographical school for young men, generally sons of soldiers, who are selected for this service. In this bureau is a large map of the Russian empire, with all the practicable roads and distances marked, which exhibits by inspection at all times the position of all the troops in the army according to the latest reports. Regiments and battalions of each army are designated by colored wafers, marked with appropriate numbers, which are stuck on the map in the proper position, and moved as occasion requires. A specimen of one of these maps has been furnished to the War Office. Regimental officers are also employed as aides-de-camp; orderly officers, (*officiers d'ordonnance;*) or on special service under the several chiefs of staff.

The Bureau of Inspections, directed by a general, is charged with the musters and returns of troops and the recruiting.

There are no officers specially employed as inspectors general. The troops are usually inspected and mustered by the immediate commanders of regiments and brigades, and occasionally by officers sent from headquarters for that purpose.

The Artillery Bureau, directed by the general officer, is charged with the administration of affairs relating to the supply of munitions of war, such as the arsenals for the construction and preservation of artillery material; cannon founderies; manufactories of small arms; laboratories for ammunition, &c., corresponding with our Ordnance Department. There is also a general staff of the artillery for the administration of the personnel, the chief of which may be also the head of the Artillery Bureau, as was the case in 1856; but the two directions are usually distinct.

An artillery board is charged with examining and trying new inventions and with making improvements in the material.

The Engineer Bureau conducts the business relating to the construction of fortifications and their dependencies, and the preparation of the bridge trains and other material used by the engineer troops. The chief of this bureau is a general officer, who acts under the immediate direction of the Minister of War, but is also subordinate to the inspector general of engineers, a post which, like that of grand master of the artillery, is often filled by a member of the imperial family. A board of engineers is charged with the examination of new plans of fortifications and of improvements in the engineer service.

The Clothing Bureau, or commissariat, is charged with the supply of clothing, camp equipage, and accouterments for the troops of all arms, including horse furniture for the cavalry. The Commissary General at the head of this bureau is a general officer of the army.

The Subsistence Bureau directs the supplies of provisions and forage for the troops. The chief is usually a general officer of the army.

The Medical Bureau, directed by a Surgeon General, has the same functions as in our own service.

The Judge-Advocate's Bureau is under the direction of a Judge-Advocate General, a civil officer, who is assisted in the administration of justice by a corps of judge-advocates educated for the purpose in the school of law, and attached to the staff of the several army corps, or separate bodies of troops. Sentences of courts-martial in cases of importance are subject to revision, not only at the headquarters of the corps, but also at the board of justice in the War Department, before being submitted for the decision of the Emperor.

The Bureau of Military Colonies is directed by a general officer, assisted by other military officers and by civil counselors. Besides the administration of the military colonies, this bureau has charge of the buildings and military domains belonging to the crown which are not included in the attributions of the artillery, engineer, or other special departments.

THE ACTIVE ARMY.

In the organization of the regular forces of Russia, the troops forming the active army, or principal army of operations, are distinct from those destined for garrison or other local service. The active army consists generally of:

1. The corps of Guards,
2. The corps of Grenadiers,
3. The six army corps called Infantry corps,
4. The two corps of Cavalry Reserve,
5. The corps, or army of the Caucasus.

The corps of guards, the corps of grenadiers, and each of the six infantry corps are organized like a separate army corps, composed of three divisions (or twelve regiments) of infantry, a division of cavalry, and one division of artillery, with battalions of sharpshooters or riflemen, engineer troops, (sappers and pontonniers,) and troops of the train. The cavalry corps consist of divisions of heavy or light cavalry and horse artillery. The corps of the Caucasus is a separate army composed of more than 100,000 men of all arms, with many peculiar bodies of troops destined especially for service on that frontier. The six infantry corps, each about 60,000 strong, forming the main body of the active army, have been generally stationed on the western frontier of the empire. The corps of guards, also about 60,000 men, is stationed habitually at or near St. Petersburg; and the corps of grenadiers, about 50,000, at Novogorod. The cavalry reserve corps, each about 16,000 strong, are quartered in the southern provinces of European Russia, where the nature of the country furnishes ready means for their support. Some general remarks will be made respecting the organization of the troops of the several arms composing the active or principal army.

1. INFANTRY.—The infantry includes the regiments of the guard, and of the grenadiers, infantry of the line, light infantry, or chasseurs, riflemen, and sharpshooters; besides a great number of independent battalions attached to the several army corps.

The Infantry of the Guard forms three divisions, making three brigades and twelve regiments; besides three regiments of chasseurs, a battalion of sharpshooters, and a battalion of sappers. Each regiment consists of three battalions, exclusive of one battalion of reserve, and one depot battalion; it is usually commanded by a general officer. A battalion consists of four companies, making about one thousand men, and is commanded by a colonel, and a lieutenant colonel; a company has a first captain, a second captain, a lieutenant, a second lieutenant, two ensigns, twenty non-commissioned officers, and about two hundred and fifty men, including drummers, &c.

The Infantry of the corps of Grenadiers forms also three divisions, or six brigades, and twelve regiments; with three regiments of riflemen, and battalions of chasseurs, sappers, &c. The organizations of regiments, battalions, and companies is the same as in the corps of the guard. Each of the *six infantry corps* consists also of three divisions, forming six brigades, and twelve regiments; one regiment in each brigade is of chasseurs, or light infantry. There is also a battalion of riflemen and one of the train. A regiment of the line or of chasseurs consists of four battalions, (exclusive of the reserve and depot battalions,) and is commanded by a colonel. Each battalion has a lieutenant colonel and major, and contains about one thousand men, in four companies; a company is officered by a captain, a lieutenant, and second lieutenant, and two ensigns, twenty non-commissioned officers, and about two hundred and forty men, including musicians. Besides the above and the army of the Caucasus, there are important corps of local infantry for service in Finland, the eastern part of European Russia, and in Siberia; altogether the infantry force of the active army, before the late war, was about five hundred battalions, or 500,000 men.

2. CAVALRY.—The regular cavalry consists of cuirassiers, lancers, hussars, dragoons, and Cossacks. *The cavalry of the guard* forms three divisions; one division of cuirassiers, in two brigades, of two regiments each; two divisions of light cavalry, in four brigades, or eight regiments; one battalion of the train.

In the two divisions of light cavalry are included several regiments or corps of irregular cavalry, Tartars, Cossacks, Circassians, &c., forming the *Emperor's guard of honor*. Thus the cavalry of the guard contains specimens of all the mounted troops of the empire, producing by the variety of their costumes, equipments, and maneuvers, a highly picturesque appearance in the field. A regiment of cavalry of the guard contains six squadrons, forming three divisions, and numbering about twelve hundred men; a squadron has eight officers and about two hundred men.

The Cavalry of the corps of Grenadiers and of the six Army Corps.—To each of these corps there is attached a division of light cavalry, consisting of one brigade or two regiments of lancers, and one brigade of hussars, with a battalion of the train.

Two corps of Cavalry of Reserve, each of three divisions, with one battalion of the train:

First corps: One division of three brigades of lancers, hussars, and dragoons, making six regiments; two divisions of cuirassiers in four brigades, or eight regiments.

Second corps. One division of lancers, two brigades, or four regiments; two divisions of dragoons, in four brigades, or eight regiments. A regiment of lancers and hussars consists of eight squadrons, and a regiment of dragoons contains ten squadrons, exclusive of one squadron of reserve and one depot squadron in each of these regiments. Total cavalry force about 80,000.

3. ARTILLERY.—The usual organization of the field artillery is in batteries of eight pieces. Both for horse and foot artillery there are heavy and light batteries; the former consisting of pieces which correspond very nearly to our 12-pounder guns and 24-pounder howitzers; the latter, of 6-pounder guns and 12-pounder howitzers. A heavy battery of foot artillery, consisting of four guns, and four howitzers, is manned by seven officers, of whom two are field officers, and about 200 men; a light battery of foot artillery has six guns and two howitzers, seven officers, and about 200 men. A heavy battery of horse artillery has four guns and four howitzers, (or

eight howitzers,) eight officers, and about 280 men; a light battery of horse artillery, four guns and four howitzers, seven officers, and 220 men. On the war establishment, each piece in a heavy battery of horse artillery is drawn by eight horses; in a light battery by six; in a heavy battery of foot artillery by six horses, and in a light battery by four. The Russian ammunition wagon is a large, two-wheeled, covered cart, drawn by three horses abreast; contains seventy-seven rounds of 6-pounder ammunition. The limber-chest of the gun carriage contains sixteen rounds of 6-pounder ammunition. In the war establishment, two ammunition wagons are attached to each piece of light artillery, and three to each piece of heavy artillery; in the *horse artillery*, the gunners are all mounted; in the foot batteries they march after the pieces; but for rapid movements and short distances, they occasionally mount the limbers and ammunition wagons. In general, four batteries of artillery form a *brigade;* four *brigades, a division*. In the corps of guards, the division of artillery consists of five brigades of three batteries each, making 120 pieces, viz: three brigades of foot artillery, each of two heavy and one light battery; one brigade of three light batteries of horse artillery; one reserve, consisting of a heavy and a light battery, of horse artillery; and a rocket battery. In the corps of grenadiers, and in the sixth infantry corps, the brigade of horse artillery contains two light batteries; of foot artillery, four batteries. In each of the cavalry corps the division of artillery consists of six batteries of horse artillery, two heavy and four light. A section of the train is attached to each battery, and a park of reserve to each division in the field. Total of artillery in the active army, (exclusive of the army of the Caucasus,) about 100 batteries of foot, and thirty batteries of horse artillery, making about 1,000 pieces and 30,000 men.

A battery of mountain artillery, attached to the army of the Caucasus, consisting of ten 12-pounder mountain howitzers and four 12-pounder light mortars, manned by about 300 men.

4. ENGINEER TROOPS.—Under this head are embraced the sappers, pioneers, and pontonniers, formed in companies, battalions, and divisions, which are commanded by officers of the corps of engineers. These troops form eight battalions of sappers, miners, and pontonniers, and eight bridge trains, of forty-two pontons each. A battalion consists of four companies, and a company contains four officers, and 250 non-commissioned officers and privates. There are also divisions of mounted pioneers, of four squadrons each, attached to the guard, and to the two cavalry or dragoon corps. Each squadron has a train of eight light pontons.

The Reserve.

The corps composing the principal army of operations consist of disciplined troops, prepared always for active service. The old soldiers and the recruits form the reserve corps. The term of service of a soldier of the line is twenty-five years; but in time of peace he is allowed to retire from the active army, on an indefinite furlough, after a continuous service of fifteen years. These furlough men constitute the troops of reserve with whom the recruits are associated, until they are prepared to join the active force. The reserve is divided into two classes: *the first reserve* consists of the men who have been retired less than five years; it comprises troops of all arms, each regiment of infantry furnishing a battalion; each regiment of cavalry, a squadron; and each brigade of artillery, a battery of reserve. There is also a proportion of engineer troops. *The second reserve* consists of the remainder of the men on furlough, up to the completion of their term of service. It is composed, like the first reserve, of depot battalions, squadrons, and batteries from the several regiments and brigades of infantry, cavalry, artillery, and engineers. The men composing the troops of reserve retire, without pay, to civil occupations, unless called again into active service. Those of the first reserve assemble about a month in each year, for exercise; those of the second reserve, only by special order. They are not formed into brigades or divisions, but are commanded by retired officers, under the general supervision of the garrison commanders in the principal towns. During the late war, the force of the troops of reserve was very much augmented; the regiments of infantry were duplicated, each regiment having (nominally at least) as many reserve as active battalions.

GARRISON TROOPS.

The garrison troops, corps of invalids, veterans, and gend'armes, perform the local military services of the interior of the Empire: such as the guards of fortresses and open cities, or of certain disturbed districts; services connected with the civil and military administrative departments, and with the arsenals and workshops of the artillery and engineers. They consist of infantry, artillery, and engineer troops: *the infantry* is formed into battalions, and distributed as guards in the principal cities and districts of the interior; in the imperial palaces, depots of military stores, &c. In those duties they are assisted by companies of veterans and invalids. *The artillery* is organized into companies of artillery for garrison service in fortresses, and the service of great parks; and companies of workmen and artificers, employed in the forts, arsenals, cannon founderies, manufactories of arms, powder mills, laboratories, &c. *The engineer troops* are formed into companies of workmen, united with companies of discipline, (men sentenced to hard labor,) for work on fortifications, service of the parks, &c. The gend'armes are distributed in the principal towns and military districts, as a military, mounted police.

IRREGULAR TROOPS.

The irregular troops of the Russian army are usually embraced in the general denomination of Cossacks, but they include also Tartars, Calmucks, Circassians, Georgians, and other tribes inhabiting the frontier countries of the Empire. The Cossacks, properly so called, furnish, however, much the greater part of this force, inhabiting the southern provinces of European Russia, whose fertile plains and mild climate are favorable to the maintenance of the horse, and whose inhabitants are habituated in early life to the management of that animal. The Cossack troops consist chiefly of cavalry and horse artillery, with a small proportion of infantry. These tribes enjoy an exemption from conscription and taxes, and from the operation of many government monopolies; in consideration of which privileges, they are bound to perform military service, furnishing their own arms and horses. They are organized into regiments, battalions, and batteries; the regiments and battalions are divided into squadrons or companies (called sotni or centuries) of 120 to 150 men, six of which usually form a regiment. The country is divided into districts, each of which is required to furnish a certain number of battalions, regiments, or companies, which serve for three years, and are replaced by others from the same district. The corps, or district, supplies the equipment of the men who are unable to furnish themselves; they receive no pay or allowances until called into service, but the government supplies the material for the artillery. Each army of Cossacks manages its own funds, and has its own arsenals, &c. The recruiting takes place among all the men whose turn it is to serve. Those who do not wish to go may, under certain restrictions, hire substitutes, who offer themselves to the highest bidders. Some regiments of Cossacks are attached to the corps of the guard; there are also Cossacks of the line. They serve not only as guards on the frontiers of the Empire, but also in the police of the interior, the service of the customs, or with armies in the field. They have, therefore, gradually acquired, in their equipments and exercises, whilst embodied, much of the character of regular light troops. The disciplined Cossack horseman, mounted on his hardy, well-formed, and active horse, appears to be a perfect specimen of a light cavalry soldier. We were particularly struck with the fine personal appearance of the men, both in the ranks and seen on detached service, as guards or attendants in the public establishments. "There are found among the Cossacks," says a well-informed German writer, "not only the bravest, but the handsomest soldiers of the Russian army. It is not by chance that we find in their ranks so many fine, well-developed forms, oval faces, bold profiles, large dark eyes, and finely-chiseled lips." The Russian officers also praise highly their character for honesty and fidelity; accordingly, they are found generally employed as servants in the public bureaus, civil and military. The Circassians, Mussulmans, and other bodies of irregular cavalry are allowed to exercise a good deal of latitude in their dress, equipments, and even in their arms. Whilst the national costume of the tribe may be preserved in the general style and fashion of dress of the men composing a squadron, each individual is permitted to exercise his own fancy in the color of his garments; and, as the colors selected are generally gay and brilliant, the appearance of one of these corps of cavalry is in the highest degree picturesque. The effect is heightened by their manner of riding and of using their weapons, when exercised as skirmishers. Their high saddles and short stirrups give them great facilities for changing position on horseback; and they may be seen firing in rapid succession to the front and to the rear, or to either side, or hanging by one leg to the saddle, until the body of the rider is nearly covered by that of his horse. Besides a carbine slung on the back, and a saber by his side, each horseman will have two or four pistols in his holster, and as many, perhaps, in his belt; so that, whilst his horse is in rapid motion, he discharges six or eight shots without reloading. In many respects, these troops resemble those of our Indian tribes who are accustomed to live and fight on horseback; and the sight of them naturally suggests the idea of trying to ingraft bodies of these active and hardy warriors on our military organization, and of making available, for the protection of the frontier, the men who are now the terror of the emigrant and the pioneer settler.

By their fitness for making forced marches, by their ability to overcome the obstacles of a difficult country, by the sagacious use of their natural faculties, and their address under all circumstances, these irregular troops are especially adapted for the service on which they are usually employed: that of detached escorts, messengers, guards, flankers, videttes, and skirmishers. The Circassians of the guard carry their arms in such a manner that their movements make very little noise, especially as their horses are not usually shod. The officers are armed with bows and arrows, which enable them, in a surprise, to kill the enemy's sentinels without alarming the camp. "Think," says the German writer before quoted, "of posting as a sentinel, in front of such men, a stupid German peasant, or a Parisian tailor." Besides the infantry, (about thirty battalions, stationed chiefly in Siberia,) the irregular troops comprise nearly 100,000 cavalry, and more than 200 pieces of horse artillery; the latter in light batteries, composed of 6-pounder guns and 12-pounder howitzers. The Cossacks of the Don furnish about one half of this mounted force.

THE MILITIA.

During the late war a large addition was made to the military force of Russia by a levy of about 200,000 militia. These men were designed to form a local force for service in the provinces to which they belonged, or in the adjoining provinces, to assist in the protection of the maritime and other frontiers, or to perform the duty of garrisons in the towns, so as to render a larger portion of the regular force disposable for distant service. The ranks were filled by serfs drafted to serve during the war. At the expiration of their time of service they were not to be liberated from serfdom, like regular soldiers, but to return to the estates by which they were furnished. The proprietors of these estates supplied these men with clothing, arms, and equipments at their own expense, and appointed the battalion and company officers: of the latter there are four to a company of two hundred and fifty men. Many of the officers were members of noble families who had retired from the army. With the exception of some of the inhabitants of maritime provinces who were drafted for service in the fleet, the militia were formed into battalions of infantry or riflemen, and armed accordingly with the ordinary musket or rifle; besides which, each man carried an ax, the habitual working tool of the Russian peasant, in the use of which he is remarkably expert. Their dress consisted of the national caftan, or full frock coat, made of dark gray cloth, confined around the waist by a red sash; loose trowsers, of the same material as the coat, were gathered below the knee into long leather boots. The head was covered with a simple forage cap, also of gray cloth, having no other ornament than a Greek cross of sheet brass in front, forming altogether a simple and serviceable uniform, which differed very little, except in color, from the habitual costume of the wearer at home. The accouterments, which were of black leather, consisted of shoulder belts and a waist belt, supporting the knapsack, cartridge-box, bayonet scabbard, and a sheath for the ax. The officers were dressed in the same style as the private soldiers, and wore their swords suspended to shoulder belts. The men were further distinguished from regular soldiers by the privilege of wearing the beard, which is an almost invariable appendage to the chin of the Russian peasant, but is strictly prohibited to be worn, by the officer or soldier, on the lower part of the face. These troops were quartered in the towns and villages, or encamped for instruction in the vicinity. We saw a body of about 5,000 militia reviewed by the Emperor at St. Petersburg, equipped in complete marching order, with baggage, ammunition wagons, &c. They made a very good appearance, and went through their exercises in a highly creditable manner, after having been embodied only two or three months. During our stay in St. Petersburg, instances were several times reported in which the militia did good service to the country by repelling marauding parties which had landed on the coasts of Finland. Some of them, it was understood, were also attached to the army in the Crimea.

RECRUITING.

The Russian army is recruited principally by conscription among the class of serfs or peasants. The government orders a levy of so many men in every thousand in a certain district of country, and it is the duty of the proprietors of estates to furnish the requisite number. This is generally done by lot; but it is said that the lot is apt to fall on those men whose services on the estate can be most easily dispensed with. Some peculiar circumstances are attended with exemption from the conscription; as, for instance, being the only male in a family, or being the father of three or more children, &c. A conscript may redeem himself from the obligation of service by the payment of a considerable sum of money, (a sum fixed by the government,) in consideration of which the proprietor or the government procures a substitute. This is not a mere nominal privilege, as many, even of the class of serfs, are engaged in commerce or other business by which they may have acquired considerable fortunes, without being able or willing to emancipate themselves. The business of recruiting is superintended by a military commission for the district, who verify the fitness of the recruit for service, and the sufficiency of pleas for exemption.

Voluntary enlistments furnish some soldiers to the army, but the principal source of recruits, after the conscription, is a class who may be said to be born to military service: these are the sons of soldiers and of military colonists. As the engagement for military service excuses the peasant from his obligation to the estate to which he belonged, the rights of the proprietor are in some sort transferred to the crown, and all the children born to the soldier after he enters the army become the property of the crown, and are destined to the military life, if capable of performing its duties. The military colonist receives certain portions of land from the crown, and enjoys exemption from service, and certain other privileges, on condition of maintaining a soldier who is quartered on him. These privileges and exemptions descend with the land to his eldest son, but his other sons are subject to military service, and are educated for that purpose.

In this sparsely-populated empire no impediment is thrown in the way of marriage of officers or soldiers. On the contrary, every encouragement consistent with the convenience of the service is held out for the marriage of soldiers. In permanent barracks, as much space as can be spared is set apart for families, and, when circumstances permit of it, separate dwellings are provided for them. At a proper age the children are placed in regimental or garrison schools, where they receive the theoretical and practical instruction requisite for a non-commissioned officer or intelligent soldier; accordingly it is from this class that the army is supplied with its best sergeants, clerks, and musicians, and the hospitals, veterinary surgeons, topographical corps, &c., with able assistants. The number of soldiers' children under instruction at the cost of the State amounts to at least 50,000.

The period of service in the Russian army is, for the line, twenty-five years; for the guard, twenty-two; and for military colonists, (cantonists,) twenty years; but after continuous, faithful service of fifteen years with their regiment, (those from some portions of the Empire after ten years,) they are allowed to retire from the active army, and constitute thereafter the armies of reserve, as before explained.

As soon as a recruit is received, his hair is cut close and his beard shaven off, by which he is at once distinguished from his fellow peasants. He is then marched, under an escort, to the nearest depot, where he usually undergoes a course of instruction in military exercises before he joins the active battalions of his regiment. In the distribution of recruits, the finest-looking men are selected for the guard and special corps; in other respects, the assignment to regiments is usually made according to the wants and convenience of the service. As the mechanical occupations are pursued in Russia almost exclusively by the peasant class, it follows, from this general conscription, that some men of every trade will be found in each body of troops; but such is the docility of the Russian peasant, that but little regard is paid to previous preparation for the duties assigned to him. Peter the Great's maxim, that "a man is fit for anything," is practically acted on: just as one man becomes an artillerist, and another a rifleman, so one learns to be a tailor, another a shoemaker, and a third a musician. At St. Petersburg we saw men employed in the operations of the Military Laboratory, (making percussion primers,) who were detailed daily from the garrison for that service, just as they would have been for guard or any other duty.

The Russian soldier is remarkable for physical qualities, well adapted to his profession; an athletic form, broad shoulders, small waist, erect, muscular frame, little encumbered with fat; accustomed to a life of labor, and to be nourished by the most simple diet: add to these qualities, and to the aptitude before mentioned, the habit of implicit obedience to superiors, and the strong religious sentiment which leads to blind and enthusiastic devotion to the Emperor, as the head of both Church and State, and to unquestioning submission to the delegated authority of the officer. Such are the principal elements of the military character of the Russian soldier.

APPOINTMENT AND PROMOTION OF OFFICERS.

Just as every peasant is held to be liable to service in the ranks of the army, so every nobleman is subject to be called on for the duty of an officer. Even those young nobles who do not design to pursue always the profession of arms, are expected to serve for a short term; and the army offers the surest road to preferment in the higher branches of the civil service of the government.

These young men are prepared for the service, either by being educated at one of the military schools, or by practical instruction in the ranks. For the latter purpose, they serve six months in the active army as privates, and three years as ensigns of infantry or cornets of cavalry, a sort of intermediate position between that of officer and non-commissioned officer. They live in the same manner, and perform the same duties, as other soldiers, from whom they are, however, distinguished by a mark of honor—a strip of gold lace on the shoulder. After the above service, they may present themselves to be examined for promotion to the grade of officer. There is also another source which furnishes a small number of officers from the ranks: after twelve years of faithful service as non-commissioned officer, the soldier, if found to be qualified for promotion, becomes an officer; those thus promoted serve, generally, in the garrison regiments. In an army where the greater part of the officers are of noble families, and where the very moderate pay of the officer requires the aid of private means, it may be supposed that the social position of men raised from the ranks is not the most desirable; accordingly, the honor of promotion is often declined by those who are entitled to it, and the government accords to such non-commissioned officers a distinctive honorary mark, and an advance of pay nearly, or quite, equal to that which they would receive as officers.

Promotions are ordinarily made by seniority. In the guards, promotions are made regimentally to the grade of lieutenant colonel, inclusive; in the infantry of the active army, regimental promotions are made to the rank of captain, inclusive; above that grade, the promotion is by divisions of four regiments; in the artillery, the promotions are made by brigades of four batteries; officers of artillery not attached to batteries are promoted separately. Above the grade of colonel, promotions are made through the whole army at the pleasure of the Emperor; so are extraordinary promotions for distinguished services, in any grade. There exists, also, in some corps, a system of promotion for a certain length of continued service in each grade. Officers of the corps of guards have exclusive privileges with regard to rank, as in the British service; thus, a captain of the guard ranks as a lieutenant colonel in the army, and may be transferred, with that rank, to an army corps. These officers are chiefly from noble and wealthy families; their corps form a sort of army of reserve, which is sent to the frontier, or called into active service, only in extreme cases. During the late war, none of this force served in the Crimea. But, in order to obtain experience in actual warfare, most of the officers are attached, for a short time, to an army which may be engaged in active operations, as in the war of the Caucasus, which furnishes a fine practical school of instruction for the Russian army, like that afforded to the French troops by the operations which have been carried on ever since 1830 in Algeria.

Among the rewards of service must be mentioned the *decorations*, which are so highly prized and so liberally bestowed in all European countries, and especially in Russia. These marks of distinction (crosses and medals) are conferred for meritorious services, on privates as well as officers. They are not always merely honorary emblems; the crosses of some orders, which are granted for distinguished service, or which accompany the attainment of a certain grade in the army, confer the rank and privileges of nobility, if the wearer is not already entitled to them. These outward marks of distinction excite the highest emulation in all classes; as to be without a decoration, where they are so generally worn, seems to imply a deficiency of merit. It may be mentioned here that marks of honor, by means of medals or of special insignia, are often conferred on regiments or bodies of troops who have signalized themselves by some brilliant action or remarkable service.

Retirement of Officers and Soldiers from Service.

It has been stated above that after a continuous and faithful service of ten or fifteen years, (according to circumstances,) the Russian soldier may retire from active service. He remains for five years attached to the first reserve, and until the expiration of his term of twenty or twenty-five years to the second reserve, in which situation, although liable in time of need to be recalled into service, he ordinarily returns to the employment of civil life. After the expiration of their term of service, able-bodied men generally return to their provinces and support themselves by any occupation which may present itself. Many discharged soldiers are employed in the imperial palaces, military schools, &c., and many are supported by the religious and charitable institutions of the country; others make use of the advantages which the government offers for an establishment in the military colonies. There are also military asylums provided for the support of those who are superannuated or disabled by wounds or disease. Two of these institutions, which we visited, at St. Petersburg and at Moscow, are well arranged, and appear to be admirably conducted for the comfortable maintenance of the inmates. But this mode of existence is not much to the taste of the Russian soldier; he prefers to live among his own people, and thanks to the abundance and cheapness of the necessaries of life in the country, and the habit of hospitality among the peasants as well as the nobles, even the wounded and disabled soldier generally finks it easy to maintain himself on his small pension. Numerous companies of invalids are employed too in the service of the interior, as guards for depots of military stores, escorts of recruits and prisoners, &c. Officers, after a certain length of service, may retire on an indefinite furlough, or may obtain leave to resign. Those on furlough constitute the officers of the corps of reserve, the ordinary duties of which force interfere very little with their freedom of action. Many officers, who have perhaps entered the army as a means of advancement in civil employment, retire at an early age. Those who remain long in service, or who are disabled by wounds, retire on pensions proportioned to their rank and term of service. Some of the aged or disabled officers who are too poor to maintain themselves, may enter the military asylums, where comfortable accommodations suitable to their rank are provided for a small number of officers. The asylum at St. Petersburg accommodates sixteen officers and 400 soldiers; that at Moscow thirty officers and 400 soldiers; neither of these establishments was quite full at the time of our visit.

PRUSSIA.

Ever since the reign of Frederick the Great this kingdom has occupied the position of one of the great powers of Europe; and to maintain this position she is obliged to keep up a military force commensurate with that of the great military States by which she is surrounded, although disproportionate to her resources and her population of 14,000,000 of souls. In order to effect this object, without imposing too great a pecuniary burden on the country, a peculiar military organization has been adopted, (in 1814,) which has reference to the defense of the kingdom, rather than to offensive operations beyond its boundaries.

This organization is based on the principle that every able-bodied man is bound to serve in defense of his country, (fatherland,) and that the army is the great school of military instruction for the whole nation. In conformity with this principle, the land forces of Prussia are composed of four classes, viz:

1. The Standing Army.
2. The Landwehr (militia) of the first ban.
3. The Landwehr of the second ban.
4. The Landsturm, or "levy en masse."

1. The standing army consists of all the able-bodied men of twenty years of age, who serve three years.

2. The landwehr of the first ban comprises all the men from twenty to thirty-two years old not belonging to the standing army. It constitutes an army of reserve, to reinforce and coöperate with the standing army for all service in time of war. This force is completely organized and equipped, and is embodied twice a year for instruction, sometimes by battalions, sometimes to join the regular troops in the great manœuvres and exercises. Their arms, clothing, and equipments are kept in storehouses provided for them, and a few officers and men of each battalion and squadron are retained permanently in service to take care of the depot.

2. The landwehr of the second ban is composed of the men from thirty-two to forty years of age who do not belong to the standing army; this force forms the garrisons of fortresses in time

of war, or it may be called to the support of the active army of operations. It is not called out in time of peace.

4. The landsturm embraces all the men from seventeen to fifty years of age who are not included in the three other classes. The force is not regularly organized, and would only be called out, in case of invasion, for the defense of the country in the last resort.

GOVERNMENT OF THE ARMY.

The King, as Commander-in-Chief of the army, has a personal staff (in 1855) of eight general officers, aides-de-camp; four genéfals à la suite, and ten field officers and captains, orderly officers. The administration of military affairs is conducted through—

THE MINISTRY OF WAR.

The Minister of War is an officer of the army; in 1855 the place was held by a general of brigade, (major general.) Besides the Central Bureau of the minister, (the chief of which is a major of the army,) there are two principal departments, each divided into several sections. The distribution of duties, and the rank of the chief of each section, in 1855, were as follows:

A.—THE GENERAL WAR DEPARTMENT,

Under the direction of a colonel, who was also, in 1855, the chief of the Engineer Bureau. This department is charged with the business relating to the organization and instruction of the troops, and to the distribution and employment of the personnel and materiel of war. It is divided into four sections:

1. *The Section of Army Affairs*, under a lieutenant colonel, is charged with the distribution and movements of the army, the discharge and recruiting of troops, &c.
2. *The Section of Artillery*, under a lieutenant colonel, has charge of all that relates to supplying arms and ammunition.
3. *The Section of Engineering*, under a colonel, has the direction of fortifications, &c.
4. *The Section of the Personal Affairs*, under a major general, is charged with the care of petitions and memorials to the King, distribution of honors and rewards, and other personal matters relating to officers. In connection with this section is—

The Private Military Chancelry, under a lieutenant colonel, charged with making out commissions, collecting information relative to officers, preparation of the Army Register, &c. Besides the chief, there are several officers of the army detailed for duty in each of these bureaus or sections.

B.—THE DEPARTMENT OF MILITARY ADMINISTRATION,

Under the direction of a major general and privy counselor, has charge of all that relates to the pay, subsistence, clothing, and lodging of the troops. The department is divided into four sections:

1. Of Funds and Expenditures.
2. Of Subsistence and Transportation.
3. Of Clothing and Field Trains.
4. Of Camp Equipage and Hospital Service.

The chiefs of the first and second sections, in 1855, were civilians, with the title of privy counselor; the chief of the third section was a lieutenant colonel, and of the fourth a major.

Besides these, there are attached to the War Ministry, a Bureau of the Affairs of Invalids, under the direction of a colonel; a Bureau of Remounts, under a major general; a Judge-Advocate's Bureau, under a judge-advocate general; a Paymaster's Department, or General Military Chest, under direction of a paymaster general. The Minister of War has also the

MILITARY ORGANIZATION—PRUSSIA.

direction of affairs relating to the military marine force. For the immediate command of the troops, under the Minister of War, there are nine commanding generals, one for the corps of guards, and one for each of the eight army corps, distributed into as many geographical districts; an Inspector General of Artillery; an Inspector General of Artillery Manufacturing Establishments; an Inspector of Riflemen.

The staff of a commander of an army corps consists of two or three officers of the general staff corps, (one as chief of the staff,) two aids-de-camp, an intendant, and four sub-intendants, a judge-advocate, a surgeon-in-chief, and a military chaplain general. The inspector general of artillery has a staff consisting of one officer of the general staff and three aids-de-camp. There are four inspection districts, in each of which is a general or field officer as inspector, with two aids. The inspector general of engineers has no staff officer, but three aids. There are three inspection districts, in each of which is a general officer as inspector, with two aids, and other officers of engineers, as sub-inspectors of fortresses and engineer troops, (pioneers;) there being in each inspection district two sub-divisions of fortresses and three pioneer detachments. The artillery and engineer troops are incorporated with the respective army corps for tactical purposes only. In what relates to their materiel, in their interior service and instruction, they are under their own inspectors.

ORGANIZATION OF THE ARMY.

Military Grades.

GENERAL OFFICERS .... Field Marshal.
                                             Colonel General of Infantry.
                                             Master General of Artillery.
                                             General.
                                             Lieutenant General.
                                             Major General.
FIELD OFFICERS .... Colonel.
                                             Lieutenant Colonel.
                                             Major.
CAPTAINS .... First, second, and third class.
SUBALTERNS .... First Lieutenant.
                                             Second Lieutenant.
NON-COMMISSIONED OFFICERS—
            Wearing sword knots ...... Master Artificer of Artillery.
                                             Orderly Sergeant.
                                             Vice Orderly Sergeant.
                                             Ensign.
                                             Master Workman of Artillery Company.
                                             Mounted Field Jäger.
            Without sword knots ...... Artificer of Artillery.
                                             Sergeant or Quartermaster of Cavalry and Horse Artillery.
                                             Corporal.
                                             Gensd'armes.
                                             Bombardier or Pioneer.
PRIVATES .... Lance Corporals, (Gefreiter.)
                                             Reënlisted soldiers, (Kapitulanter.)
                                             Common soldier.
                                             Pupil of the school section.

The *Medical Corps* of the army, since 1850, contains the following grades:
  Surgeon General, with rank of Colonel.
  Chief Surgeon, with rank of Major.
  Surgeon, with rank of Captain.
  Surgeon, with rank of First Lieutenant.
  Assistant Surgeon, with rank of Second Lieutenant.
  Under Surgeon, with rank of Ensign.
  Volunteer (one year) Surgeon, without rank.
  Hospital assistants, non-commissioned officers or privates.

The medical officers are denominated according to their employment: corps, regimental, battalion, or garrison surgeons. Other military employés (judge-advocates, intendants, paymasters, &c.) have no established military rank.

THE INFANTRY.

The infantry of the standing army consists of—

Four regiments of guards, of three battalions each	12	battalions.
One regiment of reserve	2	"
One rifle battalion	1	"
One battalion of chasseurs	1	"
Thirty-two regiments of the line, of three battalions each	96	"
Eight regiments of the reserve, of two battalions each	16	"
Eight reserve battalions	8	"
Eight rifle battalions	8	"
	144	"

The infantry of the landwehr of first ban—

Four landwehr regiments of the guard, of three battalions each	12	battalions.
Thirty-two landwehr regiments of districts, of three battalions each	96	"
Eight reserve battalions	8	"
	116	"

And the same for the landwehr of the second ban.

A regiment consists generally of three battalions, as above. A battalion contains four companies, and has twenty-four officers, viz:

One field officer, six captains, four first lieutenants, and thirteen second lieutenants, of whom one is adjutant.
  Seventy non-commissioned officers, (including drummers.)
  Sixteen musicians.
  Five hundred privates, (mean number in time of peace.)
  Two surgeons.
  One paymaster.
  One armorer.

As about two hundred recruits join the battalion in the spring, and the like number of men are discharged in the autumn, the force of the battalion is four hundred in winter and six hundred in summer. The staff of a regiment consists of one commander, (colonel or lieutenant colonel,) one major, one lieutenant as adjutant, one regimental surgeon, one non-commissioned officer as clerk, and ten musicians.

Of each landwehr battalion there are retained in service at the depot, in time of peace: one paymaster, one assistant surgeon, fourteen non-commissioned officers, and sixteen privates. Taking the battalion at 500 men, the whole force of infantry, on the peace establishment, is about 72,000 men and 3,600 officers, besides 3,712 men for the 116 skeleton battalions of the landwehr of the first ban. On the war establishment the strength of a company is 250 men, and of a battalion 1,002, except the landwehr of the second ban, in which it is 802. Thus the infantry force in time of war will be:

Standing army, 144 battalions...	144,288 men.
Landwehr, first ban, 108 battalions...	108,216
	252,504
Add: Reserve battalions and companies, 38¼ battalions...................................	37,834
Landwehr of second ban, 116 battalions...	93,032
Total infantry force, 406¼ battalions...	383,370

CAVALRY.

1. *Standing Army, thirty-eight regiments.*

	Of the guard.	Of the line.
Cuirassiers...	2	8
Dragoons...	1	4
Hussars...	1	12
Lancers...	2	8
	6	32

Each regiment consists of four squadrons, having twenty-five officers, viz: two field officers, (one colonel, lieutenant colonel, or major commanding, and one major,) six captains, four first lieutenants, and thirteen second lieutenants.

A squadron has five officers, (one captain, one first and three second lieutenants,) fifteen non-commissioned officers, one orderly sergeant, one ensign, one quartermaster, twelve sergeants, three trumpeters; a squadron of the guard has 132 privates; of the line, 127. Each regiment has also one paymaster, one chief trumpeter, one clerk, one surgeon and two or three assistant surgeons, three veterinary surgeons, and, in the line regiments, one assistant, with rank of orderly sergeant. For the corps of guards (cavalry and artillery) there is one chief veterinary surgeon.

2. In the landwehr of the first ban, thirty-four regiments, viz: eight of heavy cavalry, four dragoons, twelve hussars, eight lancers, and eight squadrons attached to the reserve infantry regiments. On the peace establishment there are kept in service one officer, one orderly sergeant, one sergeant, and two corporals, to each squadron; on the war establishment the force is the same as for the standing army—602 men to a regiment, and 150 to a squadron. Thus, the cavalry force in war is:

38 regiments of the army, or 152 squadrons .... 22,876 men.
34 regiments of the landwehr of the first ban, 136 squadrons... 20,468
8 regiments reserve infantry................................. 1,690
                                                            44,944
To which add: The reserve cavalry, 40 squadrons 7,600
              Landwehr of second ban, 104 squadrons 12,480

     Total of cavalry force .... 65,024 men, with 2,400 officers.

ARTILLERY.

The artillery consists of nine regiments, (one of the guards, and one for each of the other army corps,) and a section or battalion of artificers. A regiment of artillery consists of *four battalions and one company of workmen.* The latter are employed in the various arsenals of construction, &c. There are:

One battalion of horse artillery, with three 6-pounder batteries.
Two battalions of foot artillery; one with two 12-pounder and two 6-pounder batteries; one with one 12-pounder and two 6-pounder and one howitzer battery.
One battalion of garrison artillery, with four companies; making eleven field batteries, four garrison companies, and one company of workmen.

The field pieces are of three calibers: 6 and 12-pounder guns, corresponding in size and weight with ours, and 7-pounder howitzers, corresponding in caliber with our 24-pounders; Prussian howitzers and mortars being denominated by the weight of a stone-shot of the caliber of the piece. This field howitzer is of nearly the same weight as the 6-pounder gun, the bore being only six calibers long, exclusive of the chamber. A 6-pounder battery of horse or foot artillery consists of six 6-pounder guns and two 7-pounder howitzers; a 12-pounder battery of foot artillery, eight 12-pounder guns; a howitzer battery of foot artillery, eight 7-pounder howitzers. In the 12-pounder batteries there are eight horses to a gun; in the 6-pounder and howitzer batteries, six horses. In time of peace, each battery has but four pieces horsed, and none of the ammunition or train wagons are horsed. A regiment on the peace establishment consists of:

    1 Commander, (a colonel or lieutenant colonel.)
    4 Field Officers, (lieutenant colonels or majors.)
   21 Captains.
   15 First Lieutenants.
   50 Second Lieutenants.
    1 Chief Surgeon.
   10 Chief Artificers.
   16 Orderly Sergeants.
    1 Paymaster.
   20 Artificers.
   241 Sergeants.
   118 Gunners.
    7 Veterinary Surgeons.
   118 Lance Corporals.
 1,087 Privates.
   32 Trumpeters.

1,642 men, exclusive of officers; 556 horses.

There are also five reserve companies of garrison artillery attached to certain regiments and fortresses, each of which forms the nucleus of two or three garrison companies on the war establishment; and reserve or depot companies of about 500 men, with three batteries of four pieces each.

There is no artillery of the landwehr; but the men who have belonged to the artillery serve to complete the batteries and companies on the war establishment, and are occasionally exercised in field and garrison service.

Composition of batteries equipped for the field.

	7-pounder howitzer.	Horse artillery.	FOOT BATTERIES.	
			12-pounders.	6-pounders.
Guns and carriages...	8	8	8	8
Ammunition wagons..	10	6	10	6
Store wagon, (for repairs, &c.)...	1	1	1	1
Forge..	1	1	1	1
Baggage wagon..	1	1	1	1
Men, (including five officers)..	210	178	210	172
Horses..	159	238	175	135
Number of rounds of ammunition in limber chest..................	24	48	24	48
Number of rounds of ammunition in one ammunition-wagon chest.......	48	96	56	96
Whole number to each piece in the battery............................	114	156	133	156

To a regiment of artillery in the field there is a *park division* of thirty-three wagons, for artillery and infantry ammunition, spare gun carriages, store wagons, &c.; also, a laboratory division, with six wagons; a division of workmen, with eight wagons; a reserve company, with supernumerary men and horses. The whole force of a regiment of field artillery on the war establishment is about 2,100 men, with eighty-eight pieces of artillery; making, for the nine regiments, 18,900 men, and 792 pieces.

ENGINEERS.

The corps of officers of engineers consisted, in 1855, of:

 1 Lieutenant General, chief of the corps.
 3 Major Generals.
 7 Colonels.
 3 Lieutenant Colonels.
 19 Majors.
 81 Captains.
 38 First Lieutenants.
 77 Second Lieutenants.
 44 Second Lieutenants, supernumerary.

Total............ 273 officers.

Besides the construction and preservation of fortresses, and the buildings belonging to them, these officers commanded the pioneer troops, which include the pontonniers. There are three engineer inspection districts, each containing two subdivisions of fortresses, and three battalions of pioneers, each of two companies. The force of a company on the war establishment is four officers and about 225 men; on the peace establishment, 125 men. The pioneer soldiers of the landwehr are not organized separately, but serve to recruit the standing companies and are exercised with them. There are also two standing reserve companies of pioneers, 231 strong, and on the war establishment a garrison company to each battalion, besides a reserve garrison force to be called out in case of need. Thus the peace establishment of pioneers is about 2,400 men. The war establishment consists of:

Nine battalions of 452 men	4,068
Nine garrison companies of 225 men	2,025
Two reserve pioneer companies of 125 men	250
Garrison reserve	1,400
Total	7,743 men.

besides the landwehr and the train. Each pioneer battalion has a ponton train, consisting of thirty-four ponton wagons, (for a bridge of 500 feet,) five store wagons, and one forge; with 238 horses and 119 soldiers; besides, one officer and six non-commissioned officers of the train. There is also to each battalion a light trestle-bridge train of ten wagons, for service of the advance guard.

THE GENERAL STAFF.

The duties of the staff relate to the quartering and sheltering of the troops in peace and war; the orders and arrangements for movements, marches, and maneuvers, under all circumstances; the service of advanced and rearguards; direction of passage of rivers, &c.; reconnoissances of the ground and of the enemy; surveys and knowledge of the geography and topography of the country and field of operations, means of communication, &c.

The staff corps consisted, in 1855, of:

    1 Lieutenant General, chief of the general staff.
    1 Major General.
    8 Colonels.
    6 Lieutenant Colonels.
    29 Majors.
    18 Captains.
    ―――
    63 officers.

They are distributed into the great general staff of the army, and the staffs of army corps and divisions.

The great (central) general staff consisted of the major general, who was also director of the trigonometrical section, a colonel, three lieutenant colonels, six majors, and seven captains, besides several regimental officers detailed for staff duty. Under the direction of officers of the general staff are the trigonometrical section, the topographical section, the depot of maps and plans, and the Lithographic Institute. There are also three sections, each under the direction of a colonel, charged with collecting and arranging geographical and statistical information relative to military operations in other countries of Europe, and a bureau for the collection and preservation of archives and materials for the military history of the country.

The staff of an army corps or military (geographical) district is charged with all the correspondence and records relative to the business of the commanding general. In case of the sickness or sudden death of the general, the chief of the staff is authorized to conduct the business of the command until the King's orders can be taken in the case. The business is divided into four sections:

    1. The business of the general staff proper.
    2. The business of adjutants of regiments and corps: reports and returns of troops, arms, &c.

3. The business of the judge-advocate's department.
4. The business of intendance, (supplies,) medical, and chaplain's department.

THE TRAIN.

On the peace establishment there is only a depot of the train belonging to each army corps, in charge of an officer and thirty soldiers attached to the artillery regiment, and two special officers of the train. On the war establishment the train is divided into several parts. Each army corps has:

A park train for the artillery and a bridge train for the engineers, as before stated.

For the service of the administration and supplies: *A provision train,* consisting of five divisions of thirty-one wagons each; a forge; a bakery with two wagons, or, if they carry iron ovens, with five wagons; a wagon for the staff-books and papers: *a hospital train,* consisting of one principal train for 1,200 sick, and three light trains for 200 sick; in all, sixty-two wagons. *Wagons for the military chest, the letter mail,* and incidental supplies. *The depot of horses,* with one wagon and seventy-five spare horses.

For the immediate service of the troops: To each battalion of infantry, one 6-horse, two 4-horse, and one 2-horse wagon; four pack-horses, twenty soldiers of the train; to a cavalry regiment, one 4-horse and one 2-horse wagon; four 2-horse carts, and forty-two soldiers of the train: to a battery of artillery, one 2-horse wagon: to a pioneer battalion, four 4-horse and two 2-horse wagons: to a rifle battalion, two 2-horse wagons and sixteen company pack-horses. The whole force of the train is: for an army corps, about 3,000 men; for the whole army, about 30,000 men.

SPECIAL CORPS.

1. *Company of Non-Commissioned Officers of the Guard,* composed of seventy men, employed as watchmen in the royal palaces and grounds, &c.
2. *The Invalids.*
3. *The Gend'armes,* or military police, under the Minister of the Interior.
4. *Corps of Mounted Couriers,* composed of a colonel commanding, three lieutenants, and seventy-seven men.

ESTABLISHMENTS FOR MILITARY INSTRUCTION.

Four secondary cadet schools.
One superior cadet school in Berlin, supplied from the provincial schools.
Nine division schools, for preparing ensigns of infantry and cavalry for promotions to officers.
One school of artillery and engineers.
One cavalry school at Schwedt.
One general military school, for preparing officers for the staff corps.
One battalion school, for making non-commissioned officers.
Three schools for educating orphans and other children of soldiers.
One central gymnastic school.
Garrison schools for soldiers' children.

FORMATION OF ARMY CORPS.

On the Peace Establishment.—The Prussian army is divided into nine army corps: one of the guard, and eight provincial army corps. With slight exceptions in the guards, each army corps is composed of two divisions of infantry and cavalry; one regiment of artillery; one battalion of pioneers; one rifle battalion; one "combined" reserve battalion; one infantry regiment of reserve; one landwehr battalion of reserve; one landwehr squadron of reserve cavalry; one invalid company; one train depot.

A division consists of two brigades of infantry and one brigade of cavalry. A brigade of infantry is composed of one regiment of the regular army and one regiment of the landwehr. A brigade of cavalry consists of two regiments of regular cavalry and two of the landwehr. Of the landwehr regiments of infantry and cavalry, as before stated, only a nucleus is kept on foot in time of peace; and of the regular artillery only four pieces to a battery, or forty-four to a regiment. The whole force of the regular army on the peace establishment is as follows:

Troops.	INFANTRY.		CAVALRY.		ARTILLERY.					PIONEERS.		Number of regimental officers.
	Battalions.	Men.	Squadrons.	Men.	Regiments.	Battalions.	Companies.	Pieces.	Men.	Companies.	Men.	
Of the regular army................	144	72,000	152	22,876	9	99	51	432	16,500	20	2,500	5,300
Of the landwehr, first ban.........	116	3,712	144	576			116					232
Total........................	260	75,712	296	23,452	9	99	167	432	16,500	20	2,500	5,532

Mean aggregate number of troops on foot in time of peace about 118,000.

On the War Establishment.—An army corps for the field consists of two divisions of infantry, one division of cavalry, the artillery of reserve, and a battalion of pioneers, with a bridge train if required. *An infantry division* consists of two brigades of infantry, one regiment of cavalry, one or two batteries of foot artillery, and a battalion of riflemen. *A cavalry division* consists of two brigades of three regiments each, and one battery of horse artillery. *The artillery of reserve* consists of six or seven batteries of foot and horse artillery, and the general park train. Besides these marching corps, there are reserve and garrison troops of each arm attached to the army corps.

FORCE OF THE WAR ESTABLISHMENT.

Troops.	INFANTRY.		CAVALRY.		ARTILLERY.			PIONEERS.		Total of men.
	Battalions.	Men.	Squadrons.	Men.	Battalions or companies.	Pieces.	Men.	Companies.	Men.	
Active army..........................	120	120,240	152	22,876	93	792	19,900	18	4,064	166,084
Reserve and garrison	62	61,882	48	9,200	99	140	19,108	11	2,275	91,465
Landwehr, first ban.	104	108,216	136	20,464						128,644
Active troops........................	290	290,338	336	52,544	192	932	37,008	29	6,343	386,233
Landwehr, second ban.............	116	93,032	104	12,480	116		23,000		1,400	129,912
Grand total.....................	406	383,370	440	65,024	314	932	60,008		7,743	516,145

Add to these the soldiers of the train, (about 30,000,) and the regimental officers, (about 10,000,) and other special corps, we have a total force on the war establishment of about 560,000 men.

RECRUITING.

As before remarked, military service is required in Prussia from all able-bodied men between the ages of twenty and thirty-nine. The only exempts are—

The royal family, and members of the families of mediatized sovereign princes;
The diplomatic corps;
Foreigners who have no fixed residence in the country;
Quakers and men of other religious persuasions who are excused for conscientious motives.
Convicts guilty of disgraceful crimes are not allowed to serve as soldiers.

No substitutes are allowed, and the term of service with the colors is *three years;* but a young man who can produce a certificate from his college of a certain degree of proficiency in his studies, is allowed to commute his term for *one year's* service under arms, on condition of furnishing his own clothing and equipments, and supporting himself entirely during the year. This arrangement of *"one year volunteers"* enables young men of the better classes to pursue their studies and preparation for the learned professions with little interruption, and without neglecting the military instruction which every citizen is required to possess. It is also permitted to youths over seventeen years, but who have not attained the legal age of twenty, to acquit themselves of their term of service by making a voluntary engagement for three years; by which means they are left free from the interruption of military duty after they have commenced their intended trade or occupation, and they can also choose their arm of service.

Men who reënlist in the regular army, for one to six years, after serving three years, have certain privileges with regard to duty; they wear a distinctive badge. Their number is limited to about fifty to a battalion.

The stature required for the service is:

For the guards.. 5 feet 7 inches, English.
For cuirassiers and heavy foot artillery........................ 5 " 6 " "
For other cavalry, artillery, and infantry..................... 5 " 3⅞ " "

Smaller men are taken for the *train,* &c. In other respects the recruits are assigned to corps according to the nature of their occupations or instruction. Thus, the foresters are put into the rifle regiments; mountaineers, miners, and some of the boatmen and boatbuilders in the pioneer companies; farmers, &c., into the cavalry; mechanics into the artillery. The examination and arrangements of recruiting are conducted by a *district commission* and a *department commission.* The latter is composed of a brigade-commander of infantry, a government counselor, a field officer, and a surgeon. They verify and supervise the lists of men received and rejected which are presented to them by the district commission, which is composed in a similar manner to the other, but of officers of inferior grades, military and civil. The one year volunteers are examined by a special board in certain courses of study. Their number must not, in general, exceed four to a company or squadron.

The recruits join their regiments in the spring, and in order to reduce the expenses of the army as much as possible, the discharges usually take place in the beginning of winter, so that the men are actually little more than two and a half years under arms. From the whole arrangement of the Prussian system it will be seen that more than a third of the force is renewed every year, and the changes in the personnel of the army are almost incessant; involving a degree of labor and attention from the officers and non-commissioned officers, which must tax to the utmost their devotion to duty, and the exercise of which cannot be witnessed without admiration of the manner in which that duty is performed.

APPOINTMENT AND PROMOTION OF OFFICERS.

No person can be appointed ensign or lieutenant without having passed an examination before a special commission, except in the case of promotion for brilliant service in the field.

A volunteer for one or three years, or any soldier, may present himself for examination as ensign, if he is not less than seventeen or more than twenty-three years of age, has served at least six months, and can bring a certificate from the commandant of his regiment that he is sufficiently instructed in practical exercises, and is capable of performing the duties of ensign. (*Portepée-fähnriche*.) The candidates are examined on the following subjects:

    German, Latin, and French languages.
    Arithmetic and Elementary Mathematics.
    Geography.
    History.
    Drawing and Topography.

In case of failure a second examination may be allowed in the course of six or twelve months. Those who pass the examination are nominated to vacancies by the King in the guards, and by the commanding general in the other army corps.

An ensign, who has served at least six months as such, and is not more than twenty-five years of age, may offer for examination as second lieutenant. This examination embraces the following subjects:

    1. Ordnance instruction, viz: On artillery of all kinds, small arms, gunpowder, and side arms, including their fabrication and use. A very good synopsis of this course is found in Lieutenant Hoffman's "*Waffenlehre*."

    2. Organization of the army, elementary tactics, and service in the field. See "*Die Preussiche Armée*," by Lieutenant Kalkstein.

    3. Field and permanent fortification.

    4. Surveying and military plan drawing.

    5. Composition of a military memoir, and knowledge of the regulations for the interior service and discipline of the troops.

If the candidate fail in this examination he may be allowed another six to twelve months, as before. Those who pass are nominated to the King for vacancies of second lieutenant, provided the majority of the body of officers with whom they are to serve consider them worthy of the appointment, and their immediate superiors certify that they are sufficiently proficient in practical knowledge.

The same examination is required from the pupils of the military schools. Those of the cadet schools may present themselves, from seventeen to eighteen years of age, for examination as ensigns or lieutenants. In the cadet school, at Berlin, where the course occupies two years, the most proficient pupils, called *selecta*, remain an additional year at school, and are then nominated for second lieutenants.

By this means the appointment of officers, instead of being, as formerly, confined to the nobles, is now open to men of all classes, and of all religious persuasions. But the very moderate pay of the officers, especially of the lower grades, (that of a second lieutenant being about fifteen dollars a month,) operates as a practical check to promotion from the ranks, except on the part of the volunteers, who are generally young men in easy circumstances, who enter the army in this way with a view to promotion. Non-commissioned officers without fortune, who do not wish to continue in service after twelve years, have a right to civil employment, and become officers in the landwehr.

Promotions are made according to seniority, and by regiments or corps, to the grade of *major*, except in case of incompetency on the part of the senior captain to command a battalion. Above the grade of major the promotions are made by selections; but the order of seniority is habitually followed, in time of peace, owing partly to the difficulty in such a time of determining real military merit. The Sovereign and the Minister of War are aided in this respect by the observations and reports made by the inspectors and military commanders during the exercises and maneuvers which take place every summer for the practical instruction of army corps, as well as of smaller bodies of men.

Officers of distinguished merit are sometimes promoted out of turn by being employed on the staff, and then transferred with higher rank to a different regiment from that from which they were taken.

Besides the primary schools of instruction, and the special school for engineers and artillery, there is a general military school in Berlin for the instruction of officers. The number in attendance is limited to 120 lieutenants. The candidates undergo an examination according to a certain programme of questions. The examinations take place on the same day at the headquarters of each army corps, and the selection is made of the most meritorious by a committee to whom the written answers are submitted. The course of instruction is three years. During the season of maneuvers the officers serve in different arms from that to which they belong; thus a cavalry officer exercises one year with the infantry, another with the artillery, &c. By this arrangement these officers acquire practical as well as theoretical instruction in the service of all arms, which makes them eligible to appointments in the staff corps. Some of the most proficient are attached to the topographical section of the War Department until vacancies in the staff occur; others return to their regiments.

Gymnastic exercises, which form a part of the course of instruction in all the public schools, are practiced in all the corps of the army; and an excellent swimming school, for the instruction of soldiers and others, is attached to the pioneer establishment at Berlin.

By means of the facilities afforded for theoretical attainments, and of the continual practical exercises in every department required for the instruction of the new levies, the officers of the Prussian army, formerly remarkable chiefly for attention to the minutiæ of military service, have become highly accomplished in their profession, and have made the most creditable progress in the art of engineering, in artillery, and in military science and literature.

The *Medical Staff* is recruited partly from the Frederick-William Institute, a medical college established in Berlin for the education of young men to become surgeons in the army. There is also a pharmaceutical establishment in Berlin for supplying medicines for the army. Hospital stewards are reënlisted soldiers, who are instructed by the surgeons, or else volunteers who wish to pursue the business of apothecaries.

There is at Berlin an excellent veterinary school, in which a certain number of pupils are instructed as veterinary surgeons and others as shoeing smiths for the army, and also for similar employments in civil life.

Since 1850 an assimilated rank has been assigned to officers of the medical staff. They take rank after all other officers of the same grade, and are not eligible, under any circumstances, to command of troops. Soldiers in hospital are commanded by field and company officers detailed from the garrisons for that purpose.

Discharge and Retirement from Service.

An officer may claim an unconditional discharge when he has attained the age of forty years, or has become disabled. Under other circumstances, if permitted to retire, he is liable to be recalled into service, if necessary, either in the army or the landwehr.

Soldiers, after three years' service in the standing army, are placed in the reserve, and after five years, in the landwehr. If the number of recruits in a battalion exceeds by twenty men the authorized number, some of the oldest soldiers are discharged and placed in the reserve, to be recalled whenever it may be necessary. Otherwise men are discharged before the expiration of their term of service only for total or partial disability, or on account of peculiar domestic circumstances, on the recommendation of the commanding general.

Officers and soldiers discharged for disability occasioned by wounds or contagious disease (as opthalmia, &c.,) contracted in service, are entitled to pensions according to the degree of disability and length of service, rank, &c. Those who are only partially disabled are placed in companies of invalids, or if they have been twelve years in service, in civil employment, either in the civil departments of the army, (storekeepers, barrack masters, &c.,) or in other branches of the government service.

At Berlin there is an asylum for old and disabled officers and soldiers, which was established about one hundred years ago. At the time of our visit there were fifty-six officers and four hundred soldiers at the asylum. Twenty-six of the officers were on duty in the asylum. Soldiers are admitted after twenty-one years' service, or when disabled by wounds, &c. The rooms are arranged so that they can accommodate the families of married men, of whom there were sixty in the asylum. One kitchen serves for three or four families. Chapels are provided for Protestant and Catholic worship.

Although the military pensions are on a liberal scale in comparison with the ordinary pay, they do not constitute a severe tax on the resources of the country, because of the usually short term of military service, and the facility of providing employment for soldiers who have served out their time, by the vast number of civil offices which are required in a country where all the transactions of life are so minutely regulated as in Prussia.

THE DEPARTMENT OF SUPPLIES AND DISBURSEMENTS.

The expenditures for the support of the military establishment in Prussia are about twenty millions of dollars, or more than one quarter of the whole income of the kingdom. The disbursement of this large sum, and its application to the support of the troops, are conducted, under the direction of a bureau of the War Department, by the *intendancy* in each of the nine army corps.

The intendancy consists of one chief intendant, five principal assistants, and fourteen clerks and assistants. The intendant, under the direction of the commanding general, superintends the administration of the affairs of his department in the military district to which he belongs. The business is divided into five sections, each directed by one of the principal assistant intendants, viz:

1. The examination and settlement of accounts and expenditures.
2. The furnishing and preservation of stores and materials for supplying the troops, and for the construction of fortifications.
3. The business of the train, of clothing and camp equipage, of transportation, of allowances of bread, money, &c.
4. The supplies for garrison service, for the business of military schools, and for remounts.
5. The supplies for hospitals, the business of invalid establishments, and of the military marine.

The supplies purchased by the intendants are issued to battalions or companies, and distributed by the company officers and quartermaster sergeants. Materials for clothing are furnished, and the clothing is made up by the men. The battalion commander, a captain, and the regimental or battalion paymaster constitute a clothing board. Barrack furniture belongs to the barracks, and not to companies. The heavy furniture of officers' rooms is supplied by the government. An account of the barrack furniture is kept by a barrack master, a retired soldier, under the direction of an inspector, who is a retired officer serving in the intendant's department.

Bread only of the ration is issued in kind. Other provisions are purchased out of the money allowance. The provision fund is administered by an officer, a non-commissioned officer, and a soldier who is chosen by the company.

The men are paid every ten days. The money is received by the paymaster, who is a civil officer, and is turned over to the captain, in whose presence it is paid to the men by the orderly sergeant. Each man has a book in which his account is kept. After the payment the battalion commander inquires of the men if each has received his due. At reviews and inspections the general makes the same inquiry, and examines the books of some of the men. No individual receipts are taken from them. An intendant verifies the muster roll of the men. The pay department is superintended by a paymaster general. The funds are kept by sub-treasurers as with us. The chest for the battalion fund is locked with three keys; one of which is kept by the commander, one by the senior captain, and one by the paymaster.

Intendants and paymasters have no rank, but they wear a uniform, with epaulets.

Funds for the support of a *hospital* are administered by a commission composed of three officers of the army on duty at the hospital, an intendant, and a surgeon. The intendant makes the contracts and disbursements, subject to the approval of the chief of the Hospital Bureau of the War Department.

COURTS-MARTIAL.

The numerous laws and ordinances on the subject of military discipline and the administration of justice define, as minutely as possible, the authority of the several classes of officers, and the extent of the punishment which they may inflict; the classification of offenses of more serious character, and the nature of the penalty attached to each; the constitution of the several kinds of military courts, and the extent of their jurisdiction.

The administration of justice is under the direction of the *Judge-Advocate General*, in Berlin, assisted by four superior judge-advocates, as counselors. In each army corps, division, regiment, and garrison, it is directed by the commanding officer and a judge-advocate, or a prosecuting officer.

The jurisdiction is of two classes: the *superior* embraces all cases of officers and military employés, of non-commissioned officers and privates, when the prescribed penalty is greater than arrest or degradation; the *inferior*, all other cases. The *regimental* jurisdiction is confined to the inferior class, and to persons belonging to the regiment; the *divisional* courts have the superior jurisdiction over all persons belonging to the division, and the inferior jurisdiction over those who do not belong to any regiment; the courts of an *army corps* have the superior jurisdiction over all cases not subject to the divisional courts, and the inferior over all non-commissioned officers, privates, and employés, who do not belong to any division or regiment in the corps; the *garrison* jurisdiction refers to cases relating to the police, security, and service of the place.

When a complaint or charge is made, or an offense becomes known to the proper superior officer, he orders a court of inquiry to investigate the facts, and, with the advice of the judge-advocate, he determines whether the offense is to be prosecuted; and if so, whether it shall be brought before a court-martial, or be punished as a mere breach of discipline.

The court of inquiry, as well as the court-martial, is appointed separately in each case, by the commanding officer.

A *court of inquiry* consists of a judge-advocate, a prosecuting officer, and of one or two officers, according to the grade of the accused and the nature of the charge. Thus, it may be composed of:

1. In case of a private soldier, for a slight offense: a lieutenant.
2. In case of a private, under a grave charge, or of a non-commissioned officer: two lieutenants.
3. In case of a lieutenant: a captain and a lieutenant.
4. In case of a captain: a major and a captain.
5. In case of a field officer: an officer of the next higher grade and one of the same grade, or two officers of the same grade.

A *court-martial* is composed of five classes of members and a judge-advocate or prosecuting officer. The courts are of two kinds: for the *superior* and the *inferior* jurisdictions.

A court of superior jurisdiction is composed as follows:

1. On a private: a major, two captains, two lieutenants, a non-commissioned officer, three lance corporals or privates.

2. On a non-commissioned officer: the same officers, three sergeants or ensigns, and three other non-commissioned officers.

3. On a first or second lieutenant: one lieutenant colonel, two majors, two captains, two first and two second lieutenants.

4. On a captain: a colonel, two lieutenant colonels, two majors, two captains, two first lieutenants.

In case of an offense punishable with death, or imprisonment for life, there must be *three* members of each class of *officers* under the president.

A court of inferior jurisdiction consists of—

1. On a private: a captain, two first and second lieutenants, two non-commissioned officers, and two lance corporals or privates.

2. On a non-commissioned officer: the same officers and two sergeants or ensigns, and two other non-commissioned officers.

The decision of a court-martial is confirmed by the officer appointing it, by the commanding general, by the Minister of War, or by the King, according to the nature of the offense and the rank of the offender.

The punishments inflicted by courts-martial are: death; confinement to hard labor on fortifications; sentence to companies of discipline and work in fortresses; confinement in a fortress; arrests and confinements of various degrees of severity; degradations of various kinds, such as loss of orders of merit, or of badges of honor; reduction of non-commissioned officers or soldiers to lower rank or class, or their expulsion from service, with ineligibility to any employment under the government; cashiering of an officer, with similar disability; dismissal of officers, with or without disability to be reappointed at any time. Corporeal punishment by blows, &c., is entirely prohibited since 1852.

The laws and ordinance prescribe the *nature* of the punishment for every class of offenses. The court finds the facts of the case, and prescribes the *extent* of the penalty, if the law allows any latitude in this respect.

For minor offenses against military discipline and regulations, certain penalties can be inflicted by superiors. On *officers*: private reprimand, or in presence of the other officers, either verbally or by entry on the order book; confinement to quarters for fourteen days. Mere correction with regard to duty is not to be considered a punishment. On *non-commissioned officers*: extra guards or daily duty; slight arrest and confinement to quarters for three weeks, or more strict arrest for fourteen days. On *private soldiers*: extra drills, (three to four hours a day;) extra guards or daily duty; extra work in quarters, stables, &c.; attendance at roll calls at stated times; confinement to quarters for three weeks, or closer confinement from seven to fourteen days. On marches, or in camps, instead of confinement, deprivation of certain allowances, as brandy and tobacco; and instead of close arrest, being tied to a tree, &c., so as to prevent the offender from sitting or lying down. This latter punishment must not exceed three hours a day, and must be as little as possible exposed to public gaze. Lance corporals or privileged soldiers can be deprived of their privilege. The regulations prescribe the extent to which these penalties may be inflicted by officers of the various ranks and stations of command.

The officers and soldiers of the landwehr, permanently attached and on duty, are subject to the rules and regulations of the army. The rest of the landwehr force are subject to military jurisdiction only when called out for service or exercises. At other times they are subject to the civil jurisdiction, except in cases of certain offenses against military law.

Courts of Honor.

This institution is peculiar to the Prussian army, and deserves special notice. The organization of these courts and their jurisdiction are regulated by royal ordinances. The object of the institution is to protect the honor of the corps of officers and of individuals, by reforming delinquents, or expelling them from the service. The jurisdiction of the courts extends to all actions of dishonorable or discreditable character which are not punishable by the ordinary military laws, such as—

    Want of courage or proper spirit.
    Dishonorable debts, either in amount or kind.
    Disreputable manner of living.
    Improper associations in service.
    Scandalous habits of intemperance or gambling.
    Improper conduct in public places.
    Careless performance of duty.

Courts of honor also take cognizance of private quarrels between officers not relating to the performance of duty.

With the exception of general officers, commanders of fortresses and officers who are retired without permission to wear the uniform, all the officers of the army and the landwehr, and the gend'armerie, whether in activity or retired, are subject to the jurisdiction of these courts.

The penalties which they can inflict are, with regard to officers in active service—

    A warning or reprimand.
    Dismissal.
    Expulsion with disability of ever being restored to service.

With regard to retired officers—

    Prohibition to wear the uniform.
    Interdiction of the usual residence of officers.

The court of honor for officers, up to the grade of captain, inclusive, consists of *all* the officers of the regiment or separate battalion of infantry, cavalry, or riflemen; of the brigade of artillery, or of the battalion of engineer troops, each for their own body. Officers not attached to troops appear before a court of their own arm, or the nearest court. The senior officer presides in the court.

Courts of honor on field officers consist of all the field officers of all arms serving in the division, under the presidency of the commanding general. The same courts take cognizance of cases which concern both field officers and inferiors.

In each court there is a *council of honor*, elected by the court for a year, to receive complaints, and to prepare the business for the tribunal. In a court for field officers the council consists of a commander of a regiment, a battalion commander, and a staff officer. In other courts, of a captain, a first and a second lieutenant.

Any officer can bring to the notice of the council the conduct of one of his colleagues. The council takes the order of the president of the court, who decides whether an inquiry shall be made. If so, the council ascertains the facts of the case, and reports to the president, who transmits the report to the commander of the division through the brigade commander. The division commander may annul the proceedings without appeal, or submit the case to the court of honor. If the case relates to officers of two different corps, the common commander refers it to the court of a third corps. If the officers belong to different army corps, the Minister of War designates the court to which the case shall be submitted.

In deciding the judgment of the court, the members of the *council* give their opinion first; then, the senior officer of each grade, in succession; next, the second officer in each grade, &c.;

the voting is *viva voce*; there must be thirteen members present, and in the courts for inferior officers, a majority of *two thirds* is required for a decision; in courts of field officers, a majority decides, or, if opinions are divided, a *plurality*; in case of a division, the senior officer's vote decides the question. The judgment of the court is submitted for the approval and orders of the King. The proceedings and judgment are kept secret, until published by proper authority. The accused may make his defense or explanation in writing, to accompany the record; the members are not sworn.

The adjustment of private quarrels between officers, in cases not immediately relating to military duty, and not cognizable by courts-martial, belongs to the courts of honor, and is regulated by peculiar provisions established by royal ordinance. In case of a quarrel which may give rise to a duel, the parties are bound, in the first place, to lay the matter before the *council of honor*; the council reports to the proper commanding officer, and proceeds to investigate the facts of the case, by verbal interrogatories or written statements from the parties, or by the examination of witnesses, endeavoring to obtain a complete knowledge of the origin and all the circumstances of the case, and the characters of the parties, with a view to arrange an accommodation, if practicable. If the remonstrances of the council prevail, and the proposed settlement of the difficulty is accepted by the parties, (to whom it is communicated either verbally or in writing,) the demands of honor are considered as entirely satisfied by the decision of the council. When the parties are not content to abide by the decision of the council, or when the council cannot effect an amicable arrangement, the affair is carried before the court of honor, and investigated as in other cases. The court may find: 1. That the honor of the parties is not implicated, and that no further proceedings are required. 2. That the quarrel ought to be settled by explanations and reconciliation. 3. That the officers ought to be retired or dismissed. The last decision requires, of course, the sanction of the King. In ordinary cases, the decision of the court is to be regarded as definitive, and no further satisfaction can be demanded. But, in some cases, the court may regard themselves as incompetent to settle the quarrel, and may, therefore, decline to take cognizance of it; or the parties may declare that they are not satisfied. The action of the court then ceases, and the parties become amenable to the authority of the council of honor, under the laws regulating duels.

When informed that a duel is resolved on, the council of honor has the right to be present on the field, in order to bring about a reconciliation, or to regulate the conditions of the combat, by preventing the use of improper arms, &c., and putting an end to the contest when they think proper, the combatants being bound to obedience.

After the duel, another investigation takes place, and the parties are brought before a court-martial, whose decision is immediate, and condemns the combatants, or the survivor of them, to punishment according to a prescribed scale, applicable to the several cases, according to the conduct of the affair and the results of the combat. Thus, in case of an ordinary duel, where neither of the parties is killed, the penalty is confinement from one month to two years in a fortress, according to the severity of the wound; in a mortal duel, when the survivor has caused the death of his adversary by intentional neglect of the prescribed or customary forms, confinement from ten to twenty years in a fortress, and dismissal from the army; so in other cases, of a duel without notice to the council, or one without seconds, additional penalties are prescribed; and in these cases the seconds and witnesses are punished with confinement from one to six months; in other cases, if the conduct of the seconds is irreproachable, they incur no penalty.

If the court-martial finds that one of the parties is *guilty of the duel* and the other *innocent*, the former is punished twice as severely as the latter. If the survivor of a fatal duel is declared *innocent of the duel*, his punishment is much reduced in degree. In case of a mere formal duel, where no malice is shown, and no serious results ensue, a slight penalty only is inflicted by the commanding officer.

If an officer seeks a quarrel with a member of the council on account of their decision, he incurs the same penalty as if he were guilty of the same offense towards a superior officer in the execution of his duty.

The Prussian system of military judicature has been described with some minuteness, on account of its peculiar nature and its adaptation to the character of the people and to the constitution of the military force, and because it is thought to be little known among the officers of our army. It may be worth while to quote a few decisions made by *courts of honor:*

1. An officer was sentenced to be *dismissed* for having borrowed money from his servant.
2. An officer received a *reprimand* for blaming in an offensive manner the acts of the government.
3. A retired officer addicted to gambling was deprived of the *right of wearing the uniform.*
4. An officer who said to another "*what you say is stupid,*" was sentenced to *make an apology.* But the person insulted, not satisfied with this reparation, killed the other in a duel, and was punished for it according to the laws and regulations concerning courts of honor.

REWARDS.

In Prussia, as in other German States, and among the people of Europe generally, one of the most valued rewards of merit is the decoration of an *order*, as a mark of approbation for good service or distinguished actions, either in civil or in military life. Besides foreign orders, which they may be permitted to receive, there are as many as *fifteen* crosses or medals which can be bestowed on the Prussian officer or soldier. Several of these are exclusively military, and imply the performance of some brilliant act or faithful service under difficult circumstances; and the power of conferring these distinctions, to which are often attached the benefits of pensions and nobility, forms a most important auxiliary, in the hands of European sovereigns, to the usual means of rewarding merit in a great number of cases to which it is impossible to apply the more substantial reward of military promotion.

These honorary distinctions, and the usually rapid promotion which takes place in the large armies of continental Europe, account for the absence, in those armies, of the somewhat anomalous system of *brevet promotion,* which has been ingrafted on our military code as a kind of substitute for such honors and rewards.

AUSTRIA.

During the late war in Europe the Austrian army consisted of more than 600,000 men, viz:

Infantry	489,000
Cavalry	67,000
Artillery	47,000
Engineers	11,000
Pioneers	7,000

Besides troops of the train and of special corps, and the gend'armerie, or interior police force, of about 20,000 men. The active troops, not including depot battalions, &c., amounted to 476,000 men.

The Emperor exercises the immediate direction of military affairs. There was no Minister of War; but the orders of the Emperor were conveyed to the commanders and others charged with the execution of them through the "Central Military Bureau" of the Emperor; at the head of which was his principal aid-de-camp and adjutant general, (Count Grünne,) assisted by nine officers of all grades.

There is a Bureau of General Direction of Military Affairs, (corresponding with that of a

war minister or commander-in-chief,) over which presided a member of the imperial family. It is divided into four sections—
1. The service of aides-de-camp.
2. The Bureau of Military Operations.
3. The administrative duties, of which there are twelve subdivisions: general correspondence and bureau duties, recruiting, remounts, invalids, subsistence, equipment, medical affairs, military frontiers, marine, fortifications, accounts, judicial business.
4. Establishments for instruction and education.

Each of these sections is under the direction of a general officer, assisted by the requisite number of other officers of various grades. Some of the subdivisions of the third section are under the direction of military, others of civil officers of several grades.

Other bureaus of the administration are:

General Direction of Artillery: divided into two sections, and each section into three departments, under a general of artillery and twenty-one field officers, &c.

General Direction of Engineers: in six departments, under a lieutenant general and seventy-five field officers, &c.

Superior Military Tribunal: three general officers and five judge-advocates.

Court of Appeals: one general officer, a judge-advocate general, and twelve assistant judge-advocates, &c.

General Staff Corps: consisting of one quartermaster general, one lieutenant general, two major generals, seventeen colonels, twelve lieutenant colonels, twenty-two majors, forty-one first captains, forty-two second captains.

These officers are employed—
1. In the Bureau of the Commander-in-Chief.
2. On the staffs of the four armies, and of the several army corps and military governments.
3. In the Chorographic Bureau, (description of countries.)
4. In the Bureau of Military History.
5. In the Bureau of Movements and Statistics.
6. In the military geographical corps and Geographical Institute, Vienna.
7. In the military schools as professors.
8. On the surveys and maps of various provinces.

The *pioneer* and *pontonnier* corps, and the *flotilla* corps, (for service on the lakes and rivers,) are also under the direction of the Quartermaster General.

There is a *Bureau of Inspection of Arms in the hands of the troops,* under a lieutenant general, with twelve inspection districts.

A *Bureau of the Train,* under a lieutenant general.

A *Bureau of Inspection of Gend'armerie.*

The military forces are distributed into *four armies,* occupying different districts of the empire. The army of the Danubian principalities is a separate command. The headquarters of the four armies are, respectively, at Vienna, Verona in Italy, Buda in Hungary, and Lemberg in Gallicia. The last consists of a single army corps. Each of the others contains four army corps, and a general staff, consisting of the commander, an aid-de-camp general, an orderly officer, a director of artillery, a director of engineers, a bureau of operations, a quartermaster general and staff corps, a bureau of military administration in five sections, a pay and disbursing bureau, an inspection of arms, a surgeon general, a judge-advocate general, a chaplain general.

Each army corps has a similar staff, and is composed of two or three divisions of infantry, a brigade or detachment of cavalry, a reserve of four or more batteries of artillery, a detachment of pioneers, a sanitary company for the service of hospitals and ambulances, a detachment of dragoon orderlies, a detachment of guides, a detachment of pontonniers, a detachment of the train, a detachment of bakers, a commissariat detachment. A cavalry army corps contains two divisions or four brigades of cavalry. A division of infantry consists of two brigades of infantry and two to four squadrons of cavalry. An infantry brigade consists of four battalions of infantry of the line, one battalion of light infantry, and a light foot battery of artillery. A cavalry brigade: two or three regiments of cavalry, and a battery of horse artillery. A mixed brigade is an infantry brigade with two squadrons of cavalry.

The superior grades of officers in the Austrian army are:
Field marshal.
General of artillery (feldzeugmeister) or general of cavalry.
Lieutenant general, (feld marschall-lieutenant.)
Major general.
Colonel.

The other grades are: lieutenant colonel, major, first captain, second captain, first lieutenant, second lieutenants of two classes, cadet. The whole number of officers is about 15,000.

The regiments of infantry, cavalry, and artillery, are designated by numbers; but each regiment is known and usually called by the name of its honorary chief or *proprietor*, (inhaber.) The *proprietors* are members of the imperial family, foreign sovereigns or princes, or distinguished officers of the army. Some of the regiments have permanently the names of distinguished persons, as "Nicholas I, of Russia." These regiments, and those named after foreign princes, have a "second proprietor;" but most of them change their names when they change their chiefs. The immediate military command of the regiment centers entirely in the colonel, or actual commanding officer; but the proprietor exercises certain privileges in reference to the appointment and promotion of junior officers, the marriage of officers, &c.

The colonel alone directs and controls the administrative service of the regiment; there is no council of administration. The regimental staff consists of a chaplain, or chaplains of different churches, if necessary, a judge-advocate, a surgeon, an adjutant, battalion adjutants taken from the line, accounting officer. There are also "regimental agents" in cities, for the affairs of some of the regiments, on the English system. In the administration of the interior service of the regiment, the colonel is assisted by a captain and eight quartermaster sergeants. This captain has charge of all the accounts and returns of money and supplies, as well as the muster-rolls and other records of the regiment. He receives from the captains of companies the estimates and requisitions, and forwards them to the local department of supply from which they are issued. The regimental chest has three keys, one of which is kept by the colonel, one by a field officer, and one by a captain. These officers must, therefore, be present at all deposits and issues of funds, which are handed over to the disbursing officer, and by him paid to the captains, who thus become responsible for the individual payments.

Clothing and equipments are prepared in great manufacturing establishments of the State, under a special administrative department. When desired by the regiments, materials for clothing, &c., are issued to them, and made up by regimental workmen. Arms and ammunition are furnished by the proper department of the artillery. Bread is prepared in government bakeries.

The regimental accounts and returns are submitted to examination and inspection by the "war commissary," or other officer charged with the musters and settlement of accounts. This settlement appears to be final, so far as regards the regimental officers.

The army is *recruited* by provinces or districts, each of which is required to furnish a certain number of men for certain regiments. In this manner, notwithstanding the great variety of nations and languages which are found in the Austrian dominions, each regiment preserves its nationality. The recruits must be not less than nineteen years of age; the term of service is eight years under the colors, and two years in the reserve, which is liable to be at any time recalled into active service. Substitutes are not allowed to be hired as such, but exemption from service may be obtained by the payment of a sum of money, varying from about $250 to $350.

The provinces bordering on Turkey furnish a special force for their own defense, called "the frontier infantry," of about 55,000 men, who are distributed in garrisons and small posts on the frontiers. These troops are military colonists, having lands granted to them on the condition of service, and of supporting themselves in time of peace. The civil government of these provinces is vested in the commanding general.

The *appointment of officers* is made in various ways; but care is always taken that the fitness of the candidates shall be ascertained, as far as possible, by previous examinations. A great proportion of officers are appointed from the military schools; but any young man, capable of passing the requisite examination, may offer himself for appointment. In every regiment there are many *cadets*, who enter to fit themselves for promotion. They are appointed by the proprietors of regiments, and they receive a certain stipend from their parents—about six to ten dollars a month. They form a separate mess, and they are instructed by officers of the regiment detailed by the colonel. The applications for these appointments go through the colonel, who furnishes the proprietor information as to the character, &c. The candidate must be not less than sixteen years of age, and must be able to pass an examination in the usual branches of elementary studies, before a board of a field officer and two others, appointed by the commander of the army corps to which the regiment belongs. After two years' service, he may be examined for promotion, and become a candidate for a vacancy. The graduates of the military academies have preference to appointments; but in the regiments the Emperor appoints them only in the proportion of one graduate to two cadets advanced by the proprietor. The latter may also promote competent non-commissioned officers, in the proportion of one of this class to three cadets. Sons of *soldiers* entering as cadets are supported by the State; if not competent for promotion, they serve as non-commissioned officers or privates; others are admitted, on the same terms, into the military schools.

Promotions in the army are generally made according to seniority, up to the grade of major. The proprietors of regiments have the right of nomination to the grade of captain, inclusive; from that grade promotions are made by the Emperor, according to lists of merit kept in the War Office; above the grade of major, promotions are made by selection.

The government provides, with great liberality, the means of education and instruction for officers. The system of military schools has been lately reorganized, as shown in the following tabular statement:

No.	Kind of school.	No. of pupils.	Ages of pupils.
			Years.
12	Primary schools	1,200	8 to 12
12	Upper preparatory schools	2,400	12 to 15
4	Cadet schools	840	12 to 15
6	Infantry school-companies	720	15 to 17
3	Cavalry school-squadrons	180	15 to 17
2	Frontier school-companies	240	15 to 18
5	Artillery school-companies	600	15 to 18
1	Engineer school-company	120	15 to 18
1	Pioneer school-company	120	15 to 18
1	Flotilla school-company	60	15 to 18
1	Marine school-company	120	13 to 17
1	Naval academy	100	13 to 17
1	Pupils for practice at sea	50	17 to 19
1	Neustadt military academy	400	15 to 19
1	Artillery academy	200	16 to 19
1	Engineer academy	200	16 to 19
1	Upper artillery and engineer academy, for officers	40	
1	Staff school, for officers	30	
1	Institute, for non-commissioned officers	60	
55	Whole number of pupils	7,670	

The pupils pass from the lower schools to the higher, according to their capacities and fitness.

The oldest of these institutions was established by the Empress Maria Theresa, about the year 1750, and its hall is now adorned with many portraits of Austria's most distinguished marshals and generals, who were graduates of the academy at Wiener-Neustadt. When the new system shall have been carried into complete operation, the country may well expect that its accomplished corps of officers will be unsurpassed by any others, in military science and instruction.

The despotic and military nature of the government of this Empire, its great extent, the various and heterogeneous nations which compose it, with the corresponding varieties of climate, character, and language, make it highly important for good government that the military officers, who exercise a great share in its administration, should be men of ability and accomplished education; such as were employed, at the time of our visit to Verona, to assist Marshal Radetzky in the government of Lombardy. The mere command and instruction of the troops, and the proper execution of strictly military duties, require of the officers the familiar use of several languages and dialects; for, in order to produce a harmonious action among the various nations, the government places German officers in the Italian, Hungarian, and Sclavonic regiments, and *vice versa*; and with the same view, the commands are given in German to all the troops. From obvious motives of State policy, too, the troops do not generally serve among their own countrymen. Thus, Italian and Hungarian regiments are found in the garrison of Vienna, whilst in the beautiful plains of Lombardy the people are kept in subjection by bands of Austrians and Bohemians, &c.

> "The hostile hordes
> Of many-nationed spoilers from the Po
> Quaff blood and water."

The bond of brotherhood, the kind of Freemasonry, which unites together military men, even of different nations, (as we often experienced in our travels,) is strikingly exemplified in the *bon-hommie* and cordiality of manner towards each other observable among the officers of the Austrian army, and this is encouraged by the policy of the government. In their familiar intercourse, it is the custom of the officers to address their comrades in the second person singular, as brothers, or members of one family. A similar spirit characterizes their intercourse with strangers; they take a pride in being distinguished, even from other Germans, by an elegant courtesy and amiable frankness of manner; and in no country which we visited in our journey, had we a more cordial reception than in Austria, or more agreeable association than with Austrian officers of all ranks, from the highest to the lowest grade; from the field marshal to the lieutenant.

In garrison towns the officers do not live in messes; each one takes his meals where he chooses; and single officers, or knots of four or five, may be met with at the tables of hotels and restaurants. Previously to 1848, they were not required to wear the uniform when off duty, and a good deal of confusion and inconvenience resulted from this practice during the troubles of that period, in consequence of their not being able to recognize each other. At present they are always in uniform; but when not on service, they dispense with the sash, and wear a light and neat forage cap.

The marriage of officers is not encouraged, and few junior officers are married. The government allows no pension to a widow; but, before the officer can receive permission to marry, he must deposit with the government securities to the amount of $3,000, for the support of his family in case of his death. The proprietor of a regiment can give permission to one sixth of his officers to marry; after that number, permission must be obtained from the Emperor.

The remarks made on Prussia, with respect to honorary distinctions by crosses and medals, so much valued by all the German nations, apply equally to Austria. Marshal Radetzky's splendid collection of decorations contained the crosses of *thirty orders*, received from most of the sovereigns of Europe, the British being among the exceptions. There are four great military orders in Austria, the principal being that of "Maria Theresa," which, besides honorary privileges and noble rank, confers pensions on its members.

For the education of young men intended for the medical staff, there is a fine institution at Vienna, called the "Josephinum;" it receives 300 students, who enter at eighteen, and remain three years for instruction as physicians, or two years for surgeons. The appliances for instruction appear to be excellent; and the museum of anatomical models in wax, prepared at Florence, is one of the "sights" of Vienna.

FRANCE.

The whole force of the French army in 1855, exclusive of gend'armerie, veterans, &c., was about 550,000 men, viz:

Infantry	382,000
Cavalry	86,000
Artillery	57,000
Engineers	8,000
Administration, &c	17,000
	550,000

The whole number of officers of all kinds is about 20,000.

Under the decrees and orders of the Emperor, the direction and administration of the military force are exercised by the Minister of War.

The personal staff of the Emperor consisted in 1855 of eleven aides-de-camp, (generals or colonels,) and twelve orderly officers, (majors or captains.)

The War Ministry is organized in seven divisions, besides the personal staff and cabinet of the Minister, as follows:

FIRST DIVISION.—The personnel of the army, under a lieutenant general:
    1st *Bureau.*—General Correspondence.
    2d   "   Staff and Military Schools.
    3d   "   Recruiting and Discharges.
    4th "   Justice.
    5th "   Infantry.
    6th "   Cavalry.
    7th "   Gend'armerie.

The chiefs of these bureaus are civil officers.

SECOND DIVISION.—Service of the artillery, under direction of a lieutenant general:
    1st *Section.*— The personnel, under a lieutenant colonel.
    2d   "   Matériel and accountability, under a colonel.

THIRD DIVISION.—Service of engineers, under a lieutenant general:
    1st *Section.*—Personnel, under a civilian chief.
    2d   "   Matériel and accountability, under a major.

FOURTH DIVISION.—Administration, under an intendant:
    1st *Bureau.*—Personnel, Transportation, Trains.
    2d   "   Subsistence and Fuel.
    3d   "   Medical Officers, Hospitals, Invalids.
    4th "   Clothing, Camp Equipage, Harness.
    5th "   Pay, Musters, Interior Administration.

The chiefs of bureaus are civilians.

FIFTH DIVISION.—Affairs of Algiers, under a lieutenant general:
    Four Bureaus.—Under civil chiefs.

SIXTH DIVISION.—*Dépôt de la guerre*, under a colonel:
    1st *Section.*—Geodesy, topography, drawing, and engraving maps, under a lieutenant colonel.
    2d " Military history, statistics, archives, under a colonel.

SEVENTH DIVISION.—General accountability, under a civilian chief, as are also the several bureaus:
    1st *Bureau.*—Revision of Accounts of Expenditures.
    2d " Distribution of Funds, &c.
    3d " Property Accounts.
    4th " Pensions.
    5th " Interior service of the War Office.
    6th " Laws, Archives, Decorations.

The Minister of War is further aided by several consulting committees or boards, composed principally of general officers, viz:

For the staff	13	members.
For the infantry	6	"
For the cavalry	6	"
For the gend'armerie	6	"
For the artillery	9	"
For the engineers	10	"
For the affairs of Algiers	11	"
For the medical department	5	"
For the veterinary department	10	"
For public works	18	"
For pay and allowances	15	"

The *general officers* of the army are:
    Six marshals of France, (twelve in time of war.)
    Eighty generals of division, (lieutenant generals.)
    One hundred and sixty generals of brigade, (major generals.)

There are also many generals on the reserved and the retired lists. Major generals are placed on the reserved list at sixty-two years of age; lieutenant generals at sixty-five to sixty-eight years, with *three-fifths* of their regular pay. They are liable to be called into service in the interior of the empire. They are retired with pensions only at their own request. Besides the functions of command of districts, divisions, and brigades, the lieutenant generals and major generals are employed as inspectors general, and as chiefs of the staff of armies and army corps. Generals of engineers and artillery are included in the above number.

The *staff corps* is composed of five hundred and sixty officers, from colonels to lieutenants, who are employed as aides-de-camp, and on the staffs of divisions and brigades, as professors at the military schools, and in the topographical and statistical business, of the *dépôt de la guerre*. The lieutenants are detached for four years' regimental service in the infantry and the cavalry, and another year, sometimes, in the artillery or engineers, before they are put on staff duty. There is a special school for the education of officers intended for the staff corps.

The *military intendancy* is a corps of two hundred and forty-six officers, charged with the administrative duties of the army and the accountability—that is to say, with the supplies in money and in kind for every branch of the military service: provisions and forage, clothing and camp equipage, quarters, transportation of all kinds, hospital stores, and ambulance service, military prisons, &c. The officers are taken exclusively from the army, of the several grades from colonel to captain, and they retain military rank—the principal intendant having the rank of major general.

For the performance of the various services of the intendancy there are large corps of officers and men, called " troops of the administration," composed of workmen of various trades, hospital attendants, drivers, clerks, &c., who are employed with the armies in the field, or in the establishments for constructing, repairing, and preserving the equipments and stores required for the service of the troops. There are seven companies of workmen, and six squadrons or twenty-four companies, of the train, numbering 12,000 men; and 3,000 attendants for the service of the hospitals. The companies of workmen are recruited from the other corps of the army, with men who have served one year, and not more than two years, and who have some useful trade, such as: bakers, millers, butchers, shoemakers, masons, carpenters, locksmiths, from which the nature of their service may be deduced. The troops of the train are charged with conducting ambulances and other means of transport for the sick and wounded; transporting the materials for subsistence, hospitals, clothing, and camp equipage; the military chest, the mails, the papers and archives, (except those of the artillery and engineers,) and the transportation of all supplies which the troops cannot receive at the place of distribution. In the execution of these services the officers of the corps of military intendants exercise authority over the officers and men of the troops of the administration.

The *medical department* consists of 1,277 surgeons, and 162 apothecaries. This body is now recruited by pupils of the Military Medical School recently established at Paris. The surgeons are attached to armies or districts as inspectors, or to hospitals, regiments, and corps as medical officers. They have different grades, as inspectors, principal physicians or surgeons, and assistants; but have no assimilated rank with other officers of the army, nor do they exercise any command either in hospital or in the field.

SPECIAL STAFFS.— The *garrison staff corps* consists of 341 officers and employés of various grades, who perform, in the garrisoned towns and forts, the duties of commandants, town majors, adjutants, clerks, chaplains.

The *artillery and engineers* have each a large staff of officers and employés, (guards and storekeepers, &c.,) who are charged with the direction of their respective affairs in the military districts, garrisons, schools, and manufacturing establishments, and with the care of depots of stores and supplies pertaining to the service of those corps. The officers for these staff duties are selected from the whole corps, and remain in the line of promotion. But there is a certain number of captains of artillery, called "captains with fixed stations," who are exclusively attached to the direction of artillery, and who, in consideration of a fixed residence, renounce their promotion, but retain the command of their grade. The generals of engineers and artillery select their aides-de-camp from the officers of those corps.

The *artillery establishments* are:

The central depot at Paris, (library, museum, workshops for instruments and experiments.)

Ten regimental schools for the instruction of officers, non-commissioned officers, and soldiers.

The central school of pyrotechny.

The twenty-six directions of artillery, for regulating the service of the arm in the several territorial districts.

Eight arsenals of construction.

The forges employed to furnish iron and steel for the arsenals, and shot and shells.

Four manufactories of small arms.

Three cannon founderies.

Eleven powder mills.

Seven refineries of saltpeter.

A refinery of sulphur.
A depot of sulphur.
The "school of application" at Metz is common to the officers of artillery and engineers.
The organization of the corps of artillery is explained under the head of "field artillery."

APPOINTMENT AND PROMOTION OF OFFICERS.

A candidate for the appointment of second lieutenant (or sub-lieutenant) must be at least eighteen years of age, and must have served two years as non-commissioned officer, or be a graduate of a military school.

For promotion to be a first lieutenant or captain, the officer must have served two years in the next lower grade.

For a major, or the corresponding rank of *chef de bataillon* or *chef d'escadron*, he must have served four years as captain.

A lieutenant colonel, three years in the lower grade.

A colonel, two years as lieutenant colonel.

A major general or lieutenant general, three years in the next lower grade.

A marshal, three years as lieutenant general, and the chief command of an army or army corps, *before the enemy*.

For brilliant actions, noticed in general orders, promotions are made without regard to the above rules; and generally, in time of war, the term of service required for promotion may be reduced one half.

Ordinary promotions are made partly by *selection of the Emperor*, partly by *seniority*.

For the lowest grade of lieutenant, *one third* of the appointments are made from non-commissioned officers; the others from the military schools.

In time of peace, *two thirds* of the first lieutenants and captains, and *one half* of the majors and officers of corresponding rank, are promoted according to *seniority*; in time of war, the majors, &c., are all promoted by *selection*.

All officers of superior rank to major are promoted by selection, at all times.

Selections for promotion are regulated by lists of merit prepared every year at the general inspections. No brevet or honorary rank can be bestowed. There are special rules for the promotion of officers of the medical staff and the administration, similar to those for officers of regiments and corps.

MILITARY SCHOOLS.

The most ample means are provided for the instruction of officers and non-commissioned officers, in all branches of the military service, as will appear from the following summary statement:

In the regiments of infantry and cavalry there are regimental schools for the instruction of non-commissioned officers, to prepare them for promotion, under the direction of officers. The infantry have also regimental schools of practice in firing, for the officers and non-commissioned officers.

For the artillery non-commissioned officers and soldiers there are ten regimental schools, established in fixed garrisons, with officers as instructors; and for the engineers, three similar schools.

The military schools, properly so called, are:

1. The *Preparatory School*, at La Flèche, for the education of 400 sons of officers, or of non-commissioned officers killed in action, to prepare them for the higher military schools; paying pupils are also admitted; pupils received from ten to twelve years old.

2. The *Polytechnic School*, at Paris, to prepare young men for any of the *scientific corps* of

the army, navy, or civil administration of the government; such as the artillery, engineers, staff, naval constructors, hydraulic engineers, civil engineers, mining engineers, powder manufacturers, &c., &c.

3. The *Military School of St. Cyr*, to prepare pupils for officers of infantry and cavalry, and some for the staff.

4. The *Staff School*, for officers of the staff corps, at Paris.
5. The *School for officers of Artillery and Engineers*, at Metz.
6. The *Cavalry School*, for officers and non-commissioned officers, at Saumur.
7. The *Normal School for Firing*, for infantry officers, at Vincennes.
8. The *Normal Gymnastic School*, for non-commissioned officers, at Vincennes.
9. The *Military School of Music*, at Paris.
10. The *Pyrotechnic School*, at Metz.
11. The *School of Medicine and Pharmacy*, at Paris.
12. The *Veterinary School*, at Alfort.

RECRUITING.

The French army is recruited by conscription and by voluntary enlistment. The conscription includes all Frenchmen of the age of twenty years; but certain circumstances or occupations procure exemption from service. The men required from each district are drawn out by lot. Those not drawn form a reserve, liable to be called out at any time. A council of revision decides on the qualifications, exemptions, &c. Substitutes fit for service are allowed. The minimum stature for the recruit is five feet one and a half inch. The recruits are received at depots of the corps for which they are required; the number of men and the corps being designated in the decree by which they are called out.

The term of service is seven years, but the actual service with the colors is frequently limited to four or five years. Soldiers discharged before the expiration of their term, together with the conscripts not called into the service, form the *reserve*, which amounts to about 180,000 men.

The corps of *gend'armerie* is recruited from the soldiers of the army, of which it may be considered as forming a part. The force is about 25,000 men.

The *national guard* or militia is also an important addition to the military force of the empire, amounting to about 100,000 men, who may be used to replace the regular troops in the interior of the country.

RETIREMENT FROM SERVICE.—PENSIONS—PAY.

The *retiring pensions* are regulated according to rank and length of service. The right to a pension is acquired by *thirty years* of actual service. Certain allowances are made for special services and for campaigns. For services beyond thirty years the pension is increased; and also, for service of more than twelve years in the grade on which the pension is allowed.

The retirement of general officers has been already mentioned.

Wounds or diseases contracted in the service give a right to pensions at various rates, according to the degree of disability, or to admission into the magnificent asylum for invalids in Paris.

Pensions are allowed to widows and children of officers and soldiers who have been killed in battle or in active service, or who have died on account of wounds, or of contagious diseases contracted in actual service, or who have died in the enjoyment of a retiring pension. The widow's pension is generally *one fourth* of the pension of the husband, according to grade. After the death of the mother, the pension descends to the children until the youngest is twenty-one.

The *pay of officers* in service depends on their position, whether in *actual employment* or *waiting orders*, (applied to general and staff officers unemployed,) or temporarily *retired and unemployed*, by disbandment of corps, loss of position by captivity, &c. The last class of officers are recalled as occasion offers, to fill one half of the vacancies that occur in their respective arms. Officers may be *dropped* from the rolls on account of *incurable disease*, or as a *punishment* for faults; in the latter case, the removal is made on the report of the Minister of War, after investigation by a *court of inquiry;* in some cases, the officer thus dropped from service is allowed a certain rate of pay.

The pay and allowances vary, also, with the state of the troops, whether on *peace establishment, assembled for active service,* (as in camps of instruction, or preparation for war,) or in *war.* The war pay is uniform; but the compensation in time of peace depends on the individual position of the officer or soldier in actual service; such as whether he is stationary or on a march, present or absent from his regiment, on furlough, in hospital, in confinement, or a prisoner of war. There are also supplementary allowances for pay, for peculiar circumstances, as: for length of service; for traveling allowances; for residence in Paris; for professors and instructors in the schools; for recruiting depots; for table money to certain commanding officers and others; commutation for forage, quarters, and furniture; subsistence; payment for horses and property lost, &c.

The soldiers receive only a small portion of their pay, as *pocket money,* (*centimes de poche;*) the expenditure of the remainder is regulated by the regimental council of administration, for their subsistence, clothing, repairs of arms and equipments, &c. In each regiment, a captain performs the duties of treasurer or paymaster, and another, those of clothing officer. The funds are drawn from a treasury agent, (sub-treasurer,) as in our service.

The *accountability* for all expenditures in the War Department is conducted within the Department. The accounts, when audited and settled, are reported to the "court of accounts," which registers the receipts and disbursements for the whole Empire, in all the departments of public service.

This branch of the business of the army is conducted by the corps of military intendants, whose duty it is not only to verify the muster-rolls of the troops and the property returns by actual inspection, but also to examine and verify the accounts and returns relative to the interior administration of regiments and corps, all of which must be submitted to their inspection at any time which they may appoint. In this inspection, the intendant verifies the muster-rolls, the soldiers' account books, the company books, the mess books, the quality and condition of the clothing and equipments, and countersigns the registers of the council of administration relative to these matters.

These inspections and verifications are independent of the military reviews and inspections of the troops, in relation to their instruction and preparation for service, which are made by general officers designated for that purpose, in the several arms of service and in the several military divisions of the Empire; either at annual visits, or when specially detached for the purpose by the Minister of War. Special inspections of the condition of arms in the hands of the troops are made by officers of the artillery appointed for that purpose.

FURLOUGHS.

In time of peace, regular furloughs are allowed to a certain number of officers and soldiers during *six months,* from October 1 to March 31. The proportion depends on the actual force of the command, but is generally about *one third* of the officers and *one eighth* of the enlisted men. This is partly a measure of economy, on account of the reduced pay on furlough, and its execution, in regard to time, is in some degree regulated by the state of the supplies, as well as by political circumstances. For officers, furloughs are granted only on their own requests, and the furlough time may be divided between several officers of the same grade. For field officers, administrative officers, and the medical staff, the furloughs must be sanctioned by the Minister of War. To the soldiers, furloughs are given after two years' service, to men who have completed their military instruction, and who have a fixed domicil and means of support. The furloughs are given by the council of administration, countersigned by the intendant officer and approved by the Inspector General. Generals commanding divisions may give *temporary* furloughs during the furlough season, provided the whole number absent does not exceed the limits established by the Minister of War.

Sick leaves may be granted, not to exceed *six months*, to accompany officers or soldiers, by the generals in command of territorial divisions; to field officers, or for a longer time, they must be authorized by the Minister of War, as also furloughs for private business.

MILITARY DISTRICTS.

For the command and administration of the troops, the territory of France is divided into *twenty-one* military divisions, which are subdivided into *eighty-five* districts, corresponding with the geographical departments. Algiers comprises *three divisions*.

Each *division* is commanded by a general of division, (lieutenant general,) and each district by a general of brigade, (major general,) assisted by a suitable number of staff and administrative officers. The staff of a division includes a general commanding the artillery; but with regard to the operations of the arsenals and manufacturing establishments of the artillery and engineers, the officers in charge correspond directly with their respective administrative chiefs or bureaus of the War Department. The directors of fortifications correspond, in relation to the troops under their orders, through the usual channel of the general of division.

Since our visit to France, the territory has been further distributed into five great military departments, the troops in each being under the command of a marshal.

OF THE ADMINISTRATION OF JUSTICE.

There are three kinds of military courts, viz:
        Courts-martial.
        Courts of Appeal or Revision.
        Courts of Inquiry.

In every territorial division, in every active division of an army in the field, and in every garrisoned place in a state of siege, there are *two permanent courts-martial*, called the first and second courts, which have concurrent jurisdiction, at the option of the commanding general, of military offenses committed in the division. They are composed of seven members, assisted by an imperial commissioner, a judge-advocate, (*rapporteur*,) and a secretary.

For the trial of persons below the rank of field officer, the court consists of a colonel, a major, two captains, a lieutenant, a sub-lieutenant, and a non-commissioned officer.

For field officers, the sub-lieutenant and the non-commissioned officer are replaced by two officers of the rank of the accused, and for general officers a similar rule prevails.

For the trial of officers of the intendancy, officers of that corps are associated with others on the court.

The members of courts-martial are detailed by roster, according to seniority; but a member must be at least twenty-five years old.

The imperial commissioner and the judge-advocates are taken from the rank of major or captain, either in active service or retired. The secretaries are taken from retired officers and non-commissioned officers, or citizens who have belonged to the army. All these officers are appointed by the Minister of War, and the appointments are revoked by him, on the report of the general of division.

The commissioner is particularly charged with the observance of the necessary formalities, and with attending to the correct application of the laws. The judge-advocate is the prosecuting officer; he may be assisted, if necessary, by one or more substitutes. The secretary records the proceedings, and attends to all the writing.

The commanding officer, informed of an offense, directs the judge-advocate to inquire into the evidence, and, on his report, convenes the court for the trial. A majority of five out of the seven members is necessary for conviction. The decision of the court is immediately announced: in case of conviction, the accused has twenty-four hours allowed to make an appeal, and a like time is allowed to the commissioner for the same purpose; in case of appeal, the record is sent to the court of appeal.

After the final decision, the judge-advocate makes known the sentence to the commanding officer, to be carried into immediate execution. A report of the sentence is sent to the corps to which the accused belongs, and to the Minister of War.

The penal code defines, as minutely as possible, the punishments for specified offenses. The court determines the extent of the penalty in cases where the law allows any latitude. The punishments are: death, the galleys from five to twenty years, confinement in irons from two to twenty years, imprisonment, solitary confinement, hard labor on public works, ball and chain, dismissal from service, &c. Military prisons are provided in the principal garrisoned towns, under the direction of officers of the administration.

There are *twelve courts of appeal*, established at fixed points, and one in each division of an active army and in a besieged place. The court consists of five members: a general, a colonel or lieutenant colonel, a major, and two captains. The imperial commissioner is of the rank of field officer; the duties of judge-advocate are performed by one of the members of the court. The members are appointed by the same authority as for courts-martial; their age must be at least thirty years. The courts of appeal decide, by a simple majority of votes, concerning the validity of judgments referred to them, as to the legality of the constitution of the court-martial, the competency of their jurisdiction, the violation of law in the forms of proceeding, or in the penalty adjudged. If the judgment of the court-martial is not sustained, the case is remanded to the other permanent court or to the court of another division, or other competent court, for a new trial; if the judgment is confirmed, it is returned to the court to be executed.

Courts of inquiry are instituted for the investigation of accusations against officers involving their dismissal, either as a punishment, or for being on the retired list more than three years, or for having been condemned to imprisonment for more than six months; the object of the inquiry being to decide whether the officer shall be declared incompetent for recall to active service. These courts are of three kinds: *regimental, divisional,* or *special.* The regimental courts have cognizance of the cases of company officers; the divisional courts of the cases of field officers and those not belonging to regiments or to the division; the members of both are appointed by the division commander. The special courts have cognizance of the cases of general officers and military intendants; the members are appointed by the Minister of War. These courts consist of *five members*, of whom at least *two* must be of the same corps as the accused.

An officer can be brought before a court of inquiry only by the Minister of War, in France, or the general-in-chief, abroad. In the case of a general officer, the order of the Minister is always required.

The investigation is not public; but it takes place in the presence of the accused. The decision is made by means of secret ballot, and the record is submitted for the action of the Minister of War. The decision of the court can be altered only *in favor* of the officer; the court is dissolved as soon as the judgment is given.

These *courts of inquiry* have some analogy to the Prussian "*courts of honor*," for deciding on cases of misconduct not relating strictly to the military service, nor specified in the penal code.

For the interior government of soldiers, and for minor offenses against discipline, they are amenable to a *regimental court*, appointed by the colonel, and consisting of a field officer, the three oldest captains, and the three oldest lieutenants not belonging to the battalion or squadron of the offender. In detached corps, the general of brigade appoints the court. The result of the investigation is reported to the general of division, who orders the offender, if convicted, to be confined, not more than two months, in a fort or military prison; or, in case of an old offender, to be transferred to a disciplinary company; reporting the decision in all cases to the Minister of War.

GENERAL REMARKS.

To obtain a complete knowledge of the details of the organization and administration of the French army requires an examination of an immense number of laws and decrees, which are published in the "Journal Officiel Militaire." Of this work two large volumes are usually published every year, containing not only the general laws, but the most minute regulations for every branch of the service, the forms of returns and reports, &c. It is only in this way, or by consulting the books of regulations for the several arms and departments of service, which are reprinted separately, that an idea can be formed of the vast mass of papers which are used in the administration; but a general view of the system may be obtained from the compendiums drawn up for the purpose of instruction, and especially from Vauchelle's "Cours d'Administration," in three volumes.

The organization of the French military force, like that of the other departments of the government, necessarily experienced the effect of the sweeping measures of reform which were adopted in the first revolution, by which all the old traditions and privileges of favored corps and families were obliterated, and the field opened for the adoption of a system based on the single consideration of efficiency. How well this object was attained is evinced in the almost unparalleled success of the military operations under the republic and the first empire; and no subsequent government has ventured to depart materially from the principles then established. The French army may be said to possess a truly *republican* constitution. It is true that in other countries of Europe the principle of promotion of officers from the rank of common soldier is acknowledged, but the cases of its application are rare, and seldom attended with good results; whereas in the French army it is not a barren principle, but a rule of constant and regular application; so that the son of the meanest peasant, in obeying the conscription, may hope to attain the highest rank in the army. The instances of such success are too frequent and too well known to require particular mention. In the list of Ministers of War, (marshals or lieutenant generals,) since 1798, there are *twelve* who commenced their careers as private soldiers. The influence of such considerations in promoting good conduct, desire of instruction, and zealous performance of duty, is incontestably great. Through this influence, and the ample opportunities of theoretical and practical instruction, in peace and war, which the army constantly possesses, the officers and soldiers have justly acquired the highest reputation for the scientific ability and the individual energy and self-reliance which they exhibit in their military operations. It is true that these advantages are obtained at the frequent sacrifice of refinement of character and manners on the part of a portion of the officers, even those of elevated rank; but the great condition of efficiency in the service of the State is not the less fulfilled.

This principle of promotion can only be advantageously applied, on a large scale, where the army is recruited, like the French and Prussian, by compulsory process, from the whole youthful population of the country, and where the military institutions and the nature of the service afford ample means of instruction to those who may not have possessed the advantages of early education.

In the French army a further encouragement and reward for good conduct, on the part of non-commissioned officers and soldiers, is found in the establishment of *corps d'élite*, which are recruited by selection from old soldiers; such are the small corps of *Cent Gardes*, (for service about the person of the emperor,) and the *Imperial Guard*, recently reëstablished on the model of the distinguished corps of that name under the Great Napoleon. The Imperial Guard is a division composed of brigades of picked troops of all arms: zouaves, chasseurs, voltigeurs, grenadiers, infantry of the line, horse and foot artillery, cavalry of various kinds, &c., forming in itself a complete little army. We had an opportunity of seeing a large portion of this corps reviewed in the Crimea by General McMahon, the distinguished officer who commanded the attacking force in the last assault on Sebastopol. Their fine personal appearance, good equipment, and active movements, fully justify the selection of these men for an honorable distinction.

GREAT BRITAIN.

By a sort of fiction of the British constitution the existence of a *standing army* is not recognized, and the maintenance of a regular force depends on the annual vote of supplies by Parliament, and the annual enactment of a law called the *mutiny act*, which authorizes the punishment of offenses, regulates the billeting of soldiers in private houses, and empowers the sovereign to make rules and articles of war for the government of the troops. In practice, however, there is a permanent force of nearly uniform strength and organization in time of peace, consisting of the army proper (the cavalry and infantry) and the *ordnance department*, embracing the artillery and engineers—numbering in all about 140,000 men.

The *cavalry* force is about 13,000 in twenty-seven regiments, viz:
    Two regiments of life guards.
    One regiment of horse guards.
    Seven regiments of dragoon guards.
    Seventeen regiments of dragoons, hussars, and lancers.

These are rather distinctive *names* than indications of the nature and armament of the troops.
The *infantry* consists of—
    One regiment of grenadier guards.
    One regiment of Scot's fusileer guards.
    One regiment of Coldstream guards.
    Ninety-nine regiments of foot.
    And the rifle brigade.

There are also *ten regiments* of colonial infantry forming part of the regular force for local service in the colonies. The organization of the infantry regiments is not uniform for all; some consist of two or three battalions, but they are generally of one battalion, or about 1,000 men, when full, divided into eight or ten companies. Most of the regiments have one lieutenant colonel and two majors; but many of them have two lieutenant colonels and three or four majors. The coloneley of a regiment of cavalry or infantry is a nominal rank, the position being held by a general officer. He enjoys certain emoluments derived from the privilege of supplying the clothing of the men. The actual command of the regiment is in the lieutenant colonel.

The grades of rank of company officers are captain, lieutenant, and ensign, or cornet in the regiments of cavalry. The officers of the guards have rank in the army one grade higher than that which they hold in their own regiments. It operates in the same manner as brevet rank. Promotions are made regimentally up to the grade of lieutenant colonel; above that grade all rank in the army is in the nature of a brevet. The grades above the rank of colonel are: major general, lieutenant general, general, and field marshal. The sovereign often confers local rank, which is operative only in particular armies or districts of country abroad. The appointment of brigadier general is of the nature of local rank, giving precedence only in active service.

Brevets are not conferred on officers below the grade of captain. Appointments to the regiments are made in the lowest grade by the commander-in-chief of the army. They do not require any previous service or instruction in military knowledge. Recently, however, an order has been made for the examination of candidates, and for promotion of non-commissioned officers who may have distinguished themselves in action, or by meritorious conduct. Vacancies in the higher grades, up to lieutenant colonel inclusive, occurring by death, are filled according to seniority. Voluntary vacancies by resignation or the sale of commissions are filled by purchase; the commission being taken by the senior officer in the next grade, who is qualified and able to pay for it according to an established tariff. A certain term of service in the lower grade is required before advancement. The rule of purchase does not apply to the artillery or engineers, in which appointments are made from the Military Academy, or from young men who can pass the examination required of a graduate of the academy. Promotions are made by seniority. A certain term of service in one grade also entitles the officer to advancement in the artillery and engineers. Thus a lieutenant colonel, after three years' service as such, becomes a colonel in the army. The necessary result of this system is the withdrawal of a large number of officers from active service for want of employment corresponding to their rank. The pension system is also applied with great liberality to the army. The army list for 1855 contains the names of 135 general officers, (many of them very distinguished men,) who were in the receipt of unattached, pay (from $2,000 to $3,000 a year;) of about 160 field officers and 100 company officers retired on full pay, and of about four hundred officers of various grades retired on half pay.

The *artillery* consists of one corps called the "Royal Regiment of Artillery," composed of colonels, (some of whom are also general officers,) lieutenant colonels, first and second captains, and lieutenants; with about 15,000 men. This force is distributed into fourteen battalions of eight companies or foot batteries, and the brigade of horse artillery, which includes the rocket batteries. The small body of horse artillery is one of the most splendid corps to be seen in any army—distinguished by the richness of their dress and appointments, the excellent character of their material, their fine horses, and the quickness of their maneuvers. The field batteries of foot artillery, in which the men are mounted for maneuvers on the ammunition chests of the gun carriage and caisson, are scarcely inferior in efficiency to the horse batteries. It was the admirable facility of maneuver on difficult ground, exhibited by the British artillery during the occupation of Paris, after the fall of Napoleon, which attracted the attention of the French artillery officers to the study of the British matériel, and led to the adoption of the present French system, which has been copied by several other powers of Europe, and by ourselves. The batteries of horse artillery consist of light 6-pounder guns and 12-pounder howitzers, for the usual service of instruction in time of peace; but it may be observed that in campaign they generally adopt the 9-pounder gun instead of the 6-pounder. The foot batteries have heavy 12-pounder guns and 24-pounder howitzers, and some 18-pounder guns and light 8-inch howitzers.

The headquarters of the artillery are at Woolwich, which is the depot and school of practice for the corps. Here also is the military academy for the instruction of the young men intended for the artillery or engineers. There is a military college at Sandhurst for the instruction of officers of other corps of the army, who wish to qualify themselves for staff duty; but the selections for the staff are by no means made exclusively or principally from those who have pursued their studies at this college. This institution, however, has just been remodeled.

There is no special staff corps. General officers appointed on the staff, (as it is called,) that is to say, assigned to commands or stations according to their rank, select their own aides-de-camp from any corps in the army; and officers are detailed in like manner for duty in the Adjutant General's and Quartermaster General's Departments. The duties of the Adjutant General's Department are nearly the same as in our service. Those of the Quartermaster General and Commissary relate chiefly to the movements and supplies of the troops serving abroad, in Ireland, or in the colonies. The Quartermaster General has charge also of the Topographical Department of the staff, with reference to the movements of the troops in campaign, &c. The officers of the Commissariat Department are not taken from the army, and have no military rank out of their corps, within the island of Great Britain. The Ordnance Department is charged with quartering and supplying the troops, and that department has the general charge of barracks both at home and abroad; for which purpose it has a large number of barrack masters, who are generally retired officers or non-commissioned officers. The Pay Department is one of the civil departments of the army administration. The regulations touching pay, emoluments, and the army accountability, are under direction of a civil officer, called the Deputy Secretary at War. Until the late war with Russia the command of the troops was divided between the commander-in-chief for the army proper, (the cavalry and infantry,) and the master general of the ordnance for the artillery and engineers; and these officers were independent of any common superior. The master general of the ordnance was usually a Cabinet Minister, but on account of the incongruity of this arrangement, the command of the troops is now simplified by placing those of all arms under the control of the commander-in-chief. There is no master general of the ordnance, and the functions of the Ordnance Department are confined to the administrative duties, manufacturing establishments, supplies, &c., under direction of a civil officer called the "Clerk of the Ordnance;" but the officers in charge of all these establishments and duties belong to the corps of artillery or engineers.

Another important change was made at the same time, by vesting the general control of the military establishment in a Cabinet Minister, called the "Principal Secretary of State for War;" an arrangement which centralizes, as in other countries, the chief administration of military affairs, and is intended to promote the harmonious action of the several departments in carrying out the measures adopted by the head of the government.

On account of the nature of the British government, and the jealousy of military power on the part of the people, a very small portion of the military force is habitually employed at home. Their chief service is in the numerous colonies and dependencies which are scattered over the whole face of the globe. In this service all except the household troops (guards) participate in rotation; so that all, in their turn, enjoy at home an opportunity of relaxation from foreign service. The comparatively small standing army being thus cut up into little detachments, serving chiefly in garrison, there are few opportunities for the officers or soldiers to acquire practical knowledge of the conduct of field operations on a large scale, or of the various resources for preserving their individual efficiency in campaign. Between the close of the great war of the French revolution and the opening of the war with Russia, the operations in British India afforded almost the only opportunity of this kind. The men who had served in the former wars were too old for active duty in the Russian war; and it happened that few of the officers who had served with distinction in India were employed in the Crimea. The system of appointment and promotion of officers, and the mode of life which prevails in the army, are adapted only to young gentlemen of property or of influential families; and although such a system may secure the appointment of men of refined character and high sense of honor, ready to expose their lives freely in the service of their country, it is not equally well adapted to obtain men capable of the patient endurance of labor, and the close attention to minute details of duty and instruction, which form an important part of the service required from a good officer. Again: the British soldier, accustomed to a comparatively easy life in garrison, where all the supplies and appliances of his subsistence and service are furnished to him, (as they were before he entered the army,) finds himself very much at a loss when deprived of these conveniences, which his own ingenuity does not enable him to dispense with. Under these circumstances, it cannot be expected that the army should be always prepared for an expedition into a foreign country; nor should we be surprised at the losses and sufferings experienced, in men and animals, during the early part of the Crimean campaign, which were painfully exhibited in the reports of several commissions appointed to inquire into them. Whilst the French and Sardinian armies maintained their communications and supplies by means of their organized corps of troops of the train and administration, assisted by the labor of the other troops, the want of such a force had to be supplied in the British army, after great losses, by the employment of a contractor for making a railroad, and by the creation of a civil force under the designations of "land transport corps" and "army works corps," to the number of more than *one fifth* of the effective strength of the army.

When the wants and sufferings of the army in the Crimea became known at home, the concerted action of private enterprise, by which such great results are always produced in England, was brought to the aid of the government; and at the time of our visit to the Crimea, near the close of the war, the British army was in fine condition; well clothed, well lodged in huts sent from England, and abundantly supplied with the necessaries of life, and even many luxuries.

The want of concentration and harmonious action, on the part of the administrative departments of the army, in the Crimea, induced the commanding general to institute the office of "*chief of the staff.*" This was an officer of high rank, whose duty it was to receive and digest the reports from the several departments of the staff, &c., in order to be prepared to give the general full information as to the state and movements of the troops and of their supplies, and to assist him in arranging the details of operations; he was assisted only by his aides-de-camp in his bureau duties. The other officers of the general staff were: the military secretaries and aides-de-camp of the general-in-chief; the adjutant general, with assistants and deputy assistants; the quartermaster general, assistants and deputy assistants; the commanders of artillery and engineers; the commissary general, the medical inspector general, and the judge-advocate general. Each division staff consisted of the general of division, with his aids; the commanders of brigades, each with an aid and a brigade major; an assistant adjutant general and deputies; an assistant quartermaster general and deputies; together with medical and commissary chiefs. All these officers (except the medical officer, commissary, and judge-advocate general) were detailed temporarily for staff duty, at the choice of the commanding general, or the immediate commander under whom they served. The assistant adjutant generals and assistant quartermasters are field officers; the deputies are generally captains. The regimental staff includes an adjutant, (lieutenant;) a paymaster, who is usually a lieutenant or a retired officer; a surgeon and one or more assistant surgeons; a quartermaster, who is an old non-commissioned officer, and performs also the duty of commissary.

The faults of organization developed in the Crimean campaign demonstrated the necessity of important changes in the military establishment, in order to place it on the footing which the power and position of Great Britain demand. Some of the changes adopted have been mentioned above, and others are in progress. Commissioners had been sent, at the time of our visit, to examine and report on the organization of other European armies, and on the *military schools*, with a view to the adoption of improvements, which have been since instituted. Camps of instruction have been formed, in which the officers and men may be exercised in manœuvers of large bodies of men. Recent events in India will also undoubtedly affect, in an important manner, the constitution of the military force, in connection with the government of that country, by making it necessary to amalgamate the Indian troops with the Queen's army.

In considering the military strength of Great Britain, especially for the *defense* of the kingdom, the militia force must not be overlooked. In Great Britain, Ireland, and the channel islands, there are about 150 regiments of organized infantry militia, in which the principal officers are appointed by the Crown; the others by the lord lieutenants of counties. If the voluntary enrollments are not sufficient, the ranks are filled by lot among the young men. The militia are armed by the government, and are called out for a short time every year for exercise, during which time they receive army pay. Many of the officers have formerly belonged to the regular army, or to that of the East India Company. They are not subject to be sent out of the kingdom, but they are called into service, on occasion, to replace the regular troops who are sent abroad; and during the late war, many militia regiments volunteered for service in the garrisons in the Mediterranean islands, from which the regular troops were sent to Turkey and the Crimea. A large portion of the force is organized as "*yeomanry cavalry*," of which there are about fifty regiments, in addition to the 150 regiments of foot; the cavalry force is recruited by voluntary

MILITARY ORGANIZATION—GREAT BRITAIN.

enrollment from the sons of farmers of the better class, who furnish their own horses; they are called out for exercise two weeks in the year, and many of them make a very respectable appearance as soldiers. In the dockyard cities the workmen are formed into "*dockyard corps*," of various strengths, who are more carefully drilled than the other militia force, for the protection of the establishments in case of invasion. The total force is about 10,000 men.

Still another auxiliary force for the defense of the kingdom is the body of "*out-pensioners*," consisting of old soldiers on pensions, but not discharged from the obligation of service. They are organized by officers of the army appointed for the purpose, and may constitute a force of about 20,000 men fit for service. The names of the officers of the militia, yeomanry, &c., are all registered in the official "Army List."

The British army is recruited by voluntary enlistment, the term of service being ten or twelve years. The country is divided into nine recruiting districts—four in England, two in Scotland, and three in Ireland—each with a suitable staff. Each regiment has a depot at home, in which a detachment is left when the regiment is ordered on foreign service. The territory of the kingdom is also divided into military districts, each commanded by a general officer, who is charged with the inspection of the troops stationed in his district, and with the direction of the movements of the troops, or of other military operations in his command.

The regiments of all arms are designated and usually known by their numbers; but many of them have special names derived from royal personages or other eminent individuals. Thus the Thirty-third Foot, once commanded by the Duke of Wellington, is permitted, by special order, to retain his name. The pride and ambition of regiments and corps is also fostered by the practice of permitting them, by general orders, to bear inscribed on their colors the names of actions in which they have distinguished themselves. This seems to be a perfectly unexceptionable distinction to confer, even in a republican country; having nothing personal or mercenary in its nature, and appealing to the most honorable feelings of the soldier, by offering a high inducement to good conduct, in order to deserve and retain this mark of approbation. Whatever may be the material with which the ranks of a regiment are filled, it cannot be doubted that the men would be sensible of the obligation to maintain a reputation acquired on the field of battle by the regiment to which they belong, if its individuality were retained by any mark of distinction. It has been before remarked that in the Austrian army the regiment is known by the name of its proprietor. A regiment of dragoons, which had acquired a high reputation under the name of Latour, had its designation changed, by a change of proprietor, to Vincent. At the battle of Essling the Archduke Charles, seeing this regiment give way before a French battalion, called out to it: "Ah, Vincents! you are no longer Latours." Under this appeal the regiment rallied and performed its duty.

Even in our little army such an incentive to duty might be applied by permitting a regiment, which had received the thanks of Congress for distinguished service, to retain its number and its colors under any changes in the strength of the army. What brilliant action, for instance, might not a general expect at this day from a regiment which should have been always designated as the *Twenty-first Infantry*, with "*Niagara*" inscribed on its colors; and with its gallant leader's pithy answer, "*I'll try!*" for a motto?

PART II.

ORDNANCE AT THE SIEGE OF SEBASTOPOL.

It is curious to remark that, notwithstanding the activity of contrivance and experiments in ordnance during the long peace in Europe which preceded the Russian war, scarcely any novelties in artillery were brought into use, or even tried, at the siege of Sebastopol. No cannon of extraordinary caliber or range, no breech-loading guns, no rifled cannon, (except the Lancaster gun,) were put to the test of actual service. This must have resulted chiefly from a want of confidence in any of the new inventions proposed. It cannot be attributed to mere reluctance of trying even the best esteemed novelties, in a case where the consequences of a failure would be highly disastrous; for the failure of several experiments of this kind, like that of the Lancaster gun, would have detracted very little from the vast armament of the attack. It is the immense quantity of this armament, and the unexampled proportion of guns of large caliber, which especially distinguish the artillery operations of the siege of Sebastopol from any other of the kind. Perfect immunity from attack at home, the undisturbed command of the seas, and the possession of heavily-armed ships and capacious transports, permitted and enabled the Allies to accumulate in the Crimea ordnance and stores of all kinds to an extent which need be limited only by their means of employing them. Thus, before the *impromptu* fortifications of Sebastopol, which were, in great part, created during the siege, the Allies placed in battery, at various times, more than 2,000 pieces of heavy ordnance, besides the hundreds of field pieces with which the troops were armed. The first siege train with which the French army presented itself before the place, consisted of sixty pieces of the calibers usually employed in such operations—16 and 24-pounder guns, 8-inch howitzers, 8 and 10-inch mortars. These being soon found insufficient, were followed by other trains amounting to 250 pieces. Many guns of heavier caliber were drawn from the fleet; but the armament which, at last, appears to have been most efficient in rendering the works untenable, was a train of mortars, of which the French alone had 120 13-inch, the same number of 10-inch, and about 100 8-inch. Add to these the English siege train of more than 900 pieces, consisting chiefly of 68-pounder and 32-pounder guns, 13-inch, 10-inch, and 8-inch mortars, a considerable proportion of which were in battery at the close of the siege, and some idea may be formed of the storm of shot and shells which was poured upon the works during the bombardment of three days preceding the last assault. The appearance of the ground within the Malakoff and Redan bastions, after the retreat of the Russians, showed the impossibility of serving the guns of the place during that bombardment. It was scarcely possible to plant a foot on a spot on the terreplein of those works, which was not marked by a cannon ball or by the explosion of a shell; and the defenders could only remain there under cover of their bomb-proof shelters, which, although mostly constructed rudely of timber, fascines, and earth, seemed to have generally resisted the fire of the besiegers. The French ordnance (guns, howitzers, and mortars) of the regular siege parks was entirely of bronze, and very few of the pieces (about forty in all) were disabled by the firing. They were all of the usual patterns, and mounted on the regulation carriages, except some special 8-inch bronze howitzers, which were heavier than the ordinary siege howitzers, and were mounted on a simple *bracket* carriage, consisting of two cheeks resting on an axletree supported by strong wheels. These were no doubt designed for firing with larger charges, and at higher elevations than the stocktrail carriage admits of. A few (twenty) 8-inch iron sea-coast howitzers, mounted on their appropriate garrison carriages, were used in arming the defensive lines.

French Mortars.—Nearly all the 13-inch mortars were bronze siege mortars, (weighing 25 cwt.;) the beds, of the usual pattern, of two cheeks, with wooden transoms; the cheeks were in some cases of bronze, but generally of iron. The trunnion holes of the latter were not lined, and it was observed that the rear corners were often chipped off by firing the mortars at low angles. Many of the wooden transoms of the 13-inch mortar beds were badly split and rendered nearly unserviceable by the firing. The platforms for these mortars were made with four sleepers, 8-inch square, covered with a floor of the same scantling. Range at 45°, with full charge, (twelve pounds,) about 3,200 yards.

Some (eighteen) sea-coast iron mortars were employed for long ranges. These mortars are such as are also used on board of mortar vessels; they are cast in one piece with the *sole*, with which the axis of the mortar makes an angle of $42\frac{1}{2}$°. The whole weighs 86 cwt. The range, with a full charge of thirty pounds, is about 4,440 yards. The shell is 2.3-inches thick, and weighs 200 pounds. A good deal of use was made of the 24-pounder light mortar, which the French have substituted for the Coehorn mortar; it weighs 150 pounds, and is carried by two men; range 650 yards, with a charge of five ounces. The English also made use of Coehorn mortars. In this connection it may be mentioned that the French had no stone mortars, and that since 1854 that piece of ordnance has ceased to form a part of their system. They substitute for it the fire of 12-pounder shells and hand grenades (3-inch shells) from the ordinary mortars; but the siege of Sebastopol furnished little occasion for the use of such projectiles, the range of which is from 100 to 200 yards. Both in the Russian batteries and those of the besiegers, 8-inch and 32-pounder guns, which had their trunnions broken off, or were otherwise dismounted, were fired as mortars. The gun was placed in a trench so as to elevate it to about 45°, and in this way great ranges were obtained by using moderate charges of powder—the 24-pounder gun, with a charge of six pounds, giving a range of 4,500 yards. The front of the British camp, on Cathcart's hill, was two and one-sixth miles from the most advanced Russian works; an occasional shot or shell would pass over this rising ground and fall into the camp in rear.

Navy Guns.—Next to the mortars the most effective part of the battering train of the allies consisted of the heavy guns drawn from the fleets. Of these the French batteries had eight 50-pounders, three hundred and thirty-eight 30-pounders, (corresponding to our 32's,) and seventy-one 8-inch bomb cannon of 72 cwt.—all furnished with ship carriages, implements, and equipments. It is only under the peculiar circumstances which distinguished this siege that such means could be employed. It was not only necessary that the fleet should be so secure from insult as to be able to spare this armament, but that the siege operations should be carried on at such a convenient distance from the station of the fleet as to permit the establishment of batteries of such cumbrous ordance; the transportation of which, to any considerable distance inland, would have been almost impossible. Notwithstanding the difficulties presented by the nature of the soil and climate of the Crimea, many of these heavy guns were dragged into position on their truck carriages, over the open fields, by the force of men alone. The "naval brigades," French and English, not only aided in the establishment of these batteries, but they served the guns throughout the siege with great effect. An example of a similar operation had been given, on a small scale, by our own navy in 1847, at the siege of Vera Cruz, where the officers and sailors of the fleet armed and served two batteries of heavy guns and bomb cannon, which rendered most efficient service.

The British Batteries were armed chiefly with 24-pounder and 32-pounder guns, and 8-inch and 10-inch bomb cannon, besides 13-inch, 10-inch, and 8-inch mortars—in all, 911 pieces.

Most of the 8-inch guns were of 65 cwt.; they were mounted partly on ship carriages, partly on traveling carriages; but the most efficient guns for range and accuracy were the 32-pounder, and especially the 8-inch bomb cannon of 95 cwt. The latter were mounted on ship carriages; they were used both for shells and solid shot, but principally shells, and they were considered as decidedly the best guns in position for accuracy and regularity at long ranges. Some of the 8-inch guns of both kinds were Lancaster guns; but those of 65 cwt. were too light to throw so heavy a projectile. The effective force of this large shell, thrown from the heavy Lancaster gun, was very great, and its range was occasionally immense, (between 5,000 and 6,000 yards;) but the fire, even at 1,500 yards, was said to be often very wild. This want of accuracy, and the bursting of several of the guns, caused the use of these peculiar shells to be abandoned, and the Lancaster guns were chiefly used for firing spherical shells, for which they answered very well, although not equal to the ordinary guns of the same caliber. Some of the 32-pounder guns were mounted on ship carriages; most of them are bracket carriages, like the 18 and 24-pounder siege carriages, of the Gribeauval system, or those of General Miller. These carriages are simple and strong; they allow a much greater elevation than the French siege carriages, and were preferred to them by the English artillerists. They are not as well adapted as the French carriage to the transportation of the gun on the march, and therefore, perhaps, not as well suited for the lower calibers up to the 24-pounder. But we must hereafter regard the 24-pounder as the lowest caliber to be used in a siege train, and the besiegers must be prepared to meet the heavy armament of modern fortresses with ordnance of corresponding weight and range. For this purpose it is necessary to be prepared to mount heavy 32-pounder and 64-pounder guns on such carriages as, retaining sufficient strength for service, may be adapted to be placed conveniently in battery. It may be found that rolled iron can be adopted in the construction of these carriages; the disadvantage of increased weight being more than compensated by the convenience of such a combination of the parts as may permit of their being transported separately, and put together in the battery. The difficulty and risk of arming and supplying the batteries in the trenches before Sebastopol were unusually great. In consequence of the rocky nature of the ground, the dimensions of the trenches were much restricted, and it was almost impossible to smooth the bottom of the trench, so as to form a road for the transportation of heavy materials. The heavy armament was therefore carried to the batteries over the open country, with great exposure to the large force of men required for such operations. The hauling was performed chiefly by the men alone. The usual platform wagons belonging to a siege train were used for transporting mortars and their beds; heavy hand carts for carrying shot and shells, and light ones for ammunition.

The French reserve depot of ordnance, as of other supplies, was at Kamiesch, about four miles from the principal park, in the camp at general headquarters, which was about three miles from Sebastopol; there was a good paved road from Kamiesch to headquarters. The park for the French right attack was near the English siege park, on the right of the Woronzoff road, about two and a half miles from Sebastopol. The railroad from Balaklava, where the English supplies were landed, brought them up about six miles to a depot in rear of the principal camp, nearly three miles from Sebastopol, whence they were hauled, with great labor, to the front, over the open fields or bad roads. In the British batteries there were a few of the heavy 13-inch sea-service iron mortars, weighing 11,000 lbs.; but although the platforms were made with double decks of large timbers, it was exceedingly difficult to make them stand the service of these mortars, and most of the 13-inch shells were thrown from land-service mortars. The whole number of rounds fired from the British batteries during the siege was 253,000, of which more than 80,000 were fired from mortars, and about an equal number from 8 and 10-inch bomb cannon. The 32-pounder and 8-inch guns generally fired from 1,000 to 1,500 rounds each, and some of the latter more than 2,500 rounds. The annexed official report, made to Parliament, relative to the guns and mortars burst at Sebastopol and Sweaborg, gives some interesting facts with regard to the endurance of their iron ordnance in service. The number of pieces burst at Sebastopol was small in proportion to the whole number used; but it was stated that about two thirds of the ordnance used in the siege was considered unserviceable at its termination. Many of the guns had been rebouched; some of them two or three times; some bouching of wrought-iron were tried, but did not last long.

The French siege trains were supplied with from 1,500 to 2,000 rounds to each piece; their batteries fired during the siege about 1,250,000 rounds of all kinds, and at the close there remained from 800 to 900 rounds of ammunition for each piece. The field batteries were supplied with about 1,000 rounds to a piece. The official report of the Minister of War, a translation of which is hereto annexed, gives, in a condensed form, a view of the immense supplies of ordnance and ammunition, &c., furnished for this remarkable siege, together with much other valuable information on the subject of the men and means used in the prosecution of the war.

The permanent fortifications constructed at Sebastopol, before the beginning of the war, were all directed to the defense of the harbor. The city itself was not fortified on the land side until the allied army prepared to besiege it; some works had been commenced on the western side, but only a portion of a detached scarp-wall was built. This being the case, the place was unprovided with a regular armament for a fortress, and most of the guns, carriages, and material used in the defense were drawn from the fleet, which was otherwise nearly useless, on account of the superior force of the Allies on the sea. Ship guns were therefore chiefly employed in the works, and they were generally mounted on ship truck-carriages, though some were siege guns on their proper carriages. The calibers were 8-inch 32, and 24-pounders, with 8-inch, 10-inch, and 13-inch mortars; but few of the latter caliber. Besides the usual shot and shells for these pieces, many stands of grape and canisters were to be seen, for guns and mortars of all calibers. Some of the stands of grape were made with iron plates, after the English plan, but many of them were quilted in bags. Canisters for 13-inch mortars were filled with 2-pound balls, in five tiers, holding about 100 balls.

The use of ship-carriages made it necessary to cut the embrasures down very low, and thus to leave the gunners much exposed in serving the pieces. In order to protect them from musket and rifle shots, an ingenious mantlet was made with ropes by the sailors to cover the embrasures, and a muff of the same material was attached to the gun, so as to cover the opening for the passage of the gun, as represented in the photographic drawings obtained at Constantinople. These mantlets, however, afforded no protection against cannon balls, the frequent marks of which were to be seen on the guns and carriages, as well as on the works of fortification. *Nine shot marks were counted on one disabled gun in the central bastion; and the number of unserviceable pieces lying there was twice the number in battery!* showing that in the defense, as in the attack, the exposed batteries had their guns several times renewed. To protect the man pointing the gun from rifle shots, the French made some use of a block of wood cut to fit the gun, with a notch to sight through, and having a long handle, which could be held by a man behind the merlon of the battery. The immense number of rounds fired by the Russians during the siege was strikingly illustrated by the quantity of shot and shells with which the ground was thickly strewed within the radius of the works of attack. One of the ravines leading to the town, on the left of the English attack, was known as "The Valley of Death;" in the bottom it, in some places, our horses literally walked on a *pavement* of cannon balls lying close together.

The Allies found in Sebastopol about 4,000 pieces of ordnance of all kinds; a few of these were of brass, but nearly all the armament of the fortifications consisted of iron pieces. A considerable proportion of the above number were guns of small caliber and obsolete patterns, lying on skids at the upper end of the inner harbor, having apparently belonged to some old vessels.

ORDNANCE AT THE SIEGE OF SEBASTOPOL.

Guns.

Return to an address of the honorable the House of Commons, dated April 14, 1856, for a "return of all those guns which have burst at the siege of Sebastopol; stating the description of the caliber of each gun, number of rounds fired when the gun became unserviceable, and supposed cause of such bursting; and like return for Sweaborg."

War Department, *June*, 1856. F. PEEL.

Land Service.

Number of guns burst.	Description and caliber.	Number of rounds fired.	Cause of bursting.
1	13-inch land-service mortar, (old pattern)	No information	No information.
2	10-inch mortars, (old pattern)	do	do.
2	68-pounder guns of 95 cwt	1st, fired over 2,000 rounds.	Fired at high elevation.
		2d, no information	Enemy's shell burst in the muzzle.
1	10-inch gun of 85 cwt	No information	No information.
1	32-pounder gun of 56 cwt	do*	do.
2	24-pounder guns of 51 cwt	do†	do.
2	Lancaster guns, 8-inch caliber	do	do.

* The 32-pounder guns employed in the siege fired, on an average, 1,500 rounds each.
† The 24-pounder guns fired, on an average, 950 rounds each.

Admiralty, *June* 2, 1856.

Sir: With reference to your letter of the 16th April last, requesting information as to the condition of the guns employed by the naval brigade in the siege of Sebastopol, I am commanded by my Lords Commissioners of the Admiralty to send you herewith, for the information of Lord Panmure, a copy of a letter from Captain Kennedy, dated May 27, reporting upon the subject.

Captain Kennedy served with the naval brigade before Sebastopol nearly the whole time it was on shore.

I am, &c.,

THOMAS PHINN.

Colonel Mundy,
War Department, Whitehall.

May 27, 1856.

Sir: In answer to their lordships' memorandum of the 16th, requesting a report of the state and condition of the ordnance employed by the naval brigade before Sebastopol, I can only give it from memory, not having retained any memoranda to refer to, as I understood official reports were forwarded from time to time from the brigade.

On the 8th September, 1855, the last day of the bombardment, our guns, with one or two exceptions, were in very good condition, better and heavier than at any previous time; many of them had been rebouched once, some of the 68-pounders, 95 cwt., twice. I do not think any of the guns, except the 68-pounders, were fired more than 1,000 times in the batteries, being generally disabled by the enemy, as every embrasure much used during the siege had at the least three sets of guns.

The 68-pounders landed from the "Terrible" were constantly in use, and I should say the least number of rounds fired from any one of them was 3,000; some of them went up to 4,000.

They were generally fired with the sixteen-pound charge, and frequently very rapidly, as from their annoying the enemy so much, a very heavy fire was always directed at them. Two or three burst, but I think it was chiefly owing to using too great elevation for old guns, it being almost impossible to prevent the men taking a long shot at a working party. The burst guns appeared a good deal worn out at the lower part of the vent, and the metal about the chamber appeared to be slightly disintegrated.

The 68-pounders, 95 cwt., are as perfect guns as can be desired, and when they can be brought into position most effective.

Their range is very great, and nearly as true as a rifle. The enemy's hollow and small solid shot used to break against the muzzle without materially injuring the piece, whilst numbers of other guns during the siege were split at the muzzle by the enemy's shot.

The 10-inch and 8-inch, 65 cwt., are both very good and true guns, and especially useful for shell. The 32-pounders, 42 cwt., medium, are too light to make any impression against earthworks; ditto the artillery 24-pounders lent to the naval brigade.

I do not think it would be out of place here to call attention to the fact of Mr. Murdoch, engineer of the "Sanspareil," having bouched the guns so well with such small means, and under the enemy's fire.

Trusting this information may be satisfactory, I remain, &c.,

JOHN J. KENNEDY,
Captain Royal Navy.

The SECRETARY OF THE ADMIRALTY.

Observations on the Sea-Service Mortars, used at the Bombardment ———— *August*, 1855.

———— 20, 1855.

The cavities in the bottom of the chambers, mentioned in ———— eport, varied in depth from one inch to one and three quarter inch.

The repairs were effected by introducing melted zinc into the cavity, which lasted usually from twelve to thirty rounds.

The mortars which burst were divided through the whole course of the vent. The cavities in the chambers were found to be larger after each repair; they inclined downwards.

The vents of the mortars incline towards the breech, and this seems in some degree the cause of those cavities.

The "Growler's" mortar, cast in 1813, answered well. Had all been equally good, it is probable that the same injury might have been done to the town in a much less time, and the mortars would still have been fit for service.

The destruction caused by the bombardment may be considered partly owing to the rapidity of the fire; it prevented the enemy (probably) from extinguishing the flames, which may have been rendered more intense by their occurring in so many places at once.

In naval bombardments rapidity of fire is very essential, the men being unprotected by epaulments, and the action being liable to be impeded by bad weather.

In the old works on naval gunnery, more particularly in that of Lieutenant Brancham, R. M. A., it appears that mortars were supposed to throw about twenty-five shells per hour. At the bombardment of Sweaborg, they averaged twenty-five to thirty shells in the first hour, and fewer in subsequent hours. The only mortar which exceeded thirty rounds in one hour was that in the "Growler," which lasted best of all. During this rapid firing every shell appeared to be effective.

The Falencienne composition seems to have been destructive.

As the mortars varied much in their powers of endurance, it is submitted that some may have been made of inferior metal.

The "Growler's" swinging mortar had its suspension gear in good order throughout 355 rounds.

In the other three, the bolts supporting the muzzle-band gave way. Two of them answered well with chain, instead of a band; for the third, new bolts were made. With perfectly good materials, this system presents great advantages, and constant elevation in a sea-way is an important consideration; but an accident causes great delay, and changing a slung mortar for another would be attended with considerable difficulty.

J. M. WEMYSS,
Captain Commanding Detachment of R. M. A., attached to Baltic Fleet.

Report of the state of Mortars on board Her Majesty's Vessels after the Bombardment of Sweaborg, on August 9, 10, and 11, 1855.

(N. B. Repairs of mortars were made by melting zinc and tin into the cavity at the bottom of the chamber.)

Second repair of mortar.—Split down the bottom of the chamber; vent blown.—"Blazer," 129 rounds.

Mortar not repaired.—Split down the bottom of the chamber; vent blown.—"Grappler," 311 rounds.

Third repair.—Vent blown +*; cavity at the bottom of the chamber deep.—"Prompt," 184 rounds.

Fourth repair.—Vent blown +; vent at the bottom of the bore, in line with the longitudinal crack in the vent; cavity at the bottom of the chamber very deep.—"Porpoise," 213 rounds.

Fourth repair.—Number of rounds between each repair, 14, 34, 30; vent blown +; suspension gear carried away first day's firing; second day fought in chains.—"Surly," swing mortar, 134 rounds.

Third repair.—Number of rounds between each repair, 22, 65; vent blown ✶; suspension gear carried away; slung in chains; trunnion rods bent.—"Drake," swing mortar, 129 rounds.

Third repair.—Number of rounds between each repair, 61, 30; vent blown +.—"Redbreast," 230 rounds.

First repair.—Bolt of muzzle strap replaced once; vent blown +.—"Havoc," swing mortar, 94 rounds.

No repair.—Disabled the first day by a large cavity at the bottom of chamber, from which a crack extends over the crown of chamber through the vent, and a crack extends from the same cavity to the lower part of chamber.—"Sinbad," 113 rounds.

Mortar burst first day; no repair; cavity in the end of bore, conical apex turning downwards.—"Pickle," 114 rounds.

Mortar burst second night; no repair; fired 355 shell without cessation; bottom of chamber slightly injured; no cavity.—"Growler," swing mortar, 355 rounds.

Mortar burst second night in four pieces, two large and two small; one of the smaller went overboard; one repair.—"Mastiff," 148 rounds.

Fourth repair.—About 16 rounds between each repair; split down the bottom of chamber; vent blown +; cavity at the bottom of bore deep.—"Carron," 289 rounds.

Second repair.—Split down the bottom of bore; five large cracks in the chamber, one of them through the vent, which is blown.—"Manly," 277 rounds.

NOTE.—The mark after " vent blown," shows the appearance of vent inside the chamber.

Sixth repair.—About 14 rounds between each repair; cavity at bottom of chamber deep; vent blown +.—"Beacon," 176 rounds.

No repair.—A large rent in the crown of chamber, extending through the vent, which is blown +; a very small cavity at the bottom of chamber.—"Rocket," 241 rounds.

Total number of rounds, 3,141.

The above report was drawn up by Captain Schomberg, R. M. A., and I consider it to be correct.

J. M. WEMYSS,
Captain Royal Marine Artillery.

PART III.

REPORT OF THE FRENCH MINISTER OF WAR TO THE EMPEROR ON THE ADMINISTRATIVE ARRANGEMENTS FOR THE WAR IN THE EAST.

PARIS, *September* 8, 1856.

This report is divided into three parts: the first relates to the *Personnel* of the army; the second to the *Matériel* of all kinds; the third, to the means of *Maritime Transportation*.

FIRST PART—PERSONNEL.

MOVEMENTS OF TROOPS.

Sent Out.

	Men.	Horses.
Number embarked from France	257,324	35,777
Number embarked from Algiers	47,983	5,967
Number embarked from Corsica	1,998	....
Number embarked from Italy	1,963	230
Total	309,258	41,974

Losses Sustained by the Army.

Deaths—Up to 30th March, 1856		2,492
From that time to the evacuation, (a period of suffering from typhus and cholera)		4,564
Total of deaths reported		67,056
Missing and prisoners during the siege	2,573	
Deduct prisoners restored by exchange	792	
Missing, not accounted for	1,781	1,781
Lost by the wreck of the Sémillante		392
Total losses		69,229

Returned.

		Men.
Sent home convalescent or on leave...		65,069
Recalled before the peace—Algerian tirailleurs...........................	1,822	
Gend'armerie of the guard...................	1,168	
Imperial Guard...................................	12,000	
Twentieth, thirty-ninth, fiftieth, ninety-seventh regiments of the line, and third battalion chasseurs..	5,400	
		20,390
Present March 30, 1856—In the Crimea.................................	120,476	
In Turkey under arms............	15,316	
In hospital........................	10,448	
	25,764	
	146,240	
Deaths during the evacuation...	4,564	
Returned from the East after the peace..................................	141,676	141,676
Total returned from the army.................................		227,135

Recapitulation.

	Men.
Sent out...	309,268
Losses of the army...	69,229
	240,039
Returned to France and Algiers..	227,135
Difference...	12,904

This last number includes all persons, even those not under the colors, who were attached to the army, and also the officers and soldiers who embarked several times for the seat of war, men who returned there from sickness or furlough, and who are borne at least twice on the return of the number embarked.

Most of the horses were taken from the Crimea to Turkey, and transferred to the Ottoman government. About 9,000 were brought back to France or Algeria.

To supply the demands of the war, and the forces assembled at various points in the interior of the empire, (Paris, Lyons, Metz, Luneville, camps of Bologne, St. Omer, and the South,) as well as to keep up the army of Africa, several new corps were formed, and others increased.

1854.

March 9.—A regiment of Algerian tirailleurs, raised for the army of the East.
April 20.—A sixth squadron added to fifty-three regiments of cavalry.
May 1.—Imperial Guard reëstablished:
    One regiment of gend'armerie, two battalions.
    Two regiments of grenadiers of three battalions.

Two regiments of voltigeurs of three battalions.
One battalion of chasseurs à pied, ten companies.
One regiment of cuirassiers of six squadrons.
One regiment of guides of six squadrons.
One regiment of horse artillery, five batteries and a depot.
One engineer company.

May 26.—Increase of the personnel of clothing and camp equipage.
June 11.—Increase of the officers of administration; bureaux of the intendants.
June 24.—Corps of light cavalry, called *Spahis*.
July 21.—Increase of surgeons and apothecaries. On the 4th of August, 1855, the number of medical officers was increased by 460 assistants.
August 12.—Additional squadron of gend'armerie of the guard.
August 14, (and June 30, 1855.)—Increase of the personnel of Subsistence Department.
September 21.—Increase of administrative officers of military hospitals.
November 15.—Restoration of the sixth company to the third battalion in the 100 regiments of infantry of the line.
December 23.—Regiment of zouaves of the Imperial Guard of two battalions.

1855.
January 9.—Creation of a second battalion of native tirailleurs in each of the three provinces of Algeria.
January 17.—A second foreign legion, composed of two regiments of two battalions, and a battalion of tirailleurs of ten companies.
February 17.—Added to the Imperial Guard:
    A third battalion in the regiment of gend'armerie.
    A fourth battalion in each regiment of grenadiers and voltigeurs.
    A sixth battery in the regiment of horse artillery.
    A second company of engineers.
    A squadron of the field train.
    A regiment of foot artillery, (six foot batteries, six park batteries, and a depot.)
March 7.—Increase of the general staff and of the staff corps.
March 16.—Increase of the intendance.
March 24.—A fourth battalion added to each of the ten regiments of the line.
April 2.—Two new regiments (Nos. 101 and 102) of infantry of the line, of four battalions.
June 27.—A seventh and an eighth squadron added to each of the four regiments of African chasseurs.
August 14.—Two new battalions, (Nos. 21 and 22) of chasseurs à pied.
November 7.—Disbanding the regiment of Algerian tirailleurs, and the six battalions of native tirailleurs, and formation of three regiments of Algerian tirailleurs of three battalions.
December 20.—Imperial Guard reorganized, and the following corps created:
    Infantry.—Third regiment of grenadiers of four battalions.
        Third regiment of voltigeurs of four battalions.
        Fourth regiment of voltigeurs of four battalions.
    Cavalry.—Second regiment of cuirassiers of six squadrons.
        Regiment of dragoons of six squadrons.
        Regiment of lancers of six squadrons.
        Regiment of chasseurs of six squadrons.

By decree of November 22, 1854, the Emperor authorized the Commander-in-Chief to fill vacancies *provisionally*, up to the grade of "*chef de bataillon*" or "*d'escadron*," inclusive; and to confer *provisionally* the decorations of officer and knight of the legion of honor, as well as to bestow military medals. This power ceased at the conclusion of the peace.

The following measures were adopted for recruiting the army:

1854.
Jan. and Feb.—The disposable contingents of the classes of 1852, 1851, 1850, and 1849, called out.
May 1.—80,000 men of the class of 1853 called out.
September 14.—The remaining 60,000 men of 1853 called out.
November 9.—The men of the class of 1847 retained.
1855.
March 5.—140,000 men of the class of 1854 called out. (They were turned out from the 25th to the 30th of March.)
November 19.—Men of the class of 1848 retained.

Measures were taken for the purchase, in France and Algeria, of the horses required for the mounted troops on the war establishment; the number was soon increased from 84,000 to 138,000 horses.

It was in the ninth military division, at Toulon and Marseilles, that nearly all the embarkations of troops and materials were made. General Rostolan, commanding the division, was charged with the direction of the operations, and performed the duty with a zeal and ability which cannot be too highly commended.

The telegraph transmitted constantly from Paris to Marseilles the orders of the Emperor, and the instructions of the Minister of War; the execution of which was accelerated by means of the railways and steamboats. By these means, seconded by the devotion of their whole time on the part of the military functionaries, the French army, at 2,000 miles from the country, constantly received its reinforcements in good time, and was never at a loss for provisions or clothing.

The troops sent from all parts, either by the roads or railways, reached Marseilles and Toulon only when the means of maritime transportation were ready. Until then they were posted, at intervals, in the eighth and ninth military divisions, generally on the lines of railway, so that they could be brought to the port of embarkation at the right moment.

A commission, under a general officer, and composed of officers of all arms, took care that the troops were established on board the vessels as comfortably as possible; and they determined the number of men and horses to be placed on each vessel, so as to protect the passengers from the dangers consequent on being too crowded. Without exceeding, in this respect, the limits marked out by experience, the embarkations were so arranged that the detachments of a corps were not distributed on different vessels, an important advantage with regard to discipline, as the men were thus kept under the orders of their own officers.

The corps and detachments received, before their departure, instructions relative to the sanitary measures to be observed on the voyage, and to the necessary arrangements for first establishing themselves in the East. Hired vessels, as well as those belonging to the government, were required to have physicians and medicines. The military intendant of the ninth division often placed on board of these vessels military surgeons or hired physicians.

From the beginning of the winter of 1854, convalescents or furloughed men arrived in considerable numbers at Marseilles, from the East; they were collected in a depot of *disembarkation*, where they received, for some days, the requisite attention, and were then sent to the depots of their corps or to their homes.

In anticipation of the sickness which the fatigues of war could not fail to produce in so numerous an army, the hospital accommodations in the military divisions on the shores of the Mediterranean were largely increased. A temporary hospital was erected at Avignon, and buildings at Marseilles, Toulon, and Montpelier, were converted into hospitals. The military hospitals at Cette and Frioul were arranged to receive 1,000 beds, making in all 3,000 beds.

The sick sent to these temporary hospitals received all necessary care, notwithstanding the difficulties caused in the medical service of the southern cities by the cholera epidemics of 1854 and 1855. As fast as the patients were able to be moved, they were sent to the military hospitals of the interior.

At the time the progress of the negotiations indicated the probable return of the troops to France, the typhus fever was raging in the Crimea and at Constantinople. To prevent the invasion of this new epidemic, measures were taken, by the orders of the Emperor, on the advice of the Council of Health of the army and the Board of Health. Besides the precautions prescribed to the army in the Crimea, such as the complete separation of the detachments for some days before embarking, it was determined to establish a quarantine for the troops at an isolated place on the coast. For this purpose, three large camps were established: at the island of Porquerolles, for 12,000 men; at the island of Ste. Marguerite, for 6,000 men; and at Cavalaire, near St. Tropez, for 12,000 men, and a large number of horses. This latter point was especially intended for the mounted troops, in order to avoid, at the expiration of the quarantine, the troublesome operation of reëmbarking the horses. In a few days wells were dug, watering places prepared, camping materials carried to the places designated; and when the troops returned to France, after the signature of the treaty of peace, the three camps of observation were ready to receive 30,000 men and 2,000 horses.

Three experienced field officers were assigned, on their return from the East, to the command of these camps. At the same time huts were built to receive comfortably 500 sick at Ste. Marguerite, as many at Porquerolles, and 250 at Cavalaire. Military and civil medical inspectors were charged with the sanitary arrangements.

Similar preparations were made in Algeria, where the corps permanently attached to the army of Africa were to be landed.

The first arrivals occurred in April, 1856, under these circumstances; and all the troops of Failly's division, and also the disbanded men of the class of 1849, remained some days in the camp at Porquerolles.

The cessation of the epidemic in the Crimea, and the excellent sanitary condition of the troops which were disembarked, soon permitted a relaxation of the quarantine rules; but all the vessels were required to stop at Porquerolles for examination, before the troops were landed at Marseilles. After the arrival of Failly's division, only two vessels were detained, one, carrying foot troops, landed them at Porquerolles; the other, with mounted men, at Cavalaire.

Although the troops were sent from the Crimea by successive detachments, the accidents of the voyage would necessarily cause simultaneous arrivals; and as they could only leave Marseilles in limited numbers, in order not to obstruct the roads, it would have been necessary, in this case, to quarter them on the inhabitants. It was desirable to avoid this, on account of the fears which the people entertained as to the health of the troops returning from the Crimea. For this purpose General Rostolan established, in a few days, in the neighborhood of Marseilles, six camps, capable of receiving 12,000 men and 2,000 horses; and it several times occurred that 10,000 men and 1,200 horses were lodged at the same time in these camps. In this manner more than 100,000 men and 5,000 horses passed through Marseilles in the course of three months without its being necessary to billet a single man or horse on an inhabitant. The health of the troops in the camps was, at the same time, perfectly satisfactory.

The return of the troops was concluded by the evacuation of the hospitals at Constantinople. The hospital frigates of the imperial navy brought over the first detachments of sick, and landed them at Ste. Marguerite and Porquerolles; the naval hospital of St. Mandrier (Toulon) received the last detachments.

The camps and temporary hospitals have been already some time emptied. The sick remaining at St. Mandrier are leaving there every day, and the hospital will soon be restored to the possession of the naval authorities.

A period of six months, from April 27th, was stipulated by the treaty of peace for the evacuation of the territories occupied by the Allies. That operation began on April 11th; and in less than three months, on July 5th, notwithstanding the delays caused by the sickness which was then raging in our army, Marshal Pélissier, who superintended the embarkation to the last, left the Crimea. On August 18th our last troops, under General Pariset, left Constantinople.

SECOND PART—MATERIEL.

ORDNANCE AND ORDNANCE STORES.

Kind.	Quantity.
SIEGE PARK.	
Ordnance.	
Guns................24-pounder siege guns...	72
16-pounder siege guns...	44
12-pounder field guns...	20
Canons-obusiers......12-pounder howitzer guns, (field)..	24
12-pounder howitzer guns, light, (9-pounders bored up)..............	12
Howitzers.............22 cent (8-inch) garrison howitzers....................................	20
22 cent (8-inch) siege howitzers..	35
16 cent (32-pounder) field howitzers..................................	20
12-pounder mountain howitzers..	12
Mortars...............32 cent (13-inch) mortars...	102
32 cent (13-inch) mortars, sea-coast..................................	18
27 cent (10-inch) mortars...	116
22 cent (8-inch) mortars...	103
15-cent (24-pounder) mortars...	24
Total of ordnance...	644
Lent to the Siege Park from the Fleet.	
Guns with carriages, implements, and equipments—	
50-pounder guns, (91 cwt.)...	6
30-pounder No. 1 guns, (50 cwt.)......................................	334
30-pounder No. 2 guns, (48 cwt.)......................................	18
30-pounder rifled guns...	6
30-pounder howitzer guns..	9
80-pounder bomb cannons, No. 1, (72 cwt.)........................	71
80-pounder bomb cannons, No. 2, (54 cwt.)........................	17
Pieces of various calibers rendered unserviceable by firing........................	138
	605
Turkish guns of various calibers, with carriages..	140
Gun carriages.	
For 24-pounder siege guns...	170
For 16-pounder siege guns...	91
For 8-inch sea-coast howitzers..	25
For 12-pounder field howitzer guns...	54
For 12-pounder field howitzer guns, light...	30
For 12-pounder mountain howitzers..	10
For 13-inch siege mortars...	129
For 13-inch sea-coast mortars..	18

Kind.	Quantity.
Siege Park—Continued.	
For 10-inch siege mortars	117
For 8-inch siege mortars	131
For 24-pounder siege mortars	31
Total gun carriages	1421
Wagons, &c.	
Gun and mortar wagons	141
Sling carts	16
Park wagons, (for tools, &c.)	250
Siege carts	220
Ammunition wagons, (caissons)	80
Battery wagons	25
Traveling forges	45
Total	779
Projectiles.	
24-pounder shot	185,800
16-pounder shot	87,020
8-inch howitzer shells	166,000
24-pounder howitzer shells	78,000
12-pounder howitzer shells	41,000
13-inch bombs, (siege mortars)	154,350
13-inch bombs, (sea-coast)	13,850
10-inch bombs	202,000
8-inch bombs	142,500
Hand grenades	75,000
24-pounder canisters	1,600
16-pounder canisters	1,500
Total	1,159,320
Gunpowder and Ammunition.	
Round shot fixed for 12-pounder gun	20,240
Shells and canister for 32-pounder howitzer	20,240
Shells and canister for 12-pounder howitzer cannon	10,000
Friction priming tubes	2,019,600
Gunpowder in barrels...........pounds	5,442,800
Field Artillery.	
Guns.	

Kind.	Quantity.
FIELD ARTILLERY—Continued.	
Ammunition.	
For howitzer cannon	45,760
For mountain howitzer	236
Infantry cartridges, spherical balls	2,527,900
Infantry cartridges, elongated balls	1,503,360
FIELD PARK.	
12-pounder howitzer guns	6
12-pounder howitzer guns, light	24
12-pounder howitzers, mountain	11
Total	41
Carriages.	
For 12-pounder guns	173
For mountain howitzer	27
Caissons for 12-pounder guns	618
Caissons for infantry cartridges	340
Park wagons	61
Battery wagons	62
Traveling forges	24
Portable forges	16
Total	1,325
Ammunition.	
Rounds for 12-pounder guns	215,996
Rounds for mountain howitzers	3,264
Infantry cartridges, with various kinds of balls; spherical, elongated, (à tige?) cupped, for the guard; Nessler.	61,606,000

This ammunition, added to that in the caissons belonging to the batteries, gave a supply of 1,107 rounds to each field piece, and 600 rounds to each mountain howitzer. The supply of infantry cartridges was 547 rounds to a man, besides sixty rounds taken with him in embarking.

To recapitulate; the artillery matériel at the disposal of the army of the East comprised:

1,676 guns of all calibers.
2,038 gun carriages.
2,740 wagons.
2,128,000 projectiles.
8,800,000 pounds of powder.

As soon as the Crimean expedition was determined on, a siege train of sixty pieces, which had been collected at Toulon, in anticipation, was sent to the East; and it was with this train that the army presented itself before Sebastopol.

The vigor of the defense, the large number of guns mounted on the works, and the want of a complete investment, leaving the place open to constant supplies for the enemy, soon showed the insufficiency of these means of attack, and rendered it necessary to increase the siege train beyond all previous estimates. Three supplementary trains were sent from Marseilles and Toulon; the first of 58 pieces, the second of 46, and the third of 150; all supplied with from 1,500 to 2,000 rounds apiece.

The school of pyrotechny, which had been employed for some months, by order of the Emperor, in preparing war rockets of large size, ranging from 5,000 to 7,000 metres, (5,500 to

7,600 yards,) had already obtained some very remarkable results. Between 7,000 and 8,000 of these rockets were sent to the siege park.

On the other hand, the Commander-in-Chief of the army drew from the arsenal of Constantinople 140 guns, shot, and a considerable quantity of powder. He also asked from the fleet for guns of heavy caliber. The number thus borrowed amounted to 605, of which 238 were in battery during the last days of the siege. The fleet also furnished such supplies and powder as could be spared from its own service.

The place still holding out, the Emperor ordered that a train of 400 mortars, furnished with 1,000 rounds apiece, should be sent out, to bombard the place incessantly, and cover the attack by rendering the Russian works uninhabitable. The employment of such formidable means promised immediate and decisive results. Imagine, indeed, what would have been the effect of 400 mortars, supplied with 1,000 rounds apiece, capable of throwing, for twenty days and nights, more than 830 shells an hour, or fourteen a minute! Only a part of these mortars arrived in time to be placed in battery during the siege.

The organization of these different trains, the collecting and embarking them at Marseilles, were attended with many difficulties; but these were overcome by the resources accumulated in the fortresses and by the activity displayed in the arsenals. Workshops for making cartridges, fuzes for shells, and ammunition for artillery, were established in places situated near the railways, and the work was continued without interruption.

To meet the enormous consumption of powder, the powder-works enlarged their operations, and delivered, in 1854, 3,500,000 pounds of powder; in 1855, they were able to supply double that quantity, without slacking the manufacture of sporting and blasting powder.

The transportation of this immense quantity of stores, the weight of which exceeded 50,000 tons, would certainly have been impossible a few years ago; but, by means of the lines of railway connecting Marseilles with the principal cities of the Empire, impossibilities were overcome, and no delay occurred in the regularity of the shipments. Such was, also, the care bestowed on these operations that 3,000 tons of powder, 70,000,000 infantry cartridges, 270,000 rounds of fixed ammunition, 7,000 or 8,000 war rockets, and an immense quantity of fire-works, reached their destination without the occurrence of the slightest accident.

During the siege, the artillery, assisted by six companies of the regiment of marine artillery, by the sailors of the fleet, and by auxiliaries from the infantry, constructed, armed, and served 118 batteries on ground covered with obstacles, and under the incessant fire of the place, at the same time that they attended to arming and supplying the redoubts, the camp, and the lines of Kamiesch. These batteries required the use of 800,000 sand-bags and 50,000 gabions. On the day of the assault they were armed with 620 pieces of artillery; they had fired more than 1,100,000 rounds, and consumed more than 6,600,000 pounds of powder.

Notwithstanding this enormous expenditure of ammunition, of which history furnishes no other example, the park of artillery was still supplied, at the close of the siege, with about 800 or 900 rounds to each piece, besides what was dispatched every day from France; about forty pieces of ordnance only were disabled; the resources of the artillery would have enabled them to continue the contest a long time.

The ordnance and stores brought back to France may be estimated at 50,000 tons, of which 38,000 were French and 12,000 Russian.

MILITARY COMMISSION TO EUROPE.

ENGINEER MATERIALS.

Kind.	Number.	Weight.
Tools and Various Supplies.		Pounds.
Entrenching tools	72,000	363,000
Quarrying tools	7,400	48,000
Wood-cutters' tools	6,300	27,500
Miners' tools	1,500	33,440
Hooks, forks, and drags, for sappers	200	1,330
Sappers' armor	12	560
Wheel-barrows	800	40,000
Hand-barrows	1,700	44,000
Sandbags	920,000	566,000
Palisades	8,000	115,500
Chevaux-de-frise	50	33,000
Tool handles	80,000	77,000
Artificers' and workmen's tools	16,500	35,800
Machines.		
Norias, (water wheels)	8	8,800
Pile driver	1	3,670
Wooden ventilators	5	550
Machines for (boring) camouflets	3	1,950
Hand-mills	5	330
Hand-ram	1	110
Capstans	4	780
Ropes, assorted	...	16,000
Ladders	250	14,000
Fire engines	10	4,400
Wagons, &c.		
Wagons, assorted	87	153,700
Boxes, assorted	210	27,700
Wheels, axles, and other spare parts	235	10,000
Materials and Supplies of Various Kinds.		
Lumber, assorted, for siege works, temporary hospitals, huts, storehouses for provisions, &c. .... cubic feet...	681,000	17,537,000
Iron, bar	...	23,000
Steel	...	3,400
Sheet-iron	...	4,000
Spikes, nails, and tacks, assorted	...	118,000
Pitch	...	490,000
Candles	...	9,000
Pit coal	...	167,000
Blasting powder	...	202,000
Canvas, &c., for shutters and roofs, (of which one fifth was pitched canvas)..... square yards...	26,000	22,000
Surveying instruments	400	550
Huts.		
Huts for officers and soldiers	2,900	9,000,000
Huts for stables	210	840,000
Cast-iron stoves	2,800	185,000
Total weight	...	31,229,480

Or about 14,000 tons, of which about 2,400 tons were brought back to France.

The wagons, tools, and sappers' and miners' implements, were supplied, in great measure, from the engineer arsenals of Metz and Algiers; the rest from private sources. The shipping of these stores, (at least five times more than are generally required for the siege of a great fortress,) was begun in March, 1854, and the last shipments were made in August, 1855.

The supplies of lumber, iron, copper, &c., were bought at Lyons, Toulon, Marseilles, Constantinople, and Trieste.

Of the 920,000 sand-bags sent to the Crimea, 300,000 were drawn from the public stores; the rest were purchased at Paris and the places above mentioned.

As soon as it was ascertained that the army would pass the winter under the walls of Sebastopol, the Emperor ordered shelters to be sent out. Huts for men and sheds for horses were immediately ordered in France and England; 1,050 huts, capable of sheltering 30,000 men, were made at Toulon and Marseilles in January, 1855, and the shipment of them begun in the following month; 1,850 huts, to contain 45,000 men, were ordered in England at the beginning of December, 1854; and they were shipped from Southampton in the course of the next month. Each hut was provided with a stove.

Sheds for about 10,000 horses were ordered in Paris in December, 1854, and shipped from Marseilles in January, 1855.

Besides these, a supply of 50,000 frame pieces, 20,000 joists, 100,000 boards, and 9,000 bolts, were purchased at Marseilles, and shipped, in 1855, for establishing warming huts.

In this ever-memorable siege, the engineers executed 87,500 yards (fifty miles) of trenches, using 80,000 gabions, 60,000 fascines, and nearly 1,000,000 sand-bags. They covered the right of our attacks with defensive works of more than five miles in extent, and the left with an entrenchment of the same extent, almost in one line, called the "*Lines of Kamiesch*," resting at both extremities on the sea, covering, against all the chances of war, the bays of Kamiesch and Kazatch, and securing the possession of a vast space, containing all the supplies of the army. These lines consisted of a strong parapet, with a ditch cut in the rock, and flanked by eight strong redoubts armed with heavy guns.

But the siege of Sebastopol was especially distinguished from any other by the immense difficulties of the works of approach, which were excavated almost entirely in rock, by means of powder, before a fortress garrisoned by a large army, and constantly open to fresh supplies of men and provisions.

We had also to contend against a subterranean defense, skillfully arranged, and ramified into more than 6,500 yards of mining galleries, cut in the rock in several tiers, the lowest of which was more than fifty feet below the surface.

SUBSISTENCE—FUEL—FORAGE.

Kind.	Quantity.
Subsistence.	
Biscuit..pounds...	28,143,000
Flour...do......	48,630,000
Dry vegetables..do......	425,000
Pressed vegetables, (Chollet's preparations).....................do......	752,000
Rice..do......	7,880,000
Salt..do......	174,600
Sugar...do......	6,075,000
Coffee..do......	4,730,000
Salt pork..do......	11,533,000
Salt beef..do......	1,140,000
Preserved beef..do......	6,701,000
Hogs' lard...do......	110,000
Beeves, on the hoof...heads...	10,000
Wine..gallons...	3,080,000
Brandy and rum...do......	363,200
Fuel.	
Wood...pounds...	4,980,000
Pit coal..do......	34,700,000
Forage.	
Hay..do......	170,287,000
Barley and oats...do......	184,600,000

Of various other supplies, about 1,500 tons—making, in round numbers, about 500,000 tons measurement.

The quantity of provisions and matériel brought back to France is estimated at 50,000 tons.

The biscuit were made in the military bakeries at Paris, Rouen, Havre, Brest, Bordeaux, Bayonne, Marseilles, Toulon, Montpellier, Perpignan, Algiers, and Oran, [Lyons appears to be omitted by mistake in this enumeration,] or purchased in England and in France from the house of Packham. Two hundred and sixty thousand boxes were required to contain them.

Flour was sent from Marseilles, Toulon, Montpellier, Perpignan, Bordeaux, Algiers, and Oran.

Pressed vegetables, prepared by Chollet & Co., Paris.

Rice, mostly hulled, bought at London, Bordeaux, and the greater part at Havre.

Coffee sent from the same places as rice.

Sugar sent from Havre, except a few cargoes from Bordeaux and Marseilles; the whole of it was white sugar or loaf sugar.

Salt meats, most of them bought in England; some furnished by the Navy Department.

Preserved beef in boxes, except small quantities made in France by M. de Lignac (pressed beef) and by M. Appert, (boiled beef with soup,) almost all the rest was made in England. The statement of quantity includes 880,000 pounds of *powdered beef*, or nearly 600,000 rations.

Beef on the hoof: 4,000 beeves were obtained from Trieste, 1,500 from Algeria, 4,500 from Caramania, (Asia Minor,) by the port of Macri.

Wines: Wines for the sick were obtained from Bordeaux and Perpignan; for the troops, from the Var and Hérault.

Brandy and rum: On account of the high price of brandy and its doubtful quality, rum from the best sources of supply was used in preference; it was purchased at London and Marseilles.

Coals were obtained from England.

Wood was shipped for stowage without extra charge.

Hay, shipped from Nantes, Marseilles, Montpellier, Perpignan, Algiers, Mostaganem, Bouno, Philippeville; and abroad, from Antwerp, Genoa, Leghorn, Naples, Messina, and Trieste.

Barley and oats, from Havre, Marseilles, and Algeria; also, from England, Spain, Morocco, Italy, Egypt, and Syria.

Bags: a million of bags were sent, either containing the above provisions, or as a separate supply.

Ovens: a hundred and fifty ovens, of which sixty were portable sheet-iron ovens.

Tarpaulins: 1,700 tarpaulins, measuring 244,000 square yards.

Hay presses: there were 137 of different kinds sent for pressing the hay bought in Turkey, independently of the quantities reported in the tabular statement.

It required 1,800 trips of vessels, with full cargoes, to transport the above supplies.

     460 from France.
     566 from Algeria.
       4 from Spain.
      77 from England.
       5 from Belgium.
     600 from Italy.
      88 from Egypt and Syria.

1,800

CLOTHING, CAMP EQUIPAGE, AND HARNESS.

Kind.	Number.
Clothing and Equipment.	
Flannel belts	654,802
Canvas for tente-abri	347,319
Blankets	371,787
Cotton shirts	354,527
Leather gaiters, pairs	42,527
Linen gaiters, pairs	163,419
Pantaloons of gray linen	9,000
Shoes, pairs	398,268
Boots and spurs, pairs	32,396
Drawers	139,336
Kitchen frocks, (blouses)	200
Stable frocks, (blouses)	25,010
Pantaloons, for kitchen use	300
Caps of chasseurs d'Afrique	717
Cap covers	3,000
Gun slings	525
Tent poles, tente-abri	183,265
Cap peaks	2,000
Buttons, assorted	20,620
Cotton cravats	300,000
Special Articles.	
Wooden shoes, pairs	208,597
Woolen socks, pairs	189,162
Cloaks with capes and hoods	231.390
Woolen stockings, pairs	220,000
Woolen gloves, pairs	215,000

CLOTHING, CAMP EQUIPAGE, AND HARNESS—Continued.

Kind.	Number.
Special Articles—Continued.	
Chachias (?)	253,576
Leggins of sheepskin, pairs	90,000
Bulgarian gaiters, pairs	163,729
Sheepskin greatcoats	15,000
Camp Equipage.	
Wedges	16,440
Lance heads	60
Dowels	15,512
Poles for council tents	68
Poles for officers and men's tents	30,852
Ridge poles for council tents	21
Do for tents for sixteen men	9,190
Do for officers' tents	1,500
Do for conical tents for twenty men	6,500
Shelves, with cheats	11,009
Shelves, without cheats	18
Tent pins, large and small	587,971
Camp stools, folding	3,424
Tables	24
Curtains	4
Mallets	23,316
Frames for covers of company arms	540
Frames for covers for pickets	30
Canvas for covers of company arms	540
Canvas for pickets	14
Large kettles	40,973
Small tin kits, with straps, (bidons)	248,714
Bowls	43,193
Soup kettles	40,941
Cases for kits	1,019
Cases for bowls	1,061
Cases for kettles	1,019
Straps for kits and kettles	1,612
Straps for bowls	632
Sickles	16,460
Scythes	1,499
Axes	17,226
Shovels	15,746
Picks	16,721
Bill hooks	8,341
Picket ropes, for cavalry ......feet..	9,000
Harness.	
Horse-shoe nails	6,193,400
Horse shoes	817,915
Bags, bound with leather	16,922
Hobbles	7,567
Cords for hobbles	310
Watering bridles and bits	2,039
Light cavalry saddles, new pattern	636
Light cavalry saddles, old pattern	1,004
Bits	900
Parade halters	279
Double snaffles	368

The events of the war having placed the army in a country nearly destitute of resources, and under an extraordinary climate, it was necessary to send from France everything required to clothe and shelter them, and even the nails for shoeing their horses.

The severity of the climate on the plains of the Chersonese made it necessary to send, besides the usual articles of clothing and camp equipage, a complete suit of winter clothing as a supplementary dress for each man, viz:

   Cloak, with cape and hood.
   Bulgarian cloth gaiters.
   Wooden shoes, with woolen socks.
   Woolen gloves, stockings, *chachia*.

All the men on guard, or on any extraordinary service, had besides sheepskin greatcoats and leggins. These articles, sent in 1854, and in the beginning of 1855, had to be renewed, for the most part, like the ordinary clothing, to provide against the winter of 1855, '56.

The camp equipage in the public stores, at the beginning of the war, was only sufficient for an army of 70,000 or 80,000 men in the field. It was therefore necessary to provide quickly a considerable quantity of these supplies, which was done in good time by contractors. All these articles were received without loss or damage, notwithstanding their great numbers and bulk.

The tents sent out were sufficient for 280,000 men, besides those alloted to the officers. The first kind of tent had two poles, and was shaped like a roof; but experience of the climate of the Crimea, and especially the storm of the 14th November, 1854, showed that the conical tent, with a single pole, which is used in Turkey, resisted better the severity of the weather, and that form was adopted for all the tents sent out in 1855. Hemp canvas was not used exclusively in making the tents; the cotton canvas was found to answer very well, with less weight and cost.

The supply of sickles and scythes enabled the troops to collect the forage found first in the Doburdsche, and afterwards in the Chersonese.

Considerable parts of the camp equipage and special articles of clothing were not used, and they were sent back to France and Algeria.

The stores above enumerated may be estimated at 12,000 tons measurement. The supplies belonging to the corps, and which they take with them in the field, are not included in this estimate. Their weight is about 7,300 tons.

The articles sent back to France and Algeria amounted to about 8,000 tons.

SUPPLIES FOR HOSPITAL SERVICE.

Kind.		Quantity.
Iron bedsteads, from France	12,000	
Wooden bedsteads, purchased in the East	15,000	(a) 27,000
Blankets, sent from France	32,000	
Blankets, from the East	7,500	39,500
Cotton coverlets, from the East		3,500
Wool mattresses and bolsters, procured in the East	pounds, 715,000 or mattresses 30,000	
Complete equipment for hospitals of 500 patients each, from France	23	
Do. do. do. purchased in the East	7	(b) 30
Medicines, utensils, and medical supplies for ditto		30
Chapel furniture for hospitals		(c) 14

MILITARY COMMISSION TO EUROPE.

SUPPLIES FOR HOSPITAL SERVICE—Continued.

Kind.	Quantity.
Ambulances.	
Light ambulance equipments (pattern of those used in Africa) for 12,000 men each................	2
Ambulance wagons with stores, in the proportion of five to each division of infantry................	(d) 110
Ambulance medicine cases................	150
Saddle-bag medicine cases................	35
Boxes of surgical instruments, assorted................	106
Cases of amputating and trepanning instruments contained in the medicine chests................	150
Cases of instruments in the hospitals................	70
Dressings.	
Linen dressings, large................pounds...	125,000
Do. small................do...	165,000
Rolled bandages................do......	70,000
Lint................do......	108,000
Linen dressings, assorted, contained in the movable hospitals, the caissons, and chests................do......	176,000
	644,000
Bandages for hernia................	5,000
Hospital Stores. (c)	
Concentrated milk................pounds...	17,600
Concentrated essence of broth................do.....	2,900
Boiled beef................do.....	6,160
Gelatine, granulated................do.....	6,600
Chollet's prepared Julienne, for officers................do.....	3,500
Do. do. for soldiers................do.....	112,200
Prepared vegetables, assorted................do.....	55,000

NOTES.

(a) These supplies, completed by purchases on the spot, were the means of establishing as much regularity in the hospital service at Constantinople as in the interior of France. The 27,000 beds, collected in the first months of the war, are a larger supply than in all the permanent military hospitals of France, in which there are only 19,000 beds, viz: For the sick, 16,500 beds; for infirm soldiers, 2,500 beds. The administration provided this material by drawing from the supplies in store and by orders to private establishments, which were promptly executed.

(b) The list in detail of the supplies for these hospitals for 500 sick is given in the regulation of April 1, 1831.—(See Official Military Journal of that year, Supplement to Part 1.) The weight for each hospital is about 26,400 pounds, (exclusive of the bedsteads,) making for the thirty hospitals established in the East a weight of 792,000 pounds.

(c) In pursuance of the orders of the Emperor, religious service and spiritual aid were always provided for the soldiers. The chaplains displayed the greatest devotion to duty, and, like the admirable sisters of St. Vincent-de-Paul, they kept up the spirits of the sick and wounded in the ambulances and hospitals. Religious service was performed in the army by Catholic priests. The central consistories of the Reformed Church and of the Hebrew worship sent ministers and rabbis for their followers. The Catholic service of the fourteen hospitals of Constantinople was intrusted to the congregation of the Lazarists, which has a college in that city, and their influence is felt all over the East; that course also resulted from the establishment of the sisters of St. Vincent-de-Paul in the hospitals, the Lazarists being their superiors.

(d) Each ambulance store wagon contained 2,000 dressings; the 110 wagons furnished, therefore, a supply for the field of battle of 220,000 dressings, the consumption of which could be replaced by shipments from Constantinople.

(e) The concentrated milk, (by Ligne's process,) the concentrated essence of broth, (obtained from England,) and the preserved vegetables, (of Chollet & Masson,) were used with complete success. These articles may hereafter be regarded as perfectly suitable for hospital stores.

The hospital stores and supplies sent out amounted to 6,430 tons measurement: about one third of which quantity was returned to France and Algeria.

MILITARY TRAINS.

Kind.	Quantity	Weight.
		Pounds.
Provision wagons for 1,250 rations	775	3,054,000
Do. 1,600 rations	143	270,000
Ambulance store wagons	118	257,000
Pack wagons, with low sides	253	466,000
Do. with raised sides	218	388,000
Traveling forges, old pattern	82	26,640
Do. new pattern	8	94,360
Draft harness, with head gear complete—near leader	1,127	
Do. do. off leader	1,148	
Do. do. near wheel horse	1,236	257,000
Do. do. off wheel horse	1,285	
Drivers' saddles, complete	1,811	
Saddles for non-commissioned officers and troopers	1,732	170,000
Saddles for non-commissioned staff	25	
Pack-saddles for mules	2,971	196,000
Horse blankets	16,611	65,000
Portable forges	21	4,390
Pairs of *cacolets*, (mule litters for the sick)	2,761	61,780
Pairs of litters	849	81,300
Spare stores of all kinds, such as grease pots, tool chests, finished wheels, poles with and without iron work, watering bridles, halters, lashing ropes, &c		3,300,000
Materials, unwrought: wood, iron, &c		2,640,000
Marseilles carts, with harness	300	
Maltese carts, with harness	400	410,000
Carts called *bonhoures*, with harness	100	
Total		12,154,010

This total represents 7,956 tons, sea measurement. One third of this quantity was sold as unserviceable; but many of the wagons and other articles made in Turkey were taken to Algeria; so that the whole quantity returned may be estimated at 7,000 tons.

Notwithstanding the strength of the trains attached to the army of the East, (11,000 men and 8,000 horses or mules,) all the administrative services could not have been performed without the assistance of several auxiliary companies made up from men and stock not belonging to the train proper. Some of these companies were raised in the East, others in France. Their stock consisted principally of:

400 Maltese carts, made at Malta, under the direction of the French consul.
300 Marseilles carts, sent from France.
100 Carts, called *bonhoures*, after a model adopted by the Emperor.
1,600 Wagons and carts, called *arabas* and *tekis*, purchased in Turkey or made in Constantinople by the workmen attached to the park of reserve of the military trains.

These companies, which were raised successively as they were required, amounted at the end of the war to nineteen, having a strength of 2,728 drivers, 11,346 draft animals, (horses, mules, oxen, and buffaloes,) and 2,425 vehicles of all sorts. These resources contributed most effectively to the good execution of the transport service.

All the abovementioned articles for the trains were not used in the performance of the different services of the army; but prudent foresight required the establishment, at a convenient distance from the seat of war, of a considerable reserve, in order to supply immediately any deficiency that might appear. For this reason a park of reserve for the military trains was established at Constantinople at the beginning of the campaign. The importance of this reserve may be estimated from the following statement of quantities remaining on hand there at the end of the war.

296 caissons, 119 park wagons, 31 forges, 166 sets of harness for four horses, 714 saddles, scabraques, &c., 398 pack saddles, 9,155 blankets, 398 pairs of cacolets, (mule litters for sick,) 578 litters.

This establishment, under the direction at first of a captain, afterwards of a major (*chef d'escadron*) of the park staff, constantly rendered the most important services during the war. It was not only charged with the repairs of the rolling stock, but assisted in regulating the accountability for funds and material.

CIVIL RIGHTS—JUSTICE—GOVERNMENT OF OCCUPIED TERRITORY.

One of the first cares of the commander-in-chief, when the army was formed, was to consult the interests of the family of the soldier, by securing the regularity of his civil registration in his corps, in hospital, and even on the field of battle.

At the same time provostships and courts-martial were established in each division to maintain order and discipline. The returns show that at no time has it been necessary to make less use of the restrictive measures authorized by law.

Interpreters, commissioned by the Minister of War, kept up the necessary communications among the different nations engaged in the contest.

As soon as the establishment at Kamiesch was made, a general administration was organized; a municipal council and a council of elders (*prud'hommes*) instituted. Soon afterwards a police force and a sanitary police were created, and the numerous followers of the camp, Frenchmen and foreigners, found in this impromptu city constant and effectual protection.

SERVICE OF THE MILITARY CHEST AND THE MAILS.

The fiscal officers of the army were at the same time charged with the care of the mail service. This double business was so completely organized that the military of all grades received their pay and allowances as regularly as if they had been in garrison in France, and they could keep up a constant, almost daily, correspondence with their families. This corps, consisting of six principal paymasters, eight special paymasters, and seventy-five assistants, and secondary agents, under the direction of a paymaster general, constantly supplied all the wants of their department, both for the army about Sebastopol and for the troops occupying the most distant points. The means of transportation were drawn from the train, and also the soldiers required for drivers; it consisted of twelve caissons or wagons, 104 draft and saddle horses, and twenty pack mules, which were employed according to the demands of the service.

The payments were made, as in former campaigns, in two ways: first, direct payments in specie; second, by drafts, negotiable on the spot. The latter method produced important advantages, and the drafts on the treasury obtained such favor in the East that it was necessary to create notes or checks of 20,000 and 10,000 francs, ($4,000 and $2,000.) The issues amounted sometimes to twelve millions of francs (say $2,400,000) a month.

The payments made in the East, from the 1st April, 1854, to 1st July, 1856, from the advances or credits of the War Department, amounted to 285,646,160.45 francs, ($57,000,000,) of which 275,457,340.64 francs ($55,000,000) were paid on the orders of the military intendance; about $400,000 on the orders of the chiefs of artillery, and about $1,600,000 on the orders of the chiefs of the engineer service.

The accounts of expenditures for the war have always been examined, audited, and definitively settled within the periods usually allowed for settlement in time of peace; a result highly advantageous in all respects, and the more remarkable as it had never been attained in any previous war.

TELEGRAPHIC SERVICE.

At the beginning of the campaign the necessity was seen of establishing between several headquarters and the detached corps means of communication which should insure the rapid transmission of orders and harmony of movement.

For this purpose there was attached to the expedition a telegraphic corps, consisting of two inspectors, five directors, four electric telegraph operators, and forty-seven signal station men, furnished with sixteen portable signal telegraphs, which could be easily set up and taken down in a short time. This corps was so distributed as to put the general in immediate communication with the different portions of his army.

During the siege, the English government having formed a plan to connect Varna with Balaklava by a submarine electric cable, the Emperor ordered a communication to be established between Varna and the German telegraphic lines. In a short time, in spite of all obstacles, the line from Bucharest to Varna, about 150 miles, was completely established, and the communication was opened some days before the completion of the submarine line; three inspectors, four directors, and thirty operators, at the four stations of Bucharest, Routschouk, Schumla, and Varna, secured a regularity in transmission of messages which placed the army within a few hours of Paris.

PRINTING.

A lithographic press at general headquarters had at first sufficed for the demands of the service; but from the beginning of the siege, on account of the constantly increasing number of orders, and the necessity of distributing them without delay to the different corps of the army, the general determined to ask for a complete printing press. This was sent out by the director of the imperial printing establishment, and, until the evacuation of the Crimea, a foreman and two compositors remained at headquarters.

THIRD PART.

TRANSPORTATION BY SEA.

The imperial navy, without relaxing its military operations, furnished the following transport vessels:

- 11 ships-of-the-line, with auxiliary steam power.
- 21 ships-of-the-line, with sails.
- 19 sailing frigates.
- 19 steam frigates.
- 24 transports, steam and sailing.
- 21 sloops.
- 17 dispatch boats.

In all, 132 vessels, which made 905 trips, and transported, for the army alone, either going or returning, 273,780 men, 4,266 horses, and 116,661 tons of stores.

The English government put at the disposal of the Emperor eight vessels of the royal navy, and forty-two merchant vessels chartered by the admiralty, which transported altogether to the East 38,353 men, 1,972 horses, and 6,624 tons of stores.

The War Department chartered, in 1854 and 1855, sixty-six steamers, and 1,198 sailing vessels of all sizes. The sixty-six steamers and twenty-two large clippers formed a kind of fleet, which, until the end of the war, was continually running between the East and the ports where supplies were collected. Finally, the steamers of the "Messageries Impériales," (passenger line,) according to arrangements made at the beginning of the war, transported foot troops and supplies at the rate of two trips a week.

For the return of the army, the War Department continued to employ forty-eight steamers and two hundred and fifty-three sailing vessels, of which fourteen were large clippers.

Altogether there were transported, by the means provided by the War Department, 224,270 men, 44,736 horses or mules, and 601,251 tons of stores.

Besides the above, the intendant general in the Crimea, and the military intendant at Constantinople, chartered a great number of vessels for victualing the army. These vessels were employed exclusively in carrying to the Crimea the provisions and forage purchased on the shores of the Black sea, and in Turkey.

Recapitulation.

	Men.	Horses.	Stores.
	Number.	*Number.*	*Tons.*
Sent out to the East	309,378	41,971	597,686
Brought back	227,135	9,000	126,850
Total going and returning	536,463	50,971	724,536
Transported by the imperial navy	273,740	4,266	116,661
Transported by English vessels	38,353	1,972	6,621
Transported by the War Department	224,270	44,736	601,251
Total as above	536,463	50,971	724,536

Much the greater part of the men and stores, embarked at Marseilles, had arrived there by the railway from Paris to the Mediterranean. If that railway had not existed, the operations of the war would certainly have lost much in concert and rapidity of movement. His Majesty, the Emperor, in looking back for a few years, may recollect with satisfaction, that one of the first acts of his energetic administration was to remove the obstacles to the completion of this great line, which was so soon to contribute to the brilliant success of his army.

The Marshal of France, Minister of the War Department,

VAILLANT.

PART IV.

ARSENALS OF CONSTRUCTION.

RUSSIA.

The Arsenal of St. Petersburg was formerly in a central part of the city, but since 1850 a new establishment has been built on the Neva, near the eastern extremity of the city, and the buildings of the old arsenal are used only as a museum and storehouses for arms, gun-carriages, &c. The plan of the new establishment is shown in the drawings kindly furnished to us by the Minister of War. The buildings are arranged in a quadrangle, fronting on a street, and extending back to the river. The center building on the street contains the offices and rooms for drawing, patterns, and models; adjoining this is a long room or gallery for the inspection of finished work, and parallel to it the finishing shops for light work. Perpendicular to the front are three lines of workshops for smiths' forges, for wood work, and for boring and finishing cannon. In the rear of these, and parallel to the front, is the cannon foundery. On the two flanks, perpendicular to the front, are storehouses, separated by court-yards from the workshops. The workshops are of one story, and the storehouses of two stories—all substantially built of brick and *vaulted*. The roofs of the storehouses are of iron. In the finishing shops the main lines of shafting are supported by cast-iron columns, from which cast-iron girders extend to the walls, and support the counter shafts. The machines used in these shops were mostly made in England. They are good and substantial, but claim no special notice; those for wood work are inferior to the tools in use with us. Among the tools for finishing cannon is a horizontal lathe for dressing the handles of brass guns, in which the cutter is guided by a pattern plate of the shape of the handle, and worked by a lever connected with a crank, as in the planing machines for short work.

Eighty smiths' forges are arranged in stacks of *four*, covered by an iron hood. There are also large forges with suitable furnaces for working up scrap iron, forging shafts, and other heavy work. The blast is obtained from fans.

In the *cannon foundery* there are the usual reverberatory furnaces for casting brass guns, and a blast furnace for iron castings. The patterns are made of bronze, divided by sections perpendicular to the axis. The moulds are made of *sand* in iron flasks. The patterns of the trunnions are removed from the inside, as are the handles which are moulded in fire clay. The flasks are not placed in pits for casting, but stand in the open air, and the furnaces are in consequence raised very high. This arrangement is no doubt made on account of the difficulty of keeping the pits free from water in the low, marshy soil, bordering the river. At the time of our visit the foundery was employed in making some heavy bronze guns for sea-coast batteries, and light 12-pounders for field service, intended to replace the present field batteries of guns and howitzers. In front of the arsenal were deposited a large number of brass field pieces, the product of this foundery.

The shops of this arsenal are employed chiefly on field and siege carriages of various kinds. Gun carriages for garrison service are mostly made in the fortresses—the iron work being prepared at the government forges in the mining regions, and sent to the fortresses to be worked up. These carriages are made of oak, pine, or any suitable timber that may be most conveniently obtained. Oak is used chiefly for field and siege carriages, but the siege gun-carriage *stocks* at the arsenal were of *pine*, somewhat resembling our southern pine, but less hard. The wheels of siege carriages are made with hoop tires, but those of field carriages with *streak tires*, or sections, breaking joints with the fellies, as still practiced in the English field carriage wheels for greater convenience of repairs in the field. In the timber stores it was observed that many of the naves for large wheels are laid up in two pieces, the strength of the nave depending chiefly on the bands.

The director of the arsenal is a colonel, who is assisted by a lieutenant colonel, several captains, and subalterns. These officers belong to the artillery, but whilst on this special service they do not count for promotion in the regiments serving with the active corps of the army. The workmen at the arsenal are partly civilians, partly soldiers belonging to companies of workmen.

On the opposite side of the street from the arsenal is another portion of the establishment, containing barracks for the companies of workmen and storehouses for timber. These buildings are also of brick. The plan of the barracks, in its general arrangement, is one which we observed frequently in the buildings for this purpose and for hospitals in Russia and Germany. The rooms communicating with a corridor running along one side of the building are conveniently arranged for warmth, ventilation, circulation, and inspection. The usual sleeping accommodations are, for each man, an iron bedstead, with a palliasse, hair or wool mattress, pillows, sheets, and blankets. Near the barracks are small houses for the married men, and a school for their children.

The storehouses for timber are of two stories. The lower floor is caulked tight as a protection against the moisture from the ground. The upper floor is formed of open gratings, supported on brick arches. The timber is partially seasoned in the open air or in sheds, before being placed in these storehouses, the windows of which are furnished with close shutters, and also with Venetian blinds. Pieces of canvas are glued on the ends of the timber, to prevent it from cracking.

The *laboratory* for preparing ammunition is situated about two miles from the city, in an open and almost uninhabited plain. The buildings, which are arranged on a rectangular plan, consist of detached workshops and storehouses. The principal buildings are of brick, but the driving rooms and percussion laboratory are of wood. The work is nearly all done by hand; the turning of shot blocks and fuzes, and other work requiring the aid of machinery, being done at the arsenal. The workshops are generally of one story, covered with sheet iron. The storehouses for materials and finished work are of two stories, the lower one vaulted. The small buildings for preparing percussion powder are surrounded by high earthen traverses. A space detached from the main square of the laboratory has been set apart for this purpose, and is fenced off by an earthen inclosure and a ditch, but is not yet occupied. Near the principal entrance are a spacious guardhouse and quarters for the commander and other officers. One building contains the furnaces for casting lead bullets, in which workmen were engaged in making several kinds described in the article on small arms. They were all cast in hand moulds, except the spherical balls, which were made in a machine worked by hand, on the plan of the Prussian machine; after which the one used for the same purpose in our arsenals was also modeled. The balls were trimmed by hand and gauged by being passed through a die. The cartridges for rifle arms were greased by dipping the lower part in tallow, according to the practice adopted everywhere in Europe for the new arms, in which the greased paper is inserted with the bullet. Waxed paper was used for bundling the cartridges. The percussion caps are not bundled with them, but are distributed separately. The cartridge cases are not tied, but are closed with paste, and each cartridge is gauged when finished. Percussion caps are made in a separate establishment, at some distance from St. Petersburg; but cannon primers are prepared at this laboratory. They are made of quills, with a wafer of chlorate of potassa at the top. These primers are used only for garrison guns, which alone are furnished with locks. For field artillery common priming tubes and portfires are used. The priming tubes are made of small reeds or rushes, inserted in cups turned out of wood, which contain the wafers of mealed powder.

The buildings for driving fuzes, portfires, &c., are of wood, and they are divided by wooden partitions into small apartments or cells, each for one workman. Fuzes, both for field and garrison service, are generally made of wood. They are cut to fixed lengths for field shells, and are fixed in the laboratory. A common way of fixing ammunition is to tie the cartridge bag over the ball; for shells the bag is gathered around the upper part and glued to the ball, leaving the fuze hole open.

The work at this establishment is done by soldiers. Some of these are permanently attached; but the greater part are obtained by daily details from the troops quartered in the vicinity, and the docility of the Russian peasant is remarkably exhibited in the readiness with which these men acquire a knowledge of the requisite manipulations. In order to aid this object the work is subdivided as much as possible, so that each man may have a simple operation to perform. The ammunition, &c., prepared in this way, though not as neatly finished as ours, is good and serviceable.

Outside of the laboratory inclosure, and near the main entrance, is an excellent barrack for the permanent workmen—a brick building of two stories, both vaulted, divided into large rooms, with a neat and comfortable hospital apartment. On each side of the road leading up to the principal entrance, are neat cottages for the accommodation of the married workmen. This laboratory establishment is quite new, and not yet completed.

The *Arsenal in the Kremlin*, at Moscow, is a large depot of cannon, small arms, and equipments, which are made at the imperial manufactories, or by contract. The storehouse for small arms can hold 500,000 stands of arms. The fire-arms in store there were made chiefly at the government manufactory of Tula, or at Liege, in Belgium. The Russian arms were superior in finish to the others.

A stock of harness for 144 pieces of artillery is kept here. The leather is not blacked until the harness is issued for service.

PRUSSIA.

The *Arsenals of Construction* which we visited at Berlin and Dantzic do not require special notice. There is very little machinery used in them, the work being nearly all done by hand. In these establishments are made not only carriages and equipments for the artilley, but saddles for the cavalry, hospital store wagons and ambulances, and baggage wagons; drawings of these were obtained at the arsenal of Berlin. These arsenals of construction are in the cities; the workmen are all soldiers, belonging to the regimental companies of workmen, and are superintended by their own officers when at work; the officers attached to the arsenals remain on that duty at least three years, but many of them have grown old in the service of the manufacturing establishments, and may be considered permanently detached from field or garrison service. At the workshops in Berlin there were three companies of 200 men each, with a captain, one first and two second lieutenants; the non-commissioned officers act as master workmen; the men receive extra pay, and work by the piece as much as possible. The system of recruiting in the Prussian army, embracing men of all trades, affords peculiar facilities for organizing companies of workmen in every department of the service.

The *Arsenal* of Berlin, properly so called, is a large and beautiful building in the center of the city, on its principal street. It is a quadrangle inclosing a court; the lower story, which is vaulted, is a storehouse for artillery carriages, and the lofty upper story contains a great number of arms in racks, and an artillery museum of ancient and modern arms, trophies, &c.

Of late years the principal manufacturing establishments for material of war have been concentrated at Spandau, about nine miles from Berlin. There are the principal *powder works*, the *manufactory of arms*, and a new *cannon foundery*. The manufactory of arms we were not permitted to see, as the government endeavors to keep secret the construction of the "needle gun;" but we were allowed to visit the other two establishments; and drawings of the cannon foundery, which the Minister of War permitted us to purchase, are among the papers of the commission.

This cannon foundery—not quite completed at the time of our visit—is arranged and constructed in an admirable manner. On the front is a building for offices and the quarters of the director; perpendicular to this are two ranges of buildings; that on the right contains the furnaces, and the other the finishing rooms. The furnaces for casting bronze guns, and some small, but very neat, cupolas and crucible furnaces for iron castings, were alone finished. The bronze furnaces are two round reverberatory furnaces, of sufficient capacity to hold 50,000 pounds of metal each; they appear to be constructed on the plan described in the French works on the subject, and the moulds are made of clay, in the French method. Very heavy sinking heads are used, and the quality of the metal appears to be very superior. The furnace building is lofty, light, and airy, and is well mounted with strong and convenient cranes. The day before our visit there were cast: six 12-pounder and five 6-pounder guns, and two 24-pounder howitzers. The metal is run directly into the moulds, without the intervention of ladles.

Railway tracks across the yard connect the furnace room with the *boring* and *finishing shop*. This part of the establishment is admirably arranged; a lofty and well-lighted room contains the boring and turning lathes, consisting of—

Boring lathes.
Machine for cutting off the sinking heads.
Lathe for turning exterior of guns and planing the part between the trunnions.
Machine for turning trunnions.
Machine for setting vent pieces.

These machines were made at Berlin, on the models generally of the English machines of like kind; they are constructed in the most substantial manner, and finished in a style of *luxury* quite unusual in such tools. Steam engines furnish the motive power of the establishment, and pine wood, which is readily procured in the sandy plains of the vicinity, is the principal fuel used in the furnaces, &c. A traveling crane on a railway over head affords the means of transporting the work with facility from one part of the shop to another. This railway extends into a spacious apartment separated from the finishing shop by a movable glass partition, and appropriated to the inspection of finished work. In this room, besides the gauges and measuring instruments, are the apparatus for testing the qualities of the metal, and a large hydrostatic balance for taking the specific gravity of the whole gun. In connection with this room is a well-mounted chemical laboratory, in which one of the officers conducts the analysis of the gun metal, before and after the casting of the gun, as well as the tests of old metal, &c., used in the foundery. The personnel of the establishment consisted of one captain director, one captain assistant, and four subalterns, with about 100 workmen, civilians.

The *powder works* at Spandau are situated a short distance from the fortress, in a piece of low ground, inclosed by an earthern rampart, and thickly planted with trees. The works are distributed into small detached buildings, constructed chiefly of wood filled in with bricks, and separated from each other by plantations of trees and by earthorn traverses. The river Spree, and a canal running through the grounds, afford the moving power for the mills, although the usual head of water is not more than three feet. There is also a steam engine, the boiler of which furnishes hot water for heating the air in the drying-house, whilst the engine works the fans for driving the hot air through the pipes in the drying-house. Careful precautions against accidents are taken, by detaching the boiler and chimney from the immediate vicinity of the drying-house; the buildings are all kept in the neatest order, and the paths connecting them are strewed with saw dust. No accident has ever occurred at the works, except once from the explosion of the gas generated in making charcoal. The furnaces for this purpose and the refinery are well separated from the other parts of the establishment.

The coal is made chiefly from *alder*, (*faul-baum*, Ger.,) which is also used in England, and in France; (*bois de bourdaine*;) willow wood is likewise used. The coal is prepared by distillation in iron cylinders by the usual process for preparing what is called "cylinder coal;" the wood is packed in the cast-iron cylinders which are built into the furnace, without the intervention of sheet-iron cylinders, as often practiced, and the distillation is carried to the degree of making *black* coal; the reddish coal, which is generally obtained by this process, is considered as imparting too great *bursting* effect to the powder, and is carefully avoided. The gaseous products of distillation and the tar are sold to dyers, &c. Peat is the fuel used in the distillation, and also for the steam engine.

The *saltpeter refinery* is managed on the same principle as the French refineries, and as this method is also pursued at our best powder works, a special account of it is not required here. The rough saltpeter is procured chiefly from the East Indies; after being refined it is said to contain not more than one part in 50,000 of other salts. It is dried in small grains, and not melted with heat, according to the English practice.

The *sulphur* is procured from Marseilles in a refined state, but is remelted at the works to make it more brittle and easier to pulverize.

The method of mixing and incorporating the materials is essentially the same as that which is known in France as "the revolutionary process," from its having been adopted as an expeditious method of making gunpowder during the French revolution. In that country it has been long discontinued, from a belief that powder made in this way is too destructive to the guns, and not susceptible of good preservation; but probably the modifications introduced in the Prussian method have removed these objections, as it is practiced in that country in preference to the stamping mills of France and the cylinder mills of England.

This method consists in pulverizing the materials in rolling barrels, mixing and incorporating them in the same manner, and forming the cake under a press. The coal is pulverized separately and is kept in iron canisters in a fire-proof room, as a precaution against spontaneous combustion, to which pulverized charcoal is known to be liable. The sulphur is mixed with an equal weight of saltpeter, to prevent it from adhering together in balls in the rolling barrel. These barrels are made of wood, and the pulverizing is effected by means of bronze balls five-eighths of an inch in diameter; the charge of a barrel being 200 pounds of materials and 200 pounds of balls. The incorporating barrels are made of leather stretched on wooden frames, and the balls used for this purpose are one quarter of an inch to five sixteenths of an inch in diameter. The composition, moistened with ten per cent. of water, is reduced to cake by being pressed between two rollers; for this purpose it is put into a hopper, from which it is deposited evenly on an endless band of coarse linen, which carries it between the rollers; the upper roller is of bronze, the lower of paper; the cake formed in this way is three eighths of an inch thick, and of extreme hardness.

The granulation is performed by the old process of the "William;" (French "*Guillaume*;") a lenticular disk of lignum vitæ revolving in a parchment sieve. The grain is of two sizes; for cannon, from 0.046 inch to 0.026; below the latter size, for small arms. After being sifted it is partially dried, then glazed, and thoroughly dried by being spread on a sheet laid on wire gauze in a drying-house, which is heated to 150° by means of air forced through cylinders containing hot-water pipes. Before being glazed it is dusted in linen bags, and after glazing is again carefully sifted to assort the different sizes of grain and separate the dust. The powder is then poured into bags of stout linen containing 100 pounds each, and inclosed in casks. It was understood that when distributed for service these bags are emptied at the depot into the casks and sent back to the powder works. This establishment makes usually from 4,000 to 5,000 casks of powder a year. The workmen are civilians, about thirty in number. The director is Major Otto, an officer of artillery, well known for his contributions to military science, who conducted us himself over the works; his dwelling-house is within the inclosure of the grounds; he had been employed about fifteen years in this special department. There is another establishment of powder works at Neisse, in Silesia, not quite so extensive as that of Spandau. Private manufactories of powder are also allowed in Prussia. This is not the case in most of the other great States on the continent of Europe, the governments of which reserve to themselves generally a monopoly of this hazardous manufacture. In England, where the manufacture is free and the government purchases a large part of its supply in time of war, there is still maintained a government factory, at Waltham Abbey, about twelve miles from London, which affords the means of regulating the standard of quality and controlling the mode of manufacture. Such an establishment in the United States would be attended with great advantages to the service. Private manufacturers find much their largest market in the supply of powder for sporting and blasting purposes, and naturally adopt the methods of manufacture adapted for meeting these demands in the best and cheapest way. But it may, and actually does occur, that the gunpowder most suitable for these objects is not the best for use in the large charges required for cannon. In France, where gunpowder is a government monopoly, the sporting powder is made in the English method, in heavy cylinder mills, whilst all the powder used for the military service is made by the old process of the stamping mills. The reason of this is that the latter kind of powder, whilst sufficiently strong for service, is considered much less destructive to the metal of cannon, whether of bronze or iron, and also is susceptible of being kept for a longer time, with less deterioration, than that made by the new process. Powder of this kind, made in 1680, has been recently found very nearly equal in strength to that just made. This consideration of the explosive or bursting force of gunpowder, distinct from its propelling effect on the projectile, (as evinced in the action of fulminating powders,) has recently assumed greater importance than ever, in view of the introduction into our armaments of great numbers of guns of large caliber, requiring heavy charges of powder, the destructive effects of which, with the powder now made for our military service, causes the most serious embarrassment.

A *laboratory* for fixing ammunition, &c., is established on an open plain, at a safe distance outside of one of the gates of Berlin. The buildings occupy a square of about 200 yards; they are of one story; the workshops are frame buildings; the store-houses of brick. No work was going on at the time of our visit, and the establishment offered little worthy of special remark. There is no machinery, except a hand press for making lead balls, the work being all done by hand. The square is inclosed with an earthen rampart; the magazines are outside of this inclosure, and surrounded also by earthen fences; they are of two stories, neatly built, lined with wood and carpeted; the lower story contained gunpowder, and the upper one fixed ammunition, with percussion primers, friction tubes, &c.

AUSTRIA.

The principal manufacturing establishments of the Austrian artillery have been recently united in the new *Arsenal of Vienna*. This magnificent establishment is situated just outside of the walls of the city, on the eastern side, and comprises the following buildings:

A museum and store-house for small arms;

A manufactory of small arms;

Workshops for artillery carriages, harness, and equipments;

A cannon foundery, and boring mills for bronze and iron cannon;
Barracks for 10,000 men;
Extensive storehouses for material and finish work.

The barracks and storehouses form the inclosure of a rectangle about 500 yards front by 700 yards deep. The accompanying plan and view (Plates 1 and 2) show the general arrangement of the several buildings: the style of architecture is exhibited by the bird's eye view of the arsenal, and in the photographs of the principal buildings, which are among the papers of the commission. These buildings were designed by eminent architects of Vienna, by one of whom, Mr. Sicandsbourg, the photographs of them were most kindly presented to the commission.

They were not all occupied, but were very nearly completed at the time of our visit. The material is chiefly brick, with some cut stone in the ornamental parts. The bricks are not red, but of various colors or shades of yellow and brown; and advantage is taken of this variety to make the work ornamental. Most of the cornices and other ornaments are made of bricks molded into suitable forms. The exterior buildings are of such solidity as to make the arsenal a sort of citadel, secure from the assaults of a body of citizens such as obtained possession of the military establishments in the city in the revolution of 1848.

The principal entrance to the arsenal is through a handsome quadrangle, containing the quarters of the commanding officer and the offices of the administration. Next to this is the museum, of which the lower floor and the central hall are to receive the fine collection of arms and armor formerly deposited in the city. The upper floor is divided by the central hall into two spacious rooms to contain small arms, in racks, some of which were put up. The racks are made of cast-iron stanchions, supporting horizontal wrought iron bars, which form as many shelves as there are tiers of arms. On these the arms are laid horizontally, the buts outward, so that the full rack presents only a close mass of but-plates. This arrangement, although less ornamental than the usual method of placing the arms upright, has the advantage of stowing a greater number of arms in a given space, and of permitting the examination and removal of any one piece without disturbing another.

Next to the museum is the manufactory of small arms, all the workshops of which are united in one building. Steam is the motive power here, as in all the other machine shops of the arsenal. The principal operations performed here are, finishing the barrels, mountings, and bayonets; making the locks, and fitting and assembling the arms. The barrels are forged in the iron regions, and are made chiefly of the excellent iron of Styria. They are bored, turned, percussioned, and rifled at the arsenal. The lock plates and bridles are made, by contract, of annealed cast-iron; the other parts of the lock, and all the finishing are done at the arsenal. Steel is used only for the springs; the other parts requiring a steel surface are case-hardened. The holes in the lock-plate for the tumbler and the rear side screw are *punched* out; the others are drilled. The screws are procured by purchase. The cones are made of steel, the upper part only being hardened. The hammers are formed in a punching press and finished in a swedge under a drop hammer of Colt's patent. Planing and milling machines are used in the finishing work, but not to the same extent as with us, most of the parts being finally fitted by hand-filing. The bayonets and mountings are forged outside, and only finished at the arsenal.

The machine for rifling the barrels is well made, but it cuts the grooves of uniform depth only. The cuts are made by notches on a steel rod. There are six of these notches or cutters arranged on a spiral corresponding with the twist of the groove, each cutting one sixth of the depth, so that the groove is finished at a single operation. The rifling rod has a straight movement in the direction of its length, and the twist is given by turning the barrel. For this purpose the barrel is adjusted in two collars, and a pinion is attached to it, which, by working in a rack at right angles to the barrel, causes the latter to turn. The rack is moved by a guide bar placed at the proper inclination with the axis of the barrel, in the manner represented in Plate 3, Fig. 1. Several barrels may be grooved at the same time. The depth of the cut is afterwards relieved or increased at the breech, for about six inches in length, by hand work, with file cutters attached to a wooden rod which has leaden guides on it.

The gun stocks are made by contract, outside of the arsenal; they are seasoned by steam. The musket stocks are made of beech, the rifle of walnut.

The armory finishes from 2,000 to 2,400 arms a week.

The proof-house for barrels is outside of the arsenal square. It has an iron bed for the barrels, and the arrangements are nearly the same as at our armories. Two hundred barrels are proved at once. The charge was said to be half a *loth*, (equal to 140 grains, Troy,) with a service ball and two wads. The failures average about two per cent., but are sometimes as high as fifteen per cent. If one third of those delivered at one time fail, the whole are rejected.

On the opposite side of the arsenal, as shown on the plan, is the practice ground for small arms, which is admirably arranged. Here each one of the arms made is tried by firing from one to five shots, from the shoulder, on a rest, at 100 yards, in order to adjust the sights. A spacious house affords shelter to the men who load and fire the arms. In another part of the same building is a musket ballistic pendulum, for proving powder and trying the force of the charges and the recoil of the arms; for the latter purpose, the suspension frame for the musket is arranged to receive the arm complete, instead of the barrel alone, as in the French pendulum. The practice ground gives a range of 600 paces, or 500 yards. It is marked by targets at 50 paces apart up to 300, and then at 100 paces. At each target is a traverse, in front of which, at one side, is a brick shelter for the marker.

The lead balls are made at the arsenal, in presses constructed in a similar manner to those used at our arsenals for making round balls. The form of the Austrian ball, which has no cavity in the base, permits the use of simple dies for forming them, and cutters for separating them from the bar. In the press, the upper half of the die is attached to a plunger about three inches in diameter, which passes through the cross head of the press, and is moved up and down by an eccentric on the working shaft. Six of these presses are placed in the center line of a large room, making each 3,000 balls an hour. Twelve cutting machines, placed along one side of the room, and working at half the speed of the presses, serve to separate the balls from the bars.

As mentioned elsewhere, the new arms are all of the same caliber; and it is worthy of remark that the *locks* for all of them are identical. It is a *bar lock*, very like ours, and adjusted to the barrel in the same manner. The implements used for the new arms are a screwdriver and cone wrench, a wiper and worm, and a ball screw. (Plate 3.) The ball screw has a brass cylinder on the screw, to keep it in the center of the barrel on the point of the ball.

Sabers are also inspected and finished at the arsenal. The blades, mountings, and scabbards are made by contract, and delivered separately at the armory, where they are proved, inspected, and put together. The blades are proved by striking them flatways on a plank, and edgeways three times on an iron block. For this purpose they are not held in the hand, but are adjusted to a shaft, which is turned suddenly by means of a spring. They are then made to bend six inches in the middle, and the thick part of the blade near the hilt is also proved by being slightly bent. The saber, which is among the patterns of arms furnished to the commission, is used by both the heavy and light cavalry; that for the foot and horse artillery is of a similar pattern, but lighter.

As fast as the new pattern arms are issued to the troops, the old arms called in are broken up, and the parts sold or worked up for other purposes.

The next grand division of the arsenal comprises the *artillery workshops* for making gun carriages and wagons for field and garrison service. The shops for the wood workers, and those for the iron workers, are in separate buildings, with a steam engine in each. The rooms are forty-five to fifty feet wide, with lofty ceilings, airy, and well lighted. Unlike most of the old arsenals of construction on the continent of Europe, these workshops, as well as all the other parts of this great establishment, are well furnished with machines for executing the work formerly done by hand. Here are Nasmyth's steam hammers, large and small; Rider's machine for forging bolts, fitted with dies of various sizes; machines for planing, punching, and slotting iron work; for sawing, planing, boring, and turning wood; sawing fellies, turning spokes, &c.; all well and strongly built, generally at machine shops in Vienna. The construction of these machines does not call for any particular description, as they are nearly all made after English or American models, well known in this country, and used in our workshops, or improved upon. The fellies are cut with a web saw out of plank fastened on a circular table which guides the cut. Oak is the timber chiefly used for gun carriages, but the spokes of wheels are made also of *ash*, and the fellies partly of *beech*.

Near these machine shops is an extensive shop for making harness and leather work, &c. Both here and in Prussia American sewing machines are used for making cartridge bags and other like work.

The *cannon foundery* is in rear of the artillery workshops. This establishment had not been put in operation. In the furnace-house or foundery proper, three very large reverberatory furnaces occupy the circumference of a semicircle, so that the metal from all of them may, if necessary, be readily conducted to a mould placed in the central pit. Some of the rooms for boring and turning cannon, on one side of the foundery, were finished, and the machines were at work and finishing iron cannon cast at the foundery in Vienna. This building is admirably constructed, and furnished with machines of the most solid kind. The rooms are vaulted, but well lighted by large windows on one side. In the basement a vaulted gallery runs along one side of the building, and in this are the main shaft and the heavy gearing connected with the machines above. The gallery is well lighted, and every part of the machinery easily accessible. The moving power is a steam engine in the center of the building. The furnaces and machines are constructed after the plan of those in the fine establishment at Liege, but with improvements in the arrangements and details. We particularly remarked here, and in most of the modern works of this kind in Europe, as compared with ours, the admirable solidity and massive construction of the buildings and machinery; in which respect they are well worthy of imitation in our arsenals and other public manufactories.

The accompanying view of the Arsenal of Vienna shows the position of the barracks for troops and the storehouses, which form the exterior line of buildings. The barracks are vaulted, and have terraced roofs covered with asphaltum. They are capable of accommodating 10,000 men, but only a small force was quartered there at the time of our visit. Some of the rooms were occupied by the enlisted workmen, of whom many are employed in the arsenal, although the greater part of the workmen were civilians. A handsome church, in the center of the rear line of buildings, is provided for the garrison.

The storehouses were occupied with materials and finished work. In one of them was an immense quantity of harness—enough, we were told, for 24,000 horses.

This magnificent arsenal is said to have cost more than *four millions* of dollars.

Another grand arsenal of construction is under way at Verona for the Italian possessions of Austria. The buildings are to occupy a space of 400 feet by 340 feet, and are intended for the manufacture and repair of artillery carriages, equipments, and for the assembling and repair of small arms. A bird's-eye view of this establishment, which is unfinished, is among the drawings belonging to the commission.

The *laboratory* for preparing ammunition and military fireworks is situated near the village of Simmering, about three miles from Vienna. The workshops are *frame buildings*, detached from each other, for the different kinds of operations; no work requiring machinery is done here. The workmen are enlisted men; some of them artillerists permanently attached to the establishment, but most of them are soldiers of the line detailed for one month at a time. About 150 men were employed, chiefly in making cartridges for the new rifle arms. The ball being inserted into the barrel with the paper around it, each cartridge is dipped at the ball end into melted mutton tallow, after it is finished, according to the general practice in Europe for these cartridges. The cartridges are filled singly with a funnel and measure, and a cylindrical stick of regulated length is inserted and left in each until the box is finished, in order to make sure that all are filled. They are packed in bundles of six, with eight caps to a bundle; and in order to prevent the grease from smearing the upper part of the cartridge, a strip of paper is laid in the folding-box and passed successively between the contiguous cartridges; the wrappers are not waxed or made water-proof. The packing boxes are made at the arsenal; the ends and sides are joined together by straight notches and tenons, so as to be nailed on both sides; the notches and tenons are cut by revolving chisels, but they are not *dovetailed* by the machine; (a dovetailing machine has been very recently introduced at our arsenals;) each box contains 2,200 cartridges.

The powder for small arms is of coarser grain than our musket powder; that for cannon, finer; both kinds are highly glazed. It is packed, as in Prussia, in linen bags, in barrels of two hundred weight. The proof of the powder, by the lever eprouvette or the mortar, is marked on each barrel, and also the weight of a cubic foot; the musket powder weighs about fifty-three and a half pounds to the foot, Austrian measure, which corresponds to sixty pounds to the foot of our measure. The powder is made chiefly by contract, but the government supplies the saltpeter and sulphur. A refinery of saltpeter is connected with the laboratory at Simmering. The crude saltpeter is procured chiefly from artificial saltpeter beds in the country; nothing peculiar was observed in the process of refining. The refined saltpeter is melted and cast into rough cakes, which are broken into lumps about the size of the fist before being sent to the powder works. We were informed that the principal powder mills of the government and a large depot of powder were near Wiener-Neustadt, about thirty miles south of Vienna. The magazines were said to be *nine* in number; each building, covered with a light brick arch, is capable of holding 1,500 barrels of powder, or 300,000 pounds; about the usual capacity of our magazines at the principal arsenals.

Percussion caps are made by private contract, principally at Prague; they are delivered at the laboratory in boxes of 65,000 each.

Connected with the laboratory is a large depot of ammunition in the buildings of an old château, the garden of which is a park for artillery. The ammunition for field guns is all *fixed;* that for *howitzers* has the cartridge separate from the ball, and several different charges are provided for each, to be used according to the effect required. The packing boxes have partitions to separate the charges, and the shot or shell rests on a small coil of rope or slow match; portfires and tubes are packed separately. The portfire, like the Russian, is smaller than ours; the *exterior* diameter is half an inch, and the case is made of only three turns of light paper; the length of composition is twelve inches; a pointed stick closes the lower end of the case.

Cartridge-bags for field service are made of a close-wove woolen stuff, which is coated with a preparation of paste and linseed oil; some of them are colored with a red earthen paint. The ammunition is fixed by tying the bag over the shot; (or around the fuze hole of the shell if fixed;) instead of a shot block, a cushion of cow's hair or tow is placed between the powder and ball. For garrison service the cartridge bags were made of common brown linen.

The field artillery do not use cannon locks, but fire with friction tubes, or common tubes and portfires; the friction tubes are made on the same plan as the French.

BELGIUM.

In passing through Liege, the commission had an opportunity of visiting some of the military manufacturing establishments of that great center of the iron works of Belgium. The government *cannon foundery* has been long established, and is well known by the excellence of its products. For about twenty-five years this foundery has been conducted by its present able and zealous director, Colonel Frédérix, of the artillery, who was previously employed there as assistant to his relative, General Huguenin, the director of the establishment during the union of Belgium with Holland. The machines and operations are described in the "*Cours Élémentaire sur la Fabrication des bouches à feu, &c.,*" by Major Coquilhat, assistant director at the foundery. The capacity of the foundery being greater than is necessary for supplying the wants of Belgium in this respect, a great deal of work is done there for other governments; drawings of iron cannon made for thirteen foreign States, presented by Colonel Frédérix, are among the papers of the commission. No novelties have been recently introduced in the furnaces or machinery of the establishment; but the constant and varied work affords opportunities which are studiously used by the intelligent director for improving the quality of the work by a judicious use and mixture of various kinds of iron, &c. Bronze cannon, and other castings of that nature, such as statues, are also made here. The mode of testing the quality of gun-iron, which has been long used in France and Belgium, by proving to extremity a trial gun, is still continued. Combined with this are other mechanical tests of the iron, similar to those which have been adopted by our Ordnance Department. These consist in comparative trials of the *hardness* of the metal; of its *strength to resist fracture* by a blow; of the *transverse strength* of a bar, and of its *tensile strength* or tenacity. The apparatus used for these purposes, which is simpler, but less powerful than ours, is shown in the drawings accompanying the reports, kindly furnished to us by Colonel Frédérix. These papers, which, on account of their special nature, it is not thought necessary to embody in this report, are the following:

1. Report of the proof of a trial gun, October 12, 1853.
2. Report of the proof of a trial gun, October 15, 1853.
3. Report of experiments on copper vent pieces for iron guns, June 16, 1855.
4. A memoir on the use of elongated cartridges, and the increased durability of iron guns by that means.
5. Note of mechanical tests of iron, made in presence of the commission, February 27, 1856, with drawings of the apparatus used.
6. Note on the condemnation of cannon worn out in service.
7. Extract from the register of the foundery, relative to the casting of a 68-pounder howitzer and an 8-inch mortar.
8. Results of the proof of a 6-pounder iron gun, fired 2,000 times, by General Huguenin, in 1820, 1821, and 1822.
9. Six sheets of drawings of cannon cast at Liege Foundery, for Belgium and foreign States.

These papers, besides conveying useful information, serve to illustrate the minute care with which the operations of this cannon foundery are conducted, and the systematic attention which is paid to recording all the particulars of them, for comparison and future reference.

There are employed at the foundery ten officers, and from 150 to 250 workmen of all kinds, according to the demands for work. With the former force, about 300 guns are made in a year; but the establishment is capable of making 500 a year.

The government *manufactory of small arms* at Liege does not require an extended notice. The work is done principally by hand; but there is a steam engine of 15-horse power for turning the lathes and the boring and rifling machines, &c. The barrel skelps are drawn out under a trip-hammer, but the barrels are welded by hand, as are also the bayonets, rammers, &c. Stocks are made by hand, a machine having been unsuccessfully tried. A full account of this armory, by a commission of Spanish officers, is among the books of our commission.

A machine for making expanding bullets has been tried, but was disused on account of the slowness of its operation, and the balls were cast in hand moulds. The machine was similar, in principle, to the one made at Alleghany Arsenal, and now used at our arsenals with some success. The die for the bullet is divided horizontally, the axis of the bullet being vertical; one-half of the die is pressed up to the other by means of a cam, whilst a punch descends to compress the lead, and to form the cavity of the ball.

The machine used for rifling the barrels with grooves of progressive depth, decreasing from the breech to the muzzle, is ingenious and effective; it is copied, with some modifications, from a French machine, first made by Mr. Manceaux, an eminent manufacturer of arms, at Paris. The principle of this machine, and its mode of operation, may be understood by an inspection of Figs. 1. and 2, Plate 3. The barrel B is fixed on the frame $A A$; the cylindrical rod C, which carries the cutter, is connected with the slide rest D; a pinion, E, is attached to this rod, and works in a rack, F, the outer end of which slides on the guide bar, G, with which it is connected by a collar or a pin working in a groove in the bar. By this arrangement it is plain that, as the slide rest D is moved on its frame, the rack will cause the pinion, and consequently the rifling rod, to turn on its axis with a motion determined by the inclination given to the guide rod G, with respect to the axis of the barrel, and will thus regulate the twist of the grooves. The ingenious contrivance for regulating the progressive depth of the groove is shown in Fig. 2; the rifling rod C is hollow at one end, and contains the hook-shaped cutter H, the back of which rests on an inclined plane in the bottom of the hollow rod, whilst the point or cutting edge projects through a mortise on the opposite side; this cutter is pressed, by the spiral spring I, against the end of another rod, K, which is screwed into the open end of the rifling rod C; the rod K is connected with a square bar, L, which slides in a square socket, M, (Fig. 1,) attached to the frame of the machine; as this bar, therefore, is prevented from turning, it follows that, by the turning of the rifling rod C, in its motion through the barrel, the end of it is screwed up on the rod K, and the edge of the cutter is thus raised on the inclined plane, causing it to cut deeper as the rod is drawn through the barrel; when the motion of the rod is reversed, its socket is unscrewed, and the cutter descends by the action of the spiral spring; to commence a new cut in the same groove, the rod is slightly turned, and the cutter fed up, by means of an index plate marked with as many divisions as there are cuts required to complete the groove; the cutter is then restored to its original position, and, by means of another index plate, it is turned into the place for the next groove; about twelve cuts are required for each groove. The drawing represents the rifling rod as being worked by hand, by means of a guide screw underneath; but this motion, as well as the successive feed motions of the cutter, are easily communicated by machine power. Two of these rifling machines were purchased for our armories, but before the receipt of them, a machine was got up, under the direction of Major Hagner, of the Ordnance Department, for performing the same work in a more expeditious manner, by cutting three grooves at once.

The barrels of small arms are proved at the factory in the usual manner; the sights of the rifled arms are adjusted by firing each one five times, at 150 meters, (165 yards.)

At Liege an immense number of arms are made for foreign governments and for the trade, and the rooms of the large manufacturers, such as Mr. Francotte, Mr. Lemille, &c., present models of almost every invention in this line of business. The barrels of all these arms are inspected and proved at the government proof-house, under the supervision of a commission, some of the members of which are elected by the manufacturers. The proof for military arms is a charge of powder equal to the weight of the ball, one round ball and two wads; for other arms, the charge of powder is two thirds the weight of the ball appropriate to the caliber, allowing a windage of 0.025 inch. The barrels and most other parts of the arms are made by men working in small shops or at their own dwellings in Liege or the vicinity; women and children may be seen at all times of day in the streets carrying these products of industry to the proof-house, or to the factories where they are finished and put together. The report of arms proved at Liege in 1854, (the latest report at the time of our visit to the proof-house,) contains the names of ninety manufacturing houses for whom arms were presented for proof. The number of arms inspected for these firms, exclusive of those rejected in the proof, was 554,000, besides 13,400 belonging to sundry barrel forgers, &c. This was the first year of the Russian war; the number of military arms, then 78,720, was no doubt greatly increased in 1855 and 1856. The British government had, in the latter years, large contracts for rifled arms at Liege, where a large factory was established, under the supervision of English officers, for the inspection and packing of the arms, and also for finishing a portion of them and adjusting the sights. For the latter purpose, a very convenient and simple apparatus was used; a cast-iron bench or frame, like the ways of a lathe, has at each end a fixed head in which the barrel is supported by mandrils fitting closely in the muzzle and the breech; the ways of the frame are carefully planed, so as to be exactly straight and parallel, and the mandrils are placed exactly in the center between them; the socket for the breech is placed so that the *flats* on the side of the barrel shall be vertical and the line of sight uppermost; this line is then marked, for the back and front sights, by means of a sliding rest which carries a scriber for this purpose, and after the sights are fixed their position may be verified by the same means.

Mr. Francotte was the contractor for the arms made for the British government. The finish boring of the barrels is done with a square steel rod, the corners of which are cut in fine file-teeth or notches; the rod is supported by rounded slips of wood; it is turned rapidly and drawn at the same time through the barrel, having the effect of fine filing.

The packing boxes for these arms are made in a simpler manner than ours, and are equally secure; two pairs of cleats are nailed on the inside of the box, forming two grooves for the packing stuff, opposite to the small of the stock; the box is about an inch longer than the musket or rifle, admitting a wedge between the buts of two pieces and against the end of the intervening barrel, to prevent the arms from turning or slipping; the bayonet is tied under the stock; the sword bayonets are lodged in notches cut in packing pieces which are screwed to those that hold the rifles.

FRANCE.

The commission visited few of the artillery manufacturing establishments of France, and those not the most important. The *Arsenal at Lyons* is a depot and a place for making and repairing gun carriages and preparing small-arm ammunition. The style of buildings adopted of late years for the French arsenals is well suited for the purpose, and has been to some extent copied in our own arsenals. At Lyons the work is done altogether by hand, even the lathes being turned by men. In the smith's shop there are forty-eight fires, and the filer's benches are in the same shop. In the well-arranged storehouses for materials and finished work, fifty field carriages for the new 12-pounder gun, with harness, are kept always on hand, besides siege and garrison carriages. The tire bolts for the wheels of these carriages are not put in until the batteries are issued, so that the tires may be more readily cut and reset if necessary.

The work is done partly by companies of workmen, (soldiers,) partly by hired mechanics. The wages of the latter class are from fifty to sixty cents a day; the enlisted workmen receive fifteen cents a day extra. Cartridges for smooth bore muskets were made by women; no paste or thread is used in making these cartridges, the paper being merely folded over the ball and pressed in a die. The balls for rifle arms were cast. Both ball and blank cartridges are packed in powder barrels of different sizes, making very heavy and inconvenient packages of the ball cartridges. The principal laboratory for ammunition is in one of the detached forts, but was not occupied at the time of our visit to Lyons.

The *Arsenal at Strasburg* is on a larger scale than that at Lyons, but here also the work is done by hand; the great number of workmen at low wages dispenses with the use of costly machinery. In the great depot of stores connected with the arsenal there were 2,800 pieces of brass ordnance, and an immense number of gun carriages, &c.

The *Cannon Foundery* of Strasburg, for brass ordnance, is one of the oldest in France, and has been managed by founders of deservedly high reputation; no modern improvements have been introduced, the operations being conducted in very nearly the same manner as in the time of

Darteins and the Kellers, a hundred years ago. The boring and turning lathes are worked by horse-power, and the trunnions finished with the chisel and file. But notwithstanding the rudeness of the machinery the products of this foundery are of superior quality, still justifying its high reputation, and the production of about 600 guns a year shows how much may be done by the steady application of small means in an establishment of this nature.

The *Laboratory of Vincennes*, situated in the forest, at a safe distance from the château, consists of several detached frame buildings, in which ammunition for cannon and small arms is prepared. The workmen are soldiers detailed for fifteen days at a time from the garrison of Vincennes; one half of them only are relieved at once.

The manner of making the cartridges for rifled arms is elsewhere described; the ball part of the cartridge is dipped in grease composed of three parts tallow and one beeswax; the heavy ball cartridges are put up in bundles of six, with eight caps; the lighter, in bundles of ten, with twelve caps. Both kinds are packed in 100-pound powder barrels, which hold 3,500 smooth bore cartridges, or 2,500 rifle musket cartridges. The chargers used were cylinders attached, in groups of six or seven, to a board; these being filled, the cartridge cases are inverted over them, and the whole being reversed, the charge is emptied into the cartridge. The cases are closed merely by folding, without being tied or pasted.

The bags for cannon cartridges (24-pounders) were made entirely of *serge*, (coarse woolen stuff,) or of a *raw silk* fabric; the latter material is not yet extensively used, being only on trial. Serge, twenty-six inches wide, costs twenty-five cents a yard.

ENGLAND.

Untoward circumstances, of a political nature, although unconnected with the immediate business of the commission, caused delay in obtaining admission to the military establishments of England.

The official permission to visit them was received on the eve of our departure from London; it was expressed in the most polite terms, and we were treated with kind attention at the few places to which we had an opportunity to make a hasty visit before the time fixed for our return home.

The *Arsenal at Woolwich* is the great establishment in which are concentrated the supplies of ordnance, munitions, and equipments for arming both the land and naval forces, and where most of these supplies are manufactured. It embraces:

1. The Proof Department.
2. The Carriage Department.
3. The Cannon Foundery.
4. The Laboratory Department.
5. The Storekeeper's Department.

These departments are nearly independent of each other, and each of them (except the storekeeper's) is superintended by officers of artillery. The storekeeper's is a civil office of great trust and importance.

The *Proof Department* is charged with the proof and inspection of ordnance and projectiles, and with conducting the experiments and trials of new inventions relating to this part of the service. There is an extensive range for cannon firing within the limits of the arsenal; but for greater safety, and for practicing at very long ranges, a practice ground on the sea-shore, at Shoeburyness, near the mouth of the Thames, is used.

All the cannon, mortars, &c., and all shot and shells which are made on contract with private founderies, are delivered at Woolwich arsenal for proof and inspection, by which means the examination of them may be conducted in a more careful and uniform manner than by our system of inspection at the foundery. But this arrangement does not combine the advantage of a supervision of the manufacture by the inspecting officers.

The *Carriage Department*, besides making the gun carriages, ammunition wagons, and other carriages and equipments required for the land service of the artillery, prepares the wagons and other means of transport for the hospital department, ship gun carriages, mortar beds for floating batteries, tanks for storing powder and cartridges in ships of war, &c. In the extensive workshops of this department, great use is now made of machinery for wood working; many of which machines for this purpose have been adopted from those used in the United States, either in the arsenals or in private factories, but generally with some modifications in the arrangement, and in almost all cases with the important improvement of possessing greater solidity in their construction than our patented machines. The principle of Blanchard's lathe is applied, as with us, to turning spokes for wheels, and it is also used for shaping gun-carriage stocks and other work of that kind. In the lathe for the latter purpose the pattern which is to be copied is placed in rear of the work, the centers of both the pattern and work being fixed, and in the same horizontal plane. The pattern, turning on its centers, causes the cutting tool to work backwards or forwards in its slide rest, as the latter moves from one end of the ways to the other. This seems to be an improvement, especially for heavy work, over our eccentric lathe, in which the cutter revolves on a fixed axis, and the frame, which supports both the pattern and the work, is moved up to it. The parts of wheels are not only made by machinery, as with us, but they are put together by the same means. For this purpose the nave is fixed on a center, on a horizontal cast-iron bed, and the spokes and fellies are put in their proper positions. On the outside of the bed are four heavy cast-iron segments, shaped to fit the circumference of the wheel when finished. Each of these segments is connected with a piston-rod communicating with the cylinder of a hydraulic press, which is worked by the steam engine of the shop. By applying this pressure, therefore, to all the segments, the tenons of the spokes are driven at the same time into the nave and the fellies. If they do not enter equally on all sides, the simple turning of a stop-cock serves to relieve the pressure on one side, or increase it on another. The operation is expeditious and effective, and would no doubt be economical when a great number of wheels of one pattern are to be made. *Streak tire*, or tire bolted on in separate segments, is still used for all wheels of field and siege batteries, on account of the supposed greater facility of effecting repairs in a campaign. Hoop tires are used only for light wagons. These tires are heated singly, lying flatways in the furnace. In setting them the wheel is laid on a cast-iron table, which is counterpoised, so that it may readily be lowered horizontally into a cistern of water, and raised again when cooled.

A *scroll-cutting saw*, made of a continuous band of steel passing over two pulleys, from one of which it receives motion, appeared to work well and rapidly.

The *foundery* was not visited in our hurried walk through a part of Woolwich arsenal; but we saw extensive buildings just constructed for extending its operations. These have been here, tofore confined to making brass cannon, all the iron ordnance having been procured by contract with private founders. Whilst the manufacture of iron guns was confided to a few establishments of this kind, such as those of Gospel Oak and Low Moor, possessing the necessary knowledge and skill, and the means of applying them so as to produce with certainty excellent results, the quality of the iron ordnance appeared to be perfectly satisfactory; but when, during the late war, it was thought necessary to extend the application of the contract system to other hands, the most disastrous results ensued; the evidence of which lay before the visitor at Woolwich, in a number of mortars which were burst in the bombardment of Sweaborg, and in experimental proofs made in England. The following remarks on this subject were made in Parliament by the Secretary of War. Mr. Monsell, to whom he refers, is the civil chief of the Bureau of Ordnance:

"Lord Panmure was sorry to say that there were too good grounds for the statement made by his honorable friend (Mr. Monsell) in the House of Commons on this subject. The statement was to the effect that certain mortars under contract from a certain firm had been delivered in an imperfect state, and were found to have been tampered with in order that they might pass the supervision of the proper authorities. He must, in the first instance, state that no danger had accrued from the circumstance to any of the troops, as no mortars, as far as he had learned, were known to have passed through the revision and investigation of the authorities, and afterwards to have been found in any way incomplete. But, with respect to five of these mortars, on Thursday last an experiment took place, and the result of that experiment induced his honorable friend to make the matter publicly known on Friday. These five mortars were, as he (Lord Panmure) had learned, part of a contract entered into by the house of Messrs. Grissell, (Regent's Canal Iron Works.) Two of the mortars stood the proof at Woolwich Arsenal, and were afterwards sent down to Shoeburyness to undergo a third proof before being placed in store for the use of the service. One of them burst after the tenth round had been fired, and this led to the detection, behind the breech, of a piece of metal screwed into the mortar in the most skillful manner in order to cover a flaw which had previously been removed. He could assure the noble earl, who thought that a fraud of this kind could scarcely be committed without immediate detection, that the piece of metal being let in with such skill that the most vigilant eye might have failed to detect it. The result of the experiment upon this mortar led to the immediate examination of the other, and in that also a piece of metal was found to have been inserted very nearly at the same part. A third mortar had already been rejected, flaws of the same nature having been detected upon the base by the authorities at Woolwich Arsenal. Similar flaws were also found upon the base of the fourth; and the fifth, although the flaws were discovered in it, burst altogether during the experiment, having been manufactured from material altogether unfitted for the service for which it was intended. The result of what had taken place was, of course, first, the rejection of the mortars; and, secondly, the erasure of the firm which had supplied them from the list of those with which contracts might in future be entered into by the government; but he had not yet been able to ascertain whether the government had power to take legal proceedings against it. His honorable friend had mentioned this circumstance not as a reason why the government should establish a foundery of its own, but as a justification of the government in having taken that step. He thought it would have been well if governments had taken that step some time ago, although he was not prepared to say that they ought to become entirely their own manufacturers either of mortars and great guns or of small arms. They ought, to a certain extent, to be independent of trade, but also to be in a position to enter into contracts; they ought to be able to keep pace with trade, and to make themselves acquainted with the improvements going on outside their own manufactory, as well as to discover improvements within it. The intention of the government was to establish a foundery in which they might cast their own mortars, manufacture their own heavy armaments, and test the material used in that manufactore, in order to ascertain whether it was fit for the purpose for which it was intended, without putting every mortar and gun to the very hard trial to which it was now subjected. There was no method of testing a mortar but that of firing it so many times. They hoped to be able to test the material of which their mortars were made, and, by trying, say one mortar out of twenty until it burst, so as to be able to trust the other nineteen without further trial. The present system of testing was very deficient with regard to many articles besides large guns. An anchor might appear, on being tested, to be perfectly sound, and yet might give way at the first strain afterwards made upon it. He thought his noble friend was quite justified in demanding that the names of the contractors who had committed this fraud should be given up, and that they should not again be employed by the government; but he had not yet been able to determine whether there was any means of visiting upon them the crime of which they had been guilty. Having, however, made this statement with regard to them, he felt it his duty to add that the government had no ground whatever of complaint with regard to the other two firms with which they had dealt during the war. The names of those firms were Messrs. Hood, of Low Moor Works, and Messrs. Walker, of Gospel Oak Foundery. Both of them had supplied several varieties of heavy armament for the use of the service, with which the government was perfectly satisfied. He would only observe, in conclusion, that he hoped greater security than at present existed would before long be attained with regard to the material from which the mortars were manufactured."

In pursuance of the intention expressed by the Secretary of War, the foundery at Woolwich Arsenal has been extended by the construction of furnaces and machinery for making iron cannon—not with a view of dispensing entirely with the employment of private founderies, but with the hope of being able to improve and to control more effectually that important branch of manufacture. Before commencing this extension of the works, the Secretary of War sent a commission of artillery officers, accompanied by the master of machinery at Woolwich, to visit some of the principal cannon founderies on the continent of Europe. The report of this commission embraces much information on the subject of founderies and other manufacturing establishments of the Ordnance Department. It was printed only for the War Department, but a copy of it was kindly presented to us by Mr. Mousell, and is among the books belonging to our commission.

The *Laboratory Department* has been remodeled and greatly extended under the direction of its present able superintendent, Captain Boxer of the artillery. The operations of this department embrace the preparation of ammunition of all kinds, making war rockets, percussion caps, and cannon primers, fuzes, fire-works (or military and other purposes, &c. The workshops, although crowded too much together in one inclosure, are spacious and well furnished with machinery. The principal building is a spacious shed of one story, the roof of which is formed of a series of ridges and valleys, framed of iron, and supported by rows of iron columns, which serve also to sustain the shafts for the machinery with which the room is filled. One half of each ridge in the roof is formed of glass, thus affording abundant light in every part of the room. This arrangement, which would be impracticable in our country on account of the danger from storms of snow, hail, and rain, is attended with no inconvenience in the more uniform climate of southern England. In this large room are machines for reaming and tapping the fuze holes of shells; for fixing the shell blocks to them; for driving war rockets; for making lead balls, and expanding plugs for them; for making percussion caps for small arms; besides lathes and tools for other like purposes. The preparation of the immense quantity of projectiles required for the land and naval forces during the Russian war, was carried on here with great rapidity. The balls were conveyed to the hands of the workmen at the machines by means of inclined iron troughs leading from the piles in the yard, whilst similar troughs served to convey them, after they were finished, to the place where they were required for further operations. Shot were conveyed by the same means to the wharves or landings, for shipment.

For fixing the sabots or wooden blocks to shells, Captain Boxer has adopted, instead of the ordinary method of strapping with tin straps, a plan of *riveting*, which is simple, and appears to be secure and effective. This method is represented in Plate 20, Fig. 7. A dovetailed hole, about two tenths of an inch deep, is bored in the bottom of the shell. This is done very rapidly by means of an inclined plane attached to the vertical mandril which carries the cutting tool; so that, as the tool descends, it is forced off from the axis of the mandril, and thus cuts the hole larger at the bottom than the top. The rivets are made of soft brass, (Fig. 8,) and require no other finishing than to trim off the gate left in casting. A single blow with a hammer suffices to expand the end of the rivet into the dovetailed hole, and thus to fasten the block to the shell. A 10-inch shell, prepared in this way, was thrown violently on the stone floor of the shop without disturbing the sabot. Whether this plan is liable to the objection of weakening the shell too much, in the part where it is most exposed to the blast of the charge, must be determined by trial; but it probably cannot be used for spherical case shot or other thin shells.

War rockets are driven by hydraulic pressure; several rocket cases are adjusted vertically into the outer part of a circular horizontal iron table which revolves on a vertical axis and is moved up and down by the action of the hydraulic press; the rockets, as they are charged, are thus brought successively under drifts of different lengths which are fixed in a frame over the revolving table.

Captain Boxer endeavors to improve the accuracy of flight of rockets by greater precision in their manufacture; for this purpose he reams the interior of the cases and turns the exterior and also the heads, so as to make the rocket as nearly as possible symmetrical and smooth; he also shortens the sticks and adjusts them carefully in the axis of the rockets. Hale's rockets seem to have found no favor with the authorities at Woolwich.

Lead bullets are made by pressure. The lead wire of which they are made is drawn out, by means of a hydraulic press, in the same manner as in making lead pipe; it is coiled on cast-iron reels as it comes from the press, and these reels are transferred to the bullet press. The latter press is too complex to understand by a description; drawings of it are in possession of our Ordnance Department; it has four dies, using four reels of lead wire and making four bullets at each stroke of the press. The shape of the English expanding bullet is well adapted for being made by pressure, as it can be formed in a solid die, being smooth on the exterior; but the same kind of die is not suitable for making our grooved bullet, and for this purpose a different kind of press is required, which will permit of the die being opened after the lead is pressed into the grooves. A press of this kind, got up at Alleghany Arsenal, is now used at that place, and also at other arsenals, with a good deal of success, although not free from defects.

Percussion caps for small arms, and *cannon primers*, are made with machines of American invention, like those used in our arsenals.

The laboratory buildings for preparing ammunition and fireworks are several detached houses built entirely of *corrugated iron;* they are warmed by steam, and lighted at night by lamps placed on the outside, shining through thick plate glass. At the time of our visit a large force was employed in preparing fireworks to celebrate the peace with Russia, in the course of which work, a short time after our departure, two very serious explosions occurred, (in July, 1856,) one in an iron building, from boring a rocket, another in a wooden shed, from percussion powder, both causing loss of life and considerable injury to the surrounding buildings. The more dangerous laboratory work was then removed to a detached position.

Connected with the laboratory department is a *foundery for making shells* and other small castings. The admirable arrangements here for moulding, by what is called the "stereotype process," deserve the attention of our founders. In moulding a shell, for instance, or other symmetrical object, the pattern is made for only one half of the mould; it is made of brass or other metal, and is attached to a vertical spindle in such a manner that it can be raised, by means of a treadle, through an opening in an iron table planed perfectly true on the upper side; thus, the half pattern projects above the surface of the table; the edges of the flasks for the half mould being also planed true, the flask is inverted over the pattern on the table, the moulding sand is packed in it and the bottom of the flask fastened on; the pattern is then lowered out of the way, the flask removed, and the other half of the mould is formed in the same manner. This method is equally applicable to moulding grape and canister shot and other small objects which is to be multiplied in the same flask; the work is rapidly done, and the moulds are accurate and solid.

The business of the *Storekeeper's Department* at Woolwich arsenal involves necessarily the movement of a vast quantity of materials and stores, and the situation of the arsenal on the bank of the Thames affords great convenience for landing and shipping them. The largest ships of war can lie near the shore, and the largest transport vessels at the wharves which line the river bank; railways are used for transporting the stores, and *hydraulic cranes* for lifting cannon and other heavy articles. The power is applied to these cranes by means of a steam engine in a central position, from which a communication is established with each of them.

It is not necessary to dwell on the great advantages afforded by such arrangements for shipping the immense quantities of stores that were sent to the Baltic and the Black sea, &c., during the Russian war, and even for the movement of the military supplies constantly required in the distant parts of the British empire. Although our military operations are on a very much smaller scale, yet the want of suitable conveniences of this kind was sensibly felt in the preparations for the Mexican war, and will, if not supplied, always cause great and injurious delays in fitting out a military expedition on the sea-board. A prudent foresight would dictate the establishment of an extensive depot of military stores in a central position, where the necessary facilities may be commanded for shipping a large supply in a short time. Such a position may be found on the lower part of James river, in Virginia, accessible to the largest ships, easily reached from sea, scarcely ever obstructed by ice, and secured from the approach of an enemy by the land and naval defenses in Hampton Roads.

Manufacture of small arms.—Until very recently all the small arms for the British army were made on contract by private manufacturers; but, as in the case of ordnance, complaints of the inferior character of these arms, both in pattern and workmanship, have caused the establishment of a large government armory. The place selected for this establishment is near Enfield, about twelve miles north of London, where some small government works of the kind, for making patterns and experiments, already existed, and where the comparative trials of various models, which led to the adoption of the new patterns of rifled arms, were made. As a preliminary step, the Board of Ordnance sent a commission of three officers of artillery and the master of machinery at Woolwich Arsenal, to examine the machines and tools used in public and private workshops of this kind in the United States; a copy of their report, printed in 1855, is among the books of our commission. On their recommendation, orders were given to several private machinists in this country for large quantities of machinery like that used at our government armory at Springfield; the names of "Ames," of Chicopee, Massachusetts, and "Robbins & Lawrence," of Windsor, Vermont, &c., are accordingly to be read on most of the machines at Enfield Armory, which are constructed in a style highly creditable to the skill of our workmen.

The buildings at Enfield were commenced in the spring of 1855, and at the time of our visit, in March, 1856, a considerable part of the machinery was in operation, and the establishment was making arms, in 1857, at the rate of 1,000 a week. The sketch of the ground plan of the armory (Plate 4) shows its general arrangement and dimensions. The principal machine room, about 220 feet square, is constructed like the one before mentioned in the laboratory department at Woolwich, of one story, with a roof, half of glass, supported by rows of iron columns which sustain the driving shafts for the machines, and contain the gas-pipes for lighting the room in the short days of winter. In the barrel-welding shop the arrangements were made for welding barrels by rolling, that method being generally adopted in England. "Ryder's" hammer is used for forging bayonets, &c.; the variety of dies which this hammer contains making it very convenient for forging work which has to be brought, by successive steps, into its finished shape. Nasmyth's steam hammer is used for forging and swedging lockplates, and Colt's drop hammers for small lock pieces.

Models of the new-pattern arms have been furnished to our Ordnance Department, in exchange for our models sent to England. The rifle, constructed on the same model as the riflemusket, with a barrel thirty-four inches long, is to be extensively used in the armament of the troops. For greater economy of manufacture, annealed cast-iron is used for the *guard*, the *trigger-plate*, the *but-plate*, and the *cap of the stock*; it was found, however, that the trigger-plate was apt to break in case-hardening, and would have to be made of wrought iron; but there seems to me no objection to making the but-plate and the cap of malleable iron. In the first model of these rifle arms the rammer was made with a *swell* near the head, which served to hold it in place, under the upper band, and this arrangement has been adopted in the model of our arms; but, when tried in the field, it was found that the rammer was apt to stick fast by the swelling of the wood when wet, and to become too loose by its shrinking when dry; the *swell* was therefore omitted, a regular taper given to the rammer, and a *rod spring* (Plate 21, Fig. 13) introduced. This spring has a small roller, to prevent it from marring the screw of the rammer, at the same time the *head* of the rammer was altered, as represented in Fig. 14, to make it serve for holding a wiping rag.

The machine used at Enfield for rifling barrels with grooves of progressive depths, was obtained from Liege, being of the same kind as those ordered from there for our armories. No machine for this purpose had been used in England, and the barrels of the government arms made at Birmingham were grooved to a uniform depth. Nearly all this work was done in the old way, by hand; one man working the rifling rod, whilst another lubricates the barrel and feeds up the cutters. In one factory there was a very good machine for cutting the grooves by steam power, but it was arranged only for cutting to uniform depth.

In order to obtain the requisite supply of the new arms for the use of the troops during the war, large contracts were made for their manufacture in Belgium and in the United States, as well as in England. At Birmingham it was said that about 150,000 arms were made in 1855; probably including sabers. The work of inspection was superintended by artillery officers; for this purpose the parts of arms were brought to a government factory, where they were proved and inspected, and where the percussioning of the barrels and some of the other finishing work were done, and the finished arms put together and packed. The sights were adjusted and fixed, as described in speaking of the English factory at Liege. The barrels are all welded under rollers; they are proved, before rifling, with a charge of seven drams (191 grains) of powder and one expanding ball; after rifling, with five drams (136 grains) of powder and one ball; a *cork* wad over the ball; each barrel is proved by itself, after being percussioned; the loss in powder-proof was less than two per cent. *Welded cast-steel* barrels had been tried, but without success, being apt to burst.

Saber blades were proved by hand before mounting; the blade was struck flatways on both sides, and on the back and edge, on a block of hard wood. Cavalry sabers are sprung six inches, infantry four inches; the point resting on the floor; sword bayonets for rifles are bent one and a half inch over a bridge under the middle of the blade. The loss in proving sabers was about five per cent.

Mr. Wilkinson, of London, used a machine for proving saber blades, one of which was in the proof-room, at Birmingham, but the inspectors preferred the hand method. In Wilkinson's apparatus, the blade is fixed in a socket in a horizontal shaft; a chain passing round the shaft or hinge of the socket, is connected with a strong coach spring which is compressed by turning the shaft backwards, and when released causes the blade to strike violently on a table or block; it is struck twice flatways on an iron table; once on the back and once on the edge on a block of hard wood; then bent sideways and thrust against an iron plate; about ten per cent. exhibit defects in this proof.

PART V.

RIFLED CANNON.

The successful application of the rifle principle to small arms for the general service of the troops naturally stimulated the efforts to improve, by the same means, the range and accuracy of artillery. Experiments of this kind have been occasionally tried from an early period; but they were unsuccessful so long as reliance was placed on the effect of a patch, or of a coating of lead or other soft metal, to give the rifle motion to a spherical ball. In the collection at the arsenal in St. Petersburg there is a breech-loading cannon, made in 1615, having a bore two and three quarter inches in diameter, and sixty-two inches long, rifled with nine grooves. Similar guns of old date are to be found in other European museums. Modern experiments on this subject have been chiefly directed to the adaptation of elongated or cylindro-conical projectiles to rifled cannon. Among the first successful attempts of this sort were those of Baron Wahrendorf, the proprietor of Aker Cannon Foundery in Sweden, and of Major (now Colonel) Cavalli, of the Sardinian artillery, each of whom applied the rifle principle to a breech-loading cannon of his own invention.

The experiments tried in Sweden in 1846, with guns of the caliber of our 32-pounder, gave such promising results as to induce a repetition of them in other countries. But it would appear that neither of these arrangements for loading cannon at the breech has been found free from the usual objections to that principle of construction—the want of solidity and the difficulty of maneuvering the movable parts after firing a few rounds. The rifling arrangements consisted in cutting two grooves in the gun to receive two ribs projecting from the cylindrical part of the shot which served to guide it in the spiral grooves.

The first grooves had a twist of one turn in twelve feet; but this was undoubtedly too quick a turn, and must have contributed much to cause the great deviation in the direction of the shot which was observed to be always to the right, the twist being from left to right.

The twist was afterwards reduced to one turn in thirty-four feet. This plan appeared to effect perfectly the object of giving the rifle motion to the projectile, and obtaining increased ranges with smaller charges in proportion to the weight of the shot. With a projectile weighing eighty-one pounds, and a charge of seven and three quarter pounds, (less than one tenth,) the first graze, at an elevation of 14°, was about 3,300 yards—nearly equal to that of our Columbiads firing round shot, with a charge of one sixth.

Other experiments made in 1854, in Piedmont, with Cavalli's guns, gave still more favorable results as to range and accuracy. They are recorded in Colonel Cavalli's "*Memoire sur Divers Perfectionnemens Militaires*," translated from the Italian in 1856; from which the following summary of them is extracted:

Practice with a breech-loading rifled gun, of Colonel Cavalli's system, 1854; *diameter of bore*, 6.49 *inches; length of bore*, 88 *inches, or about* 13 *calibers; weight of piece*, 7,280 *pounds; shell, cylindro-ogival, weighing* 66 *pounds; charge of powder*, 6.6 *pounds.*

No. of rounds.	Angle of elevation.	Range of first graze.		Time of flight.	Greatest lateral deviation from line of sight.	Mean deviation from the line of the axis of the gun.
		Greatest.	Least.			
	Degrees.	*Yards.*	*Yards.*	*Seconds.*	*Yards.*	*Yards.*
10	10	3,140	3,030	11	5.4 right.	54
15	10	4,212	4,080	16	6.5 right.	98
15	20	5,005	4,969	15	8.8 left.	153
10	25	5,627	5,537	24	11 left.	298

The axis of the gun was pointed always to the left of the line of sight, by means of horizontal scales applied to the breech and to the muzzle or the trunnions, (according to the range,) in order to allow for the "*drift*" of the shot, or the constant deviation due to its rifle motion from left to right.

The last column in the table shows the amount of this drift, or the distance between the direction of the axis of the gun and the line of sight at the several ranges.

These advantageous ranges were gained partly by a reduction of windage, which was thought to be permitted in consequence of loading the gun at the breech; but they were attended with increased risk of breaking the gun, either in consequence of the expansion (upsetting) of the projectile, or of a slight accidental obstruction in the bore, which might escape observation. This result actually occurred in the course of the experiment with Cavalli's guns in Sweden and in England. When these experiments were published, General Talcott, chief of the United States Ordnance Department, caused some trials to be made of projectiles of this kind, with a gun loaded in the usual manner at the muzzle, and the results have been sufficiently favorable to authorize a continuance of the experiments, with a view to test fully the advantage, and to improve the details of this method of giving the rifle motion to cannon shot. In England, when the gun makers were invited a few years ago to offer models of rifled small arms for the troops, Mr. Lancaster, an ingenious manufacturer, brought forward a rifle with an oval bore. He applied the same principle to cannon, and the "Lancaster gun" attained a great renown about the beginning of the late war with Russia. This plan was applied to the 68-pounder of ninety-five hundred weight, the bore being cut in the shape of an ellipse, of which the longer axis is half an inch greater than the shorter one. This elliptical bore has a twist of one quarter of a turn in its length, or one turn in forty feet; so that if the longer axis of the ellipse is vertical at the muzzle, it will be horizontal at the breech. The twist is not uniform, but increases towards the muzzle. The shell is cylindro-conical, the base of the cylindrical part being elliptical like the bore of the gun. The trials of these guns in England were so favorable as to induce the making of a considerable number of them for use both in floating and land batteries. The projectiles were at first made of cast-iron, but it was soon found that they had not the strength required to resist the shock of the proper charge of powder, and the strain which resulted from their friction against the sides of the spiral bore of the gun. The shells were then made of wrought iron, and a special factory for the preparation of them was established at Woolwich Arsenal. The factory was not open to public inspection, but some of the shells were seen at Sebastopol. The body of the shell appears to be shaped under the hammer, and the bottom wolded in. The whole surface is then finished in the lathe to the proper form and dimensions. These wrought-iron shells generally resisted the shock of the charge, although some were broken in the gun like the cast-iron ones. But a still more disastrous result attended this increased strength in the shells, for it seems to have occasioned the breaking of the guns themselves. This accident occurred to one of the guns tried in England, and to three guns in the trenches before Sebastopol, as appears by the official report. It is true that this report shows the bursting of other guns also; but this occurred generally after long continued firing, and to a small proportionate number of guns; whilst the Lancaster guns were few in number, and not furnished with a large supply of projectiles.

The shell weighs eighty-eight pounds, and for extreme ranges the charge of powder was sixteen pounds, but ordinarily ten or twelve pounds. The strain on the gun from the weight of powder and shot alone was therefore much greater than in the ordinary service of the 68-pounder gun; but other causes for the failure of the Lancaster gun suggest themselves.

In Colonel Bomford's experiments with the 10-inch Columbiad, he fired a spherical shell made of bronze, (gun-metal,) which was recovered. It was found to have assumed the form of an ellipsoid; the transverse diameter was increased to the size of the bore, and the hemisphere next to the powder was more flattened than the front part. A similar effect was no doubt produced to some extent on the wrought-iron Lancaster shells. The convex base being flattened would cause an expansion of the cylinder, thus increasing the resistance produced by the rotation of the shot in the elliptical bore of the gun, and rendering it liable to be arrested by any slight inequality or obstruction in the bore; and such inequality we know is soon produced by the action of the charge itself, causing a sensible enlargement of the bore about the seat of the shot. The resistance to the forward motion of the shot was also increased by the injudicious use of a "gaining twist" in the bore, which is admissible only when that part of the projectile which serves to guide it in the grooves is made of such a material or in such a form as to adapt itself to the varying inclination of the grooves.

In cases where the Lancaster gun and shot resist the action of the charge, the reduction or annihilation of windage, resulting from the expansion of the shot concurs with other favorable circumstances in the figure and rotation of the projectile to produce very great ranges, as high as 5,600 yards, (about three and one quarter miles,) with a charge of sixteen pounds of powder, and at an elevation of 18°. But it was found, in practice, that the frequent concurrence of these favorable circumstances could not be relied on, and that even at moderate ranges these guns were very deficient in accuracy of fire; consequently, after a short trial, in the attack on Bomarsund, and in the beginning of the siege of Sebastopol, the use of these new projectiles (which cost about $100 each) was virtually abandoned.

The Lancaster guns were removed from the war steamers, and the few retained in battery at Sebastopol were used for firing the ordinary 8-inch spherical shells. A decisive practical admission of the failure of this experiment with rifled cannon is to be found in the fact that the Lancaster gun does not enter, as was at first intended, into the armament of any of the numerous gun-boats or of the powerful iron-plated floating batteries which were fitted out in England after the first active operations of the war with Russia; nor do we learn that the experiment has been thought worth repeating in any other country.

For some time past, Mr. Joseph Whitworth, an eminent machinist of Manchester, has been engaged, in connection with Mr. Wesley Richards, the well known gunmaker of Birmingham, in making experiments and investigations, under the authority of the British government, for the improvement of rifled small arms and cannon. Mr. Whitworth was one of the commissioners to the New York Exhibition, in 1850. His special business is the making of machinists' tools for working in metals, such as lathes, planing machines, slotting machines, screw cutting, &c. He is distinguished for the accuracy of his work and the minute precision of his standard gauges. His establishment at Manchester is a model of order and neatness, contrasting strongly with the apparent confusion and wasteful neglect which characterize manufactories of the same kind generally, in England as well as in the United States. Neat railways for transporting work and materials run through the premises, and the shops and yards are entirely unincumbered by the accumulation of old castings, rejected work, useless patterns, flasks, &c., which impede the circulation in most iron works. In the foundery, flasks and patterns are kept in their proper places, and the moulds in use are arranged on the moulding floor in regular ranks with suitable passages for reaching any of them.

The tools made by Mr. Whitworth are seen in the dock-yards and other manufacturing establishments of the government, as well as in the best private workshops, and his success furnishes proof, if any were required, that systematic order and neatness contribute not only to the comfort, convenience, and economy of the establishment, but to the excellence of its products.

It is from this superior accuracy of workmanship as well as from the peculiar form and construction of his arms and projectiles, that Mr. Whitworth expects to obtain increased effect and precision in rifle firing with cannon and small arms. His peculiar arrangements for this purpose were not made known, but an account was published of some experiments made at his place near Manchester, April 12, 1856, in presence of a number of military officers and others.

It may be mentioned, that at this place Mr. Whitworth has constructed a brick shed, or shooting gallery, 500 yards long, for rifle practice, in order to get rid of the causes of deviation depending on the force and direction of the wind. At one end of this shed are rooms for loading and firing, and at the other end an iron target divided by grooves into 1-inch and 10-inch squares. The target being whitewashed, the person firing can observe with a telescope the position of each shot that strikes, and can keep his own record on a paper ruled to correspond with the target. On the day mentioned, twenty shots were fired, at the range of 500 yards, from a rifle of Mr. Whitworth's of .577 inch bore, thirty inches long; bullet weighing 530 grains; charge two and one half drams, (sixty-eight grains.)

It is only stated that all the shots struck the target, but its size and the deviation of the balls are not given. The penetration of one of these balls is said to be twelve inches in a block of elm. The experiments with rifled cannon were made with a brass gun having the exterior form and dimensions of a 24-pounder field howitzer, which weighs 1,400 pounds. The gun was bored by Mr. Whitworth to receive his peculiar projectiles. The size of the bore corresponds with that of the 9-pounder; depth fifty-two inches, exclusive, probably, of the chamber.

The projectiles are of the conoidal form, but the base or cross section is *hexagonal*. The angles of the hexagon are flattened and the intermediate sides depressed, so that the angular parts serve as guides in the gun; for which purpose they are accurately dressed to a gauge. This hexagonal body has a twist of one turn in forty inches. The projectiles are of two sizes—one eleven and one half inches long, weighing thirty-two pounds; the other sixteen and one half inches long, weighing forty-eight pounds. They fit the bore with very little windage.

The chamber of the gun being large enough to contain more than a pound of powder, the small charges used in these trials were attached to cartridge blocks, filling the chamber. In firing at high elevations, the gun was placed in a trench in the ground, the breech resting against a block of wood. The results of the firing are given in the following table:

Experiments with Mr. Whitworth's rifled gun, April 12, 1856.

No.	Weight of shot.	Charge.	Elevation.	Range.		Remarks.
				First graze.	Extreme.	
	Pounds.	*Ounces.*	*Degrees.*	*Yards.*	*Yards.*	
1	32	2	45	423	423	Charge of cannon powder, L. G., large grain.
2	32	3	45	621	621	
3	32	3	45	617	617	
4	48	3	45	420	420	
5	48	5	45	735	735	
6	48	6	20	600	600	
7	48	7	20	687	687	
8	32	3	2	92	490	
9	32	3	3	104	490	
10	48	3½	2	80	....	Shot partially stopped by striking an iron railing, about five hundred yards.
11	48	4	2	83	....	
12	48	5	1	83	....	

The shot fell point foremost. On a previous day a shot, weighing thirty-two pounds, with a charge of five ounces, at an elevation of 20°, ranged 876 yards, and penetrated three feet in a strong clay soil.

The system of rifled cannon recently adopted in the French marine appears to have been suggested by the construction of the cylindro-ogival bullet used by the Russians for the two-grooved rifle. This rifle-cannon is made on the model of the 80-pounder bomb cannon (cast-iron) as to exterior dimensions, but is bored to the caliber of a 30-pounder, (Plate 5, Fig. 1,) corresponding to our 32-pounder; diameter of bore, 6.44 inches; length from base ring to muzzle, eight feet; weight, 8,600 pounds.

The bore is rifled with two circular grooves, 0.44 inch deep, as shown in the section; (Fig. 2;) the twist of the grooves is one turn in six meters, (19.68 feet.) The projectile is cylindro-ogival, having on the cylindrical part two projections, in the form of spherical segments, which fit in the grooves of the gun.

The form and dimensions are shown in Fig. 3; weight, fifty-four pounds; windage, 0.08 inch. The shells are cast with the fuze holes down, and with a large sinking head, in order that the conical part may be perfectly sound. With a charge of powder of 7.7 pounds, the range of the shell, at 15° elevation, was said to be 5,000 meters; equal to 5,468 yards.

The trials with these guns had proved so satisfactory that a large number of them had been made for the naval service, and were to be seen at Cherbourg in the spring of 1856. Many hands were employed at the same time in reaming the fuze holes of the shells, and cutting the threads in them for screwing in the metal fuze. Several of the new gun-boats were armed with these pieces, and it was understood that the plan would be extensively applied, both for naval and land service.

The spherical protuberance on these shot has the advantage over the longitudinal ribs of Cavalli's system of affording less resistance to the rotary motion of the projectile, and therefore, probably, lessening the drift or lateral deviation; but it may be doubted whether the two points of contact of these protuberances with the grooves will always give the requisite steadiness to the shot in passing out of the bore. The particular arrangement of the fuzes used in these shells is not fully known; they are metal fuzes, screwed into the apex of the shell, and closed on the exterior, so that the explosion depends on the impact of the shell against some firmly-resisting body. If the rifle motion is given to a shell, and the point of impact thus ascertained, there is no difficulty in arranging a concussion fuze, so that the shell shall explode immediately, or at a certain short interval, after striking a solid object, such as a bank of earth or the side of a ship. A very simple contrivance for this purpose was used with success in the experiments before mentioned, which were made at Fort Monroe Arsenal, under General Talcott's direction. This incidental advantage, and the increased range and capacity of elongated projectiles, (which can be fired with effect only from rifled guns,) make it desirable that experiments should be continued with such guns, with a view to remove the practical difficulties heretofore encountered in the service of the piece, and the accuracy of direction of the shot.

Although Mr. Whitworth's experiments were on too small a scale to enable us to draw any safe conclusions as to the value of his method for effective practice, they serve to indicate the increased effect which may be expected from improved accuracy of workmanship, which it is thought may be attained without an objectionable increase of expense, if the ingenuity of our officers and others, already directed to this object, is encouraged and stimulated.

The application of the rifle principle to cannon for field batteries has not, apparently, been considered so important as for fixed batteries, and very few experiments have yet been made in this direction. Some were in progress, on a small scale, (3-pounder gun,) at Liege, at the time of our visit. The recent improvements in the range and accuracy of small arms makes it important to use every means of introducing a corresponding improvement in field artillery, without impeding the convenient service of the piece; and in this respect the rifling of field guns may be found advantageous.

Some experiments of this kind were made in 1852, by the Piedmontese artillery, with a gun rifled on Colonel Cavalli's plan. The gun was an iron 16-pounder, (corresponding to the French 12-pounder,) cast in Sweden, weighing 1,650 pounds. It was bored to the caliber of an 8-pounder, (French 6-pounder;) diameter, 3.74 inches; and had two grooves of the form of those in Cavalli's 32-pounder, having a twist of one turn in eighty-seven inches. The cylindro-ogival shell weighed thirteen pounds; the solid shot, eighteen and three quarters pounds; charge, 2.6 pounds. After firing ten rounds with shells, at the fifth with solid shot the piece burst, and the experiments have not been resumed. The bursting was attributed to the breaking of one of the wings of the shot, a piece of which was found at the seat of the shot, and is supposed to have acted as a wedge.

Such experiments might be tried more safely (as Mr. Whitworth did) with bronze field pieces, bored to a lower caliber than when designed for round shot. If it should be found that bronze is too soft a metal, and that the grooves are liable to be marred in service, we may look to the improvements in the manufacture of wrought iron or cast-steel as furnishing us, at no distant day, and at a reasonable cost, with guns possessing the requisite strength and hardness. In this connection, it may be mentioned that Mr. Krupp, of Essen, (near Dusseldorf,) in Rhenish Prussia, is the inventor of a process for making cast-steel in much greater masses than has been heretofore practiced. This material being a low steel, is sufficiently soft to be readily worked, and has, at the same time, the fine grain and the tenacity of steel. At the arsenal at Vienna, there is a 6-pounder field gun of Mr. Krupp's make, to about the same dimensions and form as our 6-pounder gun; it is well finished, and it appears to be perfect; but no use or trial had been made of it. At the Paris exhibition, in 1855, large specimens of Mr. Krupp's cast-steel gained him the premium of a gold medal. A 12-pounder gun; (one of the new system of "cannon-obusier" for field batteries) was fired 2,000 service rounds, (charge of one fourth,) and the bore remained perfect, without any marks of the balloting of the shot. The vent in the steel being worn out in 500 rounds, Mr. Krupp's guns have vent pieces of copper.

Mr. Krupp made a 68-pounder gun for trial in England, a drawing of which (Plate 6, Fig. 1) shows the great size which he has attained in his castings. The weight of the cast-steel barrel of this gun was about 4,000 pounds; thickness of metal at the seat of the shot, four inches.

This thickness was considered sufficient for strength; but, as the piece was too light to be fired by itself, the breech was encased in a mass of cast-iron, which did not touch the steel barrel, except at the base of the breech, and did not, therefore, contribute to strengthen it, but only served as a means to check the recoil.

This gun was not fired with service charges, but was fired with a charge of twenty-five pounds of powder and a cylindrical shot twenty inches long, weighing 259 pounds. On the rear part of the cylinder a shoulder was turned, on which a wrought-iron ring was fitted, as represented in Fig. 2.

Under this proof the gun burst; the steel barrel was broken, it is supposed, by the jamming of the ring about the shot, as shown in Fig. 3.

According to an account given by Mr. Krupp to the editor of the Prussian "Engineer and Artillery Journal," the cast-steel barrel broke near the vent, both longitudinally and perpendicular to the axis, and the rest of the barrel, up to the point where the wrought-iron ring was wedged in it, burst into several irregular fragments, which were thrown as far as 150 yards on one side; the cast-iron envelope was broken into three large and several small pieces, separating in the direction of the axis. The front part of the barrel was thrown forward about seventy feet; the shot was not broken, but the ring of wrought iron was torn away from it.

Mr. Krupp says, under date of January 24, 1857: "It is remarkable that the trial at Woolwich has only increased the interest manifested with regard to cast-steel cannon. I have already received several orders, others are announced, and I am to make a gun for Russia like the one made for England."

It would certainly be unfair to draw from the failure in this excessive proof any decided opinion against the good quality of Mr. Krupp's cast-steel, or to refrain on this account from encouraging his efforts for improving the strength and durability of cannon.

PART VI.

CANNON OF LARGE CALIBER.

At a very early period in the use of ordnance guns were made of greater length and larger caliber than at present, many specimens of which still exist in the museums of Europe and Asia. Drawings of some of the most remarkable of these pieces (as well as of those of modern times) are to be seen in General Marion's "*Receuil des Bouches—à feu les plus remarquables*," a copy of which is amongst the books brought out by the commission. These large guns were made generally of bronze, and they were intended for throwing stone balls. Many such guns, of calibers varying from sixteen to thirty inches, are still mounted in the forts of the Dardanelles, and furnished with their supply of stone shot; they are usually fixed in the wall, on slides which allow no lateral change of direction and little change of elevation, being arranged to throw their shot into a vessel as she passes a certain line across the channel. A considerable number of these guns have been taken to the arsenal and foundery at Constantinople, where many of them have been cut up for recasting. They are all chambered pieces; they were cast on cores, and not bored or reamed out, so that the interior of the bore and chamber is quite rough and full of large cavities. A good specimen of one of the largest pieces of this kind is the great gun of the Kremlin, in Moscow, a drawing of which is annexed, (Plate 7.) This gun, designated as of the caliber of 120 pounds, (4,333 pounds,) is thirty-six inches diameter of bore, about forty-eight inches exterior diameter, and eighteen feet long, weighing 2,700 pouds, or 97,500 pounds. Its stone ball would weigh about 2,500 pounds, and a solid iron shot 6,000 pounds; the chamber of the gun is large enough to contain 500 pounds of powder. The gun has no trunnions, but has six handles, three on each side. An inscription on it shows that it was made "at Moscow, by Andrew Tchokoff, in the year 7094, being the third year of the reign of Theodore Ivanowitch," which corresponds with the year 1586 of the Christian era.

But whatever may have been the moral influence of such an armament in early times, the cumbrous and unwieldy character and slow service of this ordnance soon caused the abandonment of it in favor of the more manageable pieces of moderate caliber, into which, as before mentioned, some of these large guns have been recently converted. The new Turkish batteries are armed with brass and iron cannon of modern patterns; among the latter may be seen at the arsenal at Constantinople (Pera) some 11-inch heavy guns, made in England for the Turkish government.

During the present century a few pieces of ordnance have been occasionally made of unusual weight and size, in order to obtain an extraordinary range or great power of destruction. Such were the long brass mortars of 9-inch and 11-inch bore made by General Villantroys for the siege of Cadiz, under Napoleon, and the iron "monster mortar," of 24-inch bore, made at Liege for the siege of Antwerp, in 1832; neither of these experiments was attended with much success; the shells of the Villautroys mortar had to be nearly filled with lead in order to obtain the required range, and the "monster mortar," which was finished only at the close of the siege, burst after firing a few rounds.

The events of the war with Russia again stimulated the ingenuity of inventors to produce ordnance of extraordinary power, but, except the Lancaster rifled guns already mentioned, none of these were brought forward in time to be used in the war.

At Woolwich Arsenal there was a heavy 10-inch mortar gun of cast iron, about seven feet long, capable of firing solid shot, and mounted so as to fire at a high elevation. It was said that a range of 6,000 yards had been obtained with this piece.

Several 18-inch cast-iron mortars were made at the works of Messrs. Forrester & Co., Liverpool; one of them had been received at Woolwich, but not tried, at the time of our visit. The form and dimensions of this mortar are shown in the drawing, (Plate 8, Fig. 1.) The mortars were cast on a core fourteen inches diameter, with a sinking head of forty-two inches; weight of metal run, twenty-four tons; allowed a fortnight to cool in the pit; weight of mortar finished, fourteen and a half tons, say 32,500 pounds. The shells are concentric, three inches thick, weighing 567 pounds; charge of powder for the mortar, forty-two pounds. We have received no account of the trial of this mortar, if any has been made.

At Woolwich Arsenal there was in April, 1856, a pile of 36-inch shells, but no gun had then been made for them. It was intended to fire them from a wrought-iron mortar designed by Mr. Maire, of Blackwall, near London. This mortar was to be made with a wrought-iron center, or chamber-piece, hooped round with two tiers of hoops, which were to be accurately turned and shrunk on, (Plate 8, Fig. 2;) the cylinder of the bore, which was very short, was to be formed of similar hoops bolted together in the direction of the axis. The great mass of wrought-iron forming the breech or chamber-piece was in course of fabrication in April, 1856, at the Mersey steel and iron works of Messrs. Horsfall & Co., Liverpool; but nothing has been yet heard of the trial or completion of the mortar.

The shell for this mortar was said to weigh about 3,000 pounds, which would give it a thickness of three and a half inches; diameter of fuze hole two and three eighths inches; four wrought-iron lugs were cast in each shell for handling it. The cost of one of them was $100 to $125. The weight of the finished mortar was stated at thirty-five tons, or 78,400 pounds. The charge of powder about 100 pounds, or one thirtieth the weight of the shell; the chamber filled would hold about 120 pounds.

In May, 1856, Messrs. Horsfall & Co. completed a 13 inch wrought-iron gun, which has been tried both at Liverpool and at the practice ground at Shoeburyness. The form and dimensions of this immense mass of hammered iron are represented in Plate 9. It was made of bars welded together from the center, and was bored out from the solid. The cuttings from every part of the bore showed a good quality of tough iron, which was perfectly malleable, and exhibited none of the *granulation* often attributed to long-continued hammering. No flaw or imperfection was visible on the exterior or in the bore.

This gun was constructed after the model of a 12-inch gun made at the same establishment for the United States, under the direction of Commodore Stockton, and which is still lying at Brooklyn navy-yard, having never been tried. The trunnions are forged in the same piece as the band to which they are attached. This band is shrunk on to its place in a recess turned for it in the body of the gun; the recess is wider than the band, to receive in front a key ring which fills up the remainder of the width of the recess, and this is secured by another band shrunk on over the ring as shown in the drawing. The body of the gun weighs about twenty-one tons, and the finished piece 48,944 pounds, or nearly twenty-two tons. The solid shot weighs 280 pounds.

This gun was made by Messrs. Horsfall & Co. on their own motion, and has been presented by them to the British government. There are very few establishments, even in England, where such a piece of work can be done, and considering the expense and the time required to produce it, the result may be regarded rather as a remarkable triumph of mechanical skill than as an example likely to be often followed in the manufacture of ordnance of extraordinary caliber. The cost of this gun is estimated at £4,750, ($23,250,) say £3,000 for the welded iron, and £1,750 for finishing. The 12-inch gun above mentioned, made by the same firm for the United States, cost $10,000.

The success attained in this case would indicate, however, the practicability of making, at probably a moderate expense, wrought-iron guns for field service, if that should be found desirable in connection with the introduction of rifled cannon for such batteries.

In May, 1856, this 13-inch gun was tried near Liverpool with the following charges, besides other practice:

No.	Charge of powder.	Weight of shot or shell.	Elevation.	Remarks.
	Pounds.	Pounds.	Degrees.	
1	10	194	1	First graze 300 yards.
2	10	194	4	First graze 600 yards.
3	20	294	4	First graze 850 yards.
4	30	294	5	First graze 1,850 yards.
5	30	294	7½	First graze 2,000 yards.
6	30	194	7½	14 seconds to first graze, whole time of flight 29 seconds.
7	30	195	10	
8	30	292	10	
9	45	314	10	Loaded shell.
10	45	318	1	Loaded shell.

In November, 1856, the gun was fired at Shoeburyness (mouth of the Thames) with solid shot and a charge of fifty pounds of powder, as follows:

Report of Experimental Practice with the 13-inch Gun, manufactured by Messrs. Horsfall at the Mersey Works, Liverpool.

No. of rounds.	Elevation.	Recoil.	Time of flight.	First graze.	Extreme range.	Deflection. First graze. Left.	Deflection. First graze. Right.	Deflection. Extreme. Left.	Deflection. Extreme. Right.	Mean of first graze.
	Degrees.	*Feet, inches.*	*Seconds, fifths.*	*Yards.*	*Yards.*	*Yards.*	*Yards.*	*Yards.*	*Yards.*	
1	Point blank.	3 7	1 6	553	4,800	In line.	In line.	....	20	
2	"	4 0	1 1	615	4,835	3	....	....	5	
3	"	3 10	1 0	631	6,000	2	....	21	....	
4	"	3 10	Not observable.	572	5,951	3	....	9	....	
5	"	3 10	1 2	646	5,798	1	....	....	20	589 3-10.
6	"	3 4	1 1	583	5,162	2	....	60	....	
7	"	3 9	1 0	590	5,000	2	....	....	20	
8	"	3 8	Not observable.	600	5,011	3	....	44	....	
9	"	2 9	1 1	580	5,613	3	....	....	10	
10	"	3 9	1 0	579	5,930	2	....	103	....	
11	1°	3 8	Not observable.	953	4,800	....	2	27	....	
12	"	3 9	Not observable.	1,017	3,915	In line.	In line.	....	19	
13	"	3 6	2 0	1,060	4,761	1	....	....	5	
14	"	3 7	2 2	1,040	4,370	4	....	....	20	
15	"	3 8	2 3	1,046	4,393	4	....	30	....	1,062 5-10.
16	"	3 8	2 1	989	4,311	In line.	In line.	....	....	
17	"	3 8	2 2	1,118	4,070	6	....	5	....	
18	"	3 8	2 1	954	4,550	....	4	40	....	
19	"	3 8	2 2	1,078	4,700	....	8	....	59	
20	"	3 6	2 2	1,057	5,000	2	....	29	....	
21	3°	3 7	Not observable.	1,871	3,914	8	....	10	....	
22	"	3 7	5 1	1,890	3,743	8	....	28	....	
23	"	3 6	5 0	1,777	4,000	19	....	8	....	
24	"	3 7	5 1	1,906	3,963	7	....	....	9	
25	"	3 7	Not observable.	1,763	3,697	....	4	....	16	
26	"	3 6	4 4	1,761	4,000	6	....	54	....	1,[illegible] 1-10.
27	"	3 5	4 4	1,781	3,950	1	....	....	19	
28	"	3 7	5 0	1,758	3,943	....	3	....	56	
29	"	3 6	5 0	1,730	4,161	....	3	....	18	
30	"	3 6	4 4	1,734	3,957	....	7	12	....	
31	5°	3 6	7 2	2,448	3,363	In line.	In line.	....	22	
32	"	3 5	7 3	2,516	3,519	....	14	....	33	
33	"	3 6	7 2	2,496	3,003	5	....	....	4	
34	"	3 3	7 1	2,400	3,650	9	....	21	....	
35	"	3 4	7 3	2,383	3,531	....	9	....	28	
36	"	3 5	7 0	2,412	3,603	9	....	17	....	2,433 2-10.
37	"	3 4	7 2	2,464	3,385	6	....	In line.	In line.	
38	"	3 5	6 4	2,388	3,709	7	....	10	....	
39	"	3 5	Not observable.	2,420	3,675	....	6	....	30	
40	"	3 4	8 4	2,381	3,640	....	14	....	28	
41	7°	3 3	9 0	2,871	3,703	....	2	4	....	
42	"	3 3	9 2	2,973	3,385	2	....	5	....	
43	"	3 3	Not observable.	3,042	3,400	....	5	....	15	
44	"	3 4	9 2	3,084	3,448	16	....	28	....	
45	"	3 3	9 2	2,951	3,450	8	....	13	....	
46	"	3 4	9 1	3,020	3,385	....	3	....	6	2,946 5-10.
47	"	3 3	9 3	2,998	3,358	19	....	9	....	
48	"	3 3	9 2	2,903	3,390	3	....	....	2	
49	"	3 4	9 2	3,045	3,413	16	....	15	....	
50	"	3 4	9 2	2,954	3,388	20	....	14	....	

J. W. MITCHELL, *Lieutenant Colonel C. R. A., Superintendent.*

PART VII.

GARRISON ARTILLERY.

For a description of the guns and carriages used in the armament of fortifications in Russia, Prussia, Austria, and Belgium, reference must be made to the books and detailed drawings in the collection of the commission, which are too numerous to be reproduced in a report. Some remarks on the novelties and peculiarities of the several systems are subjoined.

Russia.

The guns, howitzers, and mortars for garrison service are of a great variety of calibers and patterns; those of old dates being still used, and also many ship guns, especially in the temporary batteries which were constructed for sea-coast defense during the war. But the permanent forts at Cronstadt, built in the most substantial manner, of great blocks of Finland granite, are armed with new pattern guns, chiefly of the calibers of 40-pounder, 96-pounder, and 120-pounder. Fort Menschikoff mounts forty-four guns, all 120-pounders, (10-inch,) in three casemate tiers, and one barbette; Fort Paul, two hundred and seven pieces of the three calibers named above, and three of 56-pounder, on iron carriages of novel construction; Fort Alexander, one hundred and forty such pieces, also in four tiers; 40-pounders were mounted in the lower tier of casemates as being most convenient to the shot furnaces; hot shot were not provided for guns of larger caliber, these being designed chiefly for shells. The form and principal dimensions of the 120-pounder bomb-cannon are shown in Plate 10, Fig. 2. The 56-pounder gun (Plate 10, Fig. 1) resembles the English and French guns of the same caliber, but its weight is 13,700 pounds; it is intended to carry shot or shells, with a charge of sixteen pounds of powder, in order to obtain a great range. The iron carriage on which this gun was mounted is represented in Plate 11, Fig. 1. It is built of plates of boiler iron, five eighths to one half inch thick, formed into hollow beams, being riveted together by means of angle iron. The cheeks of the top carriage, formed in this way, are six inches thick, and are connected together by assembling bolts, and by transoms made in the same manner as the cheeks; the trunnion sockets are made of cast brass, riveted to the cheeks; the carriage is furnished with a compressor, which is tightened by means of a screw, so as to increase its friction on the chassis, and check the recoil. In order to facilitate the running to battery the carriage has truck wheels working on an eccentric axle, so that they may be thrown in or out of gear as required; or else there are two truck wheels under the front ends of the cheeks which do not bear on the chassis until the trail of the carriage is lifted with a roller handspike. The great weight of the gun and carriage renders the use of tackle and pulleys necessary in running from battery; the tackle is attached to an eye in the trail of the carriage, and to the rear transom of the chassis; by this means four men are enabled to run the gun back. To give some elasticity to the system under the shock of firing, wooden transoms are interposed between the upper carriage and the chassis. The chassis consists of two rails built of plate iron, like the upper carriage, and joined by two transoms constructed in the same manner; the rails are sixteen inches deep, eight inches wide, and eighteen feet long. The chassis traverses on four rollers, under the front and rear transoms, as in our casemate carriage, and has a tongue projecting from the front about two feet long. In barbette batteries the pintle is fastened in an immense block of cast-iron, which is firmly secured in the ground. In casemate batteries there is a tongue hole, but the pintle is placed much nearer the inner face of the wall than with us. This arrangement strengthens the wall, but diminishes very much the traverse of the guns, reducing it to little more than half of what is allowed for our casemate guns. Besides the bearing on the traverse wheels and circles, each rail of the chassis has a bearing in the middle by means of a piece of iron, which habitually just clears the platform, but supports the rail when it is sprung by the recoil of the piece. The traversing of this heavy gun and carriage, by means of handspikes alone, would be very difficult. To facilitate this object, the journals of the rear wheels of the chassis have pinions on them, which are geared to endless screws on a shaft parallel to the rear transoms; thus, by turning a winch, both pinions and both wheels are worked together, and the proper lateral traverse given to the gun with ease and precision.

The strength and durability of these carriages would recommend them for heavy guns in permanent batteries, notwithstanding the inconvenience attending their great weight; but their cost presents a serious obstacle to the extensive use of them, as even with the cheap labor of Russia, one of these carriages costs about $2,000. It is probable, however, that with the facilities which we have for shaping rolled iron for building purposes, a less cumbrous and more economical method of applying that material to the construction of gun carriages will be devised.

Another wrought-iron carriage for guns of smaller caliber, from 12-pounders to 36-pounders, is much used in the Russian barbette batteries. (See Plate 11, Figs. 2 and 3.) This carriage is light and of simple construction; both the upper carriage and the chassis are made of bars of hammered iron, not difficult to forge, and of moderate dimensions, combined together on the general principles adopted in our ordinary barbette carriage. To prevent the rails from being bent by the shock of the discharge, they are supported in the middle, as well as by the traverse wheels at each end—a platform of planks being laid for the middle support to rest on. The prop at the rear end of the tongue is made of two pieces joined together by a shackle and screw, so that its length can be adapted to the variable level of the terreplein. In low batteries the upper carriage may be used, separately from the chassis, on a common platform. This kind of carriage was used in most of the open batteries on the Neva, and in a battery of 124 guns on the channel side of the Island of Cronstadt, except for eleven 120-pounders in the latter battery, which were mounted on wooden carriages. The wooden top carriage for these shell guns is constructed like a ship truck carriage; the chassis has no tongue, the top carriage being directly on the rails, which are supported in the middle as well as at the ends—an arrangement which is general in all chassis. The same carriage is used also for casemate batteries. Another kind of wooden gun carriage is framed much like the French carriage which we have adopted for barbette batteries. It is either mounted on a chassis, or used on a common platform; in the latter case the notch of the trail rests on a tongue or guide piece which lies flat on the platform, and traverses on a bolt in front. In open batteries the platform for the chassis is commonly formed of round logs, bolted or pinned down to radial pieces of the same kind. On these the wooden traverse pieces are laid; the front of the chassis traverses on small cannon balls rolling in an iron trough. Some of the carriages for casemates are framed in the same manner as the barbette, modified to suit the height of the embrasure. They admit of much less lateral traverse than ours, the center of motion being near the inner face of the parapet wall or scarp. Other carriages again are made of cast-iron and wrought iron combined; the cheeks or uprights being of the former material, and the braces and trail piece of the latter. These various carriages are to be found, according to the local facilities for making them, in several fortresses, or often in the armament of the same work. In some of the permanent forts at Cronstadt a railway was laid in the pavement, running in rear of the battery, to facilitate the transportation and mounting of the guns; and for the same purpose a strong eye-bolt is inserted in the center of the casemate arch.

An ingenious arrangement for pointing the guns in an open battery, without exposing the men, was observed. A board, having a graduated circle marked on it, is placed level on the parapet, or in a position where the object aimed at can be seen; the axis, perpendicular to the crest of the parapet, is marked on this board; a ruler turning about the center of the circle, carries two sights, which are directed on the object, and marks the degrees to the right or left of the axis; the rear traverse circle of the platform is divided in a manner corresponding to the circle on the board, and the chassis carries an index, by means of which it is set in the direction indicated by the sights on the ruler.

Besides the usual quadrants and tangent scales, a simple and convenient method is adopted for giving the elevation of the gun in fixed batteries. It consists of a graduated ruler of wood or iron attached to the inside of the cheek of the carriage by a small bolt through its lower end, on which it turns, so that the graduations of the scale may be applied to a mark on the side of the breech of the gun, which is thus set at the required elevation. When not in use the ruler lies along the inside of the cheek of the carriage, resting on a hook provided for it. In some of these carriages the elevating screw is checked from running down when the gun is fired, by a strong clamping screw, which passes through the box of the elevating screw. It has a T handle, by means of which it may be pressed up against the pointing screw to prevent the latter from turning.

For pointing mortars, a frame of wood supporting *two plumb lines* is placed on the epaulment of the battery in the required direction, and the mortar is brought into the same line by means of a plummet suspended to a tripod stand; by this arrangement, it is not necessary that the pointer in rear should see the object aimed at.

For firing garrison guns locks with percussion primers, and also friction primers are used. Many of the locks are of the old French pattern, consisting of a simple hammer placed perpendicular to the axis of the piece and drawn down by a lanyard; others are like the American cannon lock of Mr. Hidden. The percussion primers are quill tubes with a percussion wafer on top; the friction primers resemble those formerly used in our service and copied after the Prussian primers. Locks and friction primers are used for garrison and siege pieces only; but matches are also kept in readiness.

Some brass guns were mounted on the batteries on the banks of the Neva, and a new 10-inch brass gun was seen at the foundery in St. Petersburg; also a few heavy brass mortars at Cronstadt; but the cannon for the armament of the forts are nearly all of iron; a great proportion of them made at the Swedish founderies. The heavy 13-inch brass sea-coast mortars are cast with a *sole*, or bed-plate, like the French "*mortiers à plaque.*" The light 13-inch brass mortars are mounted on cast-iron beds. 120-pounder shell guns are mounted in *casemate*, as well as in *barbette* batteries; they are light guns of their caliber, resembling our 10-inch sea-coast howitzers, but heavier. The heavy 56-pounders, firing charges of sixteen pounds of powder, are also placed in casemates. This indicates that we have, perhaps, been too cautious in refraining from mounting our 10-inch Columbiads in casemate batteries.

In the forts some shells were kept in readiness, with the fuzes cut to several lengths, driven into the shells and marked; at Cronstadt, where the enemy's fleet was lying near the batteries, the shot furnaces were kept warm by a small fire, ready to be fully lighted on short notice. The garrisons of these forts consisted principally of infantry; they had their proper arms, but were also exercised in manœuvering the guns.

In the batteries, near each gun, there is fixed to the epaulment a black board on which is marked, in white paint, a table of the elevation or hausse corresponding to each range of the gun.

PRUSSIA.

Garrison carriages of a novel construction have been adopted in Prussia; they are mentioned in Major Hagner's Report of Observations in 1848, the trials of them having been commenced about that time. They are made of bars of wrought iron, hammered to the required shape for forming a suitable frame-work, which is held together by bolts. The general arrangement of the carriage is shown in Plates 12 and 13; all the details of construction are exhibited in the lithographed drawings presented to us by the Minister of War. The chassis is a simple frame, consisting of longitudinal bars, forming the rails and tongue, which are united together by cross bars; the front part of it rests on the platform; the rear is raised, to check the recoil, and has two traverse wheels; the center of motion is in the middle of the front transom bar. The upper carriage, for use in casemate batteries, or behind low parapets, is placed on this chassis, the front part having two truck-wheels which travel on the rails; for barbette batteries, the carriage is mounted on an intermediate frame-work of iron (Plate 12) which rests in like manner on the chassis, the trucks being transferred to the lower frame. This arrangement appears to be deficient in the stiffness necessary for resisting the effect of long-continued firing; the considerations of strength and stability have been perhaps unduly sacrificed to simplicity of construction and to the desire of making the same system answer for different situations; it would seem to be preferable to arrange each kind of carriage with reference to the special purpose for which it is intended.

Carriages of this kind are made for guns of many different calibers; some for 6-pounders mounted in flank casemates, the pintle being fastened in a block of wood within the wall. Some 6-pounders for flank casemates are mounted on common field carriages. In the casemates, rings are fastened in the wall, to receive lashing ropes for checking the recoil of the gun; and in many of them rings are placed in the crown of the arch, to aid in mounting the piece and dismounting.

In the system of *guns* for arming the Prussian fortresses and sea-coast batteries, there seems to be nothing to demand special notice. At the arsenal of Berlin we saw two rifled cannon: one of iron, on Wahrendorff's plan; the other of bronze, on a similar principle of loading at the breech. The trials were said to have been unsatisfactory.

It is proper to mention here some late experiments made by the Prussian artillery to determine the pressure of fired gunpowder on the sides of the bore of a gun at any point; an inquiry bearing immediately on the question of the proper form of cannon. The experiments referred to, made in 1851, are recorded in the report prepared by Captain Neumann, one of the commission that conducted them, and printed in the Prussian Engineer and Artillerist's Journal for December, 1853. A French translation of the report is printed in the first part of Colonel Delobel's "*Révue de Technologie Militaire*," 1854. At the time of making that report, these experiments do not seem to have been carried far enough to effect the object of ascertaining the law of tension of the gas in the bore of a gun; but they are noticed here on account of their close resemblance to those for the same purpose which were made at the arsenal near Boston, in 1842, under the direction of Colonel Bomford, late chief of our Ordnance Department, and which have had an influence in regulating the relative thickness of metal in different parts of the bore of our guns. In Colonel Bomford's experiments, the pressure exerted on the sides of the bore was estimated by the velocity with which a pistol ball was discharged from an orifice made in the gun perpendicular to its axis, and this velocity was computed by the impact of the pistol ball on a small ballistic pendulum. The Prussian experiments were conducted in the same manner, only substituting *steel cylinders* for pistol balls. The report of Colonel Bomford's experiments was made in 1843, and recorded at that time in the Ordnance Bureau; yet the report of the Prussian experiment says: "The experiments of which we have just given an account are the first [of this kind] which have been undertaken by following the direct experimental course, and which, consequently, furnish results of indisputable accuracy." We must therefore conclude that the analogy of those two series of experiments is one of those striking accidental coincidences which often occur in scientific pursuits, and which show the importance of the early publication of inventions or discoveries, in order to obtain the just credit of originality for the first author of them.

The Prussian artillery are also pursuing a course of experiments in gunnery, by means of an *electro-magnetic apparatus for measuring the velocity of projectiles.*

At the hundredth anniversary meeting of the American Philosophical Society, held at Philadelphia, in May, 1843, Professor Joseph Henry, now Secretary of the Smithsonian Institution, read a communication "on a new method of determining the velocity of projectiles." See the proceedings of the society, vol. 3, p. 165, from which the following is an extract:

"The new method proposed by the author consists in applying the instantaneous transmission of an electrical action to determine the time of the passage of the ball between two screens, placed at a short distance from each other, on the path of the projectile. For this purpose, the observer is provided with a revolving cylinder, moved by clock work at the rate of at least ten turns in a second; and of which the convex surface is divided into a hundred equal parts; each part therefore indicating, in the revolution, the thousandth part of a second. Close to the surface of this cylinder, which revolves horizontally, are placed two galvanometers, one at each extremity of a diameter, the needles of these being furnished at one end with a pen for making a dot with printer's ink on the revolving surface. To give motion to the needles at the proper moment, each galvanometer is made to form a part of the circuit of a galvanic current, which is completed by a long copper wire passing to one of the screens, and crossing it several times, so as to form a grating through which the ball cannot pass without breaking the wire, and thus stopping the current."

The paper proceeds to give some further details as to the manner of working the proposed apparatus, but it does not appear ever to have been brought into practical operation.

About the same time, Mr. Wheatstone, of England, proposed, in general terms, the application of electro-magnetism to the above purpose, and, acting on his suggestion, Captain Constantinoff, of the Russian artillery, had an apparatus constructed, in 1843 to 1845, which was soon followed by other contrivances in France, Prussia, Hanover, &c. But it is to Captain Navez, of the Belgian artillery, that we owe the invention of a convenient and reliable apparatus for this purpose, which is described in his work on this subject, published in 1853. Without entering here into the details of his method, it may be remarked that the apparatus has been already extensively used in Belgium, and also in a series of valuable experiments by the Dutch artillery, some of which are recorded in Colonel Delobel's "*Révue de Technologie Militaire,*" vol. 1, 1854. Although the instrument has been used to measure the time occupied by a ball passing through a space of 100 feet, and is designed to record a time of less than the *hundredth part of a second*, its indications appear to be perfectly reliable, as shown by a comparison of the results with known facts, and with the indications of the ballistic pendulum.

The advantages of the electro-magnetic apparatus over the ballistic pendulum, for this purpose, consist in its cheapness, its mobility, the ease and rapidity of its use, its applicability to the firing of projectiles of any kind or caliber, at any elevation, and at any distance at which a suitable screen can be struck with certainty. Captain Navez considers it applicable also to ascertaining the varying velocity of the ball in passing along the bore of the gun, or the pressure of the elastic gases on the sides of the bore at different points. This invention is, therefore, a most valuable addition to our means of investigating the various and complex problems of gunnery, and the practical questions involved in determining the proper proportions of ordnance and the best mode of manufacture of gunpowder for military purposes.

AUSTRIA.

The drawings kindly furnished to us by General Smola, Chief of the Artillery Committee in Vienna, exhibit the kind of ordnance and the construction of the carriages for garrison and siege artillery.

The gun carriages for barbette batteries (Plate 14) are framed very much like ours, but are less elevated, being designed for a parapet about five and a half feet high; in order to adapt the carriage, when necessary, to a higher parapet of six and a half feet, wooden wheels are substituted for the iron trucks, and an intermediate frame (Plate 14, Fig. 1) is placed on the rear part of the chassis to elevate the trail of the top carriage, so that the gun may be still fired over the parapet at a depression of 9°. The chassis consists of two rails connected by transoms and bolts, and a tongue which is bolted only to the middle and rear transoms; the pintle, or center of motion, is placed about three feet inside of the parapet; the chassis traverses on two rollers under the front ends of the rails and two wheels which turn on iron axles projecting from the rear ends of the rails; the rails have no supports under the middle; the traverse circles are of wood. A peculiar arrangement for the traverse of the chassis, adapted more especially for circular towers or bastions, was observed in one of the forts at Venice; it is represented in Plate 15. The pintle, instead of being fixed is set in a truck, or pintle block, which is mounted on four cast-iron wheels; these wheels run on a railway sunk in the terreplein, parallel to the crest of the parapet; there are two other traverse wheels under the rear of the chassis, which travel on the pavement of the tower; the position of the axes of these wheels can be changed according to the movement required. By this arrangement the guns are brought together on any part of the work where they may be wanted; for small variations of direction the front truck remains stationary and the chassis is traversed on the rear wheels as in ordinary cases. The recoil of the gun is checked by a rope attached to the front transoms of the carriage and chassis.

For casemate batteries the same gun carriage is used as for barbette, (Plate 16,) but the chassis consists of a single piece, or tongue. The wheels of the gun carriage travel on the platform; the tongue or guide turns on a pintle placed in or near the inner face of the parapet wall; it runs on two rollers in rear and on the pintle block in front, or on cannon balls laid in a circular trough.

For very elevated batteries a depression carriage is made, as represented in Plate 17.

Large guns and howitzers are made of bronze, and some of these, of course, are used in the fortresses; but the greater part of the guns, howitzers and mortars, for the latter purpose, are of cast-iron; one peculiarity of these cannon is, that they all have *handles* cast on them, a practice which is hardly to be met with in the iron guns of any other country.

There are no guns of unusual caliber employed; a 50-pounder, (diameter of bore seven and a half inches,) weighing 11,400 pounds, and having a charge of seventeen pounds, seems to be designed for great ranges. Mortar beds are made solid, of wood; those for heavy mortars have very thick trunnion plates of bronze, covering the whole length of the bed on each side.

The 30-pounder "bomb-cannon" corresponds very nearly in caliber, length, and weight, with our 10-inch sea-coast howitzers; it has a cylindrical chamber to hold eight pounds of powder.

FRANCE.

The French system of fortress carriages is well known to us, having been adopted, without much change, in our service. In the details of the wooden *barbette carriage* some modifications have been recently made, which will be noticed here:

In the *gun carriage* for sea-coast batteries an important change has been made in leaving off the wheels, which are only required when the carriage is to be moved from one part of a fort to another, or when it is to be used without a chassis; both cases of rare occurrence, and for which a few wheels in each fort will suffice; for aid in manœuvering, the cast-iron rollers have holes in them for iron handspikes, like those of our casemate carriage. The rear transom is modified by reducing its greatest thickness to that of the part which bears on the tongue of the chassis, and the carriage is guided on the tongue by means of two *wrought-iron knees*, which are bolted to the under side of the transom. In some carriages for 80-pounder guns, blocks and coins are substituted for the elevating screw to support the breech.

In the *chassis* of the barbette carriage, the middle transom, instead of being held by bolts passing through it, is connected with the rails by *understraps*, which are fastened to the rails by one or two bolts on each side of the transom, according to the caliber of the piece to be mounted; also, in order to relieve the strain on the middle of the chassis, a block of wood is bolted to the transom and under the tongue of the chassis, forming a prop which just clears the floor or the circle of boards laid under it, but supports the chassis when the gun is fired; in addition to the shoulder on the transom for the rail to bear against, *iron knees* are fastened in the angles between the transom and rails. Some of the rails were made, or repaired, in two pieces; the joint was *horizontal* and the pieces were held together by two rivet bolts in addition to those used for securing the transom. The tongue of the chassis is plated with iron.

But, for sea-coast batteries, both barbette and casemate, a new system of *cast-iron carriages* has recently been adopted in France. We are unable to refer to detailed drawings of these carriages, as the French Minister of War peremptorily declined to comply with our request for information on the subject of artillery. The general arrangement of the barbette carriage is shown in Plate 13, Fig. 1. It consists of a gun carriage and a chassis, both of cast-iron, and constructed on the same principles as the wooden barbette carriage, the cheeks and rails being connected by transoms and assembling bolts. The cheeks of the gun carriage are about two and a half inches thick, with flanges around them of double that thickness; the transoms are of cast-iron, and the assembling bolts are two inches in diameter. The trunnion holes have movable sockets which have flanges of different thickness, so that by reversing their position the carriage may be adapted for guns or howitzers of different diameters, but having trunnions of the same size. The rail of the chassis is of the "fish-bellied" form, about twelve inches deep in the rear and fifteen inches in the middle; the middle transom is about fourteen inches deep; the rear, ten inches; the assembling bolts, two in each transom, are one and three quarters of an inch in diameter; the tongue is bolted to the middle and rear transoms only, each by two bolts passing through flanges on the tongue and transom. The weight of the gun-carriage is 3,600 pounds; that of the chassis 5,300 pounds. A great number of these carriage have already been made; one seen at Cherbourg is numbered 627.

The *casemate gun carriage* is similar to the barbette, but the rear transom is made of wood, seventeen inches wide and eight inches deep; the axletree forms a front transom three inches in diameter, terminating at each end in a bolt two inches in diameter. The *chassis* is made of wood, except the front transom, which is of cast-iron. On the front of the transom there is a projecting socket in which a wrought-iron tongue is bolted; in the rear are three pairs of strong flanges, forming seats for the front ends of the rails and tongue, which are fastened to these flanges by horizontal bolts through the rails and a vertical bolt through the tongue; the front rollers, which are about seven inches in diameter, turn in mortises through the transom, between the tongue and rails; there are two other rollers, as usual, under the rear transom; the middle transom projects so much below the rails as just to clear the floor of the casemate, and to form a support for the chassis when the gun is fired; this arrangement permits the use of moderate sized scantling for the rails and tongue. The top of each rail is plated with a bar of iron under the wheel, one and three eighths of an inch thick, which is bent at the front and rear to form the hurter and counter-hurter.

The gun-carriage weighs 2,900 pounds; the chassis 2,400 pounds.

In the system of *cannon* for garrison and sea-coast service no changes have been recently introduced, except to adopt some of the iron navy guns for sea-coast batteries. The heavy 13-inch iron mortars, (*mortiers à plaque*,) cast with a sole, and weighing about 9,500 pounds, are used for sea-coast as well as for floating batteries.

The *stone-mortar* has been discontinued, as a part of the system of armament, either for siege-trains or for defense of fortresses. The fire of 12-pounder shells and grenades from other mortars is to be substituted for the use of stone mortars. It has been elsewhere remarked, in this report, that Colonel Bormann, of the Belgian artillery, proposes the use of *spherical case shot*, with light charges, for the same purpose. If stone mortars are to be retained in our system, there is no reason why they may not be made, as in Austria, Prussia, Belgium, &c., of cast-iron, instead of bronze, which is so much more costly.

The *garrison gin* windlass has been lately altered, but in a manner not so advantageous for working as our new windlass; a chain is now also substituted for the rope fall.

The modification of the *sling-cart* deserves notice, as being worthy of adoption. Instead of a screw on the old mortised windlass, an iron windlass with two revolving sockets, (like those used on our gin windlass,) is employed for raising the weight to be carried; the journals of the windlass turn in two iron standards fixed on the top of the bolster; the handspike sockets are on the ends of the windlass, which is retained by a pawl in a middle.

PART VIII.

FIELD ARTILLERY.

Until very recently the same general system prevailed in the kind and caliber of cannon used in the field batteries of all the principal powers of Europe, viz: 6-pounder and 9-pounder guns, and 12-pounder howitzers for horse artillery and for light foot batteries; 12-pounder guns and 32-pounder howitzers for heavy foot batteries, or batteries of position; some in the form, length, and weight of these pieces, in different countries, but in were similar to those adopted in our service. The changes now in progress for the system of field guns will be noticed under a separate head.

The *gun-carriages* for field service may be classed under two heads: first, the English *stock-carriage*, which has been adopted, with some modification of details, in France, Belgium, Sweden, Sardinia, and other countries, including our own; second, the *bracket* carriage, (French Gribeauval carriage,) with two cheeks, united by transoms and bolts, which is used in Russia, Prussia, Austria, and some of the minor German States. The first kind possess the advantage of being to using wheels of uniform size, for both the gun carriage and limber, as well as wagons, &c.; a very important consideration with reference to the facility of exchanging in the field. Since the adoption of this system, however, the second kind of carriage has been modified so as to admit the use of uniform wheels, without giving up other advantages which the old system is thought to offer. To give a complete sketch of the systems adopted in these several countries would require several volumes and many drawings; they were described, as they existed a few years ago, by Mr. Jacobi, of the Prussian artillery, most of whose works on "the field artillery of different powers of Europe" have been translated and published in France. Some of the recent changes and peculiarities of them will be noticed here. For the system of maneuvers and interior service of batteries, reference must be made to the books on those subjects, procured in the several countries.

Russia.

[See the plates of Resvoy's Artillery.]

In the gun carriage of the new pattern, (1846,) the cheeks are parallel; the iron axletree is three inches square, not reduced in the middle, although it has a wooden axle body; the elevation of the gun is given by means of a quoin which rests on an elevating bed, on which it is moved backward or forward by means of a screw working horizontally in a geared box; the handle and winch which turn the box are on the outside of the left cheek; the trail handspike is attached to the inside of the right cheek; maneuvering hooks are attached to the front and rear ends of each cheek; the eye for the pintle is, as in the Gribeauval carriage, in the rear transom; the wheel, which is common to all field carriages, is made with twelve spokes and six felloes, and the tire is put on in three pieces; the dish of the wheel is, as usual in European wheels, very great, being two and a half inches. An *iron shoe* for locking the wheel is used instead of a lock chain; and it may here be remarked, that the same method has been adopted in the English and French field artillery, where lock chains were formerly used; experience in campaign having indicated the benefit of this change, as it is believed to have done also in our service.

The *limber* is framed like that of a common wagon, having two hounds which project to the rear of the axletree, and are joined together by a sweep-bar which supports the pintle; by this construction the pintle is placed nearly two feet in rear of the center of the axletree, and the weight of the carriage trail, acting at the end of this lever, serves to sustain the pole of the limber: the trail is secured to the hounds by a chain and ring passing over a hook in the rear transom of the carriage. The splinter-bar of the limber, besides being bolted to the hounds, is connected with the outer ends of the axletree by iron stays, which have rings that pass over the axletree, and serve as linch washers. This arrangement is characteristic of the mode of draft which prevails in all the wagons of the country, and in the droschkis and many other pleasure carriages; it brings the draft immediately on the axletree, and causes the carriage to follow quickly the motion of the horse in turning. The ammunition chest on the limber is not so large as ours, containing only twenty-one rounds of 6-pounder ammunition, instead of fifty; at each end of it, on the outside, is a large pouch, to contain implements, &c.; the top of the chest is covered with sheet iron.

By the construction of the limber and the position of the pintle, the gun carriage has great facility of turning, notwithstanding the width of the trail and the equal height of the front wheels; in rapidity and compactness of movement the manœuvering of the Russian artillery leaves nothing to be desired.

The light guns are drawn by six horses; the heavy, by eight; the harness has rope traces: those of the first pair of leaders are hooked to the end of the pole, being kept apart by a wooden stretcher; the traces of the front leaders are attached to those of the first, or middle pair, which are doubled for the purpose.

The *caisson* is a two-wheeled cart, with shafts, drawn by three horses abreast; the body contains seventy-seven rounds of 6-pounder ammunition; it has a railing, front and rear, to form seats for the men. The body of the caisson, and also the limber chest, are divided into square compartments, one for each round of ammunition, which is covered with a tin case inverted over it; the top, or closed end of this case, is marked in such a manner as to indicate the kind of ammunition under it—whether shot, shell, spherical case, or canister; spherical case is not used for the 6-pounder gun.

The field batteries are composed of 6-pounder guns and 12-pounder howitzers, 12-pounder guns and 24-pounder howitzers. The Russians were the first to use the long howitzer, under the name of "*Likorna;*" but the peculiar pattern of these pieces has lately given place to others conforming nearly to the French models, though the former are still to be seen in considerable numbers. A new light 12-pounder gun is about to be introduced for all the foot batteries. All these pieces are of bronze.

The field guns have no locks, nor are friction primers used. They are fired entirely with the match, portfire, and common priming tube.

The wagons for the artillery train are made like the ordinary wagons of the country; most of them covered with canvas, except those for ammunition, which are covered with sheet iron. The field forge is a two-wheeled cart, without a cover, except the tool chest. All artillery carriages and wagons are painted *green*.

Fixed ammunition is used for field service. The fuzes of shells are cut and driven beforehand. The shot or shell is fastened to the sabot with straps of stout linen glued on, and the cartridge bag is drawn over the shot and tied.

A battery consists of eight pieces. In the horse artillery all the men are mounted; in the foot batteries, some of them are carried, in manœuvering, on the limber chest and the caisson.

The horse artillery men wear the light cavalry saber; the foot artillery a short sword like ours. They carry no fire arms; nor is there any arrangement about the gun carriage for attaching small arms of any kind.

At Moscow we saw some ammunition carts which had been made for carrying small arm cartridges for the militia enrolled in service. They were covered two-wheeled carts, drawn by three horses. They opened at the back, and contained covered sliding drawers, with large compartments, lined with felt for cartridges, and small divisions for caps. Above these were other drawers, for camp kettles, &c. There were also bread wagons, made water-tight, and covered with sheet iron.

For *siege batteries*, a stock trail carriage, after the French model, has been adopted. The trail handspike has a roller set in the end. One is used on each side of the stock, from which bolts project, that pass through holes in the handspikes above the rollers. This arrangement serves to aid in running the piece quickly to battery.

PRUSSIA.

The Prussian field artillery was modified in 1842. All the details of the new system are shown in the description and drawings published by Mr. Kamcke in 1847, which are among the books of the commission, and in other drawings, on a larger scale, now in course of publication, and received by the Ordnance Office.

The *cannon* of this system are only three: a 6-pounder and a 12-pounder gun, and a short 24-pounder howitzer, all of bronze. The guns are of the usual pattern, weighing respectively about 900 and 1,800 pounds. The howitzer is thirty-nine inches long, from rear of base ring to muzzle, and weighs 900 pounds. It has the same trunnions as the 12-pounder gun. The 6-pounder has no handles. The vents of these guns are bored perpendicular to the axis; no doubt with a view of adapting them better to the use of friction tubes, which are employed exclusively in firing them. The axis of the trunnions is in the same plane as the axis of the bore.

The *gun carriages* are so much like the Russian, (which were probably copied from them,) that the same description applies to both. The only essential difference is in the manner of elevating the gun. Instead of a quoin, the breech of the piece rests on a pointing plate, which is moved up and down by an elevating screw. The box of the screw is set in an iron supporting piece, which turns on journals, to accommodate the varying direction of the screw.

The *limber body* is made with two hounds, diverging from the front, and connected in rear by an iron sweep-bar, which is joined also to a middle rail, that rests on the axle body and supports the pintle. The pintle is placed about twenty-eight inches in rear of the center of the axletree. The ammunition chest is somewhat larger than ours, the interior dimensions being about forty-five inches by twenty-four inches; but it is not arranged for as many rounds of ammunition, greater space being left for implements. The top of the chest is covered with sheet iron, and when open, it is supported by an iron arc on the outside of the end of the chest. Handles are attached to it for the men who ride there. They have no cushions; but they use the forage sacks for that purpose. No arrangement is made for attaching small arms or sabers to the limber-chest. The sponge is a brush made of bristles.

The *prolonge* is a *chain*, made of five-sixteen inch iron. When not in use, it is coiled around the hounds, just in front of the sweep-bar. *Pole chains* are also used, and not leather straps.

The field ammunition is all *fixed*.

The gun carriage wheels are five feet in diameter; but the limber wheels only four feet, to give greater facility in turning. They have whole, or hoop tire, two and a half inches by half an inch. The wheel boxes are not *driven*, but are set in by pressure with a screw and lever.

The *caisson* body has one ammunition chest, forty-five inches by thirty-one inches; the top covered with sheet iron. The limber is the same as for the gun carriage.

The *battery wagon* has a chest about fifty-six inches by forty-eight inches. Besides tools and spare parts attached to the wagon, and stores in the chest, it carries smaller chests, for money, and for medicines both for men and horses. The limber, instead of a chest, carries three spare wheels; two of the large size, and one of the small.

The *traveling forge* has a bellows, uncovered, placed over the axletree; a folding fireplace behind, and a tool chest in front; the anvil and vise on the rails, in front of the tool chest; bar iron suspended under the axletree. The limber is like that of the gun carriage, and the chest contains tools.

The 6-pounder carriage is drawn by six horses; the 12-pounders by eight. In maneuvering, a man is mounted on each horse, for which purpose the off horses have saddles or pads, with stirrups. The saddles are smaller and lighter than the driver's saddle. The latter is the Hungarian saddle, the same that is used by the cavalry, a pattern of which was obtained by permission of the Minister of War. For the artillery, these saddles are made of six sizes or numbers. The traces of the harness are of rope, three fourths of an inch thick, with short chains at each end. Those of the first pair of leaders are hooked to the end of the pole; those of the second pair are hooked to the front end of the first. The hitching strap of the halter is of rope half an inch thick; some of them are hair rope. For stable service, halter chains are used. The bits, stirrups, and other mountings, are of steel or iron.

The straw for stuffing collars is not cut up, but is tied together in the proper shape, and covered with the leather.

The horse carries a valise, a canteen or cooking apparatus, a bundle of forage, a shoe pouch for two shoes, the rider's cloak. There is also a pouch for comb and brushes, and a nose-bag. The nose-bag is made of strong, coarse linen, (canvas;) the bottom is strengthened by two cross belts of webbing. The saddle girth and surcingle are of leather; but the girth for the off horse's pad is of webbing. The horse of a mounted man carries a breastplate, with a pair of rope traces attached, to assist with in case of a difficulty.

In the batteries, generally, only the officers and non-commissioned officers are mounted. The gunners follow the movements of the piece on foot; and in rapid maneuvers, some of them mount on the off horses, others on the limber chest. In this manner the movements are thought to be as quick as those of horse artillery, properly so called. The mounted men wear a curved saber; the others, a straight one-edged sword, about two feet long.

AUSTRIA.

The field artillery of Austria embraces at present a great variety of cannon. There are 6-pounder, 12-pounder, and 18-pounder guns; 24-pounder and 32-pounder short howitzers; new 12-pounder and 24-pounder long howitzers, and 12-pounder mountain howitzers, on the French models, beside special guns for using gun cotton in place of gunpowder. All these pieces are of bronze, as are also the guns and mortars of the siege artillery. The field gun carriages were remodeled in some of their details in 1842; they are constructed like the French carriages of the old, or Gribeauval system, with slight alterations. In the gun carriage proper the elevating apparatus is like the Russian above described, except that the winch which turns the screw of the wedge is worked behind the wedge, instead of at the side of the carriage. Between the cheeks of the carriage there is an ammunition chest, the top of which is cushioned and furnished with a railing, to form a seat for two men. In the limber, the pintle, instead of being placed over the axletree, is about fourteen inches in rear of it, leaving room for another ammunition chest on the front part of the limber. The wheels of the gun carriage are fifty-four inches in diameter, those of the limber forty-four inches, both made with hoop tire half an inch thick; the heads of the tire bolts are not countersunk, but project beyond the tire. The leaders draw by leading bars as in ordinary wagons. In the light, or horse artillery 6-pounder gun carriage, the ammunition chest between the cheeks affords a seat, about five feet long, for four or five men.

The ammunition wagon (würst caisson) is like the Gribeauval caisson, a long chest suspended on four wheels, but the cover is cushioned, to form a seat for the men.

A battery consists of eight pieces, six guns and two howitzers. The light pieces are drawn by four or six horses; the heavy by six or eight, according to the nature of the service.

At the Arsenal of Vienna we saw carriages of a new system proposed for trial. The gun carriage is designed for a light 12-pounder gun; the cheeks are parallel, as in the Prussian carriage, but in other respects the arrangement is nearly the same as in the former Austrian gun carriage; the "würst" equipment chest, for seating two men, is retained. The wheels are fifty-eight inches in diameter; they are kept on the axletree by a cap or box, covering the end of the axle, to prevent the dirt from entering; this is retained in place by a linchpin, which is held in by a ring passing around the axletree and secured by a leather thong. The implements are fastened under the carriage by leather straps passing through mortises in the rammer-head, &c. The wheels of the limber are of the same size as those of the gun carriage; the ammunition chest, to contain seventeen rounds of 12-pounder ammunition, is covered *all over* with sheet-iron; the position of the pintle is in rear of the chest as before, with a sweep bar on the ends of the hounds.

The *caisson* body has a chest to hold sixty rounds of 12-pounder ammunition; a spare wheel is fastened under the axletree; the limber is the same as that of the gun carriage.

The *forge* has a small round bellows over the axletree, and a folding fireplace in rear; the bellows is covered by a house, in the front part of which are partitions for coal, iron, &c. The anvil and vise are carried on the middle rails in front of the bellows-house; the anvil block hangs under the carriage.* The limber is the same for all the carriages of the battery.

The *battery wagon* body is arranged to carry boxes for ammunition or stores; it is covered with a canvas roof.

All the field ammunition is *fixed* by tying the cartridge-bag over the ball without a sabot; tow or hair is placed instead between the powder and ball; for shells or spherical case, the bag is left open around the fuze hole and gathered by twine round the upper part of the shell. The friction priming tubes are made on the French plan; locks are only used by the marine artillery.

There is no arrangement about the carriage for attaching small arms; sixteen carbines are allowed to a battery for guard duty; they are carried in one of the wagons on the march.

In this new system of carriages the whole weight to be drawn by each horse is 700 pounds, requiring a total force of traction, by the dynamometer, of 250 pounds.

Pole straps of leather are used instead of chains at the end of the pole; they are hooked to short breast-straps attached to the hames; the hames are of bright iron, as are also the bits and stirrups. [*Brass* is not used for bits, stirrups, or mountings, either for artillery or cavalry, in any European service.] The collars are made of various sizes, closed together on the neck, without buckles and straps. The traces are made of leather from the hames back to the rear of the horse, the remaining portion is of rope; the ropes of the leading traces, both of the first and second pair, are carried back to join the wheel traces just behind the wheel-horse's hames; the driver's saddle is like our old driver's saddle, or the common wagon saddle; the driver's *leg guard* is a piece of flat iron two inches wide and one fourth of an inch thick, which is suspended by a leather strap to the *left* side of the pommel of the saddle, and is hooked into an eye on the stirrup; a loop is sewed to the flaps of the saddle in front for convenience of hanging it up in the stable. The saddle of the off-horse is a large pad, made on an iron tree; it has large leather flaps, with pockets to hold canvas bags for the men's effects. The bridle of the near horse has a *curb bit;* that of the off-horse, a *snaffle* only; the halter has a rope for hitching.

In the horse artillery the servants are not mounted on horses; five men sit on the carriage chest, (würst,) and two on the limber chest. In the foot artillery, three men on the carriage chest, and three on the off horses.

Our visit to Austria being in the winter season, we had no opportunity of seeing maneuvers in the field; but from an examination of the artillery riding school and the regimental school in Vienna, some idea might be formed of the excellent instruction given to officers and soldiers.

The *Artillery Riding School* is under the able direction of Lieutenant Colonel Nadosy, himself an admirable rider, and the author of a valuable work on equitation, entitled "Equitations Studium." The other instructors are also officers of artillery, and the pupils are lieutenants of artillery, who remain two years at the school, and go through a thorough training in riding and driving. We saw twelve of these go through their exercises in the fine riding hall, which is about two hundred and fifty feet by sixty, with a commodious gallery and visitors' room at one end. They rode first in a squad, on saddles without stirrups, then on saddles without either stirrups or girths, and then without saddles, leaping at the bar in each exercise. After this, they drove two gun carriages and two caissons each with six horses; maneuvering and turning in circles of half the width of the hall, (thirty feet,) and passing between stakes placed six inches further apart than the length of the axletrees, all at good speed. They next practiced to represent the cases of accidents in the field; for instance: a carriage is supposed to have lost its near wheel horse and off leader, and the driver of the middle pair; the traces of the remaining leader are brought back and fastened to the middle of the splinter bar; the middle pair remains without a driver; the driver of the wheel horses mounts the off horse without a saddle, and the carriage is maneuvered quickly under these difficult circumstances, and others of like nature. The driver had no leg guard; a leading rein from the bridles of the middle pair assisted him in driving them.

The stables in the basement of the men's barrack are perfect models of order and neatness. The stalls are about five and a half feet wide, divided by swinging bars, with straw pads; the floors are of plank, laid over an inverted arch of brick, which receives the urine, and conveys it into a covered drain running along the rear of the stalls; the litter is dried every morning, and the new litter for the night is neatly placed at the rear of the stall on each side. The whole room is dry and clean, and what is unusual in German stables, is provided with ventilators near the ceiling, which are opened or closed by means of cords. Chain halters are used for the night, and short ropes in the day time.

In the lecture room of the school, Colonel Nadosy has collected a museum of specimens illustrating the anatomy of the horse, especially the teeth and hoofs; also samples of a great variety of shoes and bits used in different countries, or under peculiar circumstances.

The *Regimental Artillery School* of Vienna is intended for the primary instruction of youths who may become officers or non-commissioned officers of artillery. It is situated in the upper story of the principal artillery barracks. The pupils are about one hundred and twenty in number, partly sons of soldiers or government employés, partly sons of citizens, who pay a small contribution (seventy-five dollars a year) for their expenses. They enter at thirteen, and pursue a course of three years' instruction in elementary mathematical and military studies; an excellent course of drawing, fencing, gymnastics, &c., under the direction of officers of artillery. At the end of the second year, some of the best scholars (say ten out of one hundred and twenty) go to the Artillery Academy, or other military academies, to become officers; the others remain to be educated for non-commissioned officers of artillery.

The artillery barracks in which this school is lodged are capable of holding 3,000 men. Attached to the same building are the rooms of the "Committee of Artillery." This committee, under the presidency of a major general, (Smola,) is composed of a colonel, three field officers, five captains, and ten lieutenants, and is charged with examination of new inventions, and with experiments, &c., for the improvement of the material of artillery and arms; a detachment of non-commissioned officers and artificers assists in their operations. Connected with their bureau is a fine collection of models of gun carriages, machines, &c., of various dates and countries.

The central *Direction of Artillery* at Vienna, under a master general of artillery, is divided into several sections.
1. Of organization, personnel, remounts, and general service.
2. Of scientific affairs, new projects and inventions, and artillery schools.
3. Of judicial affairs, supplies, and depots of stores, arms, gunpowder.
4. Fiscal affairs.

A direction of artillery in each army has a like control in the territory occupied by that army. These directions and the committee compose the general staff of the artillery.

The artillery force, as organized in 1854, consists of a *general staff*, twelve regiments of *field artillery*, a *rocket regiment*, a *sea-coast regiment*, and the *technical artillery*. Each of these regiments and corps has its own staff and administrative officers, but the names of all the officers are arranged in one list of rank in the Army Register.

On the *Peace Establishment* each regiment of *field artillery* consists of four to six field officers, about eighteen captains, of first and second class, thirty first lieutenants, fifty second lieutenants, of first and second class, five to ten cadets, and about two thousand men; divided into three battalions, with eleven batteries of horse and foot artillery, each of eight pieces; being nearly two hundred men to a battery, to serve and conduct the pieces, caissons, &c.

The *Rocket Regiment* is organized in the same manner as the other field regiments. The Austrian artillery is said to have attained great skill in the manufacture and use of rockets; but we had no opportunity of seeing their practice in the field, and strangers are not admitted to the manufactory at Wiener-Neustadt. The rockets are designated 6-pounder, 12-pounder, &c., according to the weight of the finished rocket, without the shell which it carries. From some rockets and drawings it appears that the shell, which is hemispherical or cylindrical, is of larger diameter than the rocket. The stick is not placed in the axis, as in the congreve rocket, but is fastened in a socket on the side. The diameter of a 7-pounder rocket is two and three quarter inches. A rocket stand seen at the Arsenal of Venice consists of a tripod stand, which supports a tube or arms to receive the rocket and stick. The elevation is given by means of an iron arc, which is moved by a pinion working in a circular rack and fastened by a clamp screw.

The *Sea-coast Regiment* is also constituted like a field regiment, having three battalions of four companies each, but a smaller number of officers and men.

The *Technical Artillery* corresponds with our Ordnance Department, being charged with the manufacture of all the material of artillery and the armament of the troops, and also with their distribution and storage. For the arsenals and founderies and manufacture of arms, there are, besides the staff, companies of enlisted workmen, as well as hired men. For the manufacture of rockets and cannon primers at Neustadt, two companies of workmen and a staff, under the direction of a major general. For the care and administration of the material, the empire is divided into sixteen districts, with a corps of officers and men in each.

The inspection of arms in the hands of the troops is a separate department of administration, and the duty is not performed by artillery officers.

FRANCE.

The "matériel" of the French system of field artillery being well known to us, a notice of the few modifications recently made in some of the details is all that is required here. The great change in the system is the adoption of a single caliber, which will be noticed elsewhere.

In the field *gun carriage* some of the "rondelles," of cast iron, between the stock and the cheeks, having been broken in firing, they are now made of *wrought iron*. Since 1850, a *shoe* has been adopted in place of the lock chain. The nave boxes are still made of bronze. It was observed that, in the arsenals, although the tire bolts are not put in the wheels until the carriages are issued, in order that the tires may be more readily [illegible] ary on account of the shrinking of the wood, the bolt holes are bored in the tires before [illegible] set.

In the *limber* the fork is made in *three* pieces, instead of being cut o[illegible] one [illegible] as heretofore. The pole is made so as to be more easily removed than before; i[illegible] that on the pole of an ordinary carriage, to hold back by, and it is kept in place [illegible] in passing vertically through a strap across the fork and through the pole. The prolonge is coiled on hooks projecting below the axletree of the limber, and the prolonge hooks on the carriage are consequently omitted. The ammunition chests are covered *all over* with sheet iron.

The *battery wagon* is lightened by substituting for the heavy cover one of canvas laid over a ridge pole. The sides are raised in order to increase the capacity of the wagon for carrying harness. All the field carriages have the *shoe* in place of a simple lock chain.

The *harness* was remodeled in 1854. The head gear of the near horse consists of a curb bridle and a halter with a snaffle bit attached; that of the off horse is the halter-bridle with snaffle only. This snaffle bit has straight bars or check pieces. A watering bridle and a stable halter are also provided for each horse. All the bits are of bright iron. The saddle is made a good deal after the English model, with stuffed seat and pads under the tree. It has attached to it a holster, a pouch, and a shoe pocket for two horse shoes, all covered with a shabraque. The girth and surcingle are of hemp webbing. The horse of a mounted gunner carries a breast strap with a pair of traces for occasional use. The *hames* are made of wood, and have pads stuffed with hair nailed to them instead of a *collar*. The traces are of leather in the front part and of rope in the rear. The ropes of the wheel-horse traces are doubled twice, (four ropes of half inch thick,) as the leaders draw through the same traces.

Little of this new harness was used by the artillery in the Crimea, and it probably still wants the test of active service with regard to the expediency of the change made by combining the collar and hames in one. It may be remarked, however, that this arrangement has long been used in the Swedish artillery, and the common draft harness in that country has neither a collar nor a pad on the hames. The wooden hames are made large and broad, and are shaped to fit the shoulders of the horse without the interposition of any cushion or cloth.

The personnel of the French artillery was reorganized in 1854. Besides eight generals of division (lieutenant generals) and sixteen generals of brigade, (major generals,) it consists of—

    A special artillery staff.
    5 regiments of foot artillery, not mounted.
    1 regiment of pontonniers.
    7 regiments of field (foot) artillery, mounted.
    4 regiments of horse artillery.
    12 companies of workmen.
    5 companies of armorers, (1 only kept up at present.)
    5 companies of veterans.

The *staff* consists of 315 officers; (31 colonels, 33 lieutenant colonels, 44 majors, and 210 captains;) 833 military employés; (storekeepers, master artificers, and workmen;) 147 civil employés; (directors of founderies, manufactories, &c.)

A *regiment of dismounted foot artillery* consists of a commissioned and a non-commissioned staff, 12 foot batteries, 6 park batteries, and a depot staff. The non-commissioned staff (*peloton hors rang*) contains master workmen and workmen of various trades required for the repair of clothing and equipments, clerks, and assistants to the clothing officer, and to the surgeon, veterinary surgeon, &c., numbering 54 men. The field officers are 1 colonel, 1 lieutenant colonel, 8 chefs d'escadron, 1 major. A foot battery or company has 4 officers and 100 men on the peace establishment; a park battery, 73 men; in both the number of men is doubled on the war establishment, and the number in the park batteries may, if necessary, be quadrupled so as to make mounted batteries of them. The depot staff or detachment consists of 3 officers, (one captain and two lieutenants) and 23 non-commissioned officers, sergeants, corporals, smiths, saddlers, musicians. Thus, a regiment of foot artillery, not mounted, consists, in time of peace, of 92 officers and 1,724 men; on the war establishment the number of men is doubled, and the *draft* horses of the park batteries increased from 240 to 1,200. The men of the foot batteries are cannoniers; those of the park batteries are drivers. These regiments are stationed generally in fortified towns, where they are instructed in the various branches of artillery service, and from them the companies for the special service of rocket and mountain howitzer batteries are taken.

The *pontonnier regiment* contains 12 companies of pontonniers, having 4 officers and 100 men, and 4 companies of drivers, with 3 officers and 73 men, on the peace establishment; making in all 84 officers and 1,577 men, which may be increased in war to 2,300.

A *regiment of field (foot) artillery* contains 15 batteries horsed, each having 4 officers and 122 men in peace; 234 men in war; making a total of 88 officers and 1,922 men, increased to 3,600 on the war establishment and an equal number of horses.

A *regiment of horse artillery* contains eight batteries, each having 4 officers and 122 men and 100 horses, on the peace establishment; 230 men and 264 horses, in war—making a total of 56 officers and 1,059 men, in peace; 1,923 men and 2,145 horses, in war.

The field and staff and the depot detachments of all the regiments are nearly the same; the officers' horses are not included in the above enumeration.

A *company of workmen* contains 4 officers and 70 to 100 men; they are employed in the arsenals and other manufacturing establishments of the artillery.

A *company of armorers* consists of 4 officers and 100 men, who are employed with armies in active service.

The *companies of veterans* are employed as fort-keepers, &c., in the sea-coast batteries.

The whole artillery force, (exclusive of the veterans,) under this organization, is:

On *the peace establishment:* about 30,000 officers and men, with 13,700 horses; on *the war footing:* 55,000 officers and men, with 41,300 horses, to which may be added, if necessary, the 40 park batteries of the foot regiments, doubled. The 137 field batteries, horse and foot, make 822 pieces of artillery.

The principal features of this new organization of the artillery are the suppression of the troops of the train, and the separation into distinct regiments of the troops designed for the service of different kinds of batteries. The institution of the troops of the train, which took place during the wars of the revolution, was a great improvement on the old system, in which men were hired to conduct the pieces into the field, but, being non-combatants, were not expected to maneuver them in action. But the troops of the train necessarily felt themselves in an inferior position, by having their service limited to the duties of drivers, without participation in the more honorable, though scarcely more dangerous service of the guns; they had a special organization, a particular uniform, a different pay from the battery troops, and did not serve, in case of loss, to replace the fighting men. In 1829, when the present system of artillery carriages was adopted, the corps of the train was reduced to the force necessary for conducting the reserve supplies, and the other drivers were incorporated with the men of the battery. The present arrangement amalgamates still further the two kinds of servants, and makes the battery independent of other corps for the whole of its service. The mounted batteries, both horse and foot, contain nearly an equal number of cannoniers and drivers, who are competent, by their course of instruction, to replace each other in case of need. The *dismounted* regiments have batteries or companies without drivers, and park batteries with drivers only; these troops have charge of the parks of reserve and of the heavy batteries, assist in the attack and defense of fortresses, and may serve, on occasion, to increase the force of active field batteries. The *horse artillery*, in which all the cannoniers are mounted, act with cavalry, and the *foot field artillery* with infantry. These three different kinds of troops, formerly combined in one regiment, are now organized separately; an arrangement which enables each to perfect itself in its own service, and avoids the jealousies and partialities which are apt to interfere with the harmonious action of mixed regimental commands. An organization of this kind, which existed many years ago in our service, when we had a corps of artillery (foot) and a regiment of light artillery, was perhaps unwisely departed from. It is probable that they would not have been amalgamated, if they had been really serving with their appropriate arms and equipments, instead of being both employed merely to garrison the sea-coast forts, and armed as infantry.

In the new organization of the French artillery, the regiment is always complete in its officers, its non-commissioned staff, and its depot staff; so that by a simple increase of privates the number of batteries may be immediately increased from the peace to the war establishment, or any intermediate force.

The report of the Minister of War, on which this organization was adopted, will be found in the "*Journal Officiel Militaire*, 1854."

ENGLAND.

No change has been recently made in the system of guns and carriages for field artillery. In the Crimea, the batteries, both horse and foot, consisted of six 9-pounder guns and two 24-pounder howitzers, each drawn by eight horses; the caissons were drawn by six horses; there were besides eighteen spare horses in harness to each battery, and a spare gun carriage, with spare parts; four axletrees, a caisson stock, a handspike, and a pair of shafts.

On the front of each limber chest two carbines are fastened by an iron socket, three inches wide, held by three screws, and by a strap one inch wide, held by two staples; the barrels are placed uppermost and the locks covered with leather. The drivers wore no sabers; the other men carried their sabers on their persons; two mess kettles were hung on the axletree of each gun carriage. The guns had no locks, but were provided with friction tubes, and also with common tubes and portfires; besides a sharp and a blunt priming wire, each piece had a sort of *auger* for extracting a tube that failed to fire—a case which very rarely occurs.

A *rocket carriage* attached to the battery carried 100 rockets, two and three fourth inches in diameter, (called 12-pounder rockets;) the tube for firing them is three and one fourth inches in diameter, and is supported on a tripod; the carriage is drawn by eight horses.

Pickets and ropes were strapped to the foot boards of the limber, and tools and forage were attached to the caisson and gun carriage, as prescribed in the regulations. See the "Artillerist's Manual."

An ambulance cart is attached to a brigade of two batteries; it has chests for medicines, instruments, &c., in the lower part, and "stretchers" for the wounded above; also hand-stretchers along the sides for carrying the wounded off the field; the chest is twenty-two inches long, ten and a half inches wide, and twelve inches deep. Two small chests for the same purpose were packed on a mule hitched to the cart.

A supply of reserve small-arm ammunition was carried by the artillery in caissons, which have larger chests than those for the artillery ammunition, carrying 7,700 rounds on the limber and 11,200 on the body of the wagon, packed in kegs of 700 each; there are eight of these wagons to a division, each drawn by four horses. A small supply was also carried in kegs slung on mules. The whole reserve supply with the batteries was about fifty rounds to a man. In order that a proper supply may be kept up, a weekly return, in the following form, is made to the adjutant general's office, at the headquarters in the field, which was charged with the regulation of the issues; the officer in charge of this branch tried to make his estimates so as to have always on hand about 500 rounds to a man, which required about seventeen millions of cartridges for the British force alone.

FIELD ARTILLERY—ENGLAND.

WEEKLY RETURN OF THE RESERVE AMMUNITION.

_____ Division. _____ 185_.

	ISSUES.					IN HAND AND RECEIPTS.		
Date.	Regiment.	Amount ___ bore.	Spare percⁿ sion caps.	Remarks.	Date.	Amount ___ bore.	Spare percⁿ sion caps.	Remarks.
					In hand from last return............			
					Amount now in reserve............			

Commanding Royal Artillery, _____ _Division._

PART IX.

NEW SYSTEMS OF FIELD ARTILLERY.

The present Emperor of the French, who was an officer of artillery of the Swiss Republic, and had devoted much attention to that branch of the military art, proposed, before his accession to the throne, a new system of field artillery, which has been adopted in France, and which is producing a corresponding change in other countries. With a view to simplify the service of artillery in the field, without impairing its efficiency, he proposed to use but one kind and caliber of gun for that service, viz: a 12-pounder gun, of fifteen calibers length of bore, and weighing about twelve hundred weight, to be fired with a charge of one fourth the weight of the shot. In these respects the piece corresponds with the light 12-pounder gun which was used in the British field batteries during the war of 1812, but which forms no part of their present system. Experiments in France as to the range and efficiency of this gun for the purposes for which artillery is generally required in field operations were attended with satisfactory results; as regards its *mobility* there could be no question, as the weight of the piece is very nearly the same as that of the 8-pounder, which was the lightest piece used in either the horse or foot batteries in France, and it was to be mounted on a carriage of the same weight as the 8-pounder. The only circumstance, therefore, to the disadvantage of the new 12-pounder, in comparison with the 8-pounder, is the reduced number of rounds which can be carried in the ammunition chests—twenty-six rounds instead of thirty-two. The new *"gun-howitzer"* having been adopted, a great number of them have been made, and in order to introduce the system more quickly and at less cost, the 8-pounder guns have been bored up to 12-pounder, and given to the horse artillery, under the designation of *"light howitzer gun,"* being about 175 pounds lighter than the other; the same kind of ammunition is used for both, but the proportion of solid shot is smaller for the lighter gun.

The designation of *"gun-howitzer,"* (cannon-obusier,) given to this new piece, indicates the purpose of using it for firing the several kinds of projectiles for which different sorts of ordnance are generally employed in field service, viz: solid shot, shells, spherical-case shot, and canisters; an object which has been rendered practicable by the improvements that have taken place in the manufacture and preparation of field ammunition. The great advantages that will attend this extreme simplification of field artillery must be obvious to every one who reflects on the inconveniences of the present complex system of pieces varying in kind and caliber. Not only will the preparation of supplies of ammunition be rendered more simple and easy, in anticipation of demand, but, what is of much greater importance, the batteries of an enemy, which may be separated from their park of supplies, either in advance or retreat, having consumed their ammunition, or having lost it by misfortune, will be sure to find, in the first park or depot that they meet with, a supply of ammunition adapted to their guns, and not be obliged to encumber the march of a column with useless artillery, whilst by its side are wagons loaded with ammunition of another caliber.

The following tabular statement shows the most important particulars with reference to these new pieces, and to a light 12-pounder of the same kind proposed and on trial for our own field batteries.

Description of 12-pounder Howitzer Guns.

DIMENSIONS, ETC.	French 12-pounder Howitzer gun. New.	French 12-pounder Howitzer gun. Light.	U. States light 12-pounder.
GUN.			
Diameter of bore ....inches......	4.76	4.76	4.62
Length of bore ....do.........	71.46	68.74	63.6
Length of bore in diameters of ball...............................	15.25	14.67	14
Thickness of metal at the vent..........................inches......	3.40	3	3.19
Thickness of metal at the front of the shot............do.........	3.05	2.87	3.19
Thickness of metal at the neck ....do.........	1.24	1.17	1.24
Diameter of trunnions ....do.........	4.09	4.09	4.2
Length from rear of base ring to axis of trunnions....do.........	31.97	30.29	28.5
Distance of axis of trunnions below axis of gun........do.........	.04	.35	0
Weight of the gun ....pounds......	1,361	1,186	1,220
Weight of the gun in weight of shot.................................	100	87	99
Preponderance of breech ....pounds......	176	132	105
AMMUNITION.			
Diameter of ball, large gauge.........................inches......	4.65	4.64	4.53
Weight of solid shot...................................pounds......	13.64	13.64	12.3
Weight of shell loaded....................................do.........	9.15	9.15	8.84
Weight of canister...do.........	14.9	14.9	14.8
Weight of spherical case................................do.........	11.8	11.8	11.85
Charge of powder for shot..............................do.........	3.09	2.2	2.5
Charge of powder for shells............................do.........	2.2	2.2	2
Charge of powder for canister.........................do.........	2.2	2.2	2
Charge of powder for spherical case................do.........	3.09	2.2	2.5
Weight of round shot fired.............................do.........	16.04	16	15.4
CARRIAGE.			
Width of gun-carriage stock at the head..........inches......	10.08	9.2	9.65
Depth of gun-carriage stock at the head..............do.........	9.47	9.05	9.2
Distance from axis of trunnions to axis of axletree....do.........	13.8	12.8	16.2
Vertical distance of axis of trunnions in rear of axis of axletree, the piece being in battery ....inches......	.12	.12	.25
Vertical field of fire, elevation.......................degrees......	13	11	14
Vertical field of fire, depression......................do.........	7	7	9
Number of rounds carried in one ammunition chest................	26	26	32
viz: shot...	12	6	12
shells..	8	14	8
spherical case......................................	3	3	8
canisters...	3	3	4
Number of rounds carried in caisson and limber..................	78	78	96
Weight of ammunition chest loaded.................pounds......	636	508	647
Weight of limber with chest loaded	1,460	1,432	1,342
Weight of caisson and limber loaded...................do.........	3,720	3,608	3,724
Weight of gun and carriage...............................do.........	2,590	2,413	2,348
Weight of piece limbered up, chest loaded ....do.........	4,066	3,832	3,872
Weight of trail of gun-carriage on the ground....do.........	297	246	160
Number of horses to each piece and caisson...................	6	6	6

The ammunition for the French guns is *fixed*, except the canisters, which still remain separate from the charge of powder. The fuzes for the shells are driven beforehand, and are of uniform length; for spherical case, the fuzes can be regulated for three different times of burning, at the moment of loading.

These pieces take the place of the 8-pounder gun and the 24-pounder howitzer; but for batteries of position and reserve the heavy 12-pounder gun and the 32-pounder howitzer are retained, although no new pieces of the latter kinds are now made. The field batteries in the Crimea were armed altogether with the new guns, and the experience with them in campaign was said to be satisfactory to the artillery; the great advantage of having to provide ammunition of only one caliber of each nature, and spare parts for repair of but one kind of carriage, &c., is too obvious to need further remark. It may be doubted, however, whether the experience of the Russian war was sufficient to establish the efficacy of these pieces for all the service that may be required of field artillery, in European warfare especially, when the fate of an expedition, or of a great battle, often depends on the attack or defense of a village, a château, or other position, which might demand the employment of heavier calibers.

The batteries in the Crimea consisted of six pieces, each drawn by eight horses; the caissons by six horses; spare ammunition for small arms was carried in wagons, and on pack mules, which could follow closely the movement of the troops on any ground.

The example of the French has been followed by experiments of the same kind in several other countries of the continent; but it does not appear that the *English artillery* have commenced any change in that respect. In *Belgium*, also, no change has yet been made; but a light 12-pounder gun was about to be prepared, to accompany the 6-pounder gun in batteries.

In *Austria* the new field carriages, mentioned under the head of "Field Artillery," are arranged for a 12-pounder brass gun of fourteen calibers length of bore, weighing 1,280 pounds, as the gun for field batteries. We also saw in preparation at the arsenal an experimental cast-iron 12-pounder gun of the same length and nearly the same dimensions as the brass gun, and weighing 968 pounds. (See Plate 10, Fig. 3.) The charge of these guns for shot and spherical case is two and a half pounds; for canister, three pounds. The new guns are proposed for foot batteries only; the 6-pounder being retained for the light or cavalry batteries.

The Austrian artillery officers have been for some years occupied with researches and experiments for substituting *gun cotton* for gunpowder in the service of artillery. It is thought that the preparation of gun cotton may be so modified as to reduce the intensity of its *destructive* force, without an injurious diminution of its propelling power, and thus to permit of its use with safety and effect. The experiments are still in progress, and the details are not made public; but they seem to have been sufficiently encouraging to authorize the construction of several (five) batteries of 12-pounder guns and 24-pounder howitzers for trial. Cast-iron is not capable of sustaining the action of gun cotton; these pieces were therefore made of bronze, very short and thick. (See Plate 10, Figs. 4 and 5.)

In *Prussia*, as already explained, the system of field artillery had been greatly simplified by reducing it to two guns and one howitzer; but experiments were about to be made with a very light 12-pounder gun, which we saw in the foundery at Spandau. This gun resembles our 12-pounder howitzer, without a chamber; the length of bore is only twelve calibers, and the weight 930 pounds; the form is that which has been adopted for our light 12-pounder gun, cylindrical from the breech to the front of the charge, with a regular taper thence to the chase; it is adapted to use on the 6-pounder carriage. The charge of powder is one fourth the weight of the shot, or three pounds, as we were informed; but this is too much for the weight of gun.

In *Saxony*, which possesses a well-instructed corps of artillery, the light 12-pounder has been adopted for all field batteries. The gun, which weighs about 1,000 pounds, is represented in Plate 5, Fig. 4. It is adapted to the 6-pounder carriage, and the charge is only two pounds. The gun carriage resembles that which was formerly known as the "Wadsworth carriage," having been designed by Colonel Wadsworth, formerly chief of the Ordnance Department. It has no stock. The cheeks, which are kept apart by transoms in front, are bent towards each other, at the breech of the gun, and nearly meet together at the trail, having a small block between them there, to which the lunette is attached.

The nut of the elevating screw is adjusted to a wrought-iron support, which is much bent, and turns on journals, so that its convexity may be placed downwards or upwards, as the gun is to be fired at high or low angle. By this construction of the carriage, the convenience of the English system with regard to limbering is preserved, without a great sacrifice in facility of turning and manœuvering; at the same time an advantage of considerable importance in the new system is obtained in being able to elevate the piece for firing, as a howitzer, at high angles. The breech can be lowered so as to fire the gun at an elevation of 26°, with a small charge of about eight or twelve ounces of powder, for throwing shells over an entrenchment or other shelter, or into a hollow road, &c. For this purpose, the cartridge bag is attached to a small conical block, which can be inserted in a hollow cut out of the shell sabot, in which it is retained by two little brass springs. The shell is fastened to the sabot with bands of strong linen glued on. The shells, before being fixed, are floated in mercury, and the lightest point is placed uppermost in a vertical plane through the axis of the piece; the axis of the fuze hole at an angle of 35° with the axis of the gun.

Friction primers, made like the Prussian, are used exclusively for firing the charge. In firing at high angles, the lanyard is passed under a hook attached to the gun for that purpose.

Field batteries consist sometimes of six pieces; sometimes of eight. The manner of manœuvering is like the Prussian: two men mount on the limber chest, and three on the off horses. The traces are of rope. The off horse has a snaffle bridle, and a light bit also attached to the halter head-stall.

The Saxon artillery use a fixed hausse for guns, and a pendulum hausse for howitzers; both of rather complicated construction. They are represented in the sheets of drawings most kindly presented to us by the officer in charge of the Arsenal at Dresden; showing also the guns and mortars, and the system of ambulances and other hospital wagons.

In *Russia*, the light 12-pounder gun has been adopted for all foot field batteries; 6-pounders and 12-pounder howitzers are retained for the horse artillery. The 12-pounder gun and 24-pounder howitzer will be used for batteries of position. The new system has not been fully introduced; and the guns which we saw with the troops about St. Petersburg and Moscow were of the former system; but we were told that about 200 of the light 12-pounders had been made within two years preceding our visit. The new gun is of the same general dimensions as the Saxon and Prussian pieces of the same kind, having 6-pounder trunnions, and being adapted to the 6-pounder carriage.

At the Arsenal at St. Petersburg, we saw an iron field gun carriage, proposed for trial by the Duke of Würtemberg, who is connected with the imperial family of Russia. This carriage was made on the plan of the usual field carriages of Russia; but the cheeks and transoms were formed of plate iron, riveted together on the principle of a hollow beam. The axletree and the wheels were also made entirely of iron. It had been subjected to the test of being fired at, in order to ascertain what injury might be done by the enemy's shot. One or two shot which struck the lower part of the cheek made deep indentations, and glanced, without disabling the carriage. One shot struck near the center of the wheel, and broke off the arm of the axletree, as it would have done in any other kind of carriage. The weight of this carriage and its costliness would be serious objections to this particular mode of construction; but the application of rolled iron to gun carriages and wagons for field artillery deserves attentive consideration and more extensive experiments than have been yet made. It is probable that efforts at improvement in these, as in garrison carriages, will be much aided by the recent progress made in the art of rolling iron in various shapes.

From the above remarks, it will be seen that all the principal powers of Europe, except Great Britain, are preparing to follow the example of France in simplifying their systems of field artillery, and increasing its mobility, and that the northern powers are going further than the French with respect to reducing the weight of their guns and carriages. It may well be doubted, however, whether experience will show that this great reduction of weight in the 12-pounder gun can be made without too great a sacrifice of strength and durability, in both gun and carriage, unless the charge is reduced so low (as in the Saxon plan) as to impair too much the efficiency of the piece.

In adopting our present reduced charges for field guns, which are little more than one *fifth* of the weight of the shot, we might well have made a proportional reduction in the weight of the guns, instead of retaining the weight and dimensions which were calculated for a charge of *one third* the weight of the shot. Since the return of the commission from Europe, this subject has been brought before the Ordnance Board, and, on their recommendation, a few light 12-pounder guns have been made for trial. The principal dimensions of this model are given in the above tabular statement, in connection with those of the new French guns. The piece is a medium between the latter guns and the lighter model adopted in Russia and Saxony. Its strength and weight are believed to be quite sufficient to resist the effects of our service charges; and the facility for maneuvering appears, from a preliminary trial, to be satisfactory. With six horses to a piece, little difference can be seen, in the rapidity of movement, between this and the 6-pounder; and even with four horses, the draught is not too heavy for short service, in case of need. It may not be found advisable in our service to dispense with the 6-pounder gun. The nature of the country in which most of our field operations are conducted, and the character of the operations themselves, make it desirable to increase the mobility of our light batteries, by lightening the 6-pounder gun, and also to retain the great advantage which that caliber offers, of enabling us to carry with it a larger quantity of ammunition. But a great convenience would result, both in the construction and service of field batteries, if, instead of the five kinds of guns and howitzers now constituting them, we can reduce the system to two calibers: a 6-pounder and a 12-pounder gun, each containing 100 pounds of metal to the pound of shot; and this, it is believed, may be done without loss of efficiency for all ordinary service required of our artillery. Under special circumstances, the 24-pounder or 32-pounder howitzers of our present system might be employed. The 24-pounder howitzer takes the same carriage as the new 12-pounder gun.

PART X.

SHRAPNEL SHELLS OR SPHERICAL CASE SHOT.

Although General Shrapnel's invention of spherical case shot dates from the beginning of the present century, and these projectiles were used with effect in Wellington's peninsular campaigns, it is only within a few years past that much attention has been bestowed on them by the artillery of the continental powers of Europe, with a view to their adoption. The recent improvements in the effective range of small arms have given additional value to spherical case shot as one of the most effectual means of defense for the artillery against the long-range rifles, and many ingenious plans have been tried for remedying the defects which have been observed in the preparation of them, as originally practiced in the British army, and continued until a very recent period. These defects were the liability of the Shrapnel shells to break in the gun, and the inconvenience resulting from the necessity of selecting or regulating the fuze on the field of battle, and fixing it into the shell at the moment of firing. These shells are made very thin in order to make them capable of holding the greatest possible number of balls, and their liability to break in the gun may be attributed frequently to insufficient strength of metal to resist the shock of the charge, which ought to be at least as great as for solid shot, in order that the balls may have the requisite velocity (not less than 400 feet a second) when released from the shell. But experiments on this subject have led artillerists to think that the charge of powder in the shell is liable to be ignited by the compression against the shell, produced by the inertia of the balls, and that the frequent explosions in the bore of the gun are due to this cause. The following are some of the methods adopted, either definitely or for trial, to remedy these defects.

ENGLAND.

Instead of the various fuzes, of different lengths and colors, formerly used for Shrapnel shells, a new fuze, invented by Captain Boxer, the superintendent of the Laboratory Department at Woolwich, has been adopted, and a longer one of the same kind for common shells. They are represented in Plates 18 and 19, together with Captain Boxer's new diaphragm Shrapnel shell.

Plate 18, Fig. 1, represents the fuze for spherical case, full size, and Figs. 2 and 3, sections of the same. The channel for composition ($c\ c$) is bored eccentric with regard to the exterior, and the two powder channels ($d\ d$) are bored on the thickest side. The exterior taper of all the fuzes is one tenth of an inch to one inch. The fuze composition is made to burn one inch in five seconds. The upper part of the bore is charged with mealed powder, and a hole (h) is bored through this priming to a depth of 0.4 inch from the top to insure the ignition of the fuze. The figures marked on the fuze indicate tenths of an inch below the bottom of this hole, showing the points at which the fuze is to be pierced, according to the required time of burning; the greatest length being one inch or five seconds. At each of these points a hole (c) is bored into the powder channel, (d.) The exterior of the fuze is covered with paper pasted on and varnished. The lower hole (e) is pierced through into the composition. The other holes are filled with pressed powder and a little clay. In the bottom hole a strand of quick match is inserted, which serves to retain the charge in the powder channel of the Shrapnel fuze. To effect the same object in the fuze for common shells, the bottom of the powder channel below the quick match is stopped with putty. In the Shrapnel fuze the quick match is continued from one channel to the other through a groove in the bottom of the fuze.

Fig. 4 represents a metallic cap for covering the top of the fuze. Under this cap is placed a disk of pasteboard (Fig. 5) to which a piece of tape is attached to facilitate the uncapping of the fuze.

The fuze for *common shells* is represented in Plate 19, Figs. 2 and 3. It differs from the other only in length, giving double the time of burning.

The fuze for *mortar shells* (Fig. 4) is made in the usual manner, with a channel for composition only; this being but six inches long, and charged with slow composition, the fuze answers for 8-inch, 10-inch, and 13-inch shells. The points for piercing the fuze are marked by countersunk holes, which are placed on a spiral in order to avoid the risk of splitting the fuze in boring through the wood.

Plate 18, Figs. 6, 7, and 8, represent the boring tools for small fuzes. The boring bit (Fig. 7) passes through the handle, and is held in place by the set screw e bearing on the flat place g in the bit. It projects just enough beyond the shank a to pierce through the composition, when the fuze is held in the hook b, and the handle is turned down to the shoulder. Fig. 8 is a simpler tool, to be used when the other is not at hand, or is out of order. Mortar fuzes are bored with a common iron brace and bit held against the body.

Captain Boxer's diaphragm Shrapnel shell is represented in Plate 19, Fig. 1, with a fuze prepared for a range corresponding to two seconds. The interior of the shell is divided by a wrought-iron partition (d) into two compartments, so as to separate the balls (c) from the bursting charge, (p.) The balls are made of an alloy of lead and antimony; they are inserted through the fuze hole, and the interstices are filled with coal dust. A metal socket is screwed into the fuze hole, the shoulder of which rests on the diaphragm of the shell, and prevents communication between the powder and the balls. The powder is inserted through the hole f, stopped by a screw plug. In order that the balls may be released in a uniform manner, four grooves are cast in the interior of the shell, to determine the fracture.

When the fuze composition has burnt down to the hole g, which has been bored through, the powder in the side channel is ignited, and the flame from the bottom of the fuze communicates, through a small groove, to the bursting charge by the hole a; the size of the socket is so regulated that there shall be a vacant space between the bottom of the fuze and the plug of lead (b) which closes the end of the socket.

To *fix the fuze:* the hole to regulate the time of bursting is bored, according to the range required; the fuze is then placed in the socket and struck two or three times with a small mallet, or against the gun-carriage; the cap is not removed until the shell is placed in the muzzle of the gun, to protect the fuze from accident or wet. The fuze for mortar shells is prepared and fixed in a similar manner; the solid wood at the lower end of the fuze is not to be cut off.

For use in the ordinary spherical case shot, the charge of powder is put into a tin cylinder, which is soldered to the lower part of the brass fuze plug. These fuzes were tried in the Crimean campaign, and gave great satisfaction, by the regularity and certainty of their effect; but some objections present themselves, in examining this arrangement, viz: the complicated construction of the shell, the great reduction of its capacity for balls, the peculiar boring instrument required for piercing the fuze, and the time requisite for performing this operation and adjusting the fuze in the shell on the field.

FRANCE.

The spherical case shot for the new 12-pounder field guns is 0.47 inch thick; it contains eighty musket balls, and about one sixth of a pound of musket powder. In charging the shell, forty balls are first put in, on which one fifth of a pound of sand is poured, to facilitate the dispersion of the balls when the shell bursts; the other forty balls are then put in, and one third of a pound of melted sulphur poured on them; the shell is at the same time inclined slightly in different directions, that the sulphur may cement the balls together. When it is cold the shell is filled with loose powder. The fuze is made of hard wood; it has three channels, lined with tin tubes, in which is driven the composition for three times of burning—one and a half, two and a half, and three and a half seconds; that for the longest time is left open; the others are closed by leather stoppers, covered with *red* paper for the shortest time, and *blue* for the next. These papers are marked with the distance at which the shell bursts, for each time of burning, and this distance is also marked on the top of the fuze to the right and left of each channel. The fuze is covered with a disk of parchment paper, having a piece of tape attached to it, and over that a paper cap is pasted. The fuze is uncapped by pulling the ends of the tape, and scraping off with the nail any of the paper which may have stuck to the fuze, and the proper channel is opened with an implement provided for the purpose. If a mistake is made, wet the stopper and replace it, pressing it with the handle of the extractor. The fuze is driven in, and the shot strapped like a common shell; it weighs eleven and three quarter pounds, and with the sabot about twelve and a quarter pounds.

This arrangement is simple, and requires no fixing or adjusting the fuze on the field, nor any peculiar implement, as a knife or a priming wire will serve to uncap the fuze, if the proper extractor is not at hand. But this fuze, allowing only three variations in the time of flight, seems to be deficient in the nicety required for the fire of shrapnels; a difference of one second in the time of burning would correspond to a difference of from three hundred to four hundred yards in the range. The greatest time of this fuze, three and a half seconds, is also much less than is generally allowed to shrapnels, (five seconds;) it may be sufficient for as great a distance as they can generally be advantageously employed at—say 1,200 yards; but with the charge of a fourth, used in the French 12-pounder, the balls from a shrapnel shell would be effective at the distance of a mile. The French method of charging the shell is well adapted to our paper fuzes, and to prevent the breaking of the shot in the gun.

BELGIUM.

The fuze for spherical case, invented about the year 1840, by Captain (now Colonel) Bormann, of the Belgian artillery, is one of the most ingenious contrivances yet offered for this purpose. Spherical case shot prepared either on Colonel Bormann's plan or with the modifications proposed by Captain Siemens, of the Hanoverian artillery, have been extensively tried, with complete success, in Belgium, Holland, Sweden, Saxony, Hanover, Bavaria, Wurtemburg, Nassau, and they have been adopted in most of those countries. The method of Captain Siemens having been adopted in the United States service, after satisfactory trials, need not be here described. The fuze has been objected to, in England and France, as exposing too small a surface to the action of the flame from the charge of the gun, and therefore liable to miss fire; but this objection is not sustained by the results of the ample trials above referred to, in Europe and in this country; the number of failures from this cause having been wonderfully small. An objection is also made sometimes to the use of melted sulphur, in Siemens's plan, as causing the balls to adhere together, instead of scattering, when the shell bursts. If so, a less adhesive material may be used. It is believed that rosin is more brittle, and it is also less offensive to use in the melted state; but Colonel Bormann uses nothing of this kind in filling his shells, nor does he consider it necessary. To secure them from breaking in the gun, he thinks it sufficient to pack the balls carefully in the shell, (taking care not to deform them by ramming,) so that they cannot be shaken; to encourage the men in this, he gave a premium to the one who got in the greatest number of balls. My experience confirms this assertion of Colonel Bormann. Shells cast at the Washington navy-yard, of good quality of iron, as shrapnels should always be, and well filled with balls, (ninety in a 12-pounder shell,) resisted perfectly the shock of a charge of one quarter and even one third the weight of the solid shot; but when ordinary shells, obtained from private founderies, were tried in the same manner, many of them broke in the gun, even with small charges; it was therefore thought safer to continue the use of sulphur in charging the shot. But in using this new fuze, there appears to be no objection to increase the thickness of the shell, so as to secure it against breaking in the gun, without diminishing too much its capacity. A 12-pounder shrapnel shell, of 5.5 or 0.55 inch thick, would probably be sufficiently strong, if the balls are well packed; and it would hold at least as many balls as those prepared in the old method. It may also be found that the same thickness will serve for common shells, to be filled with powder, thus dispensing with the necessity of making two kinds of shells for field service.

PRUSSIA.

The Prussian spherical case shot are cast with a cylindrical case in the center, to contain the charge of powder, and keep it separated from the balls. Plate 20, Fig. 1.

The axis of this cylinder coincides with that of the fuze hole; a fuze plug or case, of cast iron, is screwed into the fuze hole, having a small hole in the bottom for the communication of the fuze with the bursting charge. The balls are contained in the annular space around the cylinder, being inserted through a hole in the side of the shell, which is then closed with a screw plug. The fuze hole is covered with a piece of thick paper glued over it. The fuzes are cut to various lengths, and are carried in fuze pouches attached to a waist belt; each pouch is marked with the range corresponding to the length of fuze it contains, and the fuze is inserted in the shell, like our paper fuzes, at the moment of firing.

This arrangement is objectionable on account of the difficulty of introducing the balls and the great reduction of space for them in the shell.

RUSSIA.

The Russian spherical case shot are like the old English shrapnel, and are charged in the same manner. The fuzes are driven in cases of papier maché, one inch long; they are of different colors for different ranges.

AUSTRIA.

It is understood that the spherical case shot heretofore used in Austria are made and charged like the English; that the fuzes are prepared for three different lengths, and fixed in the shells at the laboratory, so that each shot could be used only at one distance; this information, however, was not obtained from the Austrian artillery. At the time of our visit to the arsenal at Vienna, some experiments were in progress with a new fuze, made somewhat on the principle of Bormann's. (Plate 20, Figs. 2, 3, and 4.) The composion is pressed, as in the latter, into a circular channel, but instead of being closed by a fixed plate of metal, the channel is closed by a movable plate, (Fig. 4,) which is pressed down by a screw in the center of the fuze. The fire is communicated to the fuze composition through an opening in this plate, which can be set, by means of an index and a graduated scale, to correspond with any given point in the channel of composition, and thus regulate the length of composition to be burnt before the communication with the bursting charge takes place. To use this fuze the only implement required is a small wrench to loosen the screw and to tighten it again after the covering plate has been set at the proper point. In trying a fuze of this kind some years ago at Washington Arsenal, it was found difficult to secure the closing of the channel by means of the movable plate, so as to produce regularity in the time of burning the fuze; the fire was apt to flash suddenly over the whole surface of the composition, and cause a premature explosion of the charge. The difficulty of making this nice adjustment of the covering plate would necessarily be still greater in the field, and it is not easy to see any advantage to recommend this modification of Bormann's fuze.

I may here mention an idea of Colonel Bormann's of using spherical case shot from mortars in the defense of fortifications, in place of stones or grenades, &c. He says that he has found by experiment that half pound balls discharged from an 8-inch shell bursting fifty or sixty feet above the ground have sufficient force to inflict a disabling wound. He uses for these shells a fuze like that for ordinary spherical case, but of larger diameter.

PART XI.

FUZES FOR COMMON SHELLS.

For mortars, and for guns and howitzers with ordinary service charges, fuzes are still made, generally in the old manner, with composition driven in a wooden case; the practice in different countries presenting only slight variations in the details of fabrication.

In *England*, Boxer's fuzes, before described, under the head of "spherical case shot" are adopted for common shells. The fuze for field service is made like that for shrapnels, except that the channel of composition is one inch longer, which gives double the time of burning—ten seconds instead of five seconds. The fuze for mortar shells is adapted to shells of all calibers, 8-inch, 10-inch, and 13-inch, by having a uniform taper on the exterior, (one tenth,) and being made short enough for the 8-inch shell, whilst the time of burning at the rate of six seconds to one inch, is sufficient for the greatest range of the 13-inch shell.

The *French* fuzes for bombs and common shells are very little changed from the former patterns. The wooden fuze case has not a uniform taper, the part which fits in the fuze-hole being more tapered than the rest of the fuze, but much less in all cases than that of the English fuzes; the taper of the fuze-holes varies from one in thirty for the 13-inch shell, to one in nineteen for the 12-pounder. Two holes, to receive strands of quick-match, are bored at right angles to each other across the cup of the fuze. The length and other dimensions of the fuzes are different for shells of different calibers, but the composition is the same for all, except the 13-inch sea-coast mortar and 12-pounder field gun, viz: mealed powder three, nitre two, sulphur one; it ought to burn one inch in 3.6 seconds. For the 13-inch heavy mortar, add one part of sulphur, which increases the time of burning to 4.3 seconds to one inch. The length of composition being 8.55 inches, the whole time of burning is thirty-six seconds, corresponding to a range of about 5,000 yards. The fuzes are not cut as formerly, but bored through with a gimlet, as practiced by us.

The fuze for shells for the new 12-pounder field gun has a priming cup or head of larger diameter than the body of the fuze. It is charged with mealed powder, driven so as to burn 2.3 seconds to one inch, which gives six seconds for the whole time of burning. The fuze is capped with paper pasted over the top, having a piece of tape under the paper to facilitate its removal. It is intended to burn always the whole length, for which purpose a gimlet hole is bored through the wood at the lower end of the composition, and the fuzes are fixed into the shells at the laboratory. As the shell is designed to produce its *explosive* effect after lodging in the object fired at, or, among troops, at the end of its flight, the difference of a few seconds in the time of explosion seems to be considered of no importance, provided that the explosion does not take place *before* the shell strikes; and this arrangement of an invariable length of fuze certainly simplifies exceedingly the use of shells in field batteries.

For *hand grenades*, the French use a fuze which is ignited by a friction primer, constructed on the same principle as the cannon friction primer; by means of a loop of small cord the primer is fired and the fuze ignited at the moment of throwing the grenade from the hand. The grenade is 3.2 inches diameter, and weighs two and a quarter pounds; the fuze burns 4.2 seconds.

The wooden fuzes used in other countries visited offer no peculiarity worthy of special remark. In the Prussian fuzes the sides of the channel for composition are roughened by little grooves cut in the wood, for the purpose of holding the composition more securely; this was formerly practiced in England, but is discontinued. In the Russian sea-coast batteries some shells were kept ready, with fuzes cut to different lengths and fixed in the shells, which were appropriately marked.

Although wooden fuzes were chiefly used on both sides in the siege of Sebastopol, some shells which had not burst were to be seen, with brass fuze plugs, which were, no doubt, English and Russian navy shells, fitted with brass fuzes on the English plan. It is well known also that both the English and French marine have *concussion shells*, designed to explode on striking the object. The construction of these shells is carefully kept secret; and as they are intended chiefly to act against shipping, the war with Russia furnished little opportunity to test their merits; but it is said that they frequently fail to explode, and that the explosion, when it does occur, is apt to take place at the very instant of impact, and, consequently, outside of the object struck.

Captain Splingard, a very clever officer of the Belgium artillery, has proposed a concussion fuze of simple construction, which appears to have succeeded remarkably well in the first experiment, and to be worthy of a careful trial. This fuze is represented, full size, in Plate 20, Fig. 5. The composition is driven in a paper case, over a spindle, which leaves a cavity (*d d*) in the center, like the bore of a rocket. The lower part of the fuze, (*f f*,) up to the top of the spindle, is filled with a slow composition, which should burn long enough for the greatest time of flight required of the shell. Over that is a solid portion of a quicker composition, (*c c*;) another still quicker, (*b b*;) and, finally, a priming of mealed powder, (*a a*.) When the fuze is drawn from the mould, the sides of the cavity in the composition are varnished with one or two coats of shellac varnish; and when this is dry, the cavity is filled with soft plaster of Paris, into which, before it sets, a needle is inserted, so as to leave a cavity (*e e*) about one tenth of an inch in diameter, around which the plaster remains one eighth or one tenth of an inch thick. This fuze cannot be driven with a mallet into the shell, for fear of breaking the tube of plaster. It is, therefore, inserted by simple pressure into the wooden case or fuze plug (Fig. 6) previously driven into the shell. The mouth of this case has a ring of cork (*m m*) surrounding the fuze, to prevent the flame of the charge from penetrating into the shell. The quickness of the compositions (*b* and *c*) in the upper part of the fuze is so regulated that they shall burn out, and also a portion of the composition, *f*, shall be consumed during the shortest time of flight that can be required. Now, when the shell is fired, the plaster tube, *d d*, being supported by the fuze composition, remains whole; but by the time the shell reaches the end of its flight the composition has burned down to a point below the head of the plaster tube, so that the latter is no longer supported; and, consequently, when the shell strikes the object, the top of the tube is broken off, and a communication opened between the burning fuze and the charge in the shell. If the tube should not be broken by the impact, the charge in the shell will still be fired when the composition has burned out.

In some trials with this fuze with a 13-inch mortar, at a range of 500 yards, it was found that of 224 shells fired, 204 exploded at the fall, thirteen after the fuze had been burnt out, two prematurely, towards the end of their flight; five did not explode, of which three fuzes did not take fire. It was found that the explosion of the shell did not occur so quickly after impact as to prevent the effect of its penetration. This remarkable success shows that this fuze is worthy of full trial, if it should even be adapted only to mortar and howitzer practice. It probably would not withstand, with the same success, the test of firing heavy guns with high charges.

Colonel Bormann thinks that his fuzes are applicable to common shells, even for mortars, by charging them with slower composition, and by enlarging the diameter of the fuze, so as to increase the length of the circular channel for composition.

The objection to the use of the slow composition is the uncertainty of its ignition, when so small a space is open to the action of the charge as in the Bormann fuze. Another method may be suggested for effecting the same object: to attach to the lower side of the fuze (or to the interior iron screw plug used for closing the fuze hole in Siemens's method) a short tube filled with fuze composition, which shall burn during the shortest time of flight that can be required for a common shell, say two or three seconds. By this means, the whole time of burning may be extended to seven or eight seconds, and the scale on the outside of the fuze may be used to graduate it for the longer ranges.

PART XII.

SMALL ARMS.

RUSSIA.

The small arms used in the Russian army appear to be all made after models selected from those of other countries. The great body of infantry is armed with the smooth-bore musket, being either a new percussion musket or a flint-lock musket altered to percussion, according to the method used in France and Belgium. The caliber of the arm is the same as ours, being the caliber of eighteen to the pound, generally used on the continent of Europe before the recent adoption of the rifle system. The pattern of the Russian musket also is essentially the same as our own; but the new percussion arms have back-action locks. (See Besvoy's Artillery, Plate XXI, and Bessel's Course of Artillery, Plates XV and XVI, for drawings of these arms.) The musket has a fixed guide on the tang of the breech screw, and the front sight is placed on the barrel, below the upper band or between the two straps of that band, and not on the band itself. The usual ammunition for the smooth-bore musket is the round ball; but of late much use has been made of the Belgian projectile known as the "Nessler" ball. This is of cylindro-spherical form, the cylinder being very short. (Plate 21, Fig. 1.) The ball is hollow at the base, to make it expand, and has a projecting point in the bottom of the cavity. Its weight is 464 grains. It is said, both in Russia and in France, where this ball has also been tried, that by the use of it the smooth-bore musket has an accurate and efficient range of 300 or 400 yards, or at least double that given by the spherical ball. The cartridge is made in the usual way as for round balls, and the ball part of it is dipped into melted tallow, the ball being inserted into the gun with the paper with which it is wrapped. Many of the percussion muskets have been rifled, by cutting in them four wide grooves, as in the French musket and ours. The ball used for these altered arms is of cylindro-conical form; also on the Belgian system, with a projecting point in the cavity at the base, (Plate 21, Fig. 2,) and having three grooves cut on the cylindrical part. Its weight is 755 grains. Colonel Huger, of the Ordnance Department, tried, in his experiments at Harper's Ferry Armory, a ball of the same form, with this interior point, not knowing that it had been tried in Belgium; but the comparative results obtained by him did not appear to warrant the adoption of this more complicated form of the ball. Rifle muskets are also made on the same plan.

Besides this rifled musket, the Russian chasseurs and riflemen are armed with rifles of several kinds. Some have the French well-known "*Carabine à tige*," with a ball also of the pattern used in France. Others have a rifle made on the model of the English two-grooved rifle, known as the Brunswick rifle. These arms are made, like many of the Russian small arms at Liege, in Belgium, exactly on the English model; but instead of the belted round ball (Fig. 3) used in England, with very unsatisfactory results, the Russians use an ogival ball, weighing 787 grains, (Figs. 4 and 5,) having two projections, which fit into the grooves, very nearly on the plan which has been tried, with success, for rifled cannon. There can be no doubt that this large-bore rifle, loaded with a ball of this kind, is effective at a very great range, as appears to have been proved by experience in the Crimea. We found on the field of Inkerman Russian balls of each of the kinds above described, and we heard, in the English camp, of a man having been killed (an accidental shot, no doubt) by a rifle ball at 1,500 yards from the nearest Russian battery. The particular kind of ball was not stated. The high sites for these arms of long range are either *leaf sites*, which fold down on the barrel, or a simple hinged-sight, which gives the required elevation by being placed at a suitable angle with the barrel.

The Russian dragoon soldier serves in the manner in which that kind of force was originally designed to act, being transported on horseback, but fighting on foot. He is therefore armed with a musket similar to that of the infantry, but a few inches shorter in the barrel, for the convenience of carrying it when mounted. The other regular cavalry troops have short musketoons, or carbines which are rifled; they are furnished with swivel bars like our own. The rammers of the rifled carbines are carried separately, suspended to the accouterments. The pistol rammer is carried in the same manner, the arm itself being of the ordinary kind, of the same caliber as the musket. In the arsenals we saw cavalry carbines and wall pieces made to load at the breech, with a movable chamber, exactly after the model adopted in France in 1831, but very soon abandoned there. No breech-loading arms appear to be used by the troops. The fire-arms of the irregular cavalry present the same variety as the clothing and other equipments. Some of them carry the long-barreled piece which is commonly used in the East; but most of them use a short carbine, which can be more conveniently slung over the shoulder and unslung on horseback; these and their pistols are usually highly ornamented according to Oriental custom. But the Cossacks of the Guard and other disciplined troops of this class use the fire-arms of the regular cavalry.

The percussion caps of the Russian military fire-arms are, like ours, of the size and kind adopted, with very slight variation, by all European nations. These are made at a special establishment near St. Petersburg, with machinery furnished by Mr. Falisse, of Liege, who is well known for having set up similar manufactories for several other governments in Europe. It may be remarked here, that as much attention was given to this branch of manufacture by Major Hagner, of the Ordnance Department, in his late visit to Europe, and as the business is well understood and successfully pursued at our arsenals, we did not think it necessary to devote any time to this special subject.

Swords and Sabers.—In the guards and grenadier corps every infantry soldier wears a sword; in the line, only the non-commissioned officers. The infantry sword is a light curved saber, with a leather scabbard, exactly like the "briquet" formerly used by the French infantry. But we were informed that the foot artillery sword like ours will also be worn by the infantry. The horse artillery saber is of the same pattern as ours, but with a leather scabbard. Some batteries however use the light cavalry saber, which is also nearly of the same pattern as our cavalry saber. The saber of the heavy cavalry is straight, with a wide, ribbed blade, and a guard of four branches. The dragoon saber is nearly of the same pattern as that of the horse artillery, but the blade is a little wider; the scabbard is of leather, and the rings by which it is suspended are fastened to the convex edge of the scabbard, instead of the concave edge as usual. The object of this arrangement appears to be to cause the hilt and guard of the saber to hang towards the rear, more out of the way of the wearer's left arm. The Cossack saber is similar to the dragoon saber, but longer, and without a guard. It has a leather scabbard, which is suspended by two rings—one attached to the inner flat side of the upper band or mouth piece, the other to the middle band on the convex edge of the scabbard. These leather scabbards are lined throughout with wood, being in fact wooden scabbards covered with leather.

Mounted officers generally wear sabers with steel scabbards. Infantry and other foot officers wear a light and slightly curved saber, with a leather scabbard. The lance is carried by the Cossacks, and also by the front rank men of the heavy cavalry.

The Russian small arms are not browned for service; the mountings are usually of brass, except those of the musket for the infantry of the line. The cuirasses for the cavalry are of bright steel, or brass plated, or black, for different corps; but they are to be hereafter all black. The mode adopted for altering muskets from flint to percussion, is similar to that used in France and Belgium; putting a rounded cone seat on the top of the barrel, into which the cone is screwed, and making the necessary alteration in the lock nearly in the same manner as in our altered arms. It does not appear that there is any question at present of adopting or trying a new or smaller caliber for small arms in Russia. Russian officers are now in the United States to procure machinery for making rifle-muskets of the same caliber as those now in use, to carry the grooved Belgian ball above mentioned.

PRUSSIA.

A great part of the infantry of the line (two battalions in each regiment) and the landwehr regiments are armed with the smooth-bore musket, altered from flint to percussion, or with the new percussion smooth-bore musket. The alteration of the flint musket is made by inserting a cylindrical cone seat, screwed into the barrel, perpendicular to its axis, in the place of the old vent; this cone seat is bored through its axis, and the outer end of the opening stopped with a screw; the cone is inserted in the top of this cylinder; the lock is altered in the usual manner; a guide or rear sight is fixed to the tang of the breech-pin; the front sight is on the upper band. The bayonet of this musket is fastened on by a spring and catch. The mountings are of brass.

The new percussion musket (model of 1839) is similar to the above, with these exceptions: it has a "patent breech," (so called,) that is to say, a breech piece with a conical chamber, having the cone seat formed out of the same piece of metal, but placed on the right hand side of the barrel, (Plate 3, Fig. 3,) so that the hammer requires to be very little bent in order to strike the cone. The priming canal is pierced through the cone seat perpendicular to the barrel, and the outer end closed with a screw as in the altered musket. The whole arrangement of the breech piece is nearly the same that has been adopted for the alteration of our musket as recently arranged for Maynard's primer. The front sight is brazed on the barrel, and the lower strap of the upper band is cut so as to pass over the sight. The mountings are of brass, except the butplate, which is of iron; the caliber is the same as that of our smooth-bore muskets; the weight of the arm is ten and one third pounds. These new muskets were said to be in process of alteration to rifle muskets.

The wall piece (*Defensions-gewehr*) is the new percussion musket rifled, with four grooves, of the same width as the lands, having a twist of five feet; a tige 0.3 inch diameter and 1.85 inch long is screwed into the chambered breech; leaf sights are placed on the barrel (one inch from the breech) marked for ranges up to 600 paces, equal to 500 yards. The weight of the cylindroconical ball is 483 grains; the charge of powder 100 grains.

One battalion of each regiment of infantry of the line, and all the infantry of the guards, are armed with—

The needle gun, (*Zundnädel-gewehr*.) Although it is endeavored to make a secret in Prussia of the construction of this arm, it is well known in other countries; it is described in several published books, and specimens of it are to be had in Liege, in New York, and in many other places. It is sufficient, therefore, to say here that it is an arm which is loaded at the breech with a cartridge in which the ball, the powder, and the priming, are all united together by means of a paper "*sabot.*" The charge is fired by a *needle*, which is acted on by a spiral spring, and which, after passing through the charge, pierces a small lozenge of friction priming placed in the rear of the paper sabot, and thus sets fire to the charge of powder at its forward end. The barrel is thirty-six inches long, and the bore 0.62 inch in diameter; there are four grooves having a twist of one turn in twenty-nine inches. The charge is fifty-six grains, or about one-eighth the weight of the conical ball. This arm is highly approved by the Prussian officers with whom we conversed respecting it, and it is understood that the use of it will be extended in their army; but they have had no opportunity of trying it in actual service, except on a small scale in the Schleswig-Holstein war. Its complicated structure, and other objections, seem to have prevented it from finding favor in any other country; even so far as to cause a trial of the arm to be made on any considerable scale (so far as we are informed) out of Prussia.

The rifle, with which the battalions of riflemen, (Jäger,) except those of the guard, are armed, is constructed on the "tige" system of Colonel Thouvenin; the barrel is octagonal, 27.6 inches long; it has eight grooves with a twist of thirty-six inches; a patent breech, with a conical chamber, like that of the new percussion musket described above, (Plate 3, Fig. 3;) in the center of this chamber is screwed the "tige," 0.27 inch diameter and 1.7 inch long. The lock has a *hair trigger*, and a *safety cap* for the cone, which is kept in place by a spring, like the battery spring of the old flint lock, and must be turned forward, off the cone, when firing. The rear sight is placed six inches from the breech of the barrel; it is made with several hinged leaves, which are marked for ranges up to 700 paces, or about 600 yards. The barrel is fastened to the stock with two loops and slides. The mountings are of brass. It has a sword bayonet twenty-two inches long.

The cavalry fire-arms offer nothing remarkable. In the dragoons and hussars twenty-four men in each squadron carry a short rifle, which weighs about six pounds; the rest of the men carry a smooth-bore carbine or musketoon, weighing about five pounds. Both of these arms are of old patterns, altered to percussion; they are suspended by swivel bars and rings, and the muzzle is carried in a boot attached by a strap to the saddle. The rammer is hung to the shoulder belt. *The pistol* has a smooth bore. The cavalry arms are nearly of the same caliber as the needle gun; spherical balls are used with them.

The *artillery* have no small fire-arms. The *pioneers* have a musketoon of old pattern altered to percussion. The musket cartridges are made like ours, by enveloping the powder and ball in the same paper, and tying them with thread.

Side arms.—The heavy cavalry wear a straight saber (blade thirty-seven inches long) with steel scabbard; the light cavalry (dragoons, lancers, hussars) and the mounted artillery wear a curved saber (blade thirty-two inches long) with a plain guard and steel scabbard. Foot officers of all corps wear a light, straight sword, with leather scabbard, suspended generally to a shoulder belt, worn under the coat. Foot artillery men and pioneers have a short, straight sword, lighter and longer than our foot artillery sword. The infantry saber is now like the Russian, or the old French "briquet;" a light curved saber (blade sixteen inches long) with leather scabbard and brass mountings; but the same pattern has been adopted for the infantry as for the foot artillery and other foot troops.

AUSTRIA.

In Austria the greater part of the foot troops are still armed with the smooth-bore musket, altered from flint to percussion, and adapted to a peculiar kind of priming. This priming consists of percussion powder placed in a copper tube of such size that it can be introduced into the vent of the flint musket. Thus inserted, the primer lies in the groove of an iron seat which is substituted for the pan of the old musket; it is there protected by a cover which corresponds to the lower part of the flint "battery," and is held down by the battery spring; the percussion hammer, substituted for the flint cock, strikes on the top of this cover, and causes a point which projects from the cover into the pan to strike the tube of percussion powder, and thus fires the charge.

The non-commissioned officers and some of the men in each company of infantry are armed with rifles of the same caliber as the musket, (0.7 inch diameter of bore.) This rifle is constructed on the Delvigne plan; the ball resting on the mouth of a cham████████ is expanded by a blow from a heavy rammer.

But new models have been recently adopted for the arms of ███ infantry and riflemen, which are now in the course of fabrication for the use of all the troops. Samples of these arms have been kindly furnished us by the Austrian government. The bore of the new arm is 0.55 inch in diameter, being somewhat smaller than the new calibers adopted in England and the United States. The musket barrel is thirty-seven and a half inches long; it is rifled with four grooves which make half a turn in the length of the barrel; the width of the grooves is the same as that of the lands; they are cut by machinery to a uniform ██pth, 0.025 inch, but the depth of the grooves and diameter of the bore are slightly increased by hand work, in a length of six inches at the breech end. The lock is of the usual kind for percussion arms, (front action,) and is the same for all the new arms; the cone and the percussion cap are substituted for the former peculiar (*Consol*) system of priming. The *lock-plate* and the *bridle* are made of *cast-iron annealed*, ("malleable iron.") The mountings are of iron; the upper band is made with a pipe for the rammer, and it has b██ one broad strap, the upper part of which ██ ██ slit cut in it to facilitate its passing over the s████. The sight is on the barrel above the ba████ the base of the sight is the bayonet stud. The ████onet, about n██ ██ inches long, has a rib on the inside of the blade as well as on the b██████ slit in the sock████ the stud is cut *spirally*, so that the bayonet makes a quarter of a turn as it goes on the b██████ which it is fastened by a ring clasp. The rammer has a swell near the head, as in our new rifle-musket, in place of a rod spring; the head of the rammer is countersunk to fit the form of the ball, and it has a hole through it to assist in drawing a ball, &c. The ball-screw (Plate 3, Fig. 4) has a brass cylinder screwed on its stem as a guide to keep it steady on the point of the ball. Weight of musket and bayonet about ten and a quarter pounds. Muskets are made with ██ kinds of rear sights; most of them have a simple fixed sight placed five inches from ██ar end of the barrel, adapted to a range of about 250 yards; these are intended for the ██ of the front and middle ranks of infantry of the line. The other rifle muskets have an e████████ ight; which turns down on the barrel, and has several notches for ranges up to 1,000 p██████ yards.) These are intended for arming the non-commissioned ██████ and the third rank █████ or sharp-shooters.

T██ *rifle* barrel is ██ty-eight inches long; it is octagonal on the exterior, and is grooved ██ principle █████ musket; but there are also two kinds of rifles. Those for arming ██████ missioned officers and the third or rear-rank men of the rifle battalions (Jäger) are m██████ "tige" in the breech-pin; those for the men of the front and middle ranks have no "tig███." The two rifles are alike in other respects and have the same kind of sight, being that which is known as the *Minié* ██ght. It is a piece of iron, bent into an arc of a circle, which slides in a curved seat on the top of the barrel, in the direction of the length of the barrel, and can thus be held by a th██ screw at any desired elevation. It is marked for distances up to 1,200 paces, (1,000 ya██ ██ he barrel is bright.

██████ barrel is connected with the stock by loops and slides, without bands. The ██████ of bright iron; the bayonet is made with a socket like that of the musket, and ██████ barrel in the same manner; but the blade is shaped like a straight sword, two ██████ rammer is made with a wooden handle; it is not attached to the rifle, but is ██████ately, suspended to the soldier's belt. The weight of the rifle is nearly the same as that of the musket.

The *carbine* for sappers and special corps is similar to the rifle; the barrel is twenty-six inches long.

A *rifle pistol* is on trial, but has not yet been definitively adopted.* The barrel is ten and a qu██ ██ inches long, and we were told that the twist of the grooves is three quarters of a turn i██ ██ gth of the barrel. It was proposed to make this pistol serve also as a carbine for ██████. For this purpose a detached stock was arranged to be connected with the pistol stock proper, by means of a [illegible] and catch, in the manner that has been adopted for our pistol. By this arrangement the [illegible] would be habitually carried in the holster, and the detached stock or but-piece alone suspended to the shoulder belts by a ring and swivel.

The same *projectile* is used for all these new arms, either with or without the "tige." It is the ball proposed by Mr. Wilkinson, of London, and tried, among others, by an English commission, at Enfield, in 1852. The form is cylindro-ogival, with two deep grooves in the cylindrical part, and no cavity in the base, (Plate 21, Fig. 6;) weight 450 grains. The charge of powder (musket grain) is sixty-two grains for the musket or rifle—the cartridge being the same for both—and forty grains for the pistol. The ball is enveloped with thin paper forming the outer covering of the cartridge, which is greased in the part round the ball, and is inserted with the ball in loading. The case for the powder is made of a cylinder of stiff paper (thin pasteboard) enveloped with a covering of thin cartridge paper, which is folded over one end of the case. The point of the ball is inserted into the lower end of this cylinder, and the whole is enveloped again in thin paper. A new ball of this form is also used for the altered musket of the former caliber; weight of ball 680 grains; charge of powder fifty-five grains.

The *cavalry saber* is the same for heavy and light cavalry. A sample of this was also furnished to us by the Austrian government. It has a curved blade thirty-three and a half inches long, a steel scabbard, guard and mountings of iron.

The *artillery saber* is similar to the cavalry, but lighter, and with a simpler guard. The artillery men carry no fire-arms; sixteen carbines are furnished to each battery for guard duty; on the march they are carried in one of the wagons.

FRANCE.

The small arms used in the French army having generally been taken as patterns for those of our own troops, are so well known as to render unnecessary a particular description of them, except with regard to recent alterations and experiments. The [illegible] body of infantry of the line are still armed with the simple percussion musket, (new or altered from flint-lock,) and use the spherical ball. The caliber of this musket has been lately increased to 0.708 inch, and the old arms have been reamed out to correspond with the new one, carrying a round ball of one ounce; but this change is regretted on account of the increased difficulty of altering the arms to the muskets for carrying the elongated balls now generally adopted. This alteration has, however, been made in some of the muskets by inserting a "tige" in the breech pin, and cutting four broad and shallow grooves in the barrel, adding a high sight graduated up to 800 meters. The grooves, which are of equal width with the bands, are 0.02 inch deep at the breech, diminishing to 0.004 inch at the muzzle; the twist is one turn in two meters, or about six and a half feet. The ball weighs seven hundred and twenty grains, and the charge of musket powder is seventy grains. This arm was used by the infantry of the guard (Zouaves) in the Crimea. An old soldier said that the recoil was not inconveniently great. The infantry of the Imperial Guard are armed with a rifled musket like the above, but without the "tige." The ball for this is cylindro-conical, with a cavity at the base, but without a "culot" or expanding [illegible] 21, Fig. 7.)

The Chasseurs are armed with the "*Carabine à tige*," which is constructed on the principle as the "tige" musket above mentioned. The barrel is thirty-four inches long, and the ball and the charge are the same as for the musket. The sight is graduated to 1,200 meters.

These are the only rifled arms, on a new system, which were used by the French troops in the Crimea. They appear to have given satisfactory results as to range and efficiency. The "tige" system has been extensively tried also in other countries in Europe, and is still used by several of them as above stated. But the practical objection to the use of the "tige" is the difficulty of cleaning the chamber, and the uncertainty of effect resulting from its being [illegible] have caused experiments to be made in France, as elsewhere, for substituting some other method of expanding the ball, which shall give the advantages without the inconveniences of this plan. For this purpose experiments are now in progress on a large scale at Vincennes, at the school of infantry practice, under the direction of Mr. Minié, instructor of the school, to ascertain the best form of ball to be used with the rifled musket and the "carabineel" without the "tige." At the time of our visit to Vincennes, three kinds of cylindro-conical balls were under trial. First, the Minié ball, properly so called, (Plate 1, Fig. 8,) having two grooves in the cylindrical part, and an iron cup (culot) in the cavity of the base—weight 604 grains. Second, the new ball of the Imperial Guard, having one large groove and a large cavity (Fig. 7) in the base, without any cup or wedge—weight 535 grains. Third, a ball on the system of Colonel Timmerhans, of Belgium, (like Fig. 2,) having one square groove, and a point projecting into the cavity of the base—weight 583 grains. These balls are all enveloped with the paper of the cartridge, which is greased and inserted with the ball. Mr. Minié thought that, so far as the trials had gone, the best results had been obtained with the first ball; but the second ball had also proved very satisfactory, and recommended itself by simplicity of form and manufacture. The musketoon, it was said, can be fired with this last ball and a charge of seventy grains of powder; but the recoil is too great. For the musketoon altered "à la tige," the charge is forty-six grains.

Experiments have been made in firing the "Nessler" ball, (Plate 21, Fig. 1,) from the smooth-bore musket, with good results up to 400 yards; this ball weighs 464 grains, and the charge of powder eighty-five grains; the paper around the ball is greased and inserted with the ball.

No alteration has been made in the arms for cavalry. It is expected that all the troops will be furnished with rifled arms, when the best kind of ball is determined; but the question of a general alteration (reduction) in the caliber of the arms does not seem to be at present entertained, owing perhaps to the existence of an immense number of arms of the present pattern.

The only arm of a new caliber, which has been recently introduced into the French service, is that of the special corps called "Cent Gardes," destined for service in the Emperor's Palace. This mounted corps is armed with a rifle-carbine, which is loaded at the breech. The arm is of very small caliber, the diameter of the bore being 0.36 inch, which corresponds to a round ball of 100 to the pound; the barrel is thirty-one and a half inches long, and is rifled with five grooves, making one turn in the length of the barrel. The ball, which is cylindro-conical and grooved, is very long in proportion to its diameter; its charge of powder, about thirty grains, is attached to the ball, and is covered at the rear end by a copper cap containing the priming. The breech-loading arrangement is somewhat similar to that of Sharp's carbine; the rear of the barrel is closed by a sliding breech-piece, which moves in a vertical groove, and is held in place by the action of the trigger guard, which forms also the lock spring. By drawing down the front end of the guard, the breech is opened for the insertion of the charge, and the piece is cocked at the same time; when the spring is released, by drawing the trigger, the breech-piece flies up, explodes the priming, and at the same time closes the breech. This carbine is furnished with a slender sword bayonet, forty inches long, with which it forms a lance seven and a half feet long. The weight of the arm, without the bayonet, is about seven pounds.

This breech-loading arrangement appears to act well, as it may in an arm of so small a caliber and charge, used only under cover of a roof; but it would not seem to be adapted to use in the ordinary vicissitudes of military service. However, M. Truille, chef d'escadron d'artillerie, proposes to make arms for the general service on the same plan, and he showed us some specimens of them which he had tried. He proposes to make barrels of different lengths, according to the service required,) of the same caliber as above; to rifle them with four grooves, having always one turn in the length of the barrel; to use a very long grooved ball, (weighing about 180 grains,) with a charge of two grammes, equal to thirty-one grains. He says that a ball of this kind penetrates, at twenty paces, through a cuirass which has been proved in the ordinary manner; that it has a range of 600 meters, (656 yards,) with an ordinary sight, and an extreme range of 2,000 meters, (2,186 yards.)

GREAT BRITAIN.

The system of small arms for the British army has, within a few years, undergone a great change. In 1840, the only rifled arm used in that service was the two-grooved gun, known as the "Brunswick rifle," from which a round, belted ball was fired. In 1851, a rifled musket was adopted, and a considerable number (28,000) of this arms were ordered for issue to the troops. This musket was of the old calibre 0.702 inch; the barrel was rifled with four grooves, having half a turn in the length of the barrel. The ball adopted was on the Minié system, (Plate 21, Fig. 9,) having an iron cup in the cavity of the base, but without exterior grooves—weight 680 grains—charge of powder sixty-eight grains. On account of the great weight of this arm and ammunition, and the consequent difficulty of the soldiers carrying the requisite number of sixty rounds, further experiments were made, with a view to adopting a lighter caliber. For this purpose a commission of officers, and the government manufactory of arms, at Enfield, in 1852, for the comparative trial of many kinds of rifled arms, offered by different manufacturers, which are described in their published report. These experaments resulted in the adoption of the "*Enfield musket*," which is now in the course of manufacture for general use in the infantry. One of these muskets has been furnished to our Ordnance Department, through the kindness of Colonel Burn, R. A., one of the commission of officers who recently visited the United States for the purpose of examining our armories and machine.shops, &c.

This musket has a barrel thirty-nine inches long, with a bore of 0.577 inch; it is rifled with three grooves, which have a twist of six and a half feet or half a turn in the length of a barrel; the grooves are 0.014 inch deep at the breech, diminishing to 0.004 inch (scarcely perceptible) at the muzzle. In the arms, made by contract, at Birmingham, the depth of the grooves is uniform; the contractors having no machinery adapted to cutting grooves of increasing depth. New and neat patterns are adopted for the details of this musket; most of the mountings are of iron, and, like the barrel, are all browned or blued. The barrel and stock are connected by bands, instead of, as formerly, by loops and slides; the bayonet is fastened to the barrel, with a clasp ring, instead of the spring hook used in the old musket. The front sight is placed on the barrel, and its base is the bayonet stud; the rear sight is made with a slider adapted for ranges up to 800 yards; it is supported in an upright position, by a spring, which allows it to fall either to the front or rear, so as to prevent it from being injured by a blow. In the first pattern, the rammer was made with a swell near the head, which, coming below the cap of the stock, held the rod in its place, by pressing it against the cap and the upper band; but objections have been found to this arrangement, as the rod is apt to be held too tight or to become loose in consequence of the swelling or shrinking of the stock. The form of the rammer has been changed to a regular taper, as represented in Plate 21, Fig. 14, and a rod spring has been placed in the stock; this spring has a roller in it, to prevent it from bruising the thread at the lower end of the rammer, (Fig. 13.) The head of the new rammer is arranged for holding a wiping rag, to clean the barrel.

The ball at first adopted for the Enfield musket was similar to the one known as the "Pritchet ball," (Plate 21, Fig. 10,) having a cavity in the base, but no expanding cup or wedge. This ball weighs 525 grains, and the charge of powder sixty-eight grains; the cartridge is made in a similar manner to that for the French tige and Minié arms; but the cases, instead of being rolled, are formed of paper pulp; the greased paper is inserted into the barrel, with the ball. A considerable number of the arms and cartridges were sent to the army in the Crimea, and were issued to some of the troops just before the assault on Sebastopol, of the 18th June, 1855. Partly, perhaps, for want of proper instruction of the men in their use; partly, also, from a want of accurate adaptation in the size of the ball to that of the bore. The trial of these muskets in service was attended with some embarrassment; it was found that the barrel became foul after a few rounds, great difficulty occurred in loading, and a new ball has been adopted, which is on the Minié system; but the expanding wedge is a conical plug of wood, instead of the cup of sheet iron, (Plate 21, Fig. 11.) The trials of this ball, at the school of infantry practice, at Hythe, are said to be highly satisfactory; but they had not been received by the troops in the Crimea at the time of our leaving there. The ball weighs 525 grains—charge of powder sixty-eight grains.

A new *rifle* has been also adopted, the construction of which differs but little from that of the musket. The barrel is thirty-four inches long, and the trigger-plate, the but-plate, and the cap of the stock, are made of "malleable iron" blued. These *trigger plates* sometimes break in case hardening, and it is thought they will have to be made of wrought iron. The bands are made of wrought iron, or low steel, blued. The upper swivel is attached to the upper band, and the lower swivel to the wood screw which passes through the lower end of the guard-plate. The charge of the rifle is the same as that of the musket. A *carbine* for the artillery has been made, on the same system as the musket and rifle, with a twenty-four inch barrel, and a sword bayonet; the charge for this arm is fifty-five grains. The new *sapper's carbine* is made on the Lancaster system; having an elliptical bore which is twisted with a "gaining twist," *i. e.*, a twist which increases from the breech to the muzzle. Experience in service has not yet tested the advantages or disadvantages of this system of military small arms.

For *the cavalry*, Colt's revolver and Deane and Adams' revolver have been extensively purchased. The Deane and Adam's revolver is a well-known pistol, chiefly in the mechanism, by which the simple pulling of the trigger causes the chambered breech to revolve, and cocks and discharges the piece at the same time. The workmanship of the pistol is very good, and the arm appears to have met with much favor; but it still wants the test of actual service, and it may be doubted whether it is expedient to arm any part of the troops with a weapon which can be discharged with such exceeding facility and rapidity. It is understood that some of these pistols have been ordered by the Ordnance Department, for trial in our service; at present, they are sold at about two thirds of the cost of Colt's revolver. A specimen of this arm has been procured by the commission from Francotte, one of the principal manufacturers of arms at Liege, in Belgium.

MISCELLANEOUS.

The Sardinian infantry of the line is armed at present chiefly with the smooth-bore musket, but some of them have a rifle-musket made like the French musket, "à tige," and having a similar ball and cartridge.

The arm of the *Sardinian riflemen (Bersaglieri)* is a chambered rifle on the Delvigne system; the barrel is about thirty-inches long, and is rifled with eight grooves, making one turn in fifty-three inches. The ball is cylindro-conical, without grooves.

The Norwegian rifle, adopted also, with some slight modification, for the navy in Sweden, is a breech-loading arm. It has a movable chamber, like Hall's rifle, which is raised by means of a side lever; the axis on which this lever and the chamber turn carries a cam or eccentric, by means of which the shoulder at the front end of the chamber is pressed up into the barrel. The cone for a common percussion cap is on the under side of the chamber, and the lock consists of a simple hammer pressed by an exterior circular spring. The ball is cylindro-ogival, having one broad groove in which the paper of the cartridge is tied.

One of these rifles has been procured at Liege, merely as a sample of an arm adopted for service. The arrangement of the mechanism does not appear to be as neat or as advantageous as that of some of the breech-loading arms which have been invented in the United States; and its principal feature, the letting in of the chamber into the barrel, has been tried without success both in this country and in France. It has thus far always been found impracticable to prevent the escape of gas at the joint between the chamber and barrel, and the obstruction of this joint by the deposit from the powder of the charge, and by other causes.

The rifled arms used in the *Belgian* army are the *rifled musket* with the Minié or Timmerhans ball, and the *carabine à tige*, with sword bayonet, both of the same patterns as the French arms. A rifled pistol is also on trial, but not yet adopted.

The *Timmerhans ball* (Plate 21, Fig. 2) is cylindro-ogival, and grooved, with a bell-shaped cavity in the base, into which a point projects from the bottom of the cavity; it is essentially the same form that has been since tried in the experiments of Colonel Huger, at Harper's Ferry. Mr. Francotte, manufacturer of arms at Liege, proposes a new arrangement for loading at the breech, which has been mentioned with approbation by experienced officers. In this plan the rear end of the barrel is closed by a *piston breech-piece*, as in Jenks's rifle and some others in America. The chamber in the barrel is long enough to contain two balls, with one charge of powder. The powder lies between the two balls, one being in front and one resting on the breech-pin in rear; when the piece is fired, the latter ball is pressed against the breech-pin, and thus forms a sort of valve to prevent the escape of gas; by a motion of the piston the ball is then pushed forward, and another charge is inserted behind it.

In Saxony, the "tige" system was at first adopted for rifled arms. The *rifle* has a "patent breech," with the tige screwed into the bottom of the chamber, as in the Prussian arms described above. In the *rifle musket*, the "tige" was screwed into the ordinary breech-pin. In the new model, however, the tige is suppressed, and the ball is expanded by the action of the powder. The caliber of this arm is 0.577 inch; the barrel is 40.4 inches long; it has four grooves, the twist of which is 64½ inches. The ball is pointed, (Plate 21, Fig. 12;) it has one deep groove, and no cavity in the base; it weighs 418 grains, and the charge of powder is 80 grains. The sights are graduated up to 600 paces, (about 500 yards.) The cartridges are made as usual for these balls, with an inner case of stiff paper for the powder, which is wrapped, with the ball, in thin paper. The outer wrapper is greased around the ball, and inserted with it in loading.

In Switzerland, the latest pattern of rifle adopted for the military service, (1853,) a sample of which is in the possession of the Ordnance Department, is of very small caliber; the diameter of the bore is 0.414 inch; length of barrel, thirty-two inches; it has eight round grooves with a twist of three feet; the breech is made with a chamber of the same diameter as the bore. The ball is cylindro-ogival, with slight grooves; it is used with a greased patch, or wrapped in greased paper. The ball weighs 240 grains, and the charge of powder sixty-two grains, or one fourth the weight of the ball. The rear sight is hinged, and is held at any required point by a thumb-screw; it is graduated to 1,000 paces, (about 830 yards.) A swell or shoulder on the ramrod prevents the ball from being pressed on the powder, and leaves a space of about one fifth of an inch between the powder and the ball.

Mr. Francotte, at Liege, mentioned as worthy of notice a new Swiss rifle, of Mr. Prélat, the principle of which was said to be applicable, in a very simple manner, to the alteration of smooth-bore arms. This new invention was not yet made known, as patents were to be taken out for it both in Europe and in this country; but through the kindness of Mr. F. we obtained a report of a trial of one of these rifles by a commission of officers, at Vincennes, which appears to be worthy of insertion here on account of the good results obtained in the practice at great ranges.

REPORT OF TRIAL OF SWISS RIFLE, NORMAL SCHOOL OF (INFANTRY) PRACTICE.

In pursuance of the orders of the Minister of War, dated 17th November, 1855, the commission of the Normal School of Practice met on the 19th November, to make a preliminary trial of the rifle offered by Mr. Prélat, gunmaker of Verez, and Colonel Burnand, of the Federal (Swiss) artillery. [The weights and measures are converted to English measures.] It was agreed between these gentlemen and the commission that the rifle should be fired—

     10 rounds at 300 meters, = 328 yards.
     10 rounds at 600 meters, = 656 yards.
     10 rounds at 900 meters, = 984 yards.
     20 rounds at 1,200 meters, = 1,312 yards.

The practice ground was not placed at our disposal until half past one, P. M., and the weather being cloudy, Mr. Prélat requested that he might begin with the greatest distance, which was agreed to. The target was twenty-six feet long and thirteen feet high, with a black center three and one fourth feet square.

The rifle was always aimed at the center of the target. At the beginning of the trial the wind was from the right and rear; at the close, from the rear direct.

The firing was off-hand. Mr. Prélat fired at 1,200, 900, and 600 meters; Colonel Burnand at 300 meters. When the last shots were fired at 300 meters, it was difficult, on account of darkness, to distinguish the bull's eye.

The rifle was of the caliber of 0.472 inch; but as Mr. Prélat held it constantly in his hands, the conjectures of the commission with regard to its mechanism are too vague to be mentioned. The only facts ascertained are: that the ball is enveloped in a patch, with which it fits close to the bore at the muzzle. The patch is not greased, but is wet with saliva just before it is inserted. When once entered its whole length in the barrel, the ball is pushed down easily to within 0.4 inch of the powder; and when it has reached that point, it requires a strong pressure to drive it home. The ball is exactly like the English ball, [the Pritchett ball?] and it weighs 431 grains, (nearly one ounce.) The charge of powder is 108 grains, or one fourth the weight of the ball. The rifle was loaded by first putting in the powder with a graduated charge; then the ball, with its patch, was driven down with a wooden rammer, having a brass head countersunk to fit the ball.

Common percussion caps were used for firing; and the exterior of the piece presented nothing remarkable.

Observations made at the Target.

At 1,300 yards: the ball reached the target one second after the report of the gun was heard. It passed through the board, and seemed to have a considerable velocity remaining when it struck the butt of earth behind. The holes made by the ball were perfectly round at this distance, as well as at all the others.

At 984 yards: the ball struck the target less than one second after the report of the piece.

At 656 yards: the ball and the report reached the target together.

At 328 yards: the ball and the report arrived together; and the ball had so great a velocity that it was scarcely heard to strike the target, which was not shaken by the blow. The examination of some balls which were taken out of the butt offered nothing remarkable.

VINCENNES, *November* 21, 1855.

Members of the Commission.

Minié, Chef de Battalion, Instructor of the School; Cap de Vielle, Captain, Assistant Instructor; Lacroix, Lieutenant Colonel, Commandant of the School; R. Maldan, Captain of Artillery, Recorder.

Extract from the tabular statement of shots.

	1,312	984	656	328
Distance in yards				
	Inches.	Inches.	Inches.	Inches.
Hausse measured from the bottom of the notch to the upper surface of the barrel	1.97	1.61	0.654	0.276
Mean deviation of ball from axis of target, horizontal	41	41	5.12	3.94
Mean deviation of ball from axis of target, vertical	44	44	8.27	21.26
Mean absolute deviation, with reference to the center of target	113		42.24	24.10
Mean absolute deviation, with reference to the center of impact	53	59	40.16	12.06
Radius of the circle containing the best half of the shots, from center of target	104	51	40.16	22.05
Radius of the circle containing the best half of the shots, from center of impact	60	53	40.16	11.42

At the distance of 1,312 yards, sixteen shots in ——— contained in a circle of ninety-seven inches radius, taking the mean of the points ——— center.

Table of Rifled Small Arms.

The following table presents a synopsis of the peculiarities of the rifled arms introduced within a few years into the military service of several of the principal powers of Europe. The particulars of the new-pattern arms recently adopted in the United States have been added to this table, for the purpose of comparison.

TABLE OF RIFLED SMALL ARMS

THE ARMIES OF DIFFERENT COUNTRIES.

TABLE OF RIFLED SMALL ARMS USED IN

DESIGNATION OF ARM.	Caliber.	Length of barrel.	GROOVES.				Twist.	TIGE.		WEIGHT.	
			Number	Width	DEPTH.			Diameter	Length	Without bayonet	With bayonet
					Breech	Muzzle					
	Inches.	Inches.		Inches.	Inches.	Inches.	Inches.	Inches.	Inches.	Pounds.	Pounds.
Russia........ Brunswick rifle...............	0.69	31.5	2	0.31	0.020	0.020	31.5	....	....	9.7	11.25
Prussia........ Needle gun...................	0.60	36	4	0.23	0.03	0.03	18	....	....	10.75	....
Rifle à tige..................	0.577	27.5	4	0.11	0.025	0.025	33.0	0.27	1.7	10	....
Wall piece...................	0.70	41	4	0.27	0.017	0.017	60	0.3	1.65	9.53	10.33
Austria........ Rifle musket, (1854).........	0.55	37.3	4	0.21	0.025	0.02	73	....	....	9.3	10.25
Do. (Jager)...............	0.55	20	4	0.21	0.025	0.02	73	....	....	9	10.3
Do. with tige...........	0.55	20	4	0.21	0.025	0.02	73	0.25	1.5	9	10.3
France........ Rifled musket à tige..........	0.700	40.64	4	0.27	0.03	0.004	78.75	0.25	1.5	9.34	10
Carabine à tige, (1846)........	0.708	34.7	4	0.27	0.04	0.012	78.75	0.25	1.5	9	10.7
Do. des Cent Gardes	0.26	31.5	5	....	....	....	31.5	....	....	7	........*
Great Britain .Minié musket, (1851).........	0.702	39	4	0.15	0.02	0.01	78	....	....	9	10.5
Enfield rifle musket, (1853)...	0.577	39	3	0.022	0.014	0.004	78	....	....	9.7	9.8
Do. do. (1855)....	0.577	34	3	0.020	0.014	0.004	78	....	....	....	....
Do. artillery carbine.......	0.577	24	3	0.020	0.014	0.004	78	....	....	6.5	9.85
Sardinia .... Rifle.......................	0.665	39.5	8	0.022	0.012	0.012	20.7	....	....	9.85	11.05
Saxony........ Rifle, (musket à tige).........	0.577	40.4	4	0.20	0.025	0.025	64.5	0.3	1.7	....	....
Switzerland ..Rifle................	0.414	28	8	0.20	0.015	0.015	36	....	....	9	9.53
Norway........ Breech loading rifle...........	0.65	28.5	....	....	....	....	54	....	....	....	....
United States.Rifle musket, (1855)...........	0.58	40	3	....	0.015	0.005	72	....	....	9.18	9.9
Rifle, (altered)...............	0.58	33	3	....	0.015	0.005	72	....	....	9.60	11.60
Pistol carbine	0.58	12	3	....	0.004	0.005	48	....	....	5*	....
Rifled musket, (altered).......	0.69	41	3	....	0.015	0.005	72	....	....	9.34	10.10

* Detached stock included.

RIFLED SMALL ARMS.

THE ARMIES OF DIFFERENT COUNTRIES.

Kind (Ball)	Diameter (inches)	(inches)	(grains)	Kind (Charge of Powder)			Remarks
Ogival, with two guides	0.625	1.10	737				English two-grooved rifle, with sword-bayonet.
Sphero-conical	0.63	1	440	Musket grain	58		Priming attached to cartridge.
Cylindro-conical, with two grooves	0.56	1.03	395	Do.	58	540	Forest breech, with conical chamber.
Cylindro-conical, with three grooves	0.66	1.04	493	Do.	100	650	Do. do.
Cylindro-ogival, with two deep grooves	5.65	1	450	... grain	60	700	Wilkinson's ball.
Do. do.	5.65	1	430	Do.	60	700	Do.
Do. do.	5.65	1	450	Do.	60	1,000	Do.
Solid, cylindro-ogival, with three grooves	0.695	1.70		Do.	70	975	
Do. do.	0.695	1.10		Do.	70	1,200	Sword-bayonet.
Cylindro-ogival, solid			700	Do.	30		Sword bayonet; ...
Conoidal, with expanding cap	0.69	1.03	600	Do.	60	1,000	
Conoidal, with expanding plug	0.568	0.10	565	Do.	60	905	
Do. do.	0.568	0.10	565	Do.	60	905	
Do. do.	0.568	0.15	565	Do.	55	300	Sword-bayonet.
Cylindro-conical, without grooves	0.64	0.83	510	Rifle	52		Sword bayonet; cylindrical chamber 0.44 inch in diameter, and 1.95 inch deep.
Cylindro-conical, with one deep groove	0.57	1	410	Rifle	60	715	Small ball used in rifles without the bay...
Cylindro-ogival, solid, with two grooves	0.41	0.94	300	Musket	60	875	Cylindrical chamber, of same diameter of the bore.
Do. do.			500	Do.			
Cylindro-ogival, three grooves, cavity in base	0.5775	1.025		Do.	60	1,000	
Cylindro-ogival, three grooves, cavity in base	0.5775	1.025	510	Do.	60	1,000	Sword bayonet.
Cylindro-ogival, three grooves, cavity in base	0.5775	1.025	450	Do.	60		
....	0.645	1.05	740	Do.	70	880	

GENERAL REMARKS ON SMALL ARMS.

A review of the various systems adopted or tried of late years, in different countries, for the improvement of small arms for the military service, shows that the suggestions made more than a century ago, by Mr. Robbins, in his "Tracts on Gunnery," with respect to the importance of perfecting the construction of rifle-barreled pieces, and of "introducing them into armies for general use," have at length received their practical application. A large portion of the infantry forces of most of the great powers of Europe are still armed with the ordinary musket, on account of the difficulty of making a general and sudden change in the arms of great bodies of men; but it may be confidently anticipated that, in the course of a few years, all these troops will be supplied with rifled arms. The long delay in the adoption of this principle in the construction of military arms has resulted from the supposed necessity of using great force in loading the rifle, and the consequent slowness of the service of that arm, which caused its use in war to be confined to a few picked troops for special service. The problem to be solved, therefore, preparatory to the general adoption of the rifle, was to contrive a method of combining the faculty of easy and quick loading with the close fitting of the ball, which is requisite to give it the rifle motion imparted by the spiral grooves in the barrel. The methods which have been adopted for the solution of this question, in nearly all the European armies, are set forth in a work by Captain J. Schön, of the Saxon infantry, entitled "*Das Gezogene Infanterie—Gewehr*," (Rifled Arms for Infantry,) Dresden, 1855; a translation of which, by Captain Gorgas, of the Ordnance Department, is appended to this report.

The great advantages of rifled arms and of the elongated and pointed ball, (which has been long used for sporting rifles in the United States,) are universally recognized; but there is, as yet, no general concurrence of opinion as to the superior excellence of any one of the systems which have been tried. The principles on which these systems have been arranged may be classed under four heads:

1. The use of the patch around the ball, to fill the grooves and destroy the windage.
2. Loading at the breech.
3. Expanding the ball in the barrel by means of the rammer.
4. Expanding or "upsetting" the ball by the action of the powder.

It has been seen above that each of the methods has been adopted for the arms of one country or another, after careful experiments, which have exhibited good and satisfactory results in each case. Arms constructed on each of these plans have been found capable of making close shooting at a distance of 500 yards, and to be effective in firing at the front of a column of troops at 1,000 yards. The choice between them is, therefore, to be determined chiefly by reference to the facility and convenience of loading and using the arm in such a manner as to make its advantage available in actual service.

1. The use of a patch round the ball renders the loading difficult and slow, especially in arms of large caliber. Accordingly we find that this method of loading is confined almost entirely to the American sporting rifles and the Swiss military rifle of small caliber, which is made confessedly on the "American system."

2. Loading at the breech, if it can be accomplished in a perfect manner, offers a complete solution of the question of easy loading and close fitting; it is not surprising, therefore, that ever since the origin of fire-arms the ingenuity of inventors should have been much exercised in accomplishing this object. But notwithstanding the acknowledged advantages of this principle, it is remarkable that no method of making a practical application of it has yet been suggested which can command general, or even extensive, approbation; mechanical ingenuity seems to have been thus far incapable of removing all the difficulties of having an opening or joint exposed to the action of the charge of powder. Prussia is the only large State in which an arm

of this kind has been extensively adopted for the military service, and the absence of any imitators of her system in this respect seems to be a tacit acknowledgment of the general disapproval of it in other countries.

Experiments are in progress in the British service to test the comparative merits of the several breech-loading arms of American origin, such as Sharp's, Perry's, and Greene's, which are also on trial by our own troops.

3. The method of expanding the ball by striking it with the rammer whilst supported on the mouth of the chamber, or on the top of a stem screwed into the chamber, has met with very great approval in Europe, having been extensively adopted in France, Belgium, Russia, Sardinia, Austria, Prussia, and nearly all the States of the German Confederation. The great ranges and accurate practice which have been obtained with the arms made on the Delvigne and tige systems, are attributed not only to the expansion of the ball into the grooves of the rifle, but partly also to the circumstance that the ball does not rest on the powder, and the latter is consequently not compressed by the ramming of the ball. The charge thus lying loosely in the chamber and occupying a uniform space, burns with greater effect and regularity than when compressed in the ordinary manner. But although these good results are produced in careful trials of arms on these systems, their use in the hands of troops in service seems to have developed serious objections to this principle. In hasty loading, the soldier is apt to ram the ball too slightly or too violently, either of which would cause irregular firing; the same result is caused by the ball being displaced in ramming, so that its axis does not coincide with the axis of the barrel. The chamber is difficult to clean, and the deposit of dirt, after a considerable number of fires, reduces its capacity so that it can no longer contain the charge; in which case some of the powder rests between the ball and its point of support, and thus interferes with its proper expansion. Whilst, therefore, the tige system is retained in some countries for the arms of special sharp-shooters, as in the new Austrian rifle for the third-rank men of the jäger battalion, we find a very general desire to dispense with the use of the tige, and to adopt the system of self-expanding balls.

4. The plan of making a rifle ball expand by the action of the powder, through the intervention of a conical plug, is mentioned by Mr. Greener, in his work on gunnery, written in 1831. In 1840, Mr. Delvigne suggested the expansion of a cylindro-conical ball by the action of the powder on a hollow in the base of the ball, but the adoption of Captain Minié's method of expanding the ball by means of an iron conical cup placed in the cavity of the base has caused the name of *Minié ball* to be generally applied to all the class of self-expanding balls, and that of *Minié rifle* or musket to the arms from which they are fired, although Captain Minié was not the inventor of any peculiar rifle. The Minié ball, properly so called, that is to say, the ball with an expanding cup or plug in the cavity of the base, (Plate 21, Fig 8,) was tried in France by a few regiments of chasseurs, but it has never been adopted for the general service, and as stated in a previous part of this report, comparative trials of this and other expanding balls are now in progress at Vincennes. The Minié system was tried with approbation in several countries, and has been adopted, with some modifications, for the new rifled arms of Great Britain. Besides the complication which the expanding plug introduces into the manufacture of the ball, an objection has been found to exist to the use of this plug, on account of its liability to be driven through the hollow part of the ball, leaving a ring of lead firmly adhering to the sides of the bore. This effect has been produced even with a plug of as light a material as cork, as stated by Mr. Wilkinson, of London, in his "Observations on Muskets, Rifles, and Projectiles;" and this general result has been confirmed, by experiments with iron plugs, at Harper's Ferry Armory.

Later experiments prove that the plug is not necessary to produce the expansion of a cylindro-conical ball, and that the action of the powder on the sides of the cavity in the base of the ball, or the "upsetting" of the lead of a grooved ball, is sufficient to cause the ball to expand into the grooves of the rifle. Austria and Saxony have adopted Mr. Wilkinson's method of expanding the ball by means of deep grooves cut in its cylindrical part. The base of the ball being solid, this form has the additional advantage of being adapted also to the arms "à tige," which are used in those countries. Russia has adopted the Belgian grooved ball with a cavity in the base, and the experiments made by the United States Ordnance Department have led to a similar conclusion as to the most advantageous form of ball. In France the question is yet undecided. The grooves in the cylindrical part of these elongated balls have been found to conduce to the regularity and accuracy of their flight, as well as to facilitate the loading. They are therefore retained in all the patterns of expanding balls, except the English; notwithstanding the additional complication of form, and consequently greater difficulty of manufacture, especially by machinery. A point which requires especial attention in arranging the form of the self-expanding ball, is the graduation of the thickness of the sides of the cavity in proportion to the charge of powder, so as to prevent *the breaking of the ball*, without obstructing its due expansion. With this view, also, it is obvious that uniformity of windage, or space between the balls and the sides of the bore, is of great importance in the use of these balls. Hence the necessity of making the balls by pressure in dies, (instead of casting them in moulds,) and likewise of introducing greater accuracy in the workmanship of the barrels of small arms. At the Arsenal of Vienna the variation allowed in the diameter of the bore is *half a point*, or 0.0038 inch. In the English arms it is said to be only 0.001 inch. At our armories the allowance of variation was formerly 0.01 inch; but in the new arms it has been properly reduced to 0.0025. The same consideration operates against the use of the patch or an envelope of paper about the ball, which makes the windage not only greater, but less uniform than that of the naked ball. There can be little doubt of the correctness of Mr. Wilkinson's opinion, that the best mode of using the expanding bullets is to dip them in grease, and use them without patch or paper. But the supposed necessity of enabling the soldier to load his weapon without handling the ball by itself, has caused the general adherence, in European armies, to the old system of loading, by inserting the ball enveloped with the paper used in forming the cartridge—the only essential change being to grease the paper around the ball, and to protect the powder from this grease by putting it in an additional envelope of paper. A great objection to this method of loading, with the expanding balls, especially with those which are grooved, is that the paper is apt to be pinched by the ball, and to cause an increased accumulation of dirt in the barrel, if it does not even produce a ruptue of the ball. If the paper remains attached to the ball in its flight, a new element of irregularity of motion is introduced.

It is therefore with good reason that, in arranging the system of expanding balls for our new arms, the plan of loading with the greased ball, without paper, has been adopted. If service in the field should develop any serious inconvenience in this method of loading, it may be reasonably expected that ingenuity, aided by experience, will contrive a method of obviating the difficulty; either by carrying the ball separated from the powder, as the huntsman does, or by attaching it to the cartridge in such a manner that it can be easily detached without actually handling it separately.

With the exception of the needle gun in Prussia, and the arm of the "Cent Gardes" in France, both of which are loaded at the breech, and have the priming attached to the cartridge, all military small arms used in European armies are primed with the common percussion cap, of the English pattern, adopted in our service. The self-feeding primer of Baron Heurteloup was at one time adopted or extensively tried in Austria. The "Consol" system of priming (above described) was substituted for it, and has been used for many years; but all the new pattern arms have cones and locks adapted to the ordinary caps. Back-action locks are used in France and Russia, and were at one time adopted in England. But the new military arms in the latter country, in Austria, and Switzerland, have the front action or "bar" lock, now generally employed in the finest sporting arms.

With regard to the *caliber* most suitable for arms on the new system, no general concurrence of opinions is evinced by the present practice of different countries; but there can be no doubt that, in several of the most powerful nations, as in France and Russia, the decision of this question is, in a great measure, controlled by the actual state of their armament, and the great quantity of arms which have been accumulated in the arsenals, and which it is highly desirable to modify on the new system. It may be also that these powers hesitate to give up the advantages which attend the use of a heavy bullet, especially for long ranges; but notwithstanding these considerations, we see that several great military powers have considered it advantageous to adopt a new caliber with the new system of rifled arms. Thus Great Britain, Austria, and Prussia have recently reduced the caliber of their arms to nearly the same standard, and this size has also been adopted for the new arms of the United States.

Long experience in war appears to have produced a very general concurrence of practice, with regard to the weight of the infantry soldier's fire-arm. In order that he may not be overcharged with the burden of his equipments, it is generally agreed that a musket or rifle, for military purposes, should not weigh more than about eleven pounds, including the bayonet. The recoil of such an arm carrying an ounce ball, with a charge of 100 grains of powder, (our established charge for a smooth-bore musket, with a spherical ball, having 0.04 inch windage,) is as great as a man can conveniently bear in long-continued firing. Formerly, when a large charge was used for the musket, the powder was not so strong, the windage of the ball was greater, and withal the men were in the habit of throwing away part of the powder, because they could not bear the recoil of the piece. If, then, the same caliber is retained for the elongated ball, the weight being very much greater than that of the spherical ball, the charge of powder must be reduced in a corresponding proportion, in order to keep the recoil within suitable limits. From this results a decreased initial velocity of the ball and a corrresponding increase of the angle of elevation necessary for striking a distant object; with greater uncertainty of fire, and fewer chances of striking intervening objects, on account of the greater curvature of the trajectory; as is shown by experiments with these arms. It is true that the ball of larger caliber is less affected than the smaller by the resistance of the air, and consequently retains a greater force of impact at long ranges; but this superiority is chiefly appreciable at distances beyond 600 yards, when the fire of small arms becomes, at the best, very uncertain. On the other hand, by reducing the caliber of the arm, it becomes practicable to increase the proportional charge of powder and lead, without unduly increasing the recoil of the piece, or the weight of ammunition which the soldier has to carry. The ball, having a greater initial velocity, and a more advantageous shape than can be given to the larger ball, describes a flatter trajectory, and retains a greater force of penetration at moderate ranges; and although the effect of the shot at great distances may be less fatal than that of the larger caliber, it can hardly be doubted that a ball of the size of that adopted for our new rifle arms will be effective to *disable* a man or a horse at as great a distance as the limit of distinct vision can enable a soldier to fire with any accuracy.

In the use of these new arms of long ranges, the habit of a correct appreciation of distances in the field becomes highly important to the soldier for the proper adjustment of the sight of his gun. Several kinds of mathematical and optical instruments have accordingly been proposed for the purpose of assisting in the prompt determination of distances; but it does not appear that much value is attached, by practical men, to the use of such instruments in war, especially on the field of battle, where circumstances are obviously unfavorable to their application. The French *Stadia*, for this purpose, is well known; it depends upon the unaided eye-sight, and cannot therefore be useful beyond the moderate distance of distinct natural vision. The optical *Diastemeters*, of Messrs. Porro, Chevalier, and others, assist the sight by having the necessary apparatus attached to a portable telescope, and may perhaps be sometimes useful to the staff-officer in reconnoitering, when he can give the requisite attention to steadying and adjusting the instrument; but for judging of the distances of troops, during the movements of an army, the most practical method seems to be that adopted in the English school of infantry practice, viz:

that of exercising the soldier to observe carefully the appearance of a man at different known distances from him, noting at each distance the particular circumstances which he can distinguish in the person, costume, or equipments, and then verifying and correcting his judgment by estimating the distances of men placed at intervals unknown to him. We were told, that by this practice, the men become very expert, after a few lessons in estimating distances; their emulation is excited, and their zeal and attention stimulated by the distribution of medals and other rewards to the most skillful men. Although great progress has undoubtedly been made of late years in the improvement of military fire-arms, both in Europe and America, the matter may still be considered to be in a transition state; and prudence would therefore dictate to us to proceed, as cautiously as circumstances permit, with our changes, until our own experience, or that of others, with arms in actual service, shall have satisfactorily demonstrated the superiority of some one method of altering the existing arms and ammunition. The successful use of the "tige" rifle by the French, in Algeria and in the Crimea, has not prevented experiments from being still carried on in France for substituting a more convenient and advantageous kind of arm and ammunition; and the first trial of the new British rifle in battle caused a change to be made in the ball, which had been adopted for it after many experiments at home.

During the late war in Europe the great body of the infantry of all the armies engaged used the ordinary musket; and this circumstance, combined with the limited scale of operations in the open field, did not allow of a full trial of the effect of the new arms, and of their influence on the tactics of armies; but the protracted siege of Sebastopol served to develop the importance of these arms of long range, as an auxiliary, in both the attack and defense of places. In proof of this, it is only necessary to refer to the extraordinary means used by the besiegers and besieged to protect their gunners from rifle-shots, which could be fired with sufficient precision to enter an embrasure at 500 or 600 yards, and which were effective at even a much greater distance; or to mention the annoyance and loss caused to the besiegers by Russian riflemen posted in the little advanced entrenchments commonly called "rifle pits."

A. MORDECAI,
Major of Ordnance.

PLAN OF THE ARSENAL AT VIENNA.

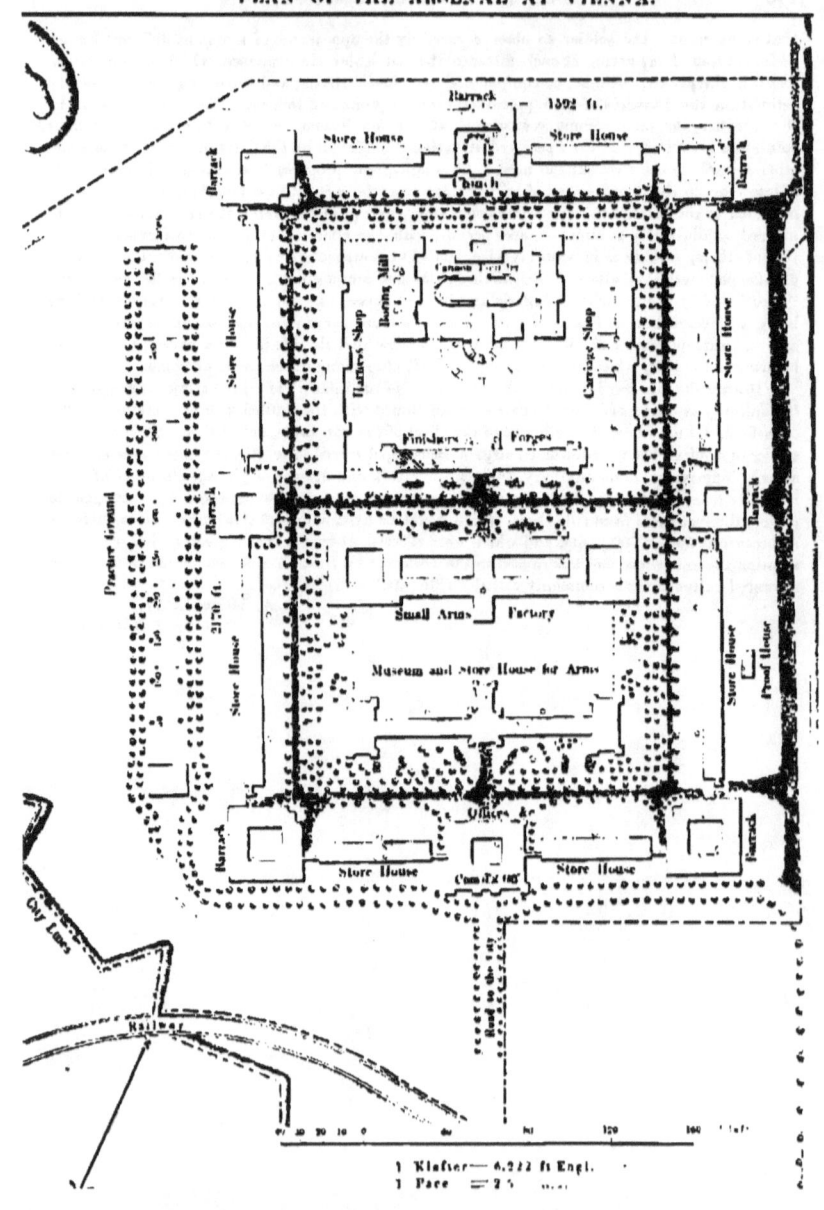

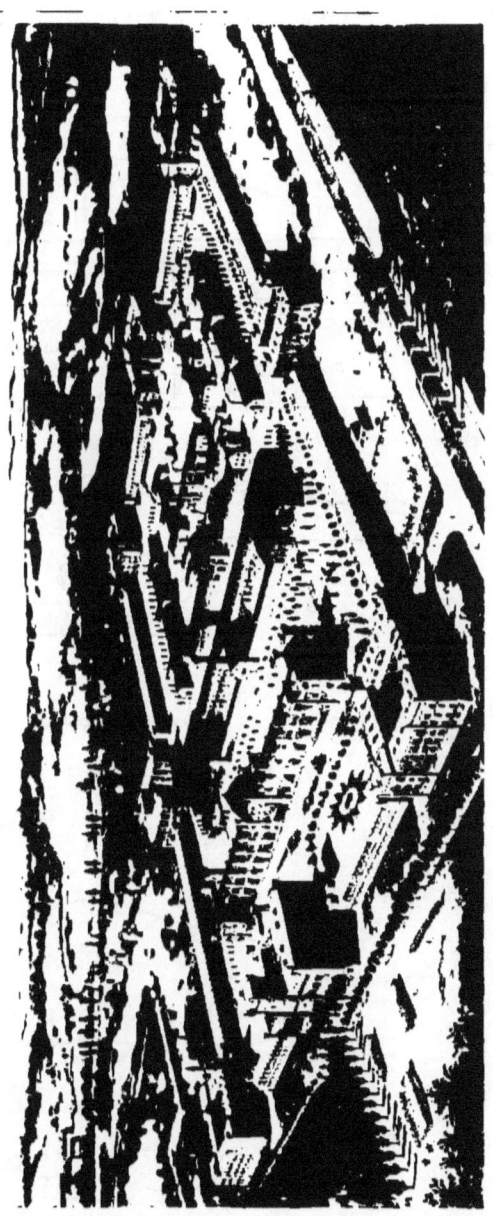

MACHINE FOR RIFLING GUN BARRELS.

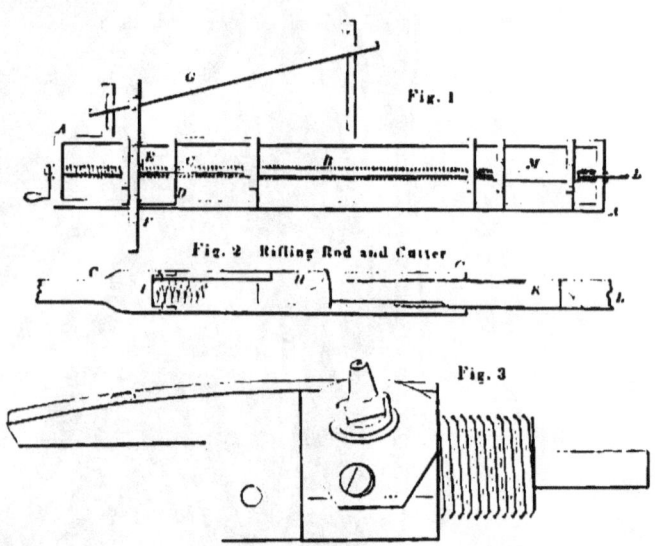

Fig. 1

Fig. 2 Rifling Rod and Cutter

Fig. 3

Implements for Austrian Rifles.

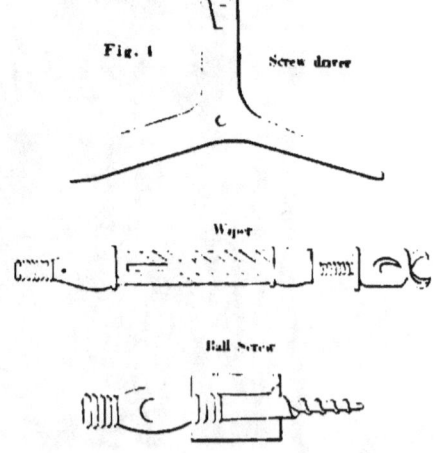

Fig. 4 Screw driver

Wiper

Ball Screw

PLAN OF ENFIELD ARMORY.

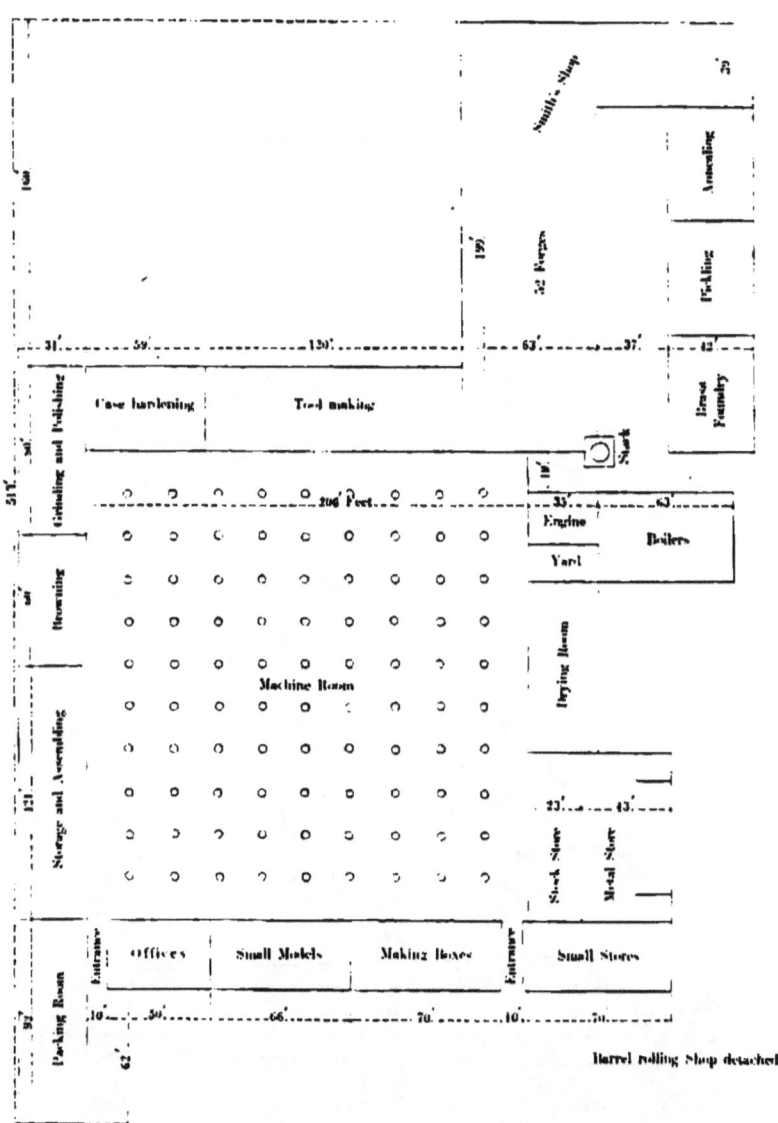

FRENCH RIFLE CANNON. Plate 5

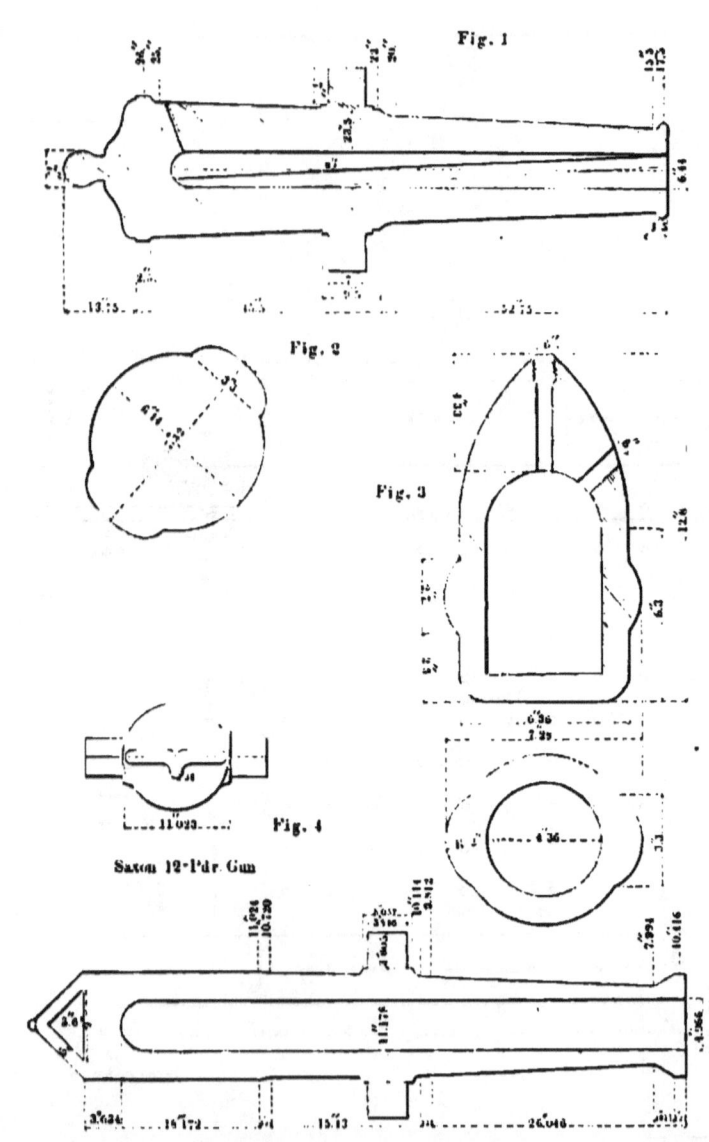

KRUPP'S CAST STEEL GUN.

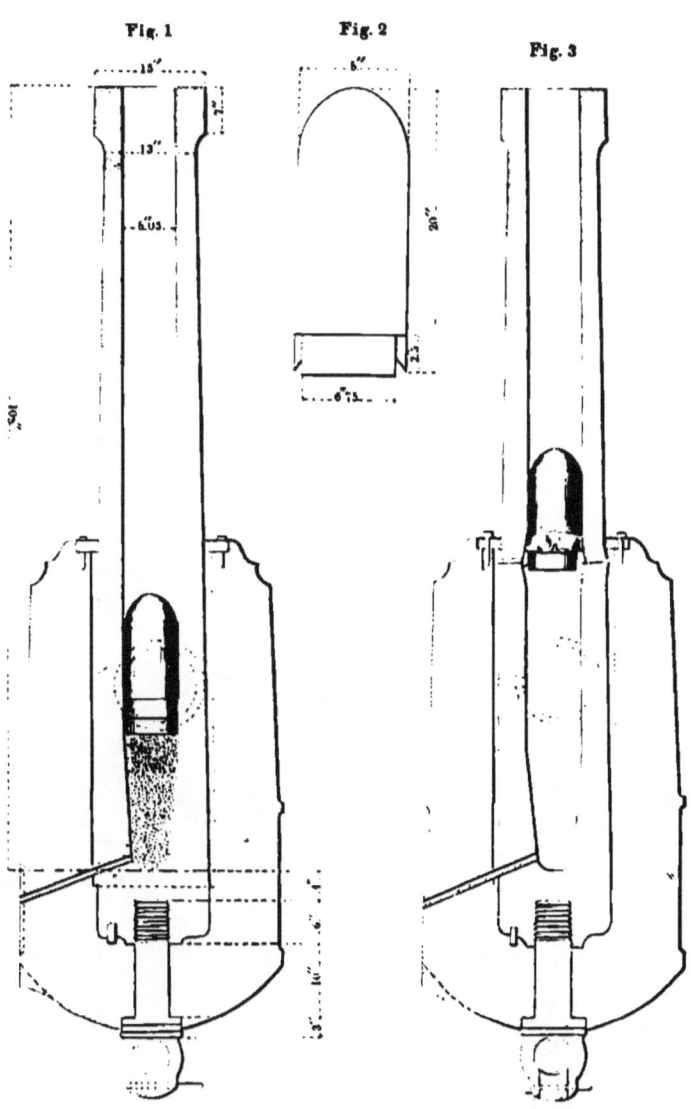

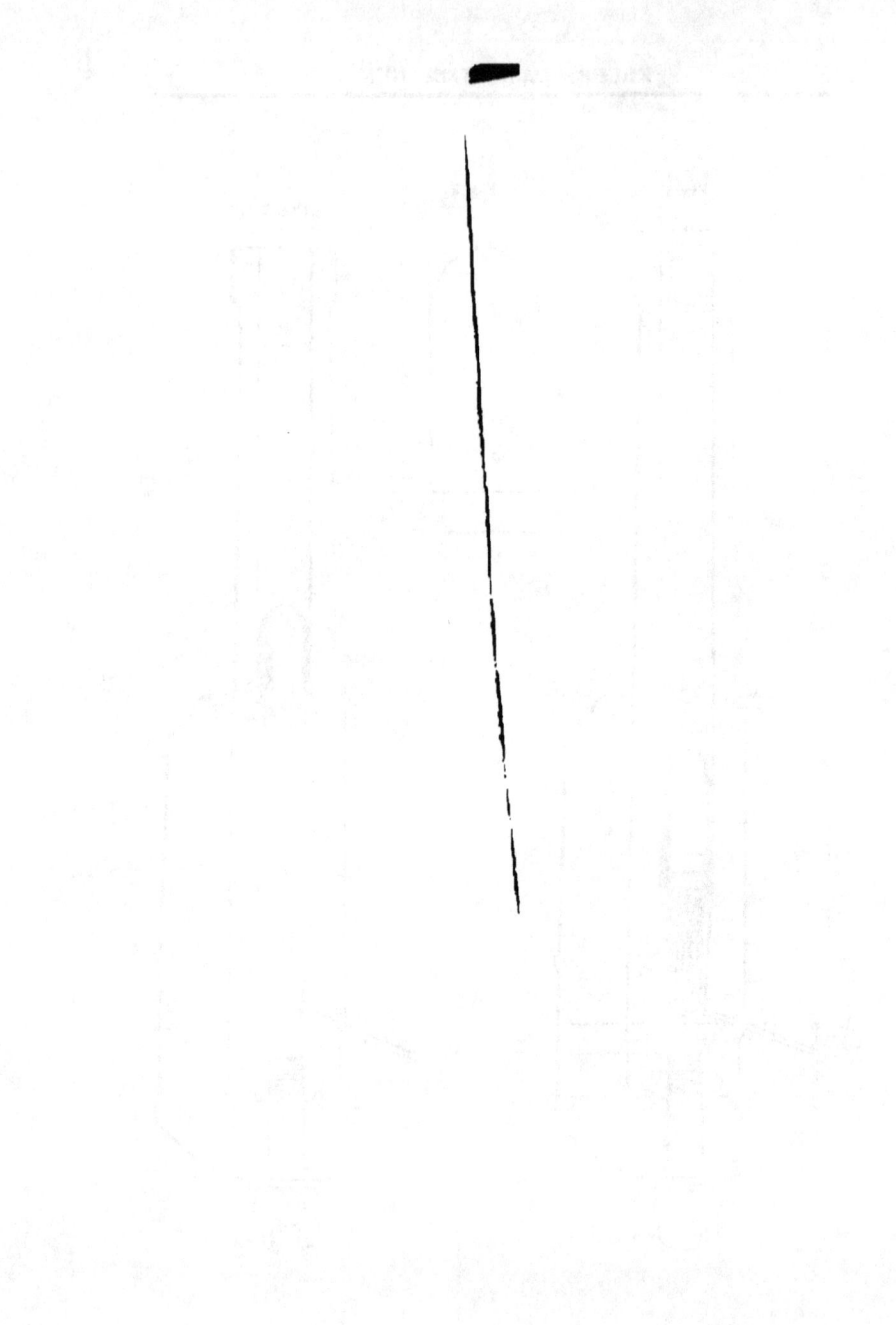

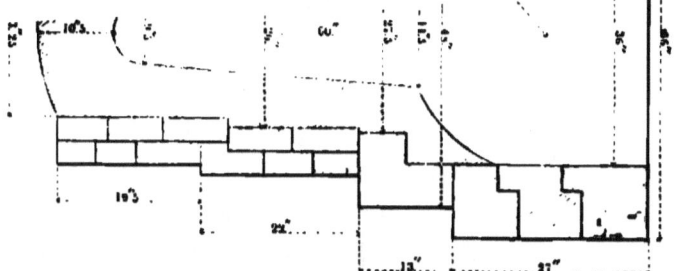

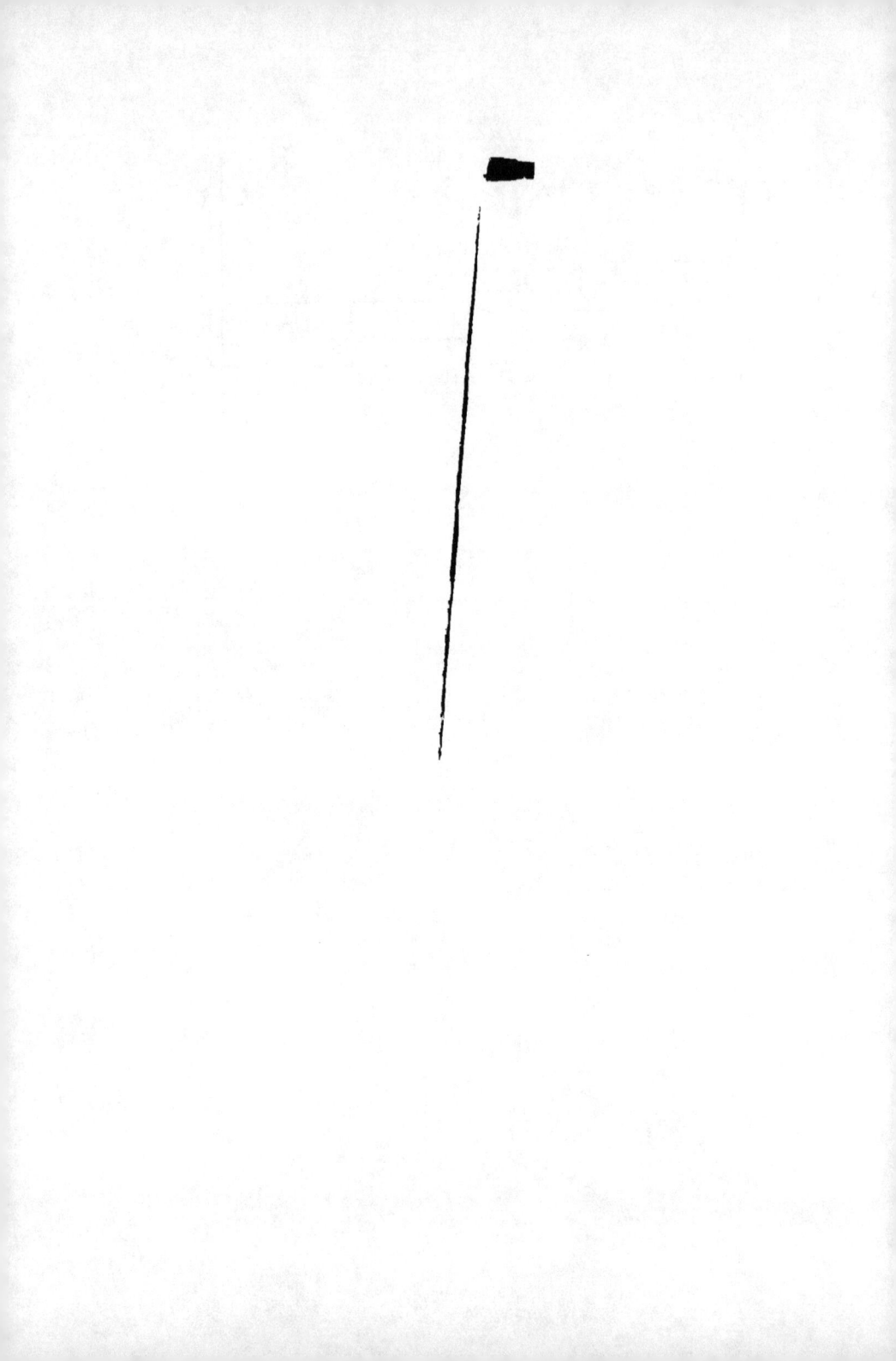

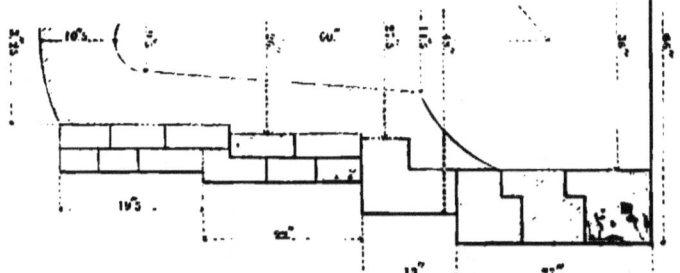

MORTARS.

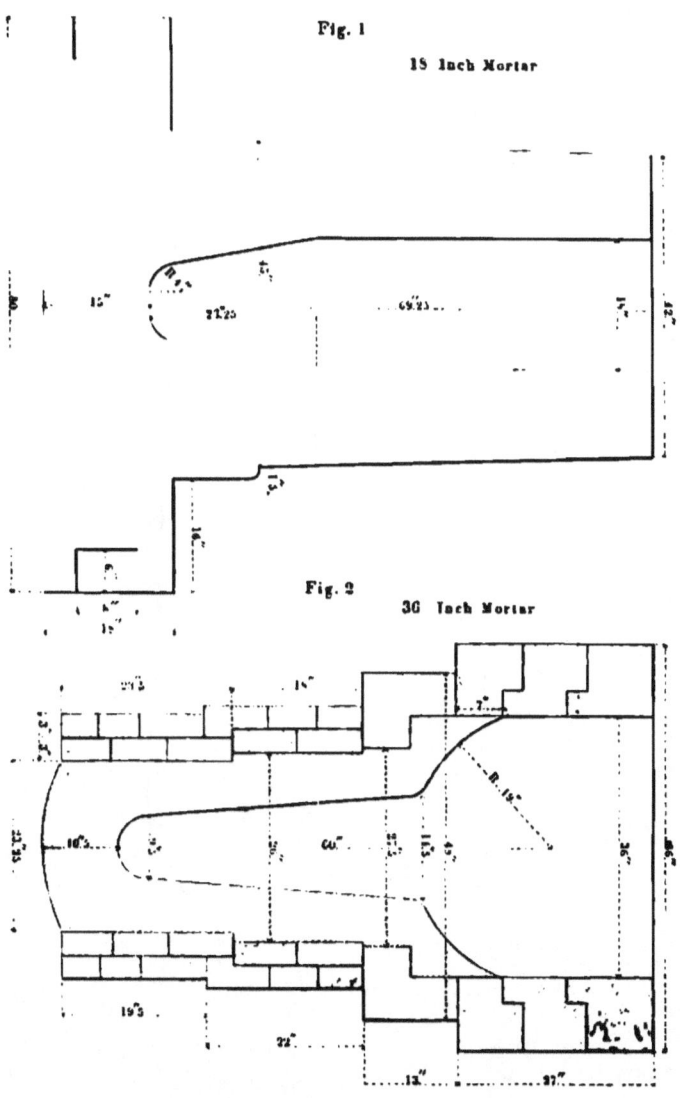

Fig. 1 13 Inch Mortar

Fig. 2 36 Inch Mortar

13 INCH WROUGHT IRON GUN. Plate

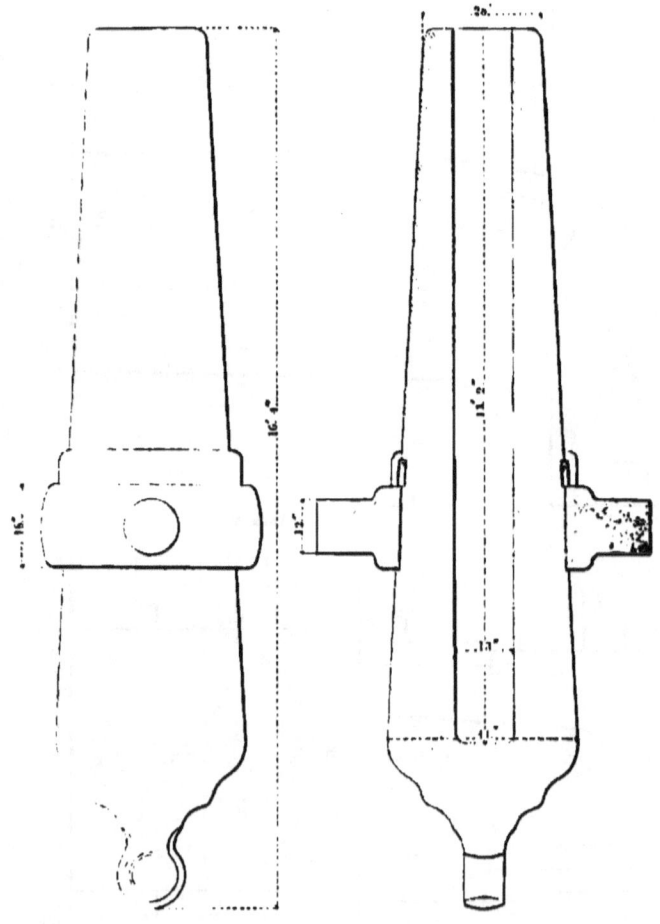

AUSTRIAN BARBETTE GUN CARRIAGES.

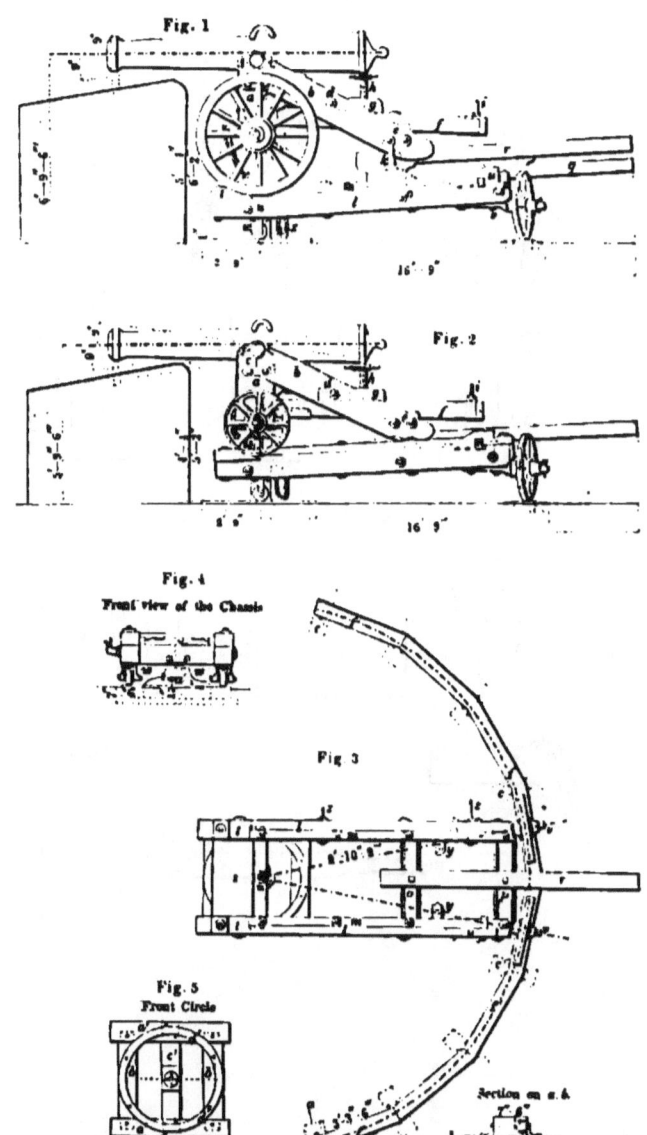

BOXER'S FUZES.

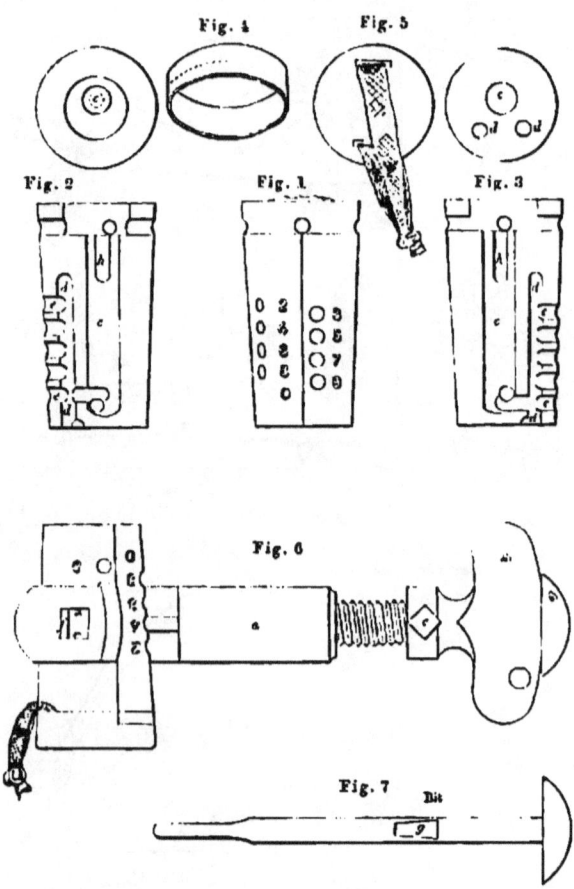

BOXER'S SHRAPNEL SHELL AND FUZES.

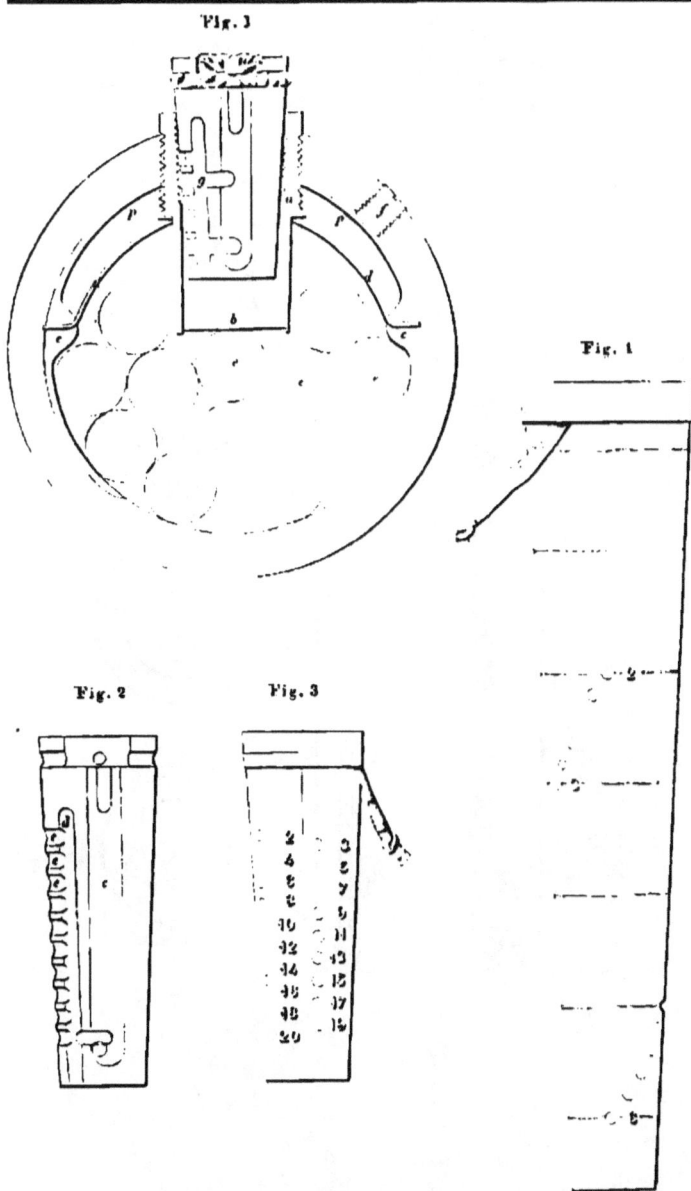

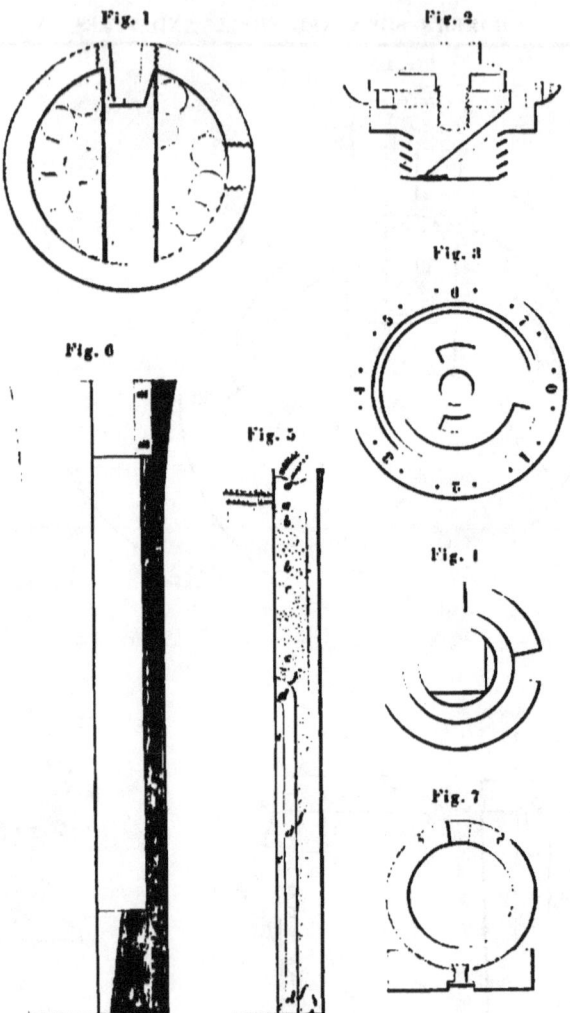

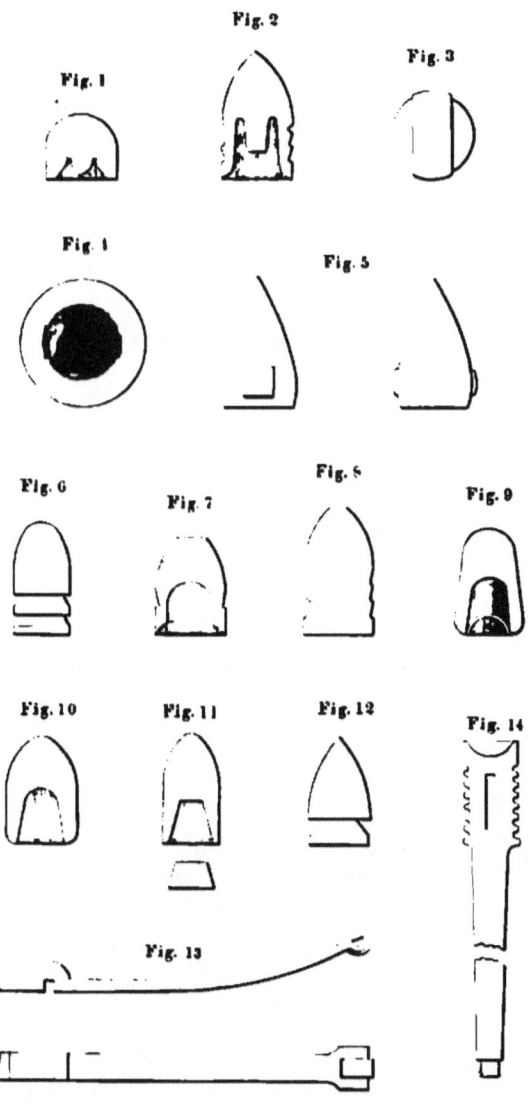

RIFLED INFANTRY ARMS.

A BRIEF DESCRIPTION

OF THE

MODERN SYSTEM OF SMALL ARMS,

AS ADOPTED IN

THE VARIOUS EUROPEAN ARMIES.

BY J. SCHÖN,

CAPTAIN IN THE ROYAL SAXON INFANTRY, HOUSEHOLD BRIGADE; KNIGHT OF THE IMPERIAL BRAZILIAN ORDER OF THE ROSE

SECOND EDITION, REVISED AND AUGMENTED,
WITH EXPLANATORY PLATES.

DRESDEN:
1855.

TRANSLATED FROM THE GERMAN
BY J. GORGAS,
CAPTAIN OF ORDNANCE, UNITED STATES ARMY.

PREFACE.

Science has within the last ten years successfully applied itself to the improvement of infantry fire-arms, and as the result of experiments stimulated by the introduction of percussion arms, thirty years ago, three systems have been originated and, with more or less modification, brought into use.

Whether military art was right in entirely abandoning the improvement of the smooth-bore arms, or whether experiments should not in time be instituted with these also, in reference to increased accuracy and force, and with improved shape of ball, is a question, the solution of which may be adverted to by the way; merely remarking now, that whoever desires to make use of the distant fire of skirmishers, recurs at once to the use of the rifled arm.

The smooth-bore arms have, on the whole, undergone but slight modifications since the first settled French model of 1777; and though they may have differed in details in the various European armies, they have agreed very generally in the caliber of 0.69 inch, and in the use of the spherical ball.

Though in these pages the systems thus far known are treated of in the order of their appearance, so as not to confuse the origin and historical development of fire-arms, they may yet be classed, notwithstanding the chequered advance of improvement in the construction of rifled arms, into three systems, according to their principles, which will be briefly sketched.

The first may be called the system of *normal form* of the ball. To this belong the Swiss system, including that of Wild, the French Minié, the English Wilkinson; and in short, all those who simply insert the ball, and endeavor to preserve it in the shape in which it has been carefully designed.

The second may be termed the system of *uniform disfiguration* of the ball, in which the ball undergoes in ramming, a regular and constant change of form before it is fired. This system, to which indeed all rifled arms belonged that were loaded with patched balls, is now represented by the system of Thouvenin, and its modifications; the round ball being now scarcely anywhere used as a missile for military service.

The *breech-loading* may be regarded as a third system, holding a middle place between the other two, in reference to the shape of the ball after the loading and after the firing. The ball is unchanged in the loading, but after the ignition of the charge is driven into the narrow part of the barrel, where it undergoes a change of shape against the sides of the bore, which is neither identical with that produced in loading nor that effected by the gases. To this system appertain the French wall piece, the Norwegian and Swedish breech-loading guns, and the Prussian needle gun, and the revolver, though the mechanism of these may vary essentially.

The construction of the bore of the rifled arms has undergone the most vital changes as well in the several systems as in its gradual development in relation to the numbers, breadth, and depth of the grooves. Beginning with twelve, eight, and even two grooves, all three systems have adopted, as most effective, four grooves, with nearly equal width of lands whilst the first system only increases their depth toward the breech. The increase of width in the same direction has been abandoned, as not being of the same utility.

It is also to be observed, that an increase of caliber toward the breech, of one thousandth part of an inch, is regarded in several services as useful, and of especial service for arms intended for expanding and compressed balls.

It appears also, that the twist of the grooves in the bore should be reduced to a minimum. The inflammation of the charge by percussion, infers an accelerated development of the gases, and a consequently accelerated action on the ball; and these conditions would seem to require the greatest possible length of twist, to insure the maximum accuracy and force.

The shape of the ball has however undergone the most marked changes.

Though the theory of the rotation of the round ball had for a long time taken into consideration the effect of the air's resistance directly on the ball, as well as that caused by the eccentricity of its figure, it is only within the last twenty years that the fullest evidence has been obtained, that the ball from a rifle does not rotate in the sense in which that expression was ordinarily understood. The rotation of the ball from a rifle is a motion about an axis, impressed on it by the twist of the grooves; and it is pretty well settled that a rotation about the center of gravity occurs only as an exception, due to a faulty construction of the missile or some accidental circumstance.

The arrow motion of the ball seems to be irrefutably established in the triumph of the elongated ball over the round one; and although the theory may have objections to encounter, even the sceptical enjoin as of the first consequence, to place the center of gravity as far to the front as possible, to employ the parabolic rather than the simple conical form of pointed ball; and to provide the ball with grooves or "connelures," the essential influence of which in directing the heel and point of the ball is acknowledged.

The requisitions which are now made on rifled arms are a consequence of the accuracy and force they possess at a distance—requirements which have only of late been made of small arms—and have constituted the riflemen and sharp shooters who use them, a powerful support to the artillery, whose advance they cover. * * * * * *

The authorities consulted in this work were the School of St. Omer, on the report of Lieutenant Panot; the "Supplement of Small Arms," of Major Schnölzl; the "Small Arms of the Royal Hanoverian Army," of Captain Gündell; "Handbook relating to the Small Arms of the imperial Austrian Infantry Regiments," by First Lieutenant Dub; "Guide to the Science of Small Arms," by Rüstow; "Reports in the Observer, of March, 1852;" the Swiss and German "Military Journals;" the "Archives of the Royal Prussian Artillery and Engineers," &c., &c. * * * * * * *

Should I succeed, in this essay, in serving any of my comrades in arms, one of my most constant aspirations will be fulfilled.

DRESDEN, *April*, 1855.

EXPLANATION OF THE PLATES.

	Figure.
System of Delvigne, the flattening of the ball, and section of the muzzle	1 a b
Pontchara's pointed ball, sabot, and patch	2
Thierry's ball, (cylindro-spherical)	3
Delvigne's ball, (cylindro-conical)	4
French chambered rifle, 1840, of the Delvigne-Pontchara system	5 a b
Austrian chambered rifle, mine system, altered by Baron Augustin	6 a b
Ball for the same, after ramming	6 c
Austrian primer, (Zünder)	6 d
OVAL BORES—	
Brunswick oval arm, cross section of chamber and muzzle	7 a b c
Brunswick oval ball	8
Brunswick patched ball	9
Brunswick rolling ball	10
English oval arm, muzzle	11
English belted ball	12
Hanoverian oval gun, muzzle	13
Patch ball to same	14
Rolling ball to same	15
SYSTEM OF BREECH-LOADING—	
Specimen of the beginning of the eighteenth century	16
Prussian needle-gun, longitudinal section, and muzzle	17 a b
Parts of the needle-gun—	
Cylinder	18
Longitudinal section of chamber	19 a
Exterior of the chamber	19 b
Needle-pipe of the chamber	19 c
Handle of the chamber	19 d
Locket, left side, longitudinal section	20 a
Locket from below	20 b
Side view of the main spring	21
Needle-socket, longitudinal section	22
Needle-stem and needle	23
Spiral spring	24
Bear spring, from above and from the right side	25 a b
Trigger	25 c
Mechanism of the needle-gun, cocked	26 a
Mechanism of the needle-gun, discharged	26 b
Prussian pointed ball for needle-gun	27
Paper for the sabot, (reduced scale)	28 a
Same, rolled up	28 b
Pressed sabot	28 c
Cartridge for needle-gun	29
Norwegian breech-loading gun, and section of muzzle	30 a b
Chamber for same, and lever	30 c d
Same, opened for loading	31
Norwegian breech-loading ball and cartridge	32 a b
English revolver of Adams & Deane, side view	33 a b
Ball for same	33 c d
Delvigne's cylindro-conical ball, improved by Minié	34
SYSTEM OF THOUVENIN—	
Breech-pin of this system	35
Ball of Tamisier	36
Ball cast with grooves	37 a b
Trajectory of the pointed and of the round ball	38, 39
French tige rifle, bayonet, ball, and cartridge	40 a b, 41, 42
Cross section of progressive grooves	43 a b
Belgian tige rifle, bayonet, ball, and cartridge	44 a b c, 45, 46

182   RIFLED INFANTRY ARMS.

	Figures.
SYSTEM OF THOUVENIN—Continued.	
Prussian tige rifle, Delvigne-Thouvenin system	47 a b
Hausse and pointed ball for same	48, 49
Prussian wall piece, Delvigne-Thouvenin system	50 a b
Ball and cartridge for same	51, 52
Bavarian tige rifle, Thouvenin system	53 a b
Ball and cartridge for same	54, 55
Saxon Jäger rifle, Delvigne-Thouvenin system	56 a b
Ball for same	57
Saxon rifled musket and hausse, Thouvenin system	58 a b
Balls of the first and second kind and cartridge	59, 60, 61
"Back action" lock of the rifled musket	62 a b
Mecklenburg gun for the pointed ball	63 a b
Ball, cartridge, and pattern for the cylinder	64, 65, 66
Hanoverian 7-grooved tige rifle	. 67 a b
Eight-grooved tige rifle, ball, and cartridge	68 a b, 69 a b
Oldenburgh Thouvenin gun, ball, and cartridge	70 a b, 71 a b
Pattern for cartridge cylinder of same	71 c
Nassau tige gun, ball, and cartridge	72 a b, 73 a b
Sardinian gun, ball, and cartridge	74 a b, 74 c d
Bersaglieri rifle and ball	75 a b c
Austrian pointed ball, cartridge, and *primer for chambered rifle*	76 a b
Luxemburg tige rifle, muzzle, and ball	77 a b c
Russian ball for the tige gun and cartridge	78 a b
Russian two-grooved gun and pointed ball	79 a b c d
THE MINIÉ SYSTEM—	
Cross-section of chamber and muzzle	80 a b
French Minié ball	80 c
Baden Minié ball and culot	81 a b
Nassau Minié ball and cartridge	82 a b
English Minié ball and cartridge	83
English balls of Purdy, Lovell, Lancaster, Wilkinson	84, 85, 86, 87 a b
English Enfield-Pritchett rifle and ball	88 a b, 88 c d e
Altered ball for the English Minié gun of 1851	89
Sections at chamber and muzzle of a *Spanish* barrel	90 a b
Spanish Minié ball	91
Cross-sections of above barrel at chamber and muzzle, with progressive grooves	92 a b
Altered Spanish Minié ball	93
Cross-section of a *Belgian* Minié barrel	94 a b
Belgian Minié ball and culot	95 a b
Altered Belgian ball of Timmerhans	96
Belgian Minié gun, hausse, and cartridge	97, 98, 99
THE SWISS SYSTEM—	
Swiss federal rifle and hausse	100 a b, 101 a b c
Swiss ball and patch, and without patch	102 a b
Ball and cartridge of the Swiss Jäger rifle	103
Danish double cartridge and pointed ball	105, 106
Incidence and deviation of air currents with the cylinder, (double size)	107
Incidence and deviation with the other forms	108, 109, 110, 111
Incidence and deviation of the same having oblique positions	112, 113, 114, 115, 116
Trajectories of pointed and spherical balls	117

CONTENTS.

I. A glance at the chief defects of the smooth and grooved arms.
   On the grooves and charges.
II. System of Delvigne.
III. System of Pontchara.
IV. The Delvigne-Pontchara system introduced into France and Belgium in 1840.
   The same system under the name of chambered arms, altered by General Augustin, introduced into Austria.
V. The oval arm introduced into Brunswick, Oldenberg, and England.
VI. System of breech loading.
   Prussian needle gun.
   Norwegian breech-loading gun.
   Swedish breech-loading gun for the marine.
   English revolver.
VII. The system of Wild in Baden and Wurtemburg.
VIII. System of Thouvenin—adoption of the elongated ball, and its trajectory compared with that of the round ball.
   Adoption of Thouvenin's system in—

France.	Oldenburg.
Belgium.	Nassau.
Prussia.	Sardinia.
Bavaria.	Austria.
Saxony.	Luxemburg.
Mecklenburg.	Russia.
Hanover.	

IX. System of Minié.

France.	Nassau.
Baden.	England.

   Experiments at Enfield in 1852. Adoption of a new gun, the Enfield-Pritchett rifle.
   Spain.   Belgium.
X. Swiss system: Stutzer, Jägergewehr.
XI. System of Wilkinson: Austria.
XII. Lancaster and American system. Conclusion.
   Extracts from experiments in Switzerland.
No. 1. Experiments on the accuracy and penetration of smooth bore, Thouvenin, and Minié arms, in Belgium.

RIFLED INFANTRY ARMS.

I. A GLANCE AT THE CHIEF DEFECTS OF THE SMOOTH AND GROOVED ARMS.—ON THE GROOVES AND CHARGES.

The improvements and discoveries recently made in infantry arms are mainly the result of endeavors to diminish or entirely eradicate the chief defects of the arm hitherto used, which, in the smooth bore, are the limited range, and in the rifle, both that and additional difficulty in the loading.

Before entering on a minute examination of these improvements and discoveries, it is proper to advert to the causes of the defects just referred to.

The smooth bore has a considerable windage to facilitate the loading, which prevents the ball, when in its place, from filling the bore, and admits currents of the generated gas at its side. This occasions a pressure of the ball against the side of the bore opposite, and not only causes it to assume an irregular rotary motion, but makes it describe a path not coincident with the vertical plane through the axis of the bore, to the great detriment of its accuracy.

In the rifles, it is true, the windage was destroyed by the use of a tight ball; but this retarded the loading, and made it so laborious as to make the firing much slower than with the smooth bore. Besides, in prolonged use the strength of the men was too much tasked to admit of a steady aim. The shape of the ball was also injured, which has a vital influence on the accuracy and range of the missile.

These defects of both species of arms became the more obvious as the effort was made to increase their range and accuracy, without, at the same time, greatly increasing the charge or elevation.

The question propounded at this day is to find a system that shall combine the advantages of the smooth bore and rifle without having their manifest defects, to which end the following chief requisites are to be kept in view:

    1. Increased facility of loading.
    2. Increased accuracy and range.
    3. The charge.
    4. The inclination of the grooves.
    5. The diameter and form of the ball.

As the first two conditions depend on the last three, it will be proper, before presenting the solutions which each of the systems offers, to examine more closely what depends upon the grooves.

The use of grooves has so much advanced the accuracy and force of small arms, that for the last half century they have been used in increased proportion for purposes of warfare; and a weapon which had formerly but an isolated existence, has attained, through improved construction, and the adoption of the pointed ball, universal favor. It is worth while, therefore, to trace more minutely their origin, and to examine their peculiar adaptation to service arms.

The grooves in use in Germany in the latter half of the fifteenth century were the result of endeavors to augment the accuracy of the arms then in use, in which, on account of the great windage* of the ball, they must have been extremely defective. Cartridges not having yet come into use, the bullet was not then, as now, enveloped in the paper of it, which would have assisted in destroying the windage, but was attacked by its sinking lead; nor did the wooden drift or rammer avail much in this respect. The bore was, therefore, furnished with a certain number of furrows or grooves running straight along the bore—that is, parallel to its axis; the ball being at the same time adapted more nearly to the diameter of the caliber.

The accuracy was, however, so little increased by these means, the improvement being only sensible at short distances, as to have but little advantage over that of the smooth bore, whilst the loading became so difficult from the increased caliber of the ball as to be nearly impracticable after a few rounds. By the introduction of the straight grooves the discovery was made, however, that the ball obeyed the grooves, and followed in its flight the direction of the axis of the bore. These observations may afterwards have caused a certain inclination to be given to them, the twist of which the ball must equally follow in the bore and retain after quitting it. The ball which in the straight grooved barrels received but one motion, that of progression, had thus a second motion impressed on it, the rotary or screw-like movement, by which it overcame with greater ease the resistance of the air. The ball was again reduced in its diameter; but in order to retain the advantage of the small windage, resort was had to greased patches, in which the ball was enveloped before loading.

With the greatly increased accuracy attained through the grooves, various weapons of the kind made their appearance, bearing such names as "target" and "deer rifles," &c., and adapted rather to the pleasures of the chase and the pastimes of target shooting than to actual service, for which they were also unsuited by their costliness. Not until the end of the sixteenth century do we find these arms (Zielbüchsen) in small numbers in the arsenals of fortresses, and used only for defense.

It was not until a later day, and first of all in Germany, that this weapon was much esteemed among the gentry; and not until the close of the eighteenth century that its merits caused it to be placed in the hands of a few troops. The great popularity it has attained in later times is to be ascribed chiefly to the use of the pointed ball. Let us now examine the different kind of grooves, and what is required of them in a service arm.

We have seen that the inclination of the grooves impresses on the ball, whether round or elongated, a motion other than the forward one produced by the action of the generated gases, which is one of rotation, in a degree greater or less, according to the inclination of the grooves. From this it would seem to follow that as the inclination or twist of the grooves is increased, or, which is the same thing, the angle diminished, the rotation of the ball would increase in the same ratio, and the accuracy of the arm improve in like measure. Theory would undoubtedly lead to this conclusion; but here another circumstance interposes unfavorably, which is the force of the gases themselves which act upon the ball. With too great a twist to the grooves, the ball which, in consequence of every impulse, endeavors to advance, cannot overcome the opposite and increased force of friction with sufficient celerity. We must also add that the lead which has been driven into the grooves in loading, in the shape of little ridges that serve as guides to the ball, is not strong enough to oppose the resistance to the impulsive force of the gases, necessary to keep the ball in the grooves. As a consequence the lead is torn off, leaving

---

* On this point, information may be found in Gryn's "Treatise on Musquets, &c.," and in Von Wolthausen's "Art of War." At the close of several directions we read: "And on top of the ball place a wad of tow or hair, or anything convenient; and see that you do not forget this matter of the wad, for it often happens, when the ball is large enough, as it ought to be, to roll in of itself, and you omit this wad on top of the charge, it will play you the trick of rolling out, and when you think you are going to bring down your enemy, you are only blazing away with harmless powder."

the ball without the direction required to produce rotation. A too great twist in the grooves diminishes also the initial velocity by the friction engendered, and consequently the range.

Hence it is evident that the degree of inclination has its limits, beyond which the advantages of twisted grooves are lost. The inquiry next arises as to what inclination is most suitable. Here, however, estimates founded on theory are indeterminate, there being too many causes, such as charge, length of barrel, depth, breadth, and even the kind of groove, which exert a greater or less effect; and hence it is that rifles of such various threads give results almost identical. This question can only be determined by actual experiments, in which the length of barrel and weight of charge must be prominent considerations, the latter being so regulated with reference to the former, that its inflammation may be complete when the bullet reaches the muzzle. So much is, however, certain, that too great an inclination of the grooves is prejudicial to the range and the penetration. We must endeavor rather to give the ball a lower and hence a more extended trajectory, and on this the shape of the ball has the greatest possible influence.

Let us next examine the accessory circumstances which exert an influence; and first, the charge.

In the determination of the charge we must reflect, in the first place, that the combustion of the powder, and consequent development of its strength, should be complete when the ball has reached the vicinity of the muzzle; a consummation influenced by the length of the barrel, quality and kind of powder, inclination, number, and depth of the grooves, not forgetting that too heavy a charge may force the ball over the lands. In the second place, the accuracy and penetration must be the greatest possible. On this point it has been pretty well established, by experiments for the purpose independent of each other—in France under Colonel Pontchara, in 1835, and in Belgium under Colonel Timmerhans, in 1839—that a medium charge, comprehended between four and six grammes, (sixty-two to ninety-three grains,) insured an adequate range and accuracy with a good barrel. A smaller charge than this is not desirable, as it makes the elevations too great and incommodes the aim. And, thirdly and lastly, the recoil is to be considered, which, while it cannot be entirely avoided, exercises a certain influence on the accuracy, and must not be made excessive by a large charge. This again requires a medium charge. A suitable angle for the butt, and a proper weight for the weapon, assist in diminishing the recoil.

The charge best suited to attain great range and accuracy being ascertained with some certainty, regard must next be had to the length of the barrel, which must fulfill the condition of a military weapon; that is, must be of a length and strength to admit of the fire of two ranks without danger to the front rank, and to form with the bayonet an offensive weapon which may be used without over fatigue.

The grooves differ in respect to the kind of twist, and in their departure, in a greater or less degree, from an uniform depth. They are classed into three kinds: the *common*, the *parabolic*, and the *progressive* grooves.

The *common* grooves proceed (supposing the bore to be developed) in right lines at a given angle from beginning to end. These are in general use, and recommend themselves especially for service arms by the ease with which they are constructed.

The *parabolic* grooves, under the same supposition in reference to the barrel, exhibit, on the other hand, a line of increasing curvature; that is, they begin at the chamber with a slight inclination, which increases to a given angle at the muzzle. The end proposed by this is to impress an increased rotation on the ball by degrees, and thus avoid forcing it over the lands. They are only used in fancy arms, and seldom even then, the fabrication being attended with considerable difficulty. According to experiments instituted, the parabolic curve, even with a slight twist, in which the first part departs but little from a right line, gradually assuming a greater twist, is inferior to the common groove. The explanation of this is, that the lead of the ball which has been pressed into the grooves must change its shape at each moment of the advance of the ball, if it keeps in the grooves; it is hence easily forced over the lands, to the detriment of the range.

The *progressive* grooves are those which are deeper at the breech than at the muzzle, where they almost disappear; but they preserve an uniform twist throughout their length. They have lately been adopted into the Minié system with advantage. Their object is, by the advance of the ball, to make it take a stronger hold on the grooves, an object undoubtedly attained.

Grooves, besides, vary essentially in their cross-section, being either *square, triangular, rounded*, or *saw-tooth*.

The *square grooves* form on either side, where they meet the lands, straight sides and sharp edges; and their defect is that the ball is forced into them with difficulty, and experiences great friction. Besides, they permit the dirt to accumulate in the angles, whence it is removed with difficulty.

The *triangular grooves* have the cross-section of an isosceles triangle, and are used only in sporting arms.

The *rounded grooves* have the shape of a quadrant, the land being where two adjacent grooves are separated by a narrow strip, which serves as a sufficient guide to the ball. These are best adapted to service, because, in the first place, the bullet in ramming more easily enters the grooves; secondly, because the sides do not create friction in the same proportion as the sharp ones; and, thirdly, because the dirt does not readily lodge in them, and is more readily removed.

The *saw-teeth (crémaillere) grooves* present on the one side an abrupt face, and on the other *die away* on the land; that is, they offer a square edge to the rotation of the ball, whilst the opposite side meets the land at a very obtuse angle. They have found favor in scarcely any service.

The *hair grooves* need no explanation, as they are not at all adapted to military uses.

As various as the form is the number of the grooves. Formerly it was the belief that an accumulation of grooves gave greater accuracy. This is, however, not found to prove true, as they produce friction, which, by diminishing the initial velocity, shortens the range; and, by being narrower, they also become more difficult to clean. The number formerly ranged from six to twelve, but is now reduced to from four to six, a limit recognized as most suitable for military purposes, since it admits of loading easily, without interfering with the desired accuracy. An odd number is affirmed by some to be most conducive to accuracy, for the reason that in this case there will be a land opposite to each groove, thus avoiding long and short transverse axes alternately, which will not be the case with an even number. For the same reason such a barrel will be more easily loaded, and the center of gravity of the ball less readily deranged. But their construction is more difficult and tedious, for which reason they are seldom used.

The proper depth of the grooves is quite as important a consideration to the effectiveness of a rifle as any of the foregoing. With grooves too shallow the ball is no longer secure in its direction, and the slightest excess of charge will force it over the lands. Equally prejudicial is too great a depth, which prevents the lead from being driven to the bottom of the grooves without crushing the powder and disfiguring the ball. The grooves not being well filled, it follows that a portion of the gases will seek to escape, thus exerting, in the first place, an unequal pressure on the ball; and, in the second place, losing the effect of a portion of the gas; both of which will have an injurious influence on the trajectory of the ball after it leaves the piece, since the ball at the instant of quitting the muzzle is unequally acted on, and the gas escaping at any point, throws the ball to the opposite side. These causes impair both the accuracy and the range.

A depth varying from 0.011 inch to 0.019 inch may be assumed as most suitable for the pointed ball, loaded without patching. This, on the one hand, will not require the ball to be too heavily rammed, and, on the other, secures adequate control over it, so that it does not *strip*.

The diminution in the number of the grooves introduces the consideration of the relation between breadth of grooves and lands. In earlier times, when the ball was driven home by the aid of a mallet, a land narrower than the grooves was introduced, it being thought that the ball thereby took a better hold on the grooves. This consideration was applicable then when a greater inclination of the grooves was used, which would be likely to cause the ball, under the effect of a heavy charge, to *strip*. Now, however, that the twist of the grooves, as well as their number, is diminished, it is the better opinion that a groove narrower than the lands is in many respects preferable, for the diminished number has, in the first place, widened the former, and, in the second place, the repairs incidental to an arm in service, such as re-rifling, &c., might soon make them too wide.

II. THE SYSTEM OF DELVIGNE.

As early as 1828, a French officer, Captain **Delvigne**, not satisfied with the principles prevalent throughout Germany, relative to the rifle loaded with the tight fitting ball and patch, proposed a new system, and thereby gave the first impulse to the essential progress recently made in the armament of infantry. His system was as follows: the bore had twelve shallow grooves of pretty rapid twist, the breadth of which nearly equaled the lands, and the breech-pin was chambered in such a manner as to leave a rim projecting about the bottom of the bore. This chamber, the diameter of which was thus smaller than the bore, served to receive the powder without, however, being filled by it, whilst the rim prevented the ball from being rammed down on the powder. The windage allowed the ball to enter the bore freely. A further advantage of this rim, combined with the limited windage, was, that the center of the ball had a position in the axis of the bore. With three blows of the rammer the windage disappeared, and the lead was driven into the grooves.

This method of loading required no exertion of strength, nor any aid such as hammer and drift, but it entailed other injurious consequences. The upper part of the ball was flattened under the blow of the rammer, whilst the lower was driven into the chamber, thus greatly changing its shape, and by the forcible projection into the chamber crushing the powder. The latter circumstance, too, took away the required empty space between the powder and the ball.

These injuries to the powder and ball must necessarily have impaired the accuracy of the weapon, and the entire closing of the chamber increased the recoil. Delvigne maintained in a publication made in 1843, "*Sur l'emploi et les effets des projectiles cylindro-conique evidees*," &c., that the flattening of the ball increased the centrifugal force, and thereby its accuracy. How far this opinion is well founded, we will not now inquire, merely remarking that the flattening of the ball causes it to take up an unsteady tremulous motion.

III. THE SYSTEM OF PONTCHARA.

To obviate the flattening of the top of the ball, Captain Delvigne countersunk or cupped the head of the rammer spherically to the depth of 0.078 inches; and to prevent the ball from being driven into the chamber, Colonel Pontchara added a wooden cylindrical sabot, which was hollowed out at one end to receive the ball, and enveloped at the other by a greased patch coming half way up its sides. (Fig. 2.) This was to facilitate the loading by removing the dirt. These contrivances only partly fulfilled their object, however; for, the bore not being well cleaned by the patch, the sabot either stuck fast or was broken in the ramming, causing still a change of figure in the ball. New shapes of balls were thereupon proposed by Colonel Thierry and Captain Delvigne, experiments with which gave still less favorable results. The ball of the former was cylindro-spherical. (Fig. 3.) It was at first approved, but experiments instituted at St. Omer being highly unfavorable to it, the common infantry cartridge, with a charge of seven grammes, (108 grains, troy,) was substituted, to be in its turn abandoned. Delvigne's ball was cylindro-conical. (Fig. 4.) Both these new balls had a cavity extending from the center of the base upwards, partly to prevent the intrusion of the ball into the chamber, partly to diminish its weight.

In September, 1841, experiments were made at Liege, by a board of Russian and Belgian officers, with a Delvigne rifle with the cylindro-conical ball, a French arm with the Thierry ball, finally an English two-grooved rifle with the belted ball, the results of which were highly favorable to the system of Delvigne. Soon after, experiments were also made in France with the Delvigne rifle and its cylindro-conical ball, as well as with the Pontchara ball and sabot, before described, (Fig. 2,) which, however, did not result to the advantage of the former, and made way for the adoption of the latter.

The causes which prevented these balls from giving results more satisfactory were in the first place the erroneous position of the center of gravity, which lay too far back, causing the ball constantly to deviate through the action of the grooves, and oftentimes to fail in reaching the mark point foremost; and second, the little resistance opposed by the cylindrical part to the air. Resort was then again had to the Delvigne-Pontchara system, despite its known defects, and it was adopted in France, Belgium, and Austria, and, with some modifications, has been retained in the service last named.

IV. THE DELVIGNE-PONTCHARA SYSTEM.

This arm, known as the "chambered rifle," with which ten battalions of French troops were armed in 1840, was of the following construction: (Fig. 5, *a*, *b*.) The barrel was 30.44 inches long, had four grooves, 0.23 inch broad and 0.019 deep, with one eighth of a turn in the length of the barrel, or an inclination of 89° 44' 15". The caliber was 0.669 inch, the breech-pin had a chamber with a depth of 2.05 inches, and a diameter of 0.55 inch, which held 6¼ grammes, (96.43 grains,) and the rim of the chamber projected 0.027 inch beyond the lands. The ball had a diameter of 0.64 inch, and weighed 395 grains, and its windage 0.029 inch. The length of this arm, without sword-bayonet, was 47.58 inches, and the weight without bayonet 9.918 pounds. The breech sight consisted of a fixed or standing sight and a leaf with several notches for different distances.

In 1842, this model, having stood the test of service but indifferently, was changed for the following: Length of barrel 33.92 inches, caliber 0.688 inch. The chamber in the breech-pin was the same as the foregoing, and there were the same number of grooves, with the same breadth, depth, and turn, or an inclination of 89° 44' 39". The diameter of the ball was 0.669 inch, and its weight 452 grains; the charge was 96 grains.

About the same time, when the experiments with these rifles had resulted successfully, the Belgian light infantry were provided with a rifle of this sort, the barrel of which was 36.03 inches long, its caliber 0.669 inch, and it had six shallow grooves. The chamber was 0.57 inch diameter, the windage was the same as that of the French model of 1842, the charge 66 grains. The cartridges for the French and Belgian rifles were pasted their whole length, and also over the ball and sabot; the latter has a patch, the former lies in contact with the powder.

The Delvigne-Pontchara System, as altered by Baron Augustin.

In Austria this system was received with equal attention; but it was so modified by Baron Augustin as to dispense with the wooden sabot. The breech-pin, instead of having the rim heretofore used, was so reamed out as to give the ball a firm bed, without impinging on the powder, from which it was separated by a considerable space.

THE OVAL RIFLE. 191

The preservation of this space is essential, as it conduces to the complete ignition of the powder instantaneously with the movement of the ball, every point of which is thereby equally pressed. As a consequence of this equal and central effort of the gases, the ball follows the grooves more smoothly, and is not so easily driven over the lands.

The barrel of this Austrian chambered rifle is twenty-six inches long, and is terminated by a breech-pin bored out to a diameter of 0.487 inch, and a depth of 1.557 inch. The bed of the ball is reamed out to a depth of 0.11 inch. The empty space between powder and ball is [...] inch. The bore has a caliber of 0.713 inch, with twelve grooves, which have half a [...] the length of the barrel, or an inclination of 88° 43′ 19″, and a depth of 0.014 inch. The breadth of the groove is nearly equal to the lands. The ball has a diameter of 0.701 in[...] a windage of 0.014 inch, (Fig. 6, a, b.) The charge is sixty-two grains. The ball sh[own in] Fig. 6, c, weighs 309 grains, and is loaded without patch, being, however, first greased in a leathern bag.

It may here be observed that, in 1841, the Austrian infantry received the Consol or percussion primer lock, as altered by General Augustin, in place of the flint lock, from which it differed, as well as from the subsequent percussion lock. In this arrangement, the barrel has no touch-hole; but in place of it, a horizontal projecting cylinder, (Fig. 6, a,) which contains the vent, and which rests on a pan similar to that of the flint lock, fastened to the lock plate. This pan is closed over the cylinder by a spring lid, having a hole in the top, and a plug passing through it; the plug having something like a screw head, and tapering to a square end. As soon as the primer is inserted, and the lid closed down on the pan, the plug rests lightly on the match by its own weight. The hammer being heavy, descends with great force on the head of the plug, driving it into the priming, which is thereby exploded. The primer (Zünder) is itself made of thin sheet brass, simply rolled together, which contains the priming of fulminate of mercury. This little tube (Fig. 6, d,) is 0.81 inch long, and 0.08 inch diameter. One end of it is pinched, and receives a fine brass wire, by which it is handled and fastened to the cartridge.

V. THE OVAL RIFLE.

Meantime similar endeavours in Germany to improve the arms of the infantry became known. In 1831, Major Berner presented a new system in Brunswick, which was to unite the advantages of the smooth-bore and rifle—the ease of loading of the first with the accuracy of the second.

To this end, he gave the barrel a length of 39.64 inches, and a caliber of 0.62 inch, with two opposite shallow grooves 0.02 inch in depth, having a twist of three fourths, or an inclination of 88° 56′ 6″. The breadth of these was so arranged as to be 0.54 inch wide at the chamber, and for a distance of 5.153 inches. From this out they were only 0.287 inch wide, and were a flat oval, (Fig. 7, a b c.) The windage was 0.01. The barrel, furnished with a standing sight and three leaves, was closed with a patent breech.

The balls for this arm were, first, patched balls; and, second, rolling balls. Both at first received an oval form, (Fig. 8.) They were formed in the same manner, of two parts, not quite hemispheres, the largest diameter being for the patched ball, 0.66 inch, and for the last, 0.59 inch; and the smaller diameter for the first 0.61 inch, and for the last 0.56 inch. In spite of the somewhat favorable results of experiments, these forms were soon abandoned for the simple sphere. Then the patched ball had a diameter of 0.61 inch, and the rolling ball 0.59 inch. The charge for the first was sixty-seven grains, and for the last eighty-four grains. The weight of the arm, without bayonet, was 10.31 pounds.

The experiments were also pretty favorable with these balls, though inferior, especially with the rolling ball, to those of the oval ball. The cartridge of the patched ball (the paper of which was red, while that of the rolling ball was blue) had a wad between the powder and the ball. The patches were carried separately in a pouch.

This arm, known by the name of the "two-grooved Brunswick infantry," or "oval rifle," has the advantage that it can be used as rifle or musket, and excels the common and the Delvigne rifle in range and accuracy; but has itself been surpassed by the still greater accuracy and symmetry of action introduced in the construction of later systems.

In *Oldenberg* the infantry were likewise wholly armed with the oval rifle, slightly altered. The Oldenberg rifle, with a patent breech-pin, has a barrel 39.14 inches long, having a caliber of 0.676 inch. The breadth of the grooves is 0.34 inch, and their depth 0.029 inch, with three fourths of a turn in the length of the barrel, or an inclination of 88° 11' 1". The roll ball has a diameter of 0.646 inch; the patch ball 0.66 inch. The charge is 113 grains; the weight 10.87 pounds.

The arm here described is borne by the privates; that of the non-commissioned officers differing only in being of the nature of a rifle, and the breech-sight is a notch on the top of the hammer.

In *England*, where, in 1837, the light brigade was armed with a weapon of this kind, known as the "two-grooved rifle," the barrel is 30.04 inches long, with a caliber of 0.704 inch, (Fig. 11.) The two rounded grooves are 0.314 inch wide, and 0.039 inch deep, and have a twist of eleven hundredths, or an inclination of 89° 42' 26". The breech-sight, a simple steel plate, is 0.117 inch high, and 3.53 inches from the breech, while the bead is 0.786 inch from the muzzle. The charge is 2.82 drams; the weight of the ball 557 grains; and that of the rifle, without bayonet, with a length of 46.67 inches, is 9.7 pounds.

Instead of the patched ball, they use the belted ball, (Fig. 7.) which measures over the sides 0.696 inch; but over the belt, (which is 0.306 inch broad,) 0.752 inch, making the projection of the belt 0.028 inch. The windage of the ball in the lands is 0.031 inch, and that of the belt in the groove is 0.04 inch. A greased patch of good brown Holland is used with the ball. In consequence of the small windage, which is further diminished by the patch, the loading is as difficult as it was with the rifles heretofore used in Germany with ball and patch. This circumstance probably gave rise to the regulation that each rifleman should carry only twelve of the belted balls, and beyond that the common infantry cartridge with the spherical ball.

After a variety of experiments *in Hanover* with the oval arm, in 1834, others were instituted in 1842, on a larger scale, with 200 of this species of arm, the barrels of which were 39.71 inches long, and the caliber 0.646 inch. The two grooves, with nearly a full turn in the length of the bore, (fifteen sixteenths,) or an inclination of 88° 59' 48", had a depth of 0.028 inch, and a breadth of 0.258 inch. The charge was seventy grains, and the weight of the arm, without the bayonet, was 9.94 pounds.

VI. The Breech-loading System.

A. *The Needle Gun.*

Prussia had, in the mean time, applied herself with great secrecy to the improvement of her infantry arms; and, though not unmindful of the systems heretofore, and which remain to be noticed, and actuated by the same motives which led to those, she instituted and perfected a system totally different from any—the system of breech-loading. This arm is known as the "Prussian needle gun." As the mechanism of this arm is not so well known, it will not be out of place to enter into a somewhat detailed description of it.

The principle of the needle gun, viz: to insert the charge at the breech, with a view to ease and facility of loading, is by no means novel, it having been employed in the amusette of Marshal Saxe, the arms of Montalembert, of Robert, and of Lafoucheux, as well as in the wall pieces of the French, and in the chamber-loading gun of the Norwegians.

[There are in the Dresden gallery of small arms several of this sort, one of which surprisingly resembles the needle gun in the method of closing the breech, with the difference that, in place of the chamber being drawn back to load, the barrel is advanced, and that the conical termination of the barrel engages over that of the chamber, both terminations being provided with the half turn of a screw. The charge lies in the fixed chamber, and is ignited by a match lock, (*feuerschloss*.) A lever attached to the barrel serves to turn and to move it back and forth. Fig. 16.]

The inventor of the present Prussian needle gun is Mr. Dreyse, manufacturer of arms at Sömmerda. As early as 1835 he sought to attain the advantage of ease and facility of loading by closing the breech with two screws behind each other, having a space between them. In this space there was a spiral spring, which carried a needle, working through the middle of the inner screw. A simple mechanism enabled this spring to be drawn back; and when let loose, the penetration of the needle into the fulminate caused the ignition of the charge.

The cartridges with spherical balls used with this arm were at first inserted at the muzzle, and had a priming of fulminate at the bottom, which frequently exploded prematurely when rammed too hard, or when the needle projected beyond the inner screw. The windage, too, had to be increased to secure sufficient ease of loading, which prevented the ball from taking a sufficient hold on the sides of the bore.

These objections induced the projector to insert the cartridge at the breech, as was done in Norway, and hence arose the new Prussian needle gun. In reference to the Norwegian breech-loading gun it may be briefly remarked, now, that the barrel is open at the rear, and there is a separate chamber for the charge, with a caliber somewhat larger than that of the barrel. The ball is cylindro-conical.

In the Prussian needle gun the cartridge is inserted at the rear; the ignition is produced by the intrusion of a needle into the fulminate attached to the cartridge, and the closing of the open barrel is effected by the fitting of the front end of the chamber to the rear of the barrel.

The barrel, the rifled part of which is 36.06 inches long, has a caliber of 0.606 inch, with four grooves, having a twist of five-elevenths in the length of the barrel, or an inclination of 88° 6' 17". The breadth of these is 0.243 inch, and their depth 0.03 inch. The unrifled portion at the rear makes a kind of chamber, or *bed of the cartridge*, the diameter of which is 0.69 inch, or several hundredths greater than the bore, and the length nearly the same as that of the cartridge. The bed of the cartridge enlarges slightly to the rear so as to admit the cartridge easily after repeated discharges; the enlargement must, however, be limited, otherwise it would interfere with the central position of the cartridge. Where the bed of the cartridge unites with the grooves and lands, which latter project on account of the smaller caliber of the bore, there is a gradual slope to prevent too sudden a compression of the ball into the bore, and to facilitate its passage. To the same end there is a slight enlargement of the lower part of the bore for the distance of 6.17 inches. The rear of the barrel terminates externally conically, and is called the *mouth-piece of the barrel*.

Over these parts the cylinder, with its six-sided head, (*a*,) is screwed. (Fig. 18.) This is cut out to such a length and breadth on its right side (*b*) as to admit of easy entrance to the cartridge, whilst to the rear the cut is continued in a zig-zag, (*c*,) so that the hind part lies exactly in the middle. Upon the right upper side of the cylinder, at the edge of the broad cut, a reinforce is left sloping toward the head, called the stoll-bed, and serves as a *point d'appui* for the *stoll* or stop of the chamber, hereafter to be described. The end projecting at *e* forms the tang by which the cylinder is fastened to the stock, by means of a screw passing through the trigger-plate. To the same end there is over the trigger-plate a second screw, the thread of which enters the barrel. And, finally, there is the trigger hole (*f*) in the under side of the cylinder. The object of the cylinder is to hold all the other mechanism of the piece.

The chamber, (Fig. 19, *a*, *b*, *c*, *d*,) which lies next to the cylinder, is reamed out conically at its front end, and thence cylindrically to the depth of 1.38 inch and 0.92 inch in diameter. The part reamed out conically is called the *chamber mouth-piece*, and fits against the rear end of the barrel, with the offset at the top of the cylindrical part, or air-chamber. The air-chamber has the needle-pipe (d) screwed into its breech, (a,) which is 0.46 inch thick. The needle-pipe is conical as far as it projects into the air-chamber, and the screw-thread is 0.46 inch long, terminated by a washer, (c;) below the washer there is the six-sided prism (b) and a short cylinder (g.) The stop (h) on the outside of the chamber is like the air-chamber breech, of one piece with the chamber, and has the breadth of the zig-zig of the cylinder. The object of this stop is to rest against the stoll-bed, which it is filed to fit, when the chamber is shoved in against the bore, and turned to the right. The handle (i) is screwed into the stop for the more convenient service of the chamber. The space (k) behind the breech of the air-chamber serves to receive the locket, (schlösschen,) to which end the inner rear parts are channeled out. On the under side of the chamber, and in rear of the air-chamber breech, is the slot of the trigger (ll,) and on the upper side is the recess (m) for the nose of the locket.

As already intimated, the locket (Fig. 20 a, b) is inserted in the empty space to the rear of the air-chamber, and contains the needle socket (Fig. 22) with its needle and spiral spring, (Fig. 24.) It is bored out cylindrically from above to within 1.8 inch of the end, where the part (a) which has the spiral spring is somewhat narrower. The bottom, 0.18 inch thick, is pierced with the hole (b) for the bolt. On the outer upper side of the locket is the recess (c) and the stop (d) for the main spring, (g,) which is held there by the part u. On the opposite side of the locket is the straight slot (e) for the trigger. The handle, (f,) projecting behind, serves partly for the better detaching of the locket, partly as a support for the mainspring, (Fig. 21,) which is filed at its front end so as to fit in the recess (d) on the inside of the locket, whilst on the under side it has a projecting tooth, (w.) The upper rear parts of the spring are furnished with offsets (x, y) which run in the grooves of the chamber. The part z is called the nose, and serves to disengage it from the rear offset of the chamber. The needle-stem (Fig. 22) is placed with the spiral spring on the inside of the locket, is cylindrical, and has two offsets (a, b) of the diameter of the locket. The forward offset touches the tooth of the mainspring, which projects inward; is reamed out on its front face, and, as it strikes the end of the needle-pipe with force, is covered with gum or caoutchouc. The other middle offset (b) serves as well for a support to the spiral spring as for a trigger in the setting of the locket. The spiral spring bears a weight of ten and a quarter to eleven and a quarter pounds. The needle stock is bored through its length to receive the needle, which is divided into the needle and its stem. The latter is of brass, and has screw threads cut on the end to screw it into the bolt. The needle is soldered into it to the depth of 0.46 inches.

The trigger-spring, with its stop and trigger, (Fig 23, a, b, c,) are on the under side of the cylinder. The first is several inches long; is fastened at one end by a screw to the cylinder, and has at the other end, on the side next to the cylinder, an upright stop, which reaches through the cylinder, the chamber, and the locket, to the offset of the needle bolt. The projection (b) is filed to receive the trigger (c.)

The trigger itself is a bow-shaped irregular lever, the short arm of which extends in the direction of the spring prolonged. By the pressure of the short arm against the cylinder the stop is drawn down, and releases the offset of the needle bolt.

The gun is loaded in this way: (Fig. 26 a, b.)

After it has been brought to a nearly horizontal position, with the but on the right hip, and the left hand at the lower band, the chamber drawn back from the mouth piece of the barrel, the cartridge is inserted through the right opening in the cylinder into its place, the chamber (a) again brought up to the mouth-piece (c) by means of the handle (d) and turned to the right. The cylinder is thus made to rest with the stop (d) against the oblique stoll-bed (e.) The chamber being shoved up engages over the mouth-piece of the barrel, and the turn to the right against the sloping face of the stoll-bed screws it up tight to its place.

The locket, which has projected somewhat to the rear, is now shoved up into the chamber,

THE NEEDLE GUN.

by which the notch of the mainspring engages the catch (*g*) at the inner rear end of the chamber; at the same time the middle offset of the needle-bolt is pressed against the trigger-stop, thus compressing the spiral spring, while the locket is prevented from returning by the catch of the mainspring just referred to.

It is to be observed here, that in turning the chamber to the right the hitherto corresponding slots of the trigger-stop are shoved sideways, and the stop enters the cross-cut *l'*.

Let now the trigger-stop be drawn down by pressure of the trigger so as to clear the offset of the needle bolt. The bolt will dart forward from the effect of the spring, and will strike the square end of the needle-pipe, which projects sufficiently to pass through the powder (*o*) of the charge and inflame the fulminate (*p*.)

The arm being loaded, to uncock it the locket must be drawn back, pressing on the mainspring.

At the time of the adoption of this new mechanism the cartridge was wholly altered, the sabot being enlarged and placed between the powder and the ball; a half round cavity being made on the upper side for the ball, and a recess in the inner side for the fulminate.

The ball (Fig. 27) is sphero-conical. The base is a hemisphere, 0.514 inch diameter, upon which is placed a cylinder 0.154 inch high and 0.639 inch diameter, terminated by a right cone 0.584 inch high, with its sides slightly curved. The weight of the ball is 450 grains. The paper sabot is made in this way: The paper intended for it is cut into strips somewhat broader than the pattern of the sabot requires. A strip (Fig. 28) is then broken into a long and a short part, which are wound on a machine and the ends pasted. The roll being completed and dry, it is pressed between two dies to give it a requisite shape, (Fig. 28, *c*,) by which it, now called a sabot, receives at the top and bottom recesses for the ball and the priming, which last is put in afterwards with considerable pressure. The bed of the ball has besides several incisions.

The paper for the cartridge, of a light quality and easily consumed, which is 2.67 inches long and 2.26 inches broad, is wrapped but once around an iron former, slightly tapering, being 0.638 inch above and 0.708 inch below. The lap is pasted and a peculiar and simple bottom made. The completion of the cartridge is not difficult, and is as follows: The cartridge having been filled and the powder slightly shaken down, the paper sabot is inserted with the priming of fulminate on the powder, the ball placed in the cavity prepared for it, and the cylinder gathered over the ball, but so as to show the point of it. (Fig. 29.) It is dipped, as far as the ball goes, in tallow. The charge of powder is fifty-six grains. The weight of a Prussian needle gun is 10.27 pounds to 11.3 pounds.

The advantages of this arm are:

First. The simplicity of the mechanism, which can be taken apart without screw driver, spring vice, &c.

Second. It can be safely and easily cleaned.

Third. The convenience and rapidity of loading in every position, especially in the contracted space of loop-holed walls and on horseback.

Fourth. The certain and uniform filling of the grooves since the ball has a diameter greater than the caliber.

Fifth. The reduced charge consequent on the entire consumption of the powder.

Sixth. The disuse of the rammer as such.

On the other hand the needle gun has its defects, among which the following are prominent:

First. A waste of ammunition from the ease and rapidity of loading, which can only be guarded against by putting it in the hands of good and experienced marksmen, who know the value of a good and well-timed shot.

Second. Weakening the spiral spring from constant use.

Third. A possibility that the needle may not penetrate to the priming, when the powder is packed too closely, or the spiral spring too weak.

B. *The Norwegian Breech-loading Rifle.*

This arm, (Fig. 30,) several times before referred to, was the forerunner of the Prussian needle gun. It is not, like that, fired by means of a needle, but with a cap, and the mechanism is quite different. The two have only the principle of breech loading in common. The arrangement is as follows: The barrel, (*a*,) which is 41.41 inches long, has six grooves 0.185 inch broad, and 0.029 inch deep, with five eighths of a turn in the length of the barrel, or an inclination of 88° 59' 48"; it terminates in a frame (*b*) 4.9 inches long; through the rear of which passes the eccentric, (*c*,) which, by the help of a handle on the outer right side, moves a cylinder (*d*.) This has a cylindrical chamber, with a spherical termination to receive the cartridge, and on the under side placed vertically the cone (*e*.) The diameter of the chamber is somewhat greater than the caliber of the bore, the latter being 0.65 inch, and the former 0.727 inch.

The parts of the lock, if it may so be called, all lie on the under side of the stock, being fastened to the trigger plate, and comprise the cock, (*f*,) the rear of which serves as a cam, the mainspring, (*g*,) the trigger, (*h*,) which also acts as a sear spring (*i*.)

The operation of these parts when the gun is cocked is as follows: The cock being drawn back against the pressure of the mainspring, by means of a projection on its right side for the thumb, the cam at the rear engages the notch (*k*) of the trigger, which is held in place by the spring *i* at *l*. The trigger being now pressed, the cam of the cock is disengaged, and the cock thrown up against the cone. As security against premature disengagement of the cock, a leather guard, fastened by a long thong to the guard bow, is laid under the raised cock, and fastened to the standard (*n*) by means of a pin.

To load, (Fig. 31,) the handle of the eccentric is turned backward, by which the cylinder, after receding 0.15 inch to 0.19 inch, is thrown upwards sufficiently to insert the cartridge and put the cap on the cone. The charging completed, the handle is again turned forward, which replaces the cylinder in the frame and closes it against the bore. To prevent the handle from turning back, of itself, a pin at the side of the frame fastens it as in the sporting needle gun.

The ball, (Fig. 32 *a*,) which is a cylinder terminated by an ogee, has but one shallow groove, and is 1.137 inch long, and 0.696 inch diameter. Its weight is 787 grains.

The cartridge (Fig. 32 *b*) is commonly of writing paper, and wound twice. One end laps over the groove of the ball, and is tied with a thick greased woolen thread, and the other end is turned down over the charge, which is 70 grains.

The arm just described must not be confounded with the breech-loading rifle constructed by First Lieutenant Von Frilitzen, and given to the Swedish marine in 1851. That differs from the Norwegian in having a sphero-conical chamber, which prevents the cone from going through, the metal being thicker, and obviates the deepening of the chamber, and the consequent accumulation of dirt. There is also on the inner face of the cone a small copper plate to prevent the direct action of the gases, and a cross-piece on the heel plate to guard the rear end of the chamber against sand, &c. Instead of the screw to the eccentric there is a bolt which admits an easier removal of the cylinder and eccentric. A projection on the side of the frame protects its side as well as the lever from external injury. Finally, the mainspring, which, in the Norwegian, is almost wholly exposed, lies within.

The dimensions of the bore are likewise different, the length of the Swedish being only 35.71 inches, and its caliber 0.514 inch. The six grooves are 0.015 inch deep, and have a half turn in the length of the bore, or an inclination of 89° 15' 10". The diameter of the chamber is 0.566 inch. The ball weighs 538 grains, and the charge 77 grains. The hausse is a leaf bent at right angles, and movable about an axis at the angle—the short arm serving for a distance of 300 Swedish ells, (195 yards,) the other for 500 ells, (325 yards.) It is retained in each position by a spring. The experiments made with this arm establish for it a much flatter trajectory than for the Norwegian—the greatest height for the range of 300 ells being two Swedish feet, (23.37 inches;) for 400 ells, three and three quarters Swedish feet, (43.82 inches;) and for 500 ells, six feet, (70.11 inches.)

To test the theory that greater accuracy was attained with a ball rounded off at the point, experiments were instituted with such and other balls; the result of which, for 540 shots, as to the deviation and the highest points of the trajectory, are recorded in the following table. The conclusion from them is, that this arm, with the rounded ball, gives greater accuracy and a flatter trajectory than the Norwegian breech-loading rifle, and that the Swedish tige rifle (*stift gewehr*) is but little behind the first in execution:

Distances.	Swedish breech-loading rifle. Pointed ball, charge 77.15 grains.			Rounded ball, charge 77.15 grains.			Pointed ball, charge [illegible] grains.			Pointed ball, charge [illegible] grains.			Norwegian breech-loading rifle.			Swedish tige.		
	Deviations in feet.																	
Swedish ells.	Horizontal.	Vertical.	Drop.	Horizontal.	Vertical.	Drop.	Horizontal.	Vertical.	Drop.	Horizontal.	Vertical.	Drop.	Horizontal.	Vertical.	Drop.	Horizontal.	Vertical.	Drop.
100 = [illegible] yards	[illegible]	[illegible]	[illegible]															
200 = [illegible] yards	[illegible]	[illegible]	[illegible]	.1046	[illegible]	[illegible]												
300 = [illegible] yards	[illegible]	[illegible]	7.794	[illegible]	[illegible]	[illegible]							[illegible]	[illegible]	[illegible]	.0919	[illegible]	[illegible]
400 = [illegible] yards	[illegible]	[illegible]	[illegible]	[illegible]	[illegible]	[illegible]	[illegible]	[illegible]	12.357				[illegible]	[illegible]	[illegible]	[illegible]	[illegible]	[illegible]
500 = [illegible] yards	[illegible]	[illegible]	[illegible]	[illegible]	[illegible]	[illegible]				1.070	[illegible]	[illegible]	[illegible]	[illegible]	[illegible]	[illegible]	[illegible]	[illegible]
600 = [illegible] yards	[illegible]	[illegible]	[illegible]	[illegible]	[illegible]	[illegible]							[illegible]	[illegible]	[illegible]	[illegible]	[illegible]	[illegible]
700 = [illegible] yards	[illegible]	[illegible]	[illegible]	[illegible]	[illegible]	[illegible]									[illegible]			[illegible]
800 = [illegible] yards															[illegible]			

C. *The Revolver Pistol.*

To this system belong the revolvers, which, for some years past, have made so much noise. This arm, known for several centuries under the name of "drehlinge,"* reappeared five or six years ago greatly elaborated, under the auspices of the American, Colonel Colt. It has since been much improved by two Englishmen, Adams and Deane, and is adopted as an arm for the English marine. The revolver of Colt is somewhat heavy, embraces several distinct parts, and requires cocking. Without further description of it, the improved one of Adams and Deane, which is decidedly preferable, will be described. The improvement consists chiefly in making the barrel and nearly all the external parts in one piece, the cylinder only being detached. The mechanism is mainly as follows: The rifle barrel, (*a*,) open at both ends, is continued to the rear, and forms an axis, (*c*,) about which the cylinder (*b*) revolves. There are five chambers in the cylinder, each of which comes in turn opposite to the barrel, and fits pretty closely to it. At the opposite end of the cylinder are, firstly, five corresponding cuts for the cones, which are screwed in; and, secondly, a five-toothed arrangement in a circle, (*d*.) The cock (*e*) is connected at its bent end (*f*) with the mainspring (*g*) by means of a swivel. On the opposite side is the notch, (*i*,) against which lies the pawl, (*k*;) here, also, is a second pawl, (*l*,) kept in place by the spring, (*m*.) The operation of the parts on each other begins with the trigger, and is as follows: The pressure on the trigger forces the pawl (*l*) into one of the notches, (*d*,) and causes the cylinder to revolve until a new chamber comes opposite to the barrel, when the revolution is arrested by the stop (*o*) on the trigger; at the same time the other pawl, (*k*,) by

* In the Dresden gallery of small arms, as well as in other collections, these "drehlinge," with wheel and match-locks, are to be seen, with dates of the last half of the sixteenth century and the first half of the seventeenth.

pressing on the notch (i) of the cock, raises it, turning it about a pivot screw. At the instant, however, that the revolution of the cylinder is arrested by the interposition of the stop, (o,) the pawl (l) glides out of the notch, (i,) and descending on the cone before it with the force of the mainspring, explodes the cap and fires the charge. The loading, which is done without a rammer, is easily effected, as the cartridge complete is put into the chamber, or else the ball, with a leather patch, is put on top of the powder. The Adams-Deane revolver has three advantages over Colt's: a more accurate fire, a greater range, said to extend to 100 meters, (109.36 yards,) greater penetration, superior rapidity of loading, and much less weight. The former weighs 2.954 pounds, the latter 4.494 pounds.

VII. The System of Wild.

In 1841, an engineer in the service of Zurich, named Wild, started, like Delvigne, with the proposition that it must be an error to drive the ball into the grooves, as was the custom with rifles, with such force as to injure its sphericity and to crush the powder under it. He aimed, likewise, at increase range and accuracy, combined with ease of loading.

With this view, he gave the bore six to eight shallow grooves, with a slight twist, and the ball a windage of 0.018 inch to 0.027 inch. The charging was done with loose powder or with cartridge. The cartridges had its ball and patch attached to its end in such a way that, when the cartridge and ball were placed in the muzzle, the patch, which was gathered over the ball by a string through the edges, could be opened again.

In loading with the powder loose, a piece of paper must be placed on the powder to prevent its adhering to the patch and burning it. When the patch is not greased, the bore is moistened with water to soften the dirt adhering from the previous discharge, and facilitate its removal by the next one. For this purpose a flask, holding perhaps three ounces of water, is carried. A contrivance at its mouth, when the flask is placed on the muzzle, supplies, with a slight pressure, the water required.

To apportion to each caliber and length of barrel the proper modicum of water, the following rules are observed: If the bore is wet at the muzzle after the discharge, there has been too much water; and if it be dry and covered with deposit from the powder, there has been too little. It should be nearly dry and quite clean after each discharge.

The ball is only moderately rammed. The rammer has a shoulder near the top, which prevents the ball from being rammed beyond a certain point; the powder cannot, therefore, be crushed.

Although the experiments instituted with this rifle in Switzerland in 1842, and later in Baden, gave favorable results, since, at 600 paces, (515 yards,) the balls were still effective, and more than 100 rounds could be fired out of the same piece without cleaning, it has been adopted in but few services. In Baden, Hesse-Darmstadt, and Wurtemburg, ten men in each company are armed with them.

VIII. The System of Thouvenin.

The Delvigne-Pontchara system did not at all answer the expectations formed concerning it in France, notwithstanding the manifold and carefully conducted experiments made. The cause of these unfavorable results was sought for in the change of figure from round to flat, which the ball undergoes in loading. A return was therefore made by Captain Minié to the cylindro-conical form of Captain Delvigne,* before described. It had now, instead of the cone, an ogee

---

* Captain Delvigne, fully aware from repeated trials of the advantages of the elongated ball, had meantime, in spite of many obstacles, unceasingly occupied himself in the improvement of his cylindro-conical ball, and had obtained many valuable results. He found, especially, that his ball must have a considerable windage on account of the barrel becoming foul. This

at the top. It terminated below in a truncated cone. Between these there was a groove, filled with a woolen thread steeped in tallow. The cavity from the base upwards was retained. These balls, however, were not approved for the rifles in use, notwithstanding the favorable results of experiments.

Meantime, Colonel Thouvenin, of the artillery, had endeavored to remedy the ascertained defects of the Delvigne-Pontchara system—which were partly the difficult fabrication of the cartridge and partly the breaking of the wooden sabot—by removing the sabot entirely, and by simplifying the construction of the cartridge, without abandoning the facility of loading with a given windage, or the correct position of the ball in the bore.

For this purpose he adopted, instead of the chambered breech-pin, the usual one, with a steel pin or stem projecting from the middle of it (Fig. 35) of half the diameter of the bore, and placed exactly in its axis. This permitted the ball to be rammed without disturbing the powder poured around it—the pin being long enough to project a certain distance above the powder. The stem or *tige*, at the same time, forced the ball when rammed into the grooves, and caused them to be filled.

Still the system did not obviate the disfiguration of the ball by the rammer, nor the consequent evils of diminished range and accuracy. The resistance of the air would still cause irregularity in the trajectory.

These considerations determined Colonel Thouvenin to adopt the cylindro-conical ball as invented by Delvigne, and altered by Captain Minié, and with far better results. In subsequent experiments the ball was altered, on the suggestion of Captain Tamisier, by abandoning the conical termination of the ball, and making the cylinder complete; and by using, instead of the one circular groove about it, a number of smaller angular grooves or "cannelures;" and above all, by placing the center of gravity nearer to the point of the ball. (Fig. 36.)

Captain Tamisier had observed in some experiments with Delvigne's ball with but one groove, (Fig. 34,) that it deviated much less from the true trajectory than the ball with smooth cylinders, and concluded that this must be due to the effect of the air on the lower sharp edge of the groove.

The adoption of this cylindro-conical ball made it necessary to cap or countersink the rammer head.

The successive alterations of the cylindro-conical ball need not be a matter of surprise. With the adoption of this form of missile arose many considerations relative to the resistance of the air, the weight of the ball, its range, and accuracy; all of which had a much smaller degree of influence on the round ball, where, when the caliber of the bore and the ball and its weight were given, nothing remained to be fixed but the charge and the elevation.

The chief consideration which weighed against the spherical and in favor of the elongated ball, and which experiments have verified, may be stated generally as follows: every ball assumes two motions, viz: a forward motion due to the impulse of the gases, and a rotary motion impressed on it by the grooves. The forward motion is prevented from exerting its full effect by the flattening of the ball, and the resulting increased atmospheric resistance; that is, the greatest range due to the impulse is not attained. The elongated ball was then hit upon. Its windage was, however, disadvantageous, because when the ball was placed in the barrel, its axis did not coincide with that of the bore, but inclined to one side, bringing the centre of gravity of the ball out of the axis of rotation, and occasioning great deviation. Did he, indeed, succeed in keeping the axis of the ball coincident with that of the bore, great range and accuracy were attained. He also remarked, that whenever the barrel became foul the great friction of the cylindrical part against the bore diminished the range and augmented the recoil. To reduce, therefore, the windage, and yet avoid the too great friction of the cylindrical part, he left a rim at the top and bottom of it, nearly the diameter of the caliber, the intervening portion being grooved out. By this means he avoided too great a windage, and attained a proper position for the ball in the bore, without being obliged to exert too much force on the ball when the barrel became foul. The grooved part was made use of to receive a patch of thread. This was the inception of the grooves, which have of late years become universal on the pointed ball, and which, as has been established by experiments, are essential to the regularity of the trajectory.

use is not recent; conical and pyramidal pointed balls having been used more than a century ago, with the difference that they were cast with grooves and lands. In the Dresden gallery are shown various rifles, with balls of this sort, (Fig. 37, *a b c d*.) Such elongated balls were, from their figure, much less influenced by atmospheric resistance than the round ones. For the same reason, they lose their velocity more slowly, and can bear an increased motion of rotation, that is a greater *twist*, without injury.* The latter will make the initial velocity smaller; but the loss of velocity will also be less than in the spherical ball.

As we have seen, the cylindro-conical ball had at first only one groove, (Fig. 34,) which was intended to receive yarn steeped in tallow. Subsequent circumstances led to the use of several grooves. The trajectory described by a ball of this kind, when discharged, is a curve, whose direction changes at each instant. The longest axis of such a ball may be regarded as tangent to the curve, from which position it departs the more, under the influence of the resistance of the air, the further the center of gravity lies to the rear; and this point will generally be found without the trajectory, *i. e.*, either above or below it. The axis of the ball must, however, be brought as near the direction of the trajectory as possible; and this is thought to be effected by the "*cannelures*," or grooves on the cylindrical part of the ball. Experiments with the grooved balls seem to justify the conclusion.

If we suppose the axis of the ball to coincide with the direction of the trajectory, the resistance of the air will be pretty equally distributed over its surface; but if the axis be, by any circumstance, deflected from this position—if, for example, the point of the ball rises—then the rear of the cylinder will be depressed, and the air will no longer act equally on all sides, but will exert a greater force against the sides of the grooves underneath, and will continue to press that part upwards until the pressure on all sides is again equalized, and the axis of the ball restored to its position tangent to the trajectory.

Theory and practice unite in this, that the groove must be in rear of the position of the center of gravity, and not in front, which the following considerations will serve to illustrate. The ball will at once rotate about its center of gravity, and will at the same time begin its deviations, revolving like the long and short arm of a lever. If now this point lies too far towards the base, and a portion of the grooves is in advance of it, the currents of air, instead of tending to restore the ball to its tangential position, will, by their effect on these grooves, still further deviate it; while the effect on those in the rear of the center of gravity, which tends to bring the ball back to its normal position, will be neutralized and overcome.

On account of their shape, which secured an easier passage through the air, the pointed balls were much less affected by it than the round balls, as well in reference to velocity as deviation; a fact which was early illustrated, and was further established by experiments made in Sweden in 1839, and in Switzerland in 1848, 1849, and 1850. The same conclusion was deduced from the experiments in Saxony in 1851. On this account they have a more uniform velocity, and greater force and penetration, and the trajectory is less curved—an essential point, when we consider that the influence of gravity is the same in both.

A comparison of the trajectories of the two species of balls will readily establish the different effect of the air on each.

Let, for example, a pointed ball, under the influence of powder alone, describe the space C to c, (Fig. 38,) in a second or a portion of a second of time, in the direction of $a b f$, the prolongation of the axis of the bore, with which the axis of the ball coincides. As, however, the resistance of the air and the law of gravity act incessantly, the ball at the end of the first instant of time will be at c', instead of c, under the influence of the first, and at c'', instead of c', under the effect of the second.

* It has lately been recommended to adopt a smaller twist, between one half and three fourths of a turn, so as not to increase the friction too much, and yet retain the desired rotation of the ball.

In the second instant of time, for the same reason, the ball will be at d', instead of d, and in the third at e', in place of e, and so on; for by the law of gravity, whether the body be moving horizontally or vertically, it will fall in the first second about 16 feet; in the second, 64; in the third, 144, and so on; or in the ratio of one, four, nine, &c.

Let us now look at the trajectory of the round ball. As it experiences a greater resistance from the air, it will not, in the first instant of time, be at e, like the pointed ball, but at g, and from the effect of gravity at g'; in the second, at h'; in the third, at g', &c. From this it will be seen that the trajectory of the pointed ball is much flatter than that of the round ball, and hence the elevations are less for the same distance.

It is to be observed, nevertheless, that the pointed ball of the *tige* arm may, by an oblique position on the tige, have a greater tendency to deviate from the direction of the axis of the bore than the old patched ball of the rifle. The deviations of the ball at the muzzle of the piece may therefore be greater in the former than in the latter; but these deviations will always be comprehended between two right lines, A C and A D, (Fig. 39,) on each side of the true direction, the resistance of the air having much less effect to deviate the pointed ball; while the path of the spherical ball, which at first departed less from the true direction, following the curved line A E or A F, will, at greater distances, lie outside of the first.*

Hence arises a peculiar relation between the degrees of deviation of these two species of ball. There is, for example, a certain distance (A G) when the deviation of each is about equal; at a greater distance, the pointed ball has less deviation, and at a smaller distance, the reverse is the case. The deviations are nearly in the ratio of their distances, so that at 500 ells they are ten times greater than at fifty ells.

In loading the pointed balls it is especially necessary to ram the balls uniformly, in order to attain uniform shots. Too light or too hard ramming will cause the ball to be unsteady. In the latter case particularly the ball will not offer the proper amount of resistance to the gases, which will escape on all sides of it, through the windage, and it will not properly follow the grooves. In the former, the ball may take a hold injuriously strong, and cause the shot to be entirely thrown away. Finally, too heavy ramming may unduly diminish or entirely obliterate the vacant space between the powder and ball, and cause the powder to be crushed.

It is no less necessary that the countersink of the rammer head should be central, otherwise the conical portion of the ball will be forced out of its position in the axis of the bore, which will necessarily cause an irregular shot.

According to every probability the motion impressed on the elongated balls by the grooves resembles in the first instance a spiral† enveloping the true trajectory, with which it coincides only at a distance, and becomes a true rotary motion.

Advantages of Thouvenin's system.

1. It is more easily and therefore more quickly loaded than the old rifle with patched balls.

2. The powder cannot be easily crushed in ramming.

3. Greater accuracy, ascribable in part to the ball not being flattened, nor the powder crushed, and in part to the pointed form of the ball.

---

* From notices of the experiments in Saxony in 1851.

† This spiral motion of a ball or shell was observed and noted in some experiments made at Old Point Comfort, early in 1852, with elongated 24-pounder flanged shells fired from a rifled cannon. Though the gun was pointed at the center of a target 400 yards distant, with the greatest nicety, by means of a long cylinder inserted in the bore, the projecting part of which was arranged with pendulum sights, yet the shell passed over a target twelve feet high and grazed the sand 200 yards in rear, in a line with the gun and target, the missile afterwards attaining an extreme range of over 1,980 yards. The theory of the spiral or helix was applied as the only satisfactory explanation of the phenomenon. The gun used had two grooves, with one turn in thirty-six feet.—*Translator.*

Defects of this System.

1. The cleaning of the bore about the tige is very difficult.
2. The ball will not always fill the grooves, which will cause irregular shooting.
3. The necessarily heavy ramming of the ball unavoidably forms a projecting ring on its conical part, which cannot but be prejudicial to the flight of the ball.
4. The occasional bending of the tige by use, which throws it out of center.
5. The accuracy is too dependent on the proper ramming of the ball.

It being now incontestible that the tige rifles, of the system of Thouvenin, with the ball of three circular grooves, satisfied the conditions of increased accuracy and range in a greater degree than any of the prior systems, some of the arms which had been altered to the Delvigne-Pontchara system were changed, by substituting for the chambered breech-pin a solid one with a steel tige 1.49 inch long, and 0.35 inch in diameter, screwed into it. The bore (Fig. 40, a, b.) 34.16 inches long had a caliber of 0.70 inch, greater by 0.011 inch than the model of 1842. It had four grooves 0.275 inch wide, and decreasing in depth toward the muzzle, being 0.0196 inch at the bottom, and 0.0118 inch at the top. The twist was changed so as to have four tenths of a turn, or an inclination of 89° 14' 19". The breech-sight, consisting of a leaf and slide, was graduated to a distance of 1,300 meters, (1,422 yards.) The weight of the arm was 8.8 pounds. Weight of ball 725 grains, and its greatest diameter 0.676 inch. The charge was sixty-nine grains.

The French cartridge consists of a cylinder of thin writing paper, into which the ball is shoved point foremost, as far as half of its cylindrical part. After the powder has been introduced, a wrapper envelopes the whole, and is folded down over the end where the ball is, and twisted at the other. It is not pasted. (Fig. 42.)

The favorable results obtained from the arm, altered to the system of Thouvenin, with the last-named ball, caused it to be applied, in part, to the smooth-bore arm of the infantry. A tige was screwed into the breech-pin, and that the metal might not be too much reduced at the muzzle, the grooves were, at the suggestion of Captain Tamisier, made only 0.019 inch at bottom, and died out at the muzzle. The twist was four tenths, or once in two meters, (6.56 feet.) The breech-sights, arranged for various distances, were soldered on at 3.14 inches in front of the chamber. The rammer head was cut off and replaced by another, cupped to suit the shape of the ball. The cartridge, with a charge of sixty-nine grains, was entirely like that of the tige rifle, both having the same caliber.

The experiments made with infantry arms, altered in this manner, gave results nearly equal to the tige rifle as to accuracy and penetration. At 800 meters, (874 yards,) at a target six meters long and two high, the hits were thirty-three per cent. At that distance the ball passed through four one-inch boards.

Beyond the limits of France, the system of Thouvenin was next received into favor in *Belgium*, and superseded the chambered rifle, hitherto used, on the Delvigne-Pontchara plan. The barrel of the new arms, which took the name of carabine à tige, was 34.08 inches long, bored with a diminishing caliber, being 17.5 mm. (0.688 inch) at the muzzle, and 17.7 mm. (0.696 inch) at the breech. The four grooves, which had one turn in two meters, or an inclination of 89° 10' 27", were 0.25 inch broad, and 0.011 inch deep. The tige was 1.18 inch long, and 0.35 inch diameter. The breech-sight, placed at 3.54 inches from the rear end of the barrel, consisted of a leaf and slide, like the French, and at its bottom a fixed sight, which served for the shortest distances when the other was lying down.

The ball (Fig. 45) approaches the conic-parabolic, and has three grooves, the upper two of which are filled with tallow. It is 1.125 inch long and 0.672 inch in its greatest diameter, where the conical and parabolic parts meet, the base having a diameter of 0.648 inch. The windage is 0.015 inch, and its weight 731 grains.

The cartridge is wound double and pasted its whole length, and the open end is drawn over the ball to the first groove to which it is tied with a woolen thread.

The charge, which contains four grammes of fine powder, (sixty-two grains,) lies against the base of the ball, and has the loose end of the cartridge, twisted only, turned down over it. (Fig. 46.)

The system also attracted so much attention in Germany, that most of the States adopted it with various modifications.

In *Prussia*, experiments were likewise instituted with tige rifles with the best results; in consequence of which this system (Delvigne-Thouvenin) was adopted for the rifles of all the Jäger battalions, except that of the guard, which had the needle gun.

The Prussian tige rifle has the following dimensions: the barrel, which is octagonal, has a caliber of 0.576 inch, and a length, exclusive of the patent breech-pin, of 27.63 inches. It has eight tray-shaped grooves, which, like the lands, are 0.112 inch wide, and are 0.025 inch deep, with a twist of three quarters, or an inclination of 88° 33′ 7″. The patent breech-pin has a conical chamber 0.927 inch deep, whose inferior diameter is 0.287 inch, and its superior 0.576 inch. The stem screwed into the bottom of the chamber is steel, with a spring tem inch long without its screw, and 0.267 inch diameter. The upper face of the tige is n flat.

The breech-sight, (Fig. 48,) which is 6.05 inches distant from the rear of the barrel, of a standing sight and two leaves; the first for distances from 200 to 250 paces, and the smaller of the second for distances up to 300 paces. The highest has three slots, with notches for 400, 500, and 600 paces; and at the top there is a notch for 700 paces, (nearly 580 yards.) The elevation measured from the axis of the base are: for the standing sight, 0.79 inch; for the smaller leaf or 300 paces, 0.91 inch; for 400 paces, 1.03 inch; for 500 paces, 1.22 inch; paces, 1.47 inch; and for 700 paces, 1.71 inch.

The ball (Fig. 49) is cylindro-conical. The cylindrical part has two dee depth, is 0.555 inch in diameter, and 0.363 inch long. The conical part h inch. The sides of the conical part are not rectilinear, but slightly curve between 0.005 inch and 0.015 inch. The caliber ball increases accord the normal caliber of 0.602 inch, to 0.617 inch. eight of the ball of n grains. The powder flask is used almost exclu ough the charge, wh fine powder, is also carried in cylinders, with the ball loosely attached.

The length of the rifle, without sword-bayonet, (*hirschfänger*,) is 49.25 inches; 10.03 pounds.

The countersink of the rammer head is conical, and does not therefore exactly fit the curved shape of the ball, but its largest diameter is somewhat greater than the corresponding part of the ball, which facilitates the forcing of the lead into the grooves.

Besides these rifles a wall piece (*defensions-gewehr*) has been adopted for fortresses. The length of the barrel is 49.91 inches, and its caliber 0.72 inch. It has four grooves rounded at the edges, with a twist of five eighths, or an inclination of 89° 0′ 46″, a breadth equal to the lands, and a depth of 0.02 inch. The patent breech-pin is chambered conically to the depth of 1.34 inch, the superior diameter being 0.72 inch, and the inferior 0.548 inch. The *tige* is 1.86 inch long, and 0.308 inch in diameter, and projects 0.51 inch above the chamber.

The ball (Fig. 51) is cylindro-conical, and is 1.23 inch long. The cylindrical part, with three grooves, is 0.694 inch in diameter, and 0.548 inch long; and the height of the conical part, the sides of which are slightly curved, is 0.617 inch. The weight of the ball is 483.88 grains.* The grooves are filled with a composition of wax, tallow, and lard. Nine balls go to

---

* Probably an error, as the weight given afterwards is nine to the pound—equal to about 777 grains.—*Translator.*

the pound. The cartridge in which the ball is placed, point inward, is tied between the powder and the ball, and both ends are turned down and not pasted. (Fig 52.) The breech-sight is 1.089 inch from the rear of the barrel. The charge is 102 grains.

In *Bavaria*, the rifles adopted in 1848 were altered to tige rifles, by increasing the caliber of the bore, (Fig. 51, *a b*,) which had a length of 26.156 inches, from 0.556 inch, to 0.566 inch. It has seven grooves 0.1419 inch broad, and 0.017 inch deep. The width of the grooves, which had a twist of three fourths in the barrel, were to the width of the lands as three to two. The tige, which terminated in a flat cone, was, as in all these arms, screwed into the breech-pin, and had a length of 1.617 inch. It projected 0.3 inch beyond the charge.

The breech sight consisted of a standing sight and two leaves, respectively for two, four, and six hundred paces, (164, 329, and 493 yards.)

The Bavarian pressed ball for this arm is as follows: Its whole length is 0.957 inch, of which 0.411 inch is cylindrical, and has three grooves. The diameter of this part corresponds to the caliber, except the lower rim, which is 0.02 inch greater. The upper part comes to a point with a considerable curve. (Fig. 54.) The weight of the ball is 478 grains.

The cylinder of the cartridge is of paper, unpasted, and contains 58 grains, from which the ball is separated by a tie. (Fig. 55.) In loading, the end folded down is not bitten off but turned, the powder poured in, the cartridge turned, and the ball shoved out of it with the rammer, which, to give a better hold, has a wooden knob. It is pushed home and rammed three times, which drives the tige from 0.15 inch to 0.09 inch deep into the lead, and fills the grooves. A space of 0.18 inch is still left between the powder and the ball.

The Bavarian rifles are of three calibers, 0.556 inch, 0.587 inch, and 0.597 inch.*

In *Saxony*, the Jäger rifles were also altered to this system in 1849, by giving the patent breech-pin a conical chamber, screwing a steel tige into the bottom, and attaching to the rammer a head, countersunk to suit the shape of the ball. To save the bore the head was inlaid with a brass ring at its greatest diameter in the middle.

The length of the barrel was 29.54 inches without the breech-pin, and its caliber 0.576 inch. The eight grooves had a depth of 0.027 inch, and a breadth of 0.073 inch, with three fourths of a turn in the length of the barrel, or an inclination of 88° 39′ 44″. The depth of the chamber inch, its inferior diameter 0.465 inch, and its superior 0.576 inch. The steel tige was 1.12 inch long, and 0.28 inch in diameter. (Fig. 56 *a b*.) The ball was a cone, with a cylindrical base, having one broad groove to receive a greased woolen thread. (Fig. 57.)

Two years after the alteration of the Jäger rifles to the Delvigne-Thouvenin plan, the long infantry arm, on the system of Thouvenin alone, was adopted. The barrel of this arm is 40.39 inches long, with a caliber of 0.576 inch. The four grooves, which are 0.023 inch deep, and 0.19 inch broad, have three eighths of a turn in the length of the barrel, or an inclination of 89° 10′ 49″.

The cylindrical tige screwed in as usual, is 1.67 inch long, and 0.287 inch diameter. It projects from 0.18 inch to 0.275 inch beyond the charge, which space the three strokes of the rammer diminishes to 0.07 inch, or 0.09 inch, leaving a vacant space between the powder and the ball of 0.185 inch. (Fig. 58 *a b c*.)

The breech-sight, which is 4.82 inches from the rear of the barrel, consists of a standing sight for a distance of 200 paces (154 yards) and two leaves; the lowest for 400, the highest for 600 paces. The height of the standing sight above the axis of the bore is 0.948 inch, that of the lower leaf 1.06 inch, and that of the higher 1.56 inch. The rammer is countersunk for the ball·

---

* At the beginning of the year 1854, the rifles thus altered to the system of Thouvenin were remodeled with favorable results. The barrel, whose caliber is the same as that of the smooth-bore arms, and increases 0.007 inch towards the breech, has four shallow grooves, with a half turn in the length of the bore. The hausse consists of a standing sight, and a leaf with a slide which works in a groove that carries it to the left as it ascends, thus correcting the deviation from "drift" by carrying the breech to the right. The sight is graduated from 200 up to 1,000 paces. The ball is of a cylindro-conical form.—*Darmstadt Military Gazette*, 1854, Nos. 141 and 148.

The ball adopted for the altered rifles was abandoned, and the Oldenburg pattern, to be described hereafter, (Fig. 59,) used instead. This had a cylindro-ogival shape, with two grooves, of which the lower was filled with a composition of suet and wax. This ball was itself afterwards changed to the parabolic, or the form which gives the greatest divergence to the opposing currents of air. It has but one groove, which is filled with yarn steeped in tallow. The greatest diameter, 0.569 inch, is above the groove, the rim below it being 0.002 less. (Fig. 60.) The weight of the ball is 359 grains, and that of the powder 79 grains.

The cartridge is of paper, with its edges pasted over each other, and its upper end tied over the point of the ball with strong twine. The charge lies against the bottom of the ball, and the paper is folded and turned down. (Fig. 61.)

To load, the fold is bitten off, the powder poured in, and the empty paper torn from the ball, which is inserted and rammed three times.*

The lock for the arm, (Fig. 62 a b,) known, from its arrangement and position on the stock, as the back-action lock, differs from those of the smooth-bore arms in a greater simplicity, and the different location of the parts. It has but one spring, which serves both as main and sear spring. Its long arm is attached to the sear by a link, which obviates the great friction between the notch of the tumbler and the main spring in the ordinary lock, and accelerates the descent of the hammer. The tumbler has two notches, the front one of which is so far forward as to elevate the hammer a very little, and prevents the cap from falling off the cone. Moreover, the lock has but two screws passing through the bridle, which secure everything except the main spring to the lock plate. The lock itself is fastened by sliding the rear end under a fixed screw, and securing the forward end to the stock with a lock screw.

About the time of the adoption of this arm in Saxony, the Delvigne-Thouvenin system was also adopted in *Mecklenburg*, and extended to their carbine and pistols—one caliber being prescribed for all three arms. They were called the "pointed-ball rifle," (pistol, and carbine.)

The length of such a rifle is 38.40 inches, exclusive of the patent breech, and its caliber 0.597 inch; which, at the distance of 6.18 inches to 7.20 inches from the rear, increased 0.003 inch. The four grooves have equal width with the lands, and are 0.02 inch deep, with an inclination of 68° 30′ 43″, or a full turn in 37 inches.

The patent breech-pin has a conical chamber of 1.43 inch deep, with a superior diameter of 0.61 inch, and an inferior diameter of 0.534 inch. The stem is screwed into the middle of the bottom from right to left. It is cylindrical at bottom, but squared towards the top, which is rounded. The length of the stem without screw is 0.206 inch, and diameter 0.28 inch, projecting 0.61 inch above the chamber. (Fig. 63 a b.)

The ball is cylindro-ogival in shape, with two grooves, the upper for tallow, the under for attaching the cartridge. Its length is 0.895 inch, of which 0.378 inch is cylindrical. The diameter of the cylindrical part is 0.586 inch, and of the lower rim 0.556 inch. The windage is 0.027 inch; the weight of the ball 451 grains, and that of the charge 56 grains. (Fig. 64.)

The cylinder of the cartridge is conical, like the Oldenburg, hereafter to be described, and is, like that, tied in the lower groove. (Fig. 65.) The shape from which the cylinder is made is of thin, but strong paper. It is convex above and concave below, with the same center. The paper wraps twice about the conical former. (Fig. 66.)

Hanover adapted the system of Thouvenin, about the same time, to two of their arms—the seven-grooved rifle-musket and the eight-grooved rifle.

The barrel of the musket is 40.26 inches long, with a caliber of 0.618 inch. Its seven grooves are 0.119 inch broad, and have an inclination of 88° 56′ 30″, or a twist of three fourths. The breech or tang screw, which has a channel for the vent, has the tige screwed into the middle of it. The tige is one and a half calibers long and half a caliber in diameter. (Fig. 67 a b.)

---

* The tige rifles first introduced are no longer retained, as the Jäger battalions have been armed with the last-named rifled infantry arm. Besides these battalions, two non-commissioned officers and sixteen privates of each company of infantry of the line, called the sharp-shooters, carry them.

The breech-sight consists of a standing sight and a leaf, and is 7.09 inches distant from the rear of the barrel.

The eight-grooved rifle is 28.758 inches long, with the same thread and caliber as the foregoing. Its grooves, which are 0.095 inch broad, differ from the last in being progressive, 0.014 inch deep at the breech, and 0.0095 inch at the muzzle. The breech is not, as in the seven-grooved rifle, closed by a tang screw, but by a patent breech, into which the tige, of the same dimensions as above, but somewhat pointed, is screwed. (Fig. 68 a b.)

The breech-sight consists of a standing sight and two leaves, and is 0.44 inch from the rear of the barrel. The charge for both arms is fifty-nine grains rifle powder.

The weight of the rifle-musket is 10.56 pounds; that of the tige rifle 11.57 pounds, without bayonets.

The rifle-musket is carried by the non-commissioned officers and riflemen of the line, and the privates of the light infantry—the rifle, by the non-commissioned officers of the light infantry alone.

The ball (Fig. 69 a) is cylindro-conical in shape, the cylindrical part being 0.8 inch high and 0.61 inch in diameter, with one groove for tying the cartridge, the loose end of which is folded twice at right angles and turned down in the Prussian manner. The cylinder itself is made of fine but strong vegetable paper, (*pflanz papier*,) not pasted. The cartridge at the ball end is dipped in tallow, as far as the tie. The ball weighs 444 grains. Each man carries in his cartridge-box sixty rounds in bundles, with seventy-two caps.

The system of *Thouvenin* has been in use in *Oldenburg* since 1847, and has entirely superseded the smooth-bore arms.

Length of bore 39.12 inches; caliber, which is slightly enlarged at the bottom, 0.688 inch. Number of grooves, four, with half a turn in the length of the bore, or an inclination of 89° 11′ 1″. Breadth of grooves 0.193 inch, depth of same 0.031 inch. The patent-breech has a chamber, the upper diameter of which is the same as the caliber, and the sides curved spherically, into which the tige, 1.53 inch long and 0.31 inch thick, is screwed. It is pointed.

The breech-sight consists of a standing sight 0.45 inch high, and two leaves; the first for 300 paces 0.67 inch high, and the second for 600 paces 1.33 inch high. In the last are two notches, for 400 and 500 paces, [the Oldenburg pace is 30.93 inches.] (Fig. 70 a b.) The weight, with bayonet, is 11.67 pounds, and without bayonet, 10.97 pounds.

The ball is of the cylindro-ogival shape, and has two grooves. Its greatest diameter, at the junction of the cylinder and ogee, is 0.658 inch, whilst the lower rim is only 0.61 inch. The cylindrical part is 0.339 inch, and the ogee 0.728 inch. The upper groove is filled with a composition of tallow and wax, whilst the lower serves to secure the cartridge. (Fig. 71 a.) Its weight is 462 grains. The cartridge is intended to be inserted entire. (Fig. 71 b.)

The cylinder is made of a piece of paper, whose upper side is convex and the lower concave, and has an offset at the bottom. (Fig. 71 c.)

After the insertion of the charge—which is 58 grains of fine powder—and the ball, the cartridge is tied in the lower groove. The bottom of this cartridge has the diameter of the tige, and cannot therefore be made to surround it, but must go between the loose powder surrounding the stem and the ball. The powder in these cartridges must be closely packed, which secures an easier bursting of the cartridge in ramming.

In *Nassau*, where, for several years, the arms of the sharp-shooters have been modeled on the system of Thouvenin, the barrel of the tige gun has a length of 39.41 inches, and a caliber of 0.69 inch. The number of the grooves is five, their inclination 88° 47′ 22″, or three fourths of a turn, and their depth 0.018 inch; width or breadth somewhat less than the lands. The length of the steel-tige is 1.21 inch, and its diameter 0.35 inch. The distance of the hausse from the bead is 28.19 inches. The weight of this arm is 9.24 pounds, without bayonet.

The ball is cylindro-ogival in shape, (Fig. 73 a,) is 1.08 inch long, of which 0.463 inch is cylindrical, and has three sharp but not deep grooves. Its diameter is 0.671 inch, and its weight 721 grains.

The cylinder is a single thickness, not pasted, (Fig. 73 *b*,) and has the ball turned point inwards. It is folded square down over the base of the ball, and dipped in tallow, as far as the cylindrical part extends. The other end of the cartridge is also folded down square, in the manner of the Saxon infantry cartridge. The charge is 69 grains, and surrounds the point of the ball.

In *Sardinia* the infantry has two sorts of rifled arms besides the smooth-bore, one of which is the short rifled infantry musket, (*Fucile di Fanteria corto. mod.*, 1844,) and the other the rifle of the Bersaglieri, (*carabina de Bersaglieri*.) The first follows the system of Thouvenin, and is modeled after the French tige rifle; the last, the Austrian chambered rifle, which has no tige, and throws a cylindro-conical ball.

The length of bore of the infantry rifle-musket is 40.43 inches, caliber 0.689 inch, number of grooves four, depth of grooves 0.021 inch, breadth 0.23 inch. The length of the tige is 1.45 inch to 1.49 inch, and its diameter 0.334 inch. The grooves have but a slight inclination, like those of the French tige rifle, which it closely resembles. The weight of the arm, with bayonet, is ten pounds.

The ball, (Fig. 74 *c*,) like the cartridge, (Fig. 74 *d*,) exactly after the French pattern, has a cylindro-ogival form, and its grooves are angular and not very deep. It is 1.12 inch long, 0.657 inch in diameter, and weighs 713 grains. Charge sixty-three grains.

The barrel of the Bersaglieri rifle (Fig. 75 *a b*) is 29.44 inches long, and has a caliber of 0.665 inch. It has eight grooves, with an inclination of 88° 46′ 28″ or fourteen twenty-fifths of a turn, in the length of the bore. The breadth of the grooves is 0.092 inch, and their depth 0.11 inch. The cylindrical chamber is, like that of the Austrian chambered rifle, chamfered at the top, and is 1.85 inch long, and 0.444 inch in diameter. The weight, with bayonet, is 11.66 pounds, and without bayonet, 9.24 pounds.

The ball (Fig. 75 *c*) is cylindro-conical in form and without grooves. Its length is 0.929 inch, and its diameter 0.641 inch. Its weight is 540 grains, and that of the charge fifty-four grains.

In *Austria*, the chamber system of Delvigne, adopted for the rifles, was partially reformed by the introduction of the pointed ball (Fig. 76 *a*) without the tige.*

The ball is pressed and weighs 652 grains. It is 1.035 inch high, and 0.692 inch in diameter. The cylindrical part is 0.518 inch high, and has a single groove 0.089 inch deep to receive a cotton thread steeped in tallow.

The rammer for these chambered rifles has a hole through the solid part of the head for a pin, to serve as a handle in drawing the ball, &c.; this hole communicates with the countersink, in order to permit the escape of the air in ramming.

The cartridge cylinder is not pasted, but folded down over the base of the ball, (Fig. 76 *b*.) The ball is turned point inwards, and is tied with a thread over the point, which prevents the access of the powder and gives the cylinder the required stiffness. The loose end is folded down and the primer attached to it. In each company of infantry of the line two non-commissioned officers and sixteen privates are furnished with these chambered rifles.

In the grand duchy of *Luxemburg* the Jäger rifles, originally designed for patch balls, were several years ago altered to the system of Thouvenin.

The length of the barrel, which is octagonal, (Fig. 77 *a b*,) is 28.74 inches, and its caliber 0.562 inch. It has eight grooves with a twist of three quarters, or an inclination of 88° 38′ 6″; they are 0.035 inch broad, and 0.019 inch deep. The tige screwed into the face of the breech-pin is slightly conical, being 0.273 inch at the lower end, and 0.255 inch at the upper; its

---

* Lately this system has been superseded by that of Wilkinson. See p. 102.

length 1.77 inch. The breech-sight, which consists of a standing sight and three leaves, is inserted 6.96 inches from the rear of the barrel.

The ball (Fig. 77 c) is cylindro-ogival in shape, and is 1.106 inch long and 0.557 inch in diameter. It weighs 494 grains, and the weight of the charge is sixty-two grains. The cylindrical part has a circular groove filled with a woolen thread.

In *Russia*, the system of Thouvenin was also adopted, and ten men to each company of Jägers were furnished with arms of this sort, having very shallow grooves and a thick tige.

The ball (Fig. 78 a) is cylindro-conical, with a total height of 1.191 inch; the greatest diameter, at the junction of the conical and cylindrical part, is 0.70 inch. The lower part, which is nearly cylindrical, has but one shallow circular groove, bounded by a rim at the base of 0.691 inch diameter. Its weight is 689 grains.

The cylinder is double, has its edges pasted, and is folded down over the base of the ball, which has its point turned inwards. It is tied in the groove with a woolen thread dipped in tallow. The other end is pinched and folded down. Another tie is made about a third way down the conical part of the ball, the object of which is to prevent the powder from shaking down.

In the experiments at St. Petersburg, in 1852, at a distance of 1,200 paces (931 yards,) out of 200 shots thirty took effect in a moderate sized target.

In addition, they have adopted for their two-grooved rifle a pointed ball with two projections or studs, in place of the belted ball. (These belted balls had a diameter of 0.692 inch over the side, and 0.728 inch over the belt.) The length of bore of these arms is 31.49 inches, and their caliber 0.689 inch. The number of the grooves is two, (Fig. 79 a b,) with a whole turn or an inclination of 87° 59′ 18″. The breadth of the grooves is 0.31 inch, and their depth 0.032 inch. The breech-sight is 3.58 inches from the rear of the barrel. The new ball (Fig. 79 c d) consists of two cones with their bases joined, the lower cone being truncated. The point of junction has the greatest diameter, which is 0.685 inch, the base being 0.673 inch. The two studs, which are intended to fill the grooves more readily on ramming, are 0.283 inch broad. Weight of the ball, 788 grains.

IX. The System of Minié.*

Of late years endeavors have been made, particularly in France, to dispense entirely with the chamber and the tige, still retaining the advantages already attained in the facility of loading, the preservation of the shape of the ball and of the grain of the powder, as well as those of increased accuracy and range.

The grooves in this system are progressive—that is, they diminish in depth from breech to

---

* The honor of originating this system belongs indisputably to Captain Delvigne, who, years ago, in his constant experiments with cylindro-conical balls, made the discovery that the lead of his balls, which, as we know, were hollow from the base upward, was forced into the grooves by the effect of the powder.

The particulars are given in his essay "*Sur l'emploi et les effets des Projectiles cylindro-coniques évidés, par Gust. Delvigne, Extrait du Spectateur Militaire, cahier d'Août, 1849,*" from which we make the following extract:

"In these researches (which referred to the position of the center of gravity of the cylindro-conical ball) I made an important discovery, viz: that the gases of the inflamed powder, which so often drive a ball not well rammed out of the grooves, may thus constrain it to follow them. I record this, as I believe, a novel idea, recommending it to the consideration of such as are inquiring into the subject of small arms. We have only to control the great force of the powder to profit by this new discovery.

"It is obvious that the form and size of the cavity must be proportioned to the charge, and regard had to the object to be attained.

"The difficulties in the way are, first: if the cavity is too great, the spread and friction will be extreme, causing the gases to force a passage through the lead. Second, is the cavity too small, then the expansion will not take place at all. In either case, unless the form of the ball and chamber in some measure prevents the gases from surrounding the ball, there will be a forcing together of the sides in proportion to the size and shape of the cavity."

muzzle. The breech-pin has neither tige nor chamber. The grooves are 0.019 inch deep at the breech, and 0.011 at the muzzle. (Fig. 80 a b.)

The ball is cylindro-ogival in shape, has three angular grooves (*cannelures*) on the cylindrical part, and a cavity conical from the base upwards, which is closed with a sheet-iron culot shaped like a cup. Its diameter, which is less than that of the bore, permits it to drop down easily on the powder—the more easily, after repeated firing, from having the "cannelures" filled with tallow. The rammer is countersunk to suit the shape of the ball. The following are the theoretical advantages which experience has fully confirmed:

That the gas evolved in the inflammation of the powder forces the culot to the extremity of the cavity, by which the sides of the ball are pressed out and driven into the grooves. As these may not, however, always be completely filled, they are, as already stated, made shallow towards the muzzle, thereby securing absolute contact between the lead and the surface of the bore, and producing the required rotation of the ball about its longer axis. Besides, the force of the powder, by its more direct action on the center of gravity of the ball, forces it to retain its original tangential position to the trajectory.

The system has, moreover, the considerable advantage that the ball retains its shape unaltered, as it is not rammed, but only pressed down, which is not the case with the other systems, (if we except the Prussian and the recent Swiss;) in all of which the effect of the rammer on the upper part of the ball is first to change the taper very appreciably; and, secondly, to form a shoulder theoretically injurious in its influence on the trajectory, since the air, instead of moving smoothly along the surface, meets with resistance there.

The initial velocity of these Minié balls is said to be inferior, as appears, indeed, from an inspection of the table annexed.

General Paixhans presents, in his "*Constitution Militaire de la France*," page 40, the following results of experiments with the new rifled carbine, with a charge of only four grammes (sixty-two grains) to a ball almost double the weight of the old round ball.

At a distance 200 meters, (218½ yards,) a target of two yards square was hit 100 times in succession with this new musket, while the ordinary smooth-bore only made forty-four hits in the same number.

At 600 meters (656 yards) there were twenty-five hits at the same target, while the smooth-bore did not reach it at all, and a field piece only hit it six times in the same number of rounds.

At 1,000 meters, (1,093½ yards,) at which distance a field piece generally deviates five to six yards from the target, there were six hits in 100 shots with the new musket, and at this excessive distance it was found that a skillful marksman put three out of four shots in a moderate sized target.

Table No. 1, annexed, affords interesting information in reference to the accuracy and penetration; the experiments recorded having been made under the same circumstances with smooth bore, tige, and Minié arms.

The advantages of this system are—

1. The ball retains its shape entire after loading.
2. Quick and convenient loading.
3. Less accumulation of dirt, and more easy cleaning than in the arms of the system of Thouvenin.
4. Any smooth-bore arm may be changed to it without materially weakening the strength.

Its disadvantages are—

1. Great inequality in the effect of the iron culot.
2. The separation of this latter from the ball in loading, which exposes men in the vicinity to injury, and produces uncertainty of execution.
3. It requires a charge somewhat heavier than the system of Thouvenin.
4. The elevations are greater, and, consequently,
5. The dangerous space* (*bestreichenen raum*) is less.
6. Should the sides of the ball be too thin, it happens not unfrequently that the force of the gases separate the hollow from the solid part, and leaves it in the gun.

For the purpose of instituting extended experiments with this system, four regiments in the French service were supplied with the arms. The adoption of the system was, however, deferred to a later day.

Like experiments were instituted in *Baden*, in 1852, but with a smaller caliber. The ball was 0.883 inch long, and the cylindrical part had three grooves and a diameter of 0.506 inch. The interior conical cavity was 0.558 inch deep, with an inferior diameter of 0.36 inch, and a superior diameter of 0.307 inch. This cavity was closed with a close-fitting sheet-iron culot. (Fig 81 *a b*.) Two battalions of fusileers, fifth and tenth, were armed with these weapons for purposes of experiment. Since then a part of the smooth-bore arms of the infantry, as well as the carbines of the artillery and the holster pistols of the cavalry, have been altered to this system.

In *Nassau*, also, where the rapid fouling of the barrel was found to be very troublesome, since it admitted but ten to twelve successive discharges in warm weather, attention was turned to the system of Minié, and experiments, with a view to its adoption, were set on foot in 1853 with his balls. The stem or tige was removed, but the grooves remained unchanged. The trials resulted favorably to the system, and showed that the arms, with Minié balls, became much less dirty, and could be fired thirty to forty times in succession. The charge, however, had to be increased 7.71 grains.

The tige was hereupon removed from the breech-pin, the grooves having already the required diminution of depth towards the muzzle.

The ball which was the subject of these experiments has a cylindro-ogival form, is 0.663 inch in diameter, and 1.2 inch long. The conical cavity closed with a sheet-iron culot, is 0.608 inch deep, and at the base 0.442 inch broad. The weight is 703 grains. (Fig. 82 *a*.)

The cartridge (Fig. 82 *b*) is very like the Belgian, hereafter to be described, (Fig. 99,) and the charging is effected in the same manner.

In *England*, also, in 1851, many experiments were instituted with this system at Woolwich. They were begun at a distance of 200 yards, and prosecuted to a distance of 400 yards, with good results, the majority of the balls being in the bull's eye or the vicinity of it. Even at 600 yards, it is said, a great number of the balls hit the target, the dimensions of which are, however, not given.

The arm with which these experiments were made (of which 23,000 were ordered in consequence) was of the following dimensions:

The length of the bore was three feet three inches, and its caliber 0.702, (subsequently reduced.) The four grooves, 0.25 inch wide, had something over half a turn in the bore, or an inclination of 89° 10′ 37″, and had a depth of 0.02 inch at the breech and 0.01 inch at the muzzle. The charge was two and a half drams, (68.35 grains.) The breech-sight,

---

* This expression is used to denote the portion of the trajectory which is intercepted by a horizontal line drawn at the height of a man on foot or on horseback. (Fig. 117.)—*Translator.*

like that of the French, was 4.7 inch from the rear end of the barrel, and graduated for distances from 200 to 900 yards.

The ball, (Fig. 83,) originally like the French, was, after some experiments, altered to a sphero-conical shape, with the omission of the grooves. It is 1.03 inch long, and has a diameter at the base, where it is greatest, of 0.69 inch. The conical cavity is 0.51 inch long, and 0.4 inch in diameter at the base. Like the Minié ball, it is closed by a culot, and weighs 22.66 drams, or about ten to the pound. The weight of this arm, with bayonet, is ten pounds eight and three quarter ounces. The height of the trajectory above the line of sight was three and a half feet in the middle, for a range of 200 yards, and for 900 yards, 110 feet.

There are ten men in each company armed with these arms.*

During the year 1852 endeavors were made to substitute a smaller caliber for the large ones which had hitherto been preserved with the adoption of the Minié ball. This would enable the soldier to carry a larger supply of ammunition without overloading himself. The shape of the ball was also to be modified, the conical part having hitherto been too great and giving the ball too little hold on the barrel, causing it more readily to assume an oblique position.

With this view a commission was in that year assembled at Enfield, who were to submit to ample experiment models furnished by the most noted gunmakers.

The arms thus presented were:
1. The two-grooved rifle.
2. The Minié arm, adopted in 1851.
3. *Purdy's* rifle, with a length of bore of 39 inches, and a caliber of 0.65 inch. The four grooves had not a uniform inclination; but started at the breech with a twist of 0.5427 of a circle in the length of the barrel, which, at the muzzle, was increased to 0.6842. This arm had two balls, one of which (Fig. 84 *a*) was 1.05 inch long, and 0.543 inch in diameter over the rim at the base. The cavity was closed with a metal plug, in lieu of the culot of Minié, and was in the same way to effect the spreading of the ball. This ball weighed 610 grains. The other ball (Fig. 84 *b*) weighed only 487 grains; was 0.91 inch long, and 0.634 inch in diameter. Both were, in other respects, essentially like the English Minié ball, and the cavity in the second was closed by an iron culot. The charge was over two and a half drams of fine powder, and the weight of rifle and bayonet, nine pounds one and a half ounce.
4. *Lovell's* rifle: its length of barrel was 39 inches, and its caliber 0.635 inch. There were two balls, the length of one (Fig. 85 *a*) being 1,145 inch, its diameter 0.63 inch, and weight 686 grains. The length of the other, (Fig. 85 *b*,) 0.95 inch, its diameter 0.628, and its weight 562 grains.
5. *Greener's* rifle, with seven sorts of balls, the results obtained with which being not favorable, are not given. The barrel had a caliber of 0.621 inch, and one of the several kinds of balls weighed nineteen to the pound.
6. *Richard's* rifle was equally unsuccessful. The caliber was 0.577 inch, and the ball weighed twenty-four to the pound.
7. *Lancaster's* rifle, which differed from all the others in the peculiar construction of the bore. It was 39 inches long, and had no grooves; but was smoothly and elliptically bored out. This elliptical bore had an increasing twist and a diminished cross-section as it approached the muzzle; the smaller axis, which is to be regarded as the caliber, being 0.543 inch at the breech, and 0.540 inch at the muzzle; while the greater axis, which takes the place of the grooves, was 0.557 inch at the breech, and 0.543 inch at the muzzle. The twist was half

---

* For more extended and uniform practice with these arms, a school of practice was organized at Hythe, near Dover, under the superintendence of Colonel Hay, whither eight or ten men from each infantry regiment were sent for instruction. After attaining proficiency these men were returned to their regiments as instructors.

Eye-witnesses affirm that at the trials here 77 shots out of 100 were put into a target eight feet square, 800 yards distant; and again, that at the same target and distance, without previous knowledge of the distance, 40 out of 50 shots hit.

a turn in the length of the bore. The ball (Fig. 86 *a b*) was cylindro-spherical in shape, 1.125 inch long, and 0.532 inch in diameter. The conical cavity at the base was closed by a plug somewhat larger, which spread out the lead the more the further it was driven up. The cylindrical part had three sharp grooves. Its weight was 542 grains, and the charge two and a half drams. The weight of the rifle and bayonet was nine pounds nine ounces.

8. *Wilkinson's* rifle, the barrel of which was also 39 inches long, and it had a decreased caliber toward the muzzle, where it was 0.530 inch, against 0.531 at the breech. It had five grooves, with half a turn in the length of the barrel. It weighed nine pounds five ounces. Its ball, (Fig. 87 *a b*,) of cylindro-conical form, was solid, 1.075 inch long, and 0.537 inch in diameter. The lower cylindrical part had two deep sharp grooves, filled with tallow. It weighed 500 grains.

9. *A rifle* made in the Royal Armory, at *Enfield*. The barrel (Fig. 88 *a b*) was 39 inches long, with a bore entirely cylindrical, of the caliber of 0.577 inch and having but three grooves, the twist of which was one half in the length of the barrel, or an inclination of $89° 19' 17''$. The depth of the grooves was 0.014 inch, and their breadth 0.262 inch. The weight of the rifle and bayonet was nine pounds three ounces. The ball adopted for it afterwards (Fig. 88 *c d e*) was not solid, but like Minié's, provided with a cavity, of limited depth, however. The length of the ball was 0.96 inch, its diameter 0.568 inch, and its weight 520 grains.

As before observed, the chief object of these trials was to determine on an arm with smaller caliber, which would enable the soldier to carry the customary sixty rounds of ammunition without fatigue. This could not be done with the Minié arm of large caliber heretofore in use. It was also to present the advantage of greater strength with less weight of metal. It was, in addition, the province of the commission to ascertain the influence of the number of grooves, to obviate the use of the culot, and to modify the objectionable shape of the ball, which was too conical; and, finally, to construct a breech-sight less faulty than the one in use on the Minié rifle.

On the second point, whether an even or an odd number of grooves is most advantageous, the experiments led to the conclusion that the latter was preferable in point of accuracy, as an odd number gave a land opposite to the groove, causing the groove to fill more readily; and when a small number of grooves only are to be used, three is a better number than four, as better preserving the cylindrical contour of the ball, which, with four grooves, inclines to become a square. Whether the last conclusion is well founded may be doubted, when we inspect the ball fired from a three-grooved bore, (Fig. 88 *c.*) It has much of a triangular shape, and a greater number of grooves would produce a much better appearance.

The adoption of a smaller caliber infers, of course, a corresponding diminution of the weight of the ball, when it is not made disproportionately long. The balls submitted were, however, in their form and arrangement, for the most part, entirely unsuited for field service. As it was one of the prominent objects of the commission to determine upon a suitable form, and the Minié ball heretofore used did not take sufficient hold on the barrel, from its too conical shape, it was agreed to alter it, the lower half being made wholly cylindrical, the upper part remaining unchanged, (Fig. 89.) The trials with these balls gave far better results. While at short distances, the elevation had to be somewhat greater than for the former balls, at 700 yards they were equal. The experiments at Woolwich, on the projecting culot, and whether any culot is advantageous, showed less accuracy by one third for the ball without culot.

These experiments also elicited the fact that the Minié or expanding ball gave better results when separated from the cartridge in loading than when united to it; and in the latter case, still better when the envelopes was well greased. It was also thought that no small influence was exerted on the expanding ball by the grain of the powder, the coarse grain giving the better results. This was ascribed to its slower inflammation, which put the ball more gradually in motion, giving time for the full expansion of the lead.

THE SYSTEM OF MINIÉ.

The use of the Minié rifle of large caliber had developed the defect of the breech-sight in use, which was, like the French, provided with a slide, to be set for each distance. After prolonged use, the slide would become loose, and would fall down, in spite of the spring; and shoving it back in the hurry of action, this would not always be correctly done. It was, therefore, abandoned in the new arms, and one adopted, hereafter to be described, the leaf of which has a slit for the sliding sight, and folds down in either direction. The reason for such an arrangement is that the sight, when raised, may yield, and not be broken by any accidental blow. It has the objection, however, that the sight, when up, may not be placed exactly perpendicular, and thus give false elevations.

For better comparison, we will here give the horizontal ranges of the various arms tried, placed at four feet seven and a half inches from the ground, and the elevations at which they must be fired:

Distances in yards.

ARMS.	Horizontal range.	100.	200.	300.	400.	500.	600.	700.	800.	1,000.
	Yds. ft ins.	o ′	o ′	o ′	o ′	o ′	o ′	o ′	o ′	o ′
Two-grooved Brunswick................	173 0 2½	0 9	0 34	0 52	1 22	1 51	2 23	3 5	3 25	....
Purdey's...................................	180 2 4	0 15	0 43	0 57	1 17	1 47	2 21	2 51	3 41	....
Lovell's, (heavy ball,).................	190 0 0	0 11	0 26	0 49	1 9	1 34	2 2	2 32	2 50	4 16
Lovell's, (light ball,)..................	176 0 0	0 14	0 26	0 52	1 18	1 47	{Beyond th is the fell off ra pidly.			results
Lancaster's...............................	194 0 11	0 11	0 26	0 49	1 9	1 34	2 2	2 32	3 1	....
Wilkinson's...............................	185 0 3½	0 14	0 28	0 47	1 5	1 25	2 0	2 29	2 44	4 31

At the distance of two hundred yards, this rifle (Wilkinson's) requires a greater elevation than that of Lancaster, but less for all greater distances; a discrepancy ascribed to the shape of the ball, which in Wilkinson's approaches more nearly to the spherical, and will, therefore, present a more uniform surface of resistance to the air, whatever the angle under which it is fired; while that of Lancaster, being more pointed, cleaves the air more easily at smaller elevations, in which more of the point and less of the side presents itself to resistance.

With the Enfield rifle, whose horizontal range and elevations are not given, the greatest height of the trajectory for a range of one hundred yards, at a distance of fifty yards from the muzzle, was nine inches; for two hundred yards, at one hundred and fifty yards, was 21.16 inches; and for three hundred yards, at one hundred and seventy-five yards, was 43 inches.

At the close of the experiments the commission were unanimously in favor of the adoption of the last named Enfield rifle, as on the whole best fulfilling the required conditions of reduced weight combined with requisite strength, diminished caliber, a ball more easily prepared than that of Minié, in which the manufacture of the culot was troublesome, and the retention of the sixty rounds of ammunition. The efficiency and accuracy of this rifle exceeded all others of the grooved arms up to 800 yards, especially when loaded with the greased envelope.

Upon this, two patterns were made at Enfield from those which had proved successful in the experiments. The one intended for the line and the militia had a standing sight for 100 yards, and two leaves for 200 yards and 300 yards, respectively; the other, for the riflemen and portions of other corps, had a standing sight for 100 yards, and two leaves, like the Prussian needle gun, which moved either way and were graduated to 800 yards.

From the statements of the experiments, in which the accuracy and penetration are not given, it appears that at first a ball was used constructed on the principles of Minié; but that at the close of the experiments it was referred to Pritchett, the gunmaker, to furnish a ball without culot, such as he had submitted at former experiments, and which had given satisfactory results. This new ball (Fig. 88 c) is cylindro-conical, has a bell-shaped cavity 0.27 inch deep and 0.43 inch diameter at the base. It is 0.568 inch caliber and 0.96 inch long. The weight is 520 grains, and the charge two and a quarter drams of fine powder. This arm, the dimensions of which have before been given, is known as the Enfield-Pritchett rifle.

In *Spain*, after favorable experiments with new rifled arms, it was likewise decided, in 1852, to adopt the Minié system. The barrel of the weapon is 33.07 inches long, has a caliber of 0.597 inch, and has four grooves with a half turn in the length of the barrel, or an inclination of 89° 10' 12''. The width of the grooves is 0.224 inch, and they are of a uniform depth of 0.019 inch, departing in this respect from the principles of the Minié system. The breech-sight is 2.24 inches from the rear of the barrel. The bead, as in the Belgian arms, serves also the purpose of bayonet-stud. Weight, without bayonet, 8.36 pounds.

The ball (Fig. 91) has a rather long cylinder, with three sharp grooves, with a diameter of 0.554 inch; it is 0.984 inch long. The cavity, closed by an iron culot, is conical, the superior diameter being 0.26 inch, and the inferior, 0.36 inch. The windage is 0.043 inch. According to late accounts the uniform depth of the grooves has been abandoned, and the depth at the breech made 0.031 inch, that at the muzzle remaining the same. The diameter of the ball is also said to have been increased to 0.568 inch, thus reducing the windage to 0.011. Weight 422 grains.

In *Belgium*, where, induced by the favorable results obtained in France, experiments were also made with entire success, the infantry were partially armed on this system. The length of the bore is 41.73 inches, and its caliber 0.689 inch. The four grooves, with something over half a turn, ($\frac{1}{2}\frac{1}{2}$,) or an inclination of 89° 13' 17'', are 0.255 inch broad, with a diminishing depth towards the muzzle; the depth at the chamber being 0.017 inch, and at the muzzle 0.005 inch. (Fig. 94 a b.)

The ball adopted, (Fig. 95 a,) but subsequently changed at the instance of Colonel Timmerhans, weighed 719 grains, and differed so far from the French (Fig. 80 c) that it was not pointed, but had a rounded termination, and it was furnished with three very shallow grooves. The diameter of the cylindrical part was 0.673 inch, and the whole length 1.165 inch. The cavity was conical 0.622 inch long, with an inferior diameter of 0.440 inch, and a superior diameter of 0.311 inch. The culot was 0.137 inch deep and 0.338 inch broad. The charge was 79 to 85 grains of musket powder.

Various reasons gave rise to renewed experiments in Belgium, in 1853, with arms of this system, under the supervision of the well-known Colonel Timmerhans. The object of these was partly to adapt this system to the smooth-bore arms, retaining their caliber; partly, also, to improve the Minié ball in some way so as to obviate the objections to the culot, which not unfrequently separated itself from the ball in loading, and endangered the men in the vicinity; and, finally, to establish more fully the relation between the weight of the ball and that of the charge.

As all experiments had shown that, with equal accuracy and penetration, these arms were much less liable to become foul than those of Thouvenin, the dirt being quite as perceptible in the latter after ten or fifteen rounds as in the former after thirty or forty rounds; as the cleaning of these arms can be effected with a simple wiper, which is serviceable under all circumstances; and as they can be loaded in much less time without any stated blows of the rammer, but simply by pushing the ball down on the powder, the favorable results of these experiments were scarcely to have been doubted.

All the advantages claimed for this system were again confirmed; but the Minié ball had its own defects which were to be obviated. Trial was then made of the Peter* ball, but it was found

---

* This ball was entirely similar to the Belgian ball (Fig. 95 a) in external appearance, but instead of the culot there was in the cavity a strong plug, forming a part of the ball, projecting and tapering downwards. The diminution of the cavity thus caused would, it was supposed, favor the effect of the gas, and cause the lead to be driven into the grooves quicker and more effectually.

that the space between the plug and the sides of the cavity did not allow sufficient action for the gases, especially when the lead was somewhat thick.

Subsequently, Colonel Timmerhans presented a ball of his own construction, in which the cavity was bell-shaped, leaving an edge somewhat thin, which yielded more readily to the effort of the gases. A plug in the cavity exerts an influence so far useful that it receives and breaks the first shock of the explosion, and prevents the separation of the hollow from the solid part, as happened with the Minié ball before described, when there was defective construction or an overcharge. The gases are thus forced to act more on the inferior parts of the cavity. Moreover, as this plug, or projection, is a sort of sinking head, the cavities caused by the escape of the air in casting will occur on it, and will exert little or no influence in displacing the position of the center of gravity, a disposition favorable to exact rotation.

This new ball, (Fig. 96,) differing from the Minié before described, (see Fig. 95, a, b,) has a cylindro-ogival form, is 1.223 inch long and 0.673 inch in diameter, and has three grooves. The bell-formed cavity has a height of 0.574 inch, and a diameter at the base of 0.598 inch. The plug (*zapfchen*) is 0.35 inch long, 0.3 inch in diameter at the base, and 0.15 inch at the end. The ball, with a windage of 0.015 inch, weighs 721 grains.

The rifle itself, (Fig. 97,) the dimensions of which are given at page 214, (Fig. 94, a, b,) remained unaltered in reference to the grooves, except that they were deepened at the muzzle from 0.005 inch to 0.009 inch. The breech-sight (Fig. 98) consists of a leaf on a hinge, at the back of which there is a spring, the foot of which, turned up, furnishes, as it rests on the hinge-bed, the standing sight for 300 paces. When the leaf, which has a slit for 400 paces, and a notch at top for 500 paces, is raised, the lower end of the spring is received into the hinge-bed, and holds the sight fast. The notch of the standing sight is 0.822 inch, the slit is 1.361 inch, and the notch at the top of the leaf is 1.739 inch above the axis of the bore. It is 3.74 inches from the rear end of the barrel. The iron bead, a quadrant in shape, with the curve turned to the muzzle, serves also as the bayonet stud.

The cartridge (Fig. 99) is made of thin card board rolled around once, and, for greater security and the preservation of the powder, is wrapped about with an envelope of common writing paper pasted, the end of which is inserted into the cylinder in such a way as to envelope the point of the ball and separate it from the powder. The whole is then surrounded by a third wrapper unpasted and folded close over the base of the ball; the other end being left long, is twisted and turned down. The cartridge is dipped in tallow as far as the cylindrical part of the ball extends.

The method of loading is as follows: The cartridge is bitten off above the powder, the powder poured in, the cylindrical part of the ball inserted, the empty cartridge torn off, and the ball shoved down without ramming on the charge, which is 85 grains of common musket powder. In loading in this way, without freeing the ball of the paper, there will be no danger of the ball's moving forward when the gun is carried with its muzzle depressed, as is often the case with skirmishers.

On comparing the experiments with smooth-bore arms with a charge one third the weight of the ball, and those made with the altered rifles with a charge only one tenth the weight of the ball, the following results have been obtained in reference to accuracy and range:

Smooth-bore Arms—100 rounds.

At 100 paces, (82 yards,) 16 hit the size of a man; 50 an infantry front of 12 meters.
At 200 paces, (164 yards,) 10 hit the size of a man; 38 an infantry front of 12 meters.
At 300 paces, (329 yards,) 18 hit the size of a man; 12 an infantry front of 12 meters.

Altered Arms—100 *rounds.*

At 100 paces, 64 hit the size of a man; 84 an infantry front of 12 men.
At 200 paces, 28 hit the size of a man; 60 an infantry front of 12 men.
At 400 paces, 16 hit the size of a man; 51 an infantry front of 12 men.
At 500 paces, 8 hit the size of a man; 43 an infantry front of 12 men.
At 600 paces, 6 hit the size of a man; 37 an infantry front of 12 men.

This arm, besides, covers a dangerous space of:
At the distance of 200 paces, 200 paces.
At the distance of 300 paces, 200 paces.
At the distance of 400 paces, 150 paces.
At the distance of 600 paces, 56 paces.

X. THE SWISS SYSTEM.

About the time of the appearance of the system just described, attention was called in Switzerland to the new American system; and, after full experiments, it was in 1850 adopted, with some modifications, for their sharp-shooters. The arm was called the "new federal stutzer," [provincial for a rifle-barreled gun.]

To this system belong a very small caliber, half-round grooves, with nearly a whole turn, and a chambered breech-pin. The ball rests neither on the powder nor on the breech-pin, and is loaded with a patch.

The stutzer has these dimensions: the length of the barrel is 32.038 inches, and its caliber 0.413 inch. The eight half-round grooves have equal breadth with the lands, and are 0.017 inch deep. The twist is once in three feet, or an inclination of 85° 56′ 54″. The chamber of the patent breech-pin is 1.004 inch deep, and 0.413 inch in diameter. (Fig. 100 *a b*.) Fig. 101 *a b* explains the breech-sight, which is 5.19 inches from the rear of the barrel. The whole length of the stutzer with bayonet is 68.89 inches; the weight, with it, ten and a half to eleven pounds.

The ball (Fig. 102 *a b*) is cylindro-conical, and has at the lower end of the cylinder one groove not very deep, chamfered at the top, in which the patch is tied with common thread. The greatest diameter of this ball is 0.409 inch, which is at the lower rim, the upper being 0.393 inch only; and the ogee part, which is 0.925 inch long, is only 0.370 inch in diameter at its junction with the upper rim. The whole length of the ball, the weight of which is between twenty-eight and thirty-two to the pound Swiss, (275.42 grains, and 237.47 grains,) is 1.1694 inch.

The charge, which must not exceed sixty-four grains, nor fall below fifty-nine grains, is contained in a cylinder made of good sized paper. The ball is carried apart from the cartridge in the hunting-pouch, wrapped with patching. The pouch carries sixty cartridges and eighty caps, besides a certain quantity of lead (2.2 pounds) and sixty patches, with the necessary thread. The patching is made of cotton cloth, steeped in grease.

The thread which binds the cartridge to the ball it is intended shall strip off on the insertion of the ball, and must therefore be of a certain thickness. A shoulder near the upper end of the rammer prevents the ball from being driven down too far, and leaves a space varying from 0.177 inch to 0.236 inch between the powder and the ball. Besides the rammer, a starter of wrought brass is carried.

At the close of 1853, a new arm was also adopted for the Jäger, after the most satisfactory experiments. It has, like the Minié arm, a light charge, weighs 1.1 pound less than that, has less recoil, and greatly excels it in accuracy. At 2,500 Swiss feet (820 yards) the small ball of this Jäger rifle penetrated three boards 1.18 inch thick each. It is nearly of the same character as the stutzer. The bore, small like the latter, is 32.038 inches long, and 0.431 inch

THE SWISS SYSTEM.

caliber, has eight rounded grooves, with a turn in 35.46 inches, or an inclination of 88° 56′ 54″, equal to 0.9023 of a turn in the length of the bore. There is a maximum of 1.0423, and a minimum of 0.8468 laid down. The depth of the grooves varies from 0.014 inch, to 0.017 inch, and the breadth is equal to that of the lands. The chamber has the same caliber as the barrel, and is 1.004 inches deep. The breech-sight, which is like that of the stutzer, is 5.2 inches distant from the rear of the barrel, and is graduated on the left side for 200, 400, 600, and 800 paces.

The heights of the sights above the axis of the bore, are—

  For 200 paces, (164 yards,) 0.744 inch.
  For 400 paces, (328 yards,) 0.897 inch.
  For 600 paces, (492 yards,) 1.086 inch.
  For 800 paces, (656 yards,) 1.347 inch.
  For 1,000 paces, (820 yards,) 1.643 inch.

The height of the bead, which is on the muzzle-band above the axis, is 0.637 inch. The length of the Jäger without bayonet is 48.82 inches, and with bayonet 68.89 inches, and its weight with bayonet 9.9 pounds.

The ball, (Fig. 103,) like that of the stutzer, is cylindro-ogival, and has a greatest diameter of 0.395 inch at the junction of the ogee and cylinder. The cylindrical part, 0.385 inch long, with two grooves, tapers toward the bottom, where its diameter is 0.379 inch. The whole length of the ball is 0.940 inch, and its weight from twenty-eight to thirty-two to the pound, (275.42 to 239.47 grains.)

The cartridge (Fig. 104) is made of writing paper closely wrapped, without pasting, and has a charge of 62 grains of musket powder. The ball is inserted point first, and separated from the powder by a small paper wad. The lower end is folded over the base of the ball, and dipped in a mixture of four parts of tallow and one of wax to a depth of 0.35 inch, the upper end being folded close and turned down. Each man carries into the field six bundles of cartridges of ten each, and seventy-eight caps, in papers of thirteen, which are packed with each bundle.

The mode of loading is the same as with the stutzer, but without the patch, the place of which is supplied by the end of the cartridge dipped in the composition, which goes in with the ball. A certain interval is preserved between powder and ball. Besides the steel rammer, a brass drift is used, 21.26 inches long, after the ball is pushed home.

The results of trials with the Jäger rifles are as follows:

As to accuracy, at 400 paces, at a target seven and three quarters feet square, out of 100 shots there were ninety-five hits. At 600 paces, at a target eleven and a half feet long and eight and three quarters feet high, with a high wind, there were sixty-three hits; and at 800 paces, in calm weather, there were eighty to eighty-seven hits in the same target.

The elevations of the Jäger rifle, the stutzer, and the Minié, are as follows:

	Jäger.	Stutzer.	Minié.
For 400 paces	0° 25′ 30″	0° 35′ 10″	0° 10′ 21″
For 600 paces	0 54 20	1 3 20	1 51 0
For 800 paces	1 21 40	1 38 50	2 43 0
For 1,000 paces	1 52 43	2 9 0	3 34 0

The smaller elevations of the Jäger rifle over the stutzer must be ascribed to the diminished friction of the ball in the bore. The Minié requires double the elevation and the balls have a similar dangerous field.

In reference to penetration, the results were equally favorable, since at 800 paces (656 yards) the penetration was through five boards 1.2 inch thick, (nearly,) and at 1,000 paces (820 yards) four boards of like thickness, while with the Minié rifle at the first distance only three to four boards were penetrated, and at 800 paces even the ball of the wall piece went through but one board.

Experiments of great interest* in reference to the penetration of the Jäger and Stutzer rifles, which agree in charge, ball, and other respects, were made on the 16th of January, 1855, at Thun, in Switzerland, under the direction of Colonel Wurstemberg and Lieutenant Colonel Wehrli, on a horse recently killed. Such an experiment on a body that remained warm all the time of the firing is the more interesting as it enables us the better to estimate the execution of a service arm than could be done from its effect on boards.

For this purpose the carcass was placed astride on a piece of wood, and the head and the neck arranged in as natural a position as possible. The results were as follows on the fore part of the body at 100 paces: One ball made a round hole in the middle of the forehead, without any splinters, traversed the brain and spheroidal bone, and passing out through the skin at the larynx, went on. A second passed through the bridge of the nose without splintering the bone; and after passing through the gums, went out at the glands of the larynx. A third went through the breast bone, wounded several principal parts, as well as the upper part of the leg and the joint, in the neighborhood of which it again passed out. Like effects were produced on the hinder parts of the body, where a ball passed through the thigh bone and came out at the hock joint.

At 300 and 400 paces balls fired against the right side smashed the ribs, passed through the body, and either passed out, or struck against a rib opposite, or hung in the tissue of the skin. The conclusion from these firings was, that at 100 paces (84 yards) the majority of the shot would produce instant death, and the rest mortal or very dangerous wounds. Two fired at this distance, and from a kneeling position, would have inflicted instant death.

At 200 paces there were no hits of note on account of a snow storm; but at 300 paces (245 yards) several shots would have produced death, and the same at 400 paces, at which distance several balls broke ribs, passed through or hung in the opposite side.

These most interesting experiments prove, in the most striking manner, the great penetration of balls fired up[...] the balls from these stutzers, which possess this advantage in a high degree, at [...] 400 paces, break through and shatter strong bones like the breast bone, the skull [...] ribs, continue their course through the great interior parts of the body, which are of an elastic and spongy nature, and either make their way on the opposite side through the skin, or bury themselves in the bones there.

XI. THE SYSTEM OF WILKINSON.

The characteristic of this system refers chiefly, like that of Minié, to the operation of the gases on the ball, and to the construction of the latter, which differs from that of Minié in being solid, not hollow, and having on the cylindrical part two deep right angled grooves. As the ball has no cavity, the action of the gases must be different. They must operate by forcing the hoop-like cylindrical part forward on the conical part, and thus effect the filling of the grooves; and this can only take place when the conical part has the necessary weight. Through the pressure of the gases on the base, the oblique sides of the grooves are pressed wedge-like into the hoop or circle in front, and spread it. But this can only happen when the sloping parts are somewhat long, and the force of the gas does not instantly overcome the inertia of the heavier conical part. It is clear that the slope of the groove must be regulated by the depth of the rifles, whilst the weight of the conical part is determined by the strength of the charge—e. g., with deep grooves, the sloping sides must be made longer than with shallow ones, since the spread required is greater; and, with a heavy charge, the conical part must be lighter, since the pressure from behind and the spread of the hoops is more violent from the greater force of the gases.

Wilkinson adopted besides a progressive caliber, a condition not essential, when the rifles are shallow and rounded, since the filling of them can be effected, as above stated, by the arrangement of the grooves of the ball.

* Taken from the "Examination of the Results obtained January 16, 1855, in the arrangement of the system of Federal Ordnance, at Thun, &c., &c.

This system, though in many respects decidedly preferable to the other, was nowhere accepted until 1854; but since then it has been adopted in Austria after the most extensive and successful trials.* Three new rifled arms have been introduced on this system, and are divided into the tige rifle for non-commissioned officers, the third rank, and the best marksmen in the Jäger battalion; the rifle, without tige, for the rest of these troops; and the rifle musket for the non-commissioned officers and sharp-shooters of the battalions of the line.

The barrels of these three arms are identical in the numbers, depth, and breadth of their grooves, the last being the same as that of the lands; but the twist of the rifle musket differs from that of the rifle.

The breech-sight is arranged according to the destination of the weapon, so that the tige rifle is sighted in the Danish manner for 1,200 paces, while the rifle without tige and the rifle-musket, after the Belgian mode, are prepared for 900 paces only.

In these weapons the Consol lock, peculiar to Austria, were abandoned, and the common percussion lock substituted.

The ball is, according to the authority just cited, modeled on that of Wilkinson, used in the English experiments in 1852, at Enfield. (Fig. 87.) The cartridge resembles the French, in which, it will be recollected, the end folded over the ball is greased and loaded like a patch with it after the part of the cartridge has been torn off.

In accuracy and penetration the system is said to excel all others, especially at great distances. At 300 paces the hits were 100 per cent. in a target the size of a man's head, and at 1,500 paces, forty-nine hits in a column target. At 1,000 paces the ball is said to have passed through six boards 1.03 inch thick, and placed 12½ inches apart; and at 2,000 paces, three of them in the same way.

In the journal already referred to, it is stated: "This system surpasses the hitherto unapproached tige arm in accuracy, penetration, ease of loading, absence of dirt, and facility of cleaning." It is, in fact, surprising that, to prevent the crushing of the powder, the tige should have been introduced into one of the stutzers, contrary to the principles of the system, whilst it was thought unnecessary in the other arms of the same system. The *tige* is no constituent of this system, and appears only to interfere with the cleaning of the barrel.

This system must eventually meet with general favor, as it unites almost every advantage conducive to accuracy and penetration.

XII. THE SYSTEM OF LANCASTER.

The peculiarity of this system, which of late has attracted great attention in England, and is adopted into the artillery of that nation, relates to the interior conformation of the barrel, which is neither round nor grooved; but the interior cross-section is an ellipse, and the bore has a certain turn in its length.† At the breech the twist becomes nearly rectilinear, but soon assumes the increasing inclination, which is uninterrupted to the muzzle; both axes of the ellipse, however, undergo a diminution, the greater of 0.066, the less of 0.029 inch.

The system thus proposed by Lancaster seems to be partially borrowed from the American smooth bore, with the addition of the expanding ball, which, enlarged by the action of the gases on the conical plug, retains its cylindrical part entire unchanged by the increased twist, and only alters when the point has left the muzzle.

Strictly speaking this twisting ellipse is nothing else than the parabolic grooves before described.

As the American system is the basis of Lancaster's it deserves a passing notice. It adopts the principle of the parabolic grooves, and a small twist; that is, the grooves do not, as usual,

---

* Karlsruhe Times, 1855; Darmstadt Military Times, Nos. 15 and 16.

† It is evident that the idea is but an extension of the two-grooved rifle, since, if we take a round smooth bore, and on opposite sides form two broad rounded grooves, the figure of the cross-section will resemble an ellipse.—*Translator.*

retain a fixed angle from breech to muzzle, but beginning with a direction nearly parallel to the axis of the bore, they assume a greater and greater inclination to it as they approach the muzzle. This species of grooves, which is called a "gaining twist," by impressing a gradual motion of rotation on the ball, effects the purpose of preventing the ball from *stripping*, or being forced over the lands by the first impulse of the gases.

The followers of this system claim for it increased accuracy and diminished recoil; assertions which are somewhat doubtful as regards the elongated ball, in which the cylindrical part encounters increased friction—a friction yet further augmented by the continued change that part undergoes from the ever increasing twist.

In Denmark, balls other than the round have for some years been in use. Figs. 105 and 106 are samples of the kinds used in the Schleswig war. In the cartridge shown at Fig. 105 both balls were sometimes of the same caliber. The cylinder was tied above the small ball, and in the groove of the plate.

CONCLUSION.

In taking a retrospect of what has been accomplished in the systems heretofore treated of the fundamental conditions laid down at page 185, in the improvement of infantry arms, must be kept in view. These were, first, increased facility of loading; second, increased accuracy and range; third, the charge; fourth, the inclination of the grooves; fifth, the diameter and shape of the ball. The first two can, it is evident, be attained only through the last three, which are to be regarded rather as the means to an end. Such has been the process in all the systems proposed since 1620, and facility of loading and increased accuracy have been, though not always in an equal degree, attained.

In the systems introduced from Delvigne to Thouvenin, the round ball was retained, but with such diminished diameter as to secure, through the increased windage, facility for loading. Delvigne, for this purpose, gave his balls a windage of 0.027 inch, the powder being kept from crushing by the use of the chamber, with a diameter less than the bore, upon which the ball rested. In loading, however, the ball was considerably disfigured, as, on the upper side, it was flattened by the face of the rammer, despite the concavity of the latter, and on the other it was forced into the chamber. The results obtained being unsatisfactory, Pontcharn, to preserve the shape of the ball, introduced a wooden sabot, which, with a patch, partly enveloped the ball. This did not wholly prevent the disfiguration of the ball, besides introducing new difficulties. This system in this state was, however, adopted in France, and attempts made to improve it by lengthening the barrel and diminishing the twist of the grooves, still retaining the same charge of ninety-six grains. The chief obstacle, however, to improved results, still lay in the disfiguration of the ball, which greatly increased the resistance of the air, and thereby diminished the range.

The system of Wild gave much better results. In this the round ball was still retained, with considerable windage, which was diminished, as desired, by a thicker or thinner patch. The preservation of the spherical shape of the ball is here, too, a condition; and this, with the method of loading, whereby the accumulation of dirt was avoided, showed, in the experiments of Baden and Hesse in 1843, the superiority of these rifles, both in accuracy and penetration over any of the systems then known. They were always observed to require a less elevation for the greater distances.

With the appearance of Thouvenin's and the accompanying pointed ball, the rifled arm assumed a different aspect, since the range of its execution was limited only by the extent of human vision. No longer can artillery, when opposed to infantry, take up its position and securely discharge its rounds of grape and canister, secure from immunity from any but a random shot from its adversary. At this distance it is now at the mercy of the rifle of the foot-soldier;

hence, when covering the artillery, the rifled arm becomes a much more efficient support than formerly, when it was not always in its power to afford the needful protection.

How profoundly these improvements have been felt and acknowledged, is shown by the speedy and general adoption of this system, which none other has supplanted without presenting the same defects. Facility of loading is attained in this system, by a sufficient windage; and increased accuracy, range, and penetration, though the charge is diminished and the weight of the ball augmented, by the use of the pointed ball. In France, for example, the charge has been reduced from 96 grains to 68 grains, whilst the weight of the ball has increased from 452 grains (the round ball of 1842) to 725 grains. The reasons for this are, in the first place, that the powder is kept by the tige from being crushed; secondly, that the powder is fully burned by the time the ball quits the muzzle; and, thirdly, the effect of the form of the ball and its grooves, ("cannelures.") The great influence of these three points is shown in the fact that rifles, formerly loaded with round balls after the old method, when brought into this system unchanged except by the introduction of the tige, acquire greatly increased accuracy and range. Still, one circumstance operates unfavorably on the latter of these two properties—that is, the partial disfiguration of the ball by the rammer, which both changes the point of the ball and forms a rim there more or less marked. This defect has been attempted to be remedied by giving, as in Prussia, to the lower part of the hollow in the rammer-head an increased width. The ball, too, when the cylindrical part is too long, may take too strong a hold on the grooves, when these are somewhat deep, by which the direction of the ball will, indeed, be secured, but the augmented friction will be injurious to the range.

In spite of all attempts to guard against deforming the projectile, it has not yet been attained; and this system must be regarded as that of *constant disfiguration* of the ball, to which all that we have treated of belong, except that of Wild.

While in the system of Thouvenin the ball is forced into the grooves by the aid of the rammer and the tige, the same is effected in that of Minié by the expansive force of the gas, which fills up the cavity of the ball and presses it equally outward. This system does not essentially increase the accuracy, and the range is diminished; but it attains two advantages, viz: a still greater facility of loading, and the preservation of the original form of the ball. An apparent contradiction is here asserted, viz: that, did the disfiguration of the ball not take place, the system of Thouvenin would insure still greater range and accuracy, while the Minié system, in which the ball retains the shape which theoretical principles have assigned to it, gives no greater accuracy, and a range even inferior. The explanation of this anomaly is to be sought in the fact that, in the Minié system, the culot does not always correctly fulfill its functions, but is separated from the ball at the moment of loading; or else, being turned edgeways, causes the total loss of the shot. The diminished range may be accounted for by supposing that a portion of the gas escapes before the ball has completely filled the grooves. These defects were sought to be remedied, in Belgium, in the ball of Timmerhans, and in a great degree successfully; but still the charge had to be augmented nearly eight grains.

A further peculiarity of this system consisted in the progressive grooves, which were not, however, indispensable, since grooves of the shallow and rounded kind gave the same result, namely: a certain and easy filling of them.

The system of Wilkinson was founded on principles similar to those of Minié, in effecting the filling of the grooves through the action of the gases; not, however, as in the latter, by pressure from the interior outwards, but by pressure from behind on the conical part, the cylindrical part being provided with deep grooves, which permitted its constituent rings to move forwards, before the inertia of the solid anterior part was overcome. Thus much is evident, from the experiments at Enfield and in Austria, that arms of this system surpass nearly every other in accuracy, range, and penetration. Ease of loading, security against crushing the powder, and preservation of the figure of the ball, are in this, as in Minié's system, prominent principles. The Swiss system fulfills, in an equal degree, all the requirements of an excellent arm for service. The loading is here effected with as little difficulty as in the other systems, the ball being shoved down to a given point only, so as to leave a space between the powder and the ball; but the filling of the grooves is effected differently. As in the system of Thouvenin, it is accomplished by the aid of the rammer; in those of Minié and Wilkinson, by the operation of the gas on the ball; so it is here brought about by the use of a greased patch, which surrounds the lower part of the ball. This system also differs from the others in having a remarkably small caliber. These peculiarities are by no means detrimental to the effectiveness of the weapon, since, in the qualities of accuracy, range, and penetration, it excels all systems yet reduced to practice, without a resort to excessive charges or high elevation. On the contrary, in the latter respect it has the advantage of the other systems, as will be seen from the table at page 217.

There remains, finally, the breech-loading system, including the French wall piece, the Norwegian breech-loading, and the Prussian needle gun, all of which differ materially from each other in their mechanism; the first two having the ordinary percussion cap, whilst the latter is fired by means of a needle, which enters the priming. This system differs from all the foregoing, in that the ball is first forced into the barrel by the gases. It is decidedly the easiest and most expeditious in loading, and equals that of Thouvenin in accuracy and range. The only disfiguration that the ball suffers, is the elongation which the cylindrical part undergoes by its forcible entry into the bore, which is of little consequence.

In all the recent systems where they have not been ingrafted on old arms, there has been a diminution in the inclination of the grooves formerly deemed necessary, except in the Prussian needle gun, the Swiss stutzer, and Jäger rifle, as also the Mecklenburg-Thouvenin rifle.

CONCLUSION.   223

...ing table, in which the twist of the grooves is given in degrees, will present
...ination of various arms more clearly, as the length and caliber of the bore must
...sidered:

Arms.	Length of barrel without breech-pin screw.	Caliber.	Grooves in—		
			Parts of a circle.	Degrees.	
	Inches.	*Inches.*		°	′ ″
English oval rifle	29.369	0.850	⅓₃	9	42 46.9
Enfield-Pritchett rifle	38.335	0.577	¼	19	17.5
Swedish marine breech-loading arm	35.614	0.514	¼	15	10.9
French tige rifle, 1846	33.512	0.704	⅕	14	49.3
Belgian Minié musket	41.432	0.694	⅓	13	17.7
Oldenburg tige musket	38.418	0.675	¼	11	1.7
Saxon rifle-musket	29.637	0.576	¼	10	49.8
English Minié musket	36.330	0.700	¼	10	36.9
Belgian tige rifle	33.227	0.692	¼	10	27.3
Spanish Minié rifle	29.447	0.597	¼	10	11.4
Prussian wallpiece	39.941	0.700	⅓	6	46.3
Norwegian breech-loading gun	26.540	0.651	¼	59	48
Swiss stutzer	31.491	0.453	⅛	56	51
Swiss Jäger rifle	31.491	0.453	⅛	56	51
Hanoverian 7-grooved tige rifle	39.435	0.617	¼	56	30.4
Brunswick oval rifle	29.100	0.625	¼	56	6
Nassau tige and Minié musket	38.505	0.699	¼	47	22.8
Bersaglieri carbine	27.364	0.665	⅓	48	58.6
Austrian chamber rifle	25.112	0.713	¼	43	19.4
Luxembourg tige rifle	30.034	0.568	¼	34	6.1
Prussian tige rifle	26.902	0.576	⅓	33	7.5
Mecklenburg rifle musket	37.412	0.597	1/638	31	43
Hanoverian 8-grooved tige rifle	27.947	0.617	¼	30	25.4
Old Bavarian tige stutzer	25.443	0.566	¼	29	45.2
Prussian needle gun	36.084	0.607	⅛	6	17.5
Russian 2-grooved rifle for pointed ball	30.795	0.699	¼	7	59 10.0

The ratio of the weight of the powder to that of the ball has also been much diminished, with advantage to the range of the rifled arm. As, however, accuracy and range are not dependent on system alone, but, besides the groove and the charge, on the figure of the ball also, we will, in conclusion, examine this part of the subject somewhat more minutely. For this purpose it will be necessary to ascertain the deviation caused by the resistance of the air on the various forms of balls.

The shapes to be examined are, first, the *cylinder*, or the bullet, as it becomes disfigured by the old method of loading; second, the purely spherical ball, as it occurs in the system of Wild; third, the conical, which, since the introduction of pointed balls, has been often adopted; fourth, that formed by the intersection of two arcs of circles; and, fifth, the parabolic form, as used in Prussia in the needle gun, and in Saxony.

Every ball, when fired, encounters a certain resistance from the air, which retards its velocity and influences its range. With equal velocities this resistance depends—

First. On the greatest cross-section perpendicular to the axis of the ball.

Second. On the figure on the pointed part.

Third. On the shape of the portion in rear of that cross-section.

In reference to the first point it must be assumed, in the comparison of any two balls, that the greatest cross-section, as also the caliber, is alike in the two. The consideration of the third point, it having formerly been discussed, may be omitted here, provided it does not materially interfere with the normal position of the ball, for the resistance of the air is assumed as being exerted in directions parallel to the longer axis of the ball. We may, then, address ourselves to the consideration of the second point.

The passage of the ball through the air necessarily infers that every particle of air lying in the path of the ball is thrust out of place; and this takes place at a certain angle with the surface of the ball. According to the law of impact of elastic bodies, the angle at which the particles of air leave the surface of the tapering part of the ball will be equal to the angle at which they impinge on it. These deflected particles of air will form themselves into conical fascicles, the axes of which will be the element of greatest deviation, the other divergent elements of each fascicle collecting around this one.

Each impinging element of air is reflected in this way, and the more the axes of the several fascicles of elements diverge from each other, the more easily the deflected elements escape, and the less will be resistance of the air. The greatest divergence exists when the axes of the fascicles, or their greatest deviations, produced to the rear, meet at a single point. This condition requires the paraboloid.

Before entering further on the consideration of these deviations it may be remarked that it will conduce to a clearer conception, and will not affect the result, to consider the ball at rest, and the air moving in parallel lines against it.

Let us now examine the different figures of balls for the purpose of ascertaining in what manner the deviation happens.

The cylindrical ball, (Fig. 107.) The ball is disfigured by the ramming so that its upper surface is flat; the elements of air will here be received at an angle of 90°, and the reflection occurring according to the law of impact of elastic bodies, it will be at the same angle. No deviation can here occur but the elements are reflected back in the same direction in which they approached, producing a continually increasing compression of the air, which, on account of its elasticity, yields, but presents to the ball such a resistance as it would encounter if moving in a denser medium.

The round ball, (Fig. 108.) In this case the element impinging on the apex of the ball will alone be reflected at the angle of 90° and return upon its path; the remaining currents will have different angles of incidence, and corresponding angles of reflection. Some of these deviations prolonged backwards will meet in a point on the axis; these belong to elements at the same distance from the apex. The elements c and c^1, for example, have the point of intersection of their deviations produced back c^a c^2 at v; g and g^1 at x; h and h^1 at y, and so forth. These points of intersection it is seen do not all lie together, since the deviation lying nearest to the greatest diameter, as l^a, l^2, meet at z, outside of the ball; whilst the deviations of the elements lying next to the apex meets at a distance of half the radius ($\frac{1}{2}$ r) from the apex, as the deviations b^a, b^2, c^a, c^2, show, which all meet in v. Hence it is that all the elements incident in the vicinity of the apex are rather thrown back than deflected, and produce a compression of the air calculated to increase the resistance. This resistance is, however, the same in every position of the spherical ball.

The law of reflection for the incident elements from the surface of the ball is the same for all balls of pointed form or curved sides.

The conical ball, (Fig. 109.) Here, too, as in the round ball, all the reflected elements produced back meet on the axis, and all under the same angle. Hence they are all parallel to each other, and, indeed, the angle is the same as that of the conical point itself. Let A B C be

the cone, a B its axis, $d\,k$ an incident element, $d^2\,k$ its reflection, $k\,z$ its prolongation backwards, we shall then have the following relation between the angles:
$$d^2 z a = d k z$$
$$= d k \text{B} + \text{B} k z$$
And as $\text{B}\,k\,z = \text{A}\,k\,d^2 = d\,k\,\text{B}$
We have $d^2\,z\,a = 2\,d\,k\,\text{B} = \text{A B C}$.

The parallel deviations demonstrate that here there is no interference among the reflected elements. The conical shape will therefore separate the incident elements of the air more easily, but the reflected ones will accumulate and increase the pressure on the sides.

The ball formed by the intersection of two arcs of circles (Fig. 110) fulfills the condition of greatest dispersion of the air currents better than either of the other two, though not equally with the paraboloid, since a part of the reflected elements produced backwards fall on the inside and part on the outside of the ball. These last correspond to the deviated elements l^2, l^2, which meet in the point y; while all the rest fall on the inside, but have various points of intersection, according to their position, unlike the round ball, where most of the elements incident near the apex met in a point $\frac{1}{2}\,r$ distant.

The paraboloid (Fig. 111) fulfills in the highest degree every requisite, as here all the deviated elements produced backward form focal lines, and unite at the focus x. This form also secures the greatest divergence of the deflected air currents, and consequently the least opposition from the resistance of the air.

Let us now look at a ball which, having been discharged, from any circumstance assumes a position different from its normal position with reference to the trajectory. It will be seen that the round ball disfigured into a partial cylinder (Fig. 112) reflects the incident elements of air from its flattened top in lines parallel to its axis, whilst the elements falling on the parts remaining spherical follow the law of the sphere, and those incident on the inclined sides are reflected as in the cone; and that a greater volume of air opposes the body than when the ball retains its normal position.

The position of the spherical ball which has not been injured in loading, whatever that position may be, will not increase the resistance of the air, which will always oppose one half of the surface, and the reflection of the elements will occur as already ascertained. (Fig. 113.)

The situation of the pointed ball is much worse, (Fig. 114,) since it receives a much greater number of impinging elements on its inclined side. These will still be reflected in parallel lines, but at an angle greater than that of the point, by the angle contained between the axis prolonged and the element incident at the point; while on the opposite side the angle of reflection is less than the angle of the point of the ball by the same quantity. Under these circumstances a ball of this kind will increase its deviation if it be not corrected by grooves on its cylindrical part.

The ball formed of two intersecting arcs, the point of which has been uninjured in loading, (Fig. 115,) is less affected by deviation from its normal position, though such deviation must always be injurious; and this because the reflection of the elements follows the rules already laid down for a figure of this kind; and from the greater dispersion of the reflected elements the ball encounters less resistance, which permits it the more readily to assume its normal position under the influence of its grooves.

Still more favorable is the situation of the ball with parabolic point, (Fig. 116,) since the divergence of the reflected elements is still greater, which arises from the circumstance that the elements deflected in the vicinity of the apex, produced to the rear, will still meet at the focus, even in the oblique position of the ball. Here also the return to the normal position is easier.

The balls designated by figures 114, 115, and 116, have, by more or less ramming, received a rim toward the bottom of the pointed part, which cannot but be injurious to the range, since it encounters air currents which are thrown back, as in the case of the flattened ball. (Fig. 112.)

Much more advantageous are those balls which undergo no alteration of their primitive shape in the loading, as is the case with the expanding ball of Minié and the compression ball of Wilkinson. Theory and practice are not in opposition here.

The novel expedient of filling the grooves of the ball, the design of which is, as we have stated, to keep the missile in its normal position in reference to the trajectory through the effect of atmospheric resistance, with a mixture of tallow and wax, was resorted to for the purpose of greasing the bore at each discharge, and preventing the accumulation and hardening of the dirt in it. The object was, however, not entirely attained in the arms of the Thouvenin system, which, after fifteen to twenty rounds, became so foul as to be unreliable. Few services retained the practice, but effected the same end of greasing the barrel by the Belgian method of dipping the end of the cartridge which envelopes the cylindrical part of the ball into grease and inserting it with the ball. If the influence of the grooves of the ball be not overrated, they are undoubtedly of service in diminishing the deviation of the ball from its normal position, provided such deviation be not the effect of one-sided ramming, or of unequal guidance as the ball leaves the muzzle.

As the charge must be considered in relation to the ball, its weight being in a great measure determined from that of the ball, and as its influence on the angles of elevation is essential, a few words in conclusion on this subject will not be out of place.

A charge of considerable strength seems always to be advisable for a service arm, so that the ball may receive the force and velocity it requires to attain its object without a resort to undue elevations. These necessarily cause very curved trajectories for the greater distances, and are in all respects objectionable. With diminished elevations the path of the ball is less curved, and its effective range at the height of a man is greater, which range is proportionately increased for the height of cavalry. The influence of error in the estimate of distances, as also that of disturbed aim, is less sensible than with arms the trajectory of which is much curved. It must also be remembered that the soldier in time of excitement, disturbed and hurried, is not in a condition to pronounce accurately on distances, and omits for the same reason to take the proper elevation. In both cases an effective charge comes to his assistance. It is of course to be presumed that the charge is not so heavy as by its recoil to render the firing fatiguing and uncertain.

The force of the charge is under all circumstances to be regulated by the weight of the ball and the length of its cylindrical part. The latter may be disproportionately long, which developes increased friction, and this in turn requires increased expenditure of force to effect the rotation. As to the first point, viz: the relation to the weight of the ball, it is to be one fourth, or at least one sixth of the latter—the proportion best calculated to produce the lowest elevations. (The weights of balls and charges are compared in the following table of elevation, page 227.)

The charge is also dependent on the kind of ball, all experiments having shown that the Minié kind requires an increased charge, which is explained on the supposition that a part of the gas escapes before the grooves can be filled.

In the annexed table of elevations of various arms whose angles it was possible to estimate correctly, it appears that those arms which, like the Swiss and Saxon, have the smallest elevations, have, aside from any consideration of form, the heaviest charges in proportion to the weight of the ball, while those of greater elevation, like the French and Belgian, present the opposite relation. The Belgian Minié musket shows, besides, the influence of the form of the ball (Fig. 95 *a*) on the height of the angles of sight. At 200, 400, and 500 paces they were higher than those of the Belgian tige rifle; at 600 equal, and at greater distances considerably less:

CONCLUSION. 227

ELEVATIONS.

Distance in paces.	Jäger rifle.	Pfutzer.	Saxon tige rifle.	Prussian tige rifle.	Oldenburg tige musket.	Tige rifle.	Minié musket.	Minié musket.	French tige rifle.		
100									150 metres =	204.9 verges	0 35 38
200	0 13 30	0 14 19	0 26 36	0 27 26	0 31 31	0 44 49		38	300 "	372.1 "	0 48 10
300	0 22 31	0 23 43		0 50 49	0 43 37				300 "	409.5 "	1 16 54
400	0 33 1	0 31 15	0 30 36	1 11 36	1 13 15	1 1 41			400 "	546.2 "	1 37 18
500	0 46 32	0 45 27		1 43 20	1 40 29	1 24 36			500 "	693.6 "	2 1 22
600	0 57 2	1 1 4	1 34 37	2 07 19	2 4 1	1 50 23		15	600 "	810.3 "	2 44 11
700	1 13 30	1 16 41		2 7 34		2 20 47	7		700 "	925.0 "	3 04 43
800	1 20 3	1 20 40				2 46 40	4 29		800 "	1,092.4 "	4 10 21
900		1 50 10				3 21 10		4	900 "	1,229.04 "	5 2 48
1,000	2 7 20	2 7 20				4 5 16	5 31		1,000 "	1,385.05 "	6 2 24

	Grains.	Grains.	Grains.	Grains.	Grains.	Grains.	Grains.		Grains.		
Weight of charge	61.72	61.72	76.89	55.31	55.31	61.72	64.65		61.42		
Weight of ball	253.85	253.85	356.74	385.88	431.73	740.64	709.10		733.21		

APPENDIX.

EXPERIMENTS IN SWITZERLAND.

The commission intrusted with the improvement of the Swiss stutzer, under the direction of Colonel Fr. Müller, began experiments for this purpose in 1847 with various rifles. The scope of these experiments embraced not only the caliber and weight of the arm, but extended also to the comparative value of round and elongated balls. The rifles put on trial were, first, the Sardinian Bersaglieri rifle; second, the French *carabine à tige* of 1846; third, the French wall piece; fourth, the French Jäger; fifth, the stutzer of Wild; sixth, a Prussian rifle; seventh, a Bernese pattern stutzer; eighth, one from Uri; ninth, one from Glarus; tenth, a rifle with a tige, from Lepage, of Paris; eleventh, a Bernese stutzer, old pattern, with tige.

The results obtained clearly gave the greatest advantage to the pointed over the spherical ball in the qualities of accuracy and penetration, especially at great distances, the ratio being two to one with but half the charge.

In consequence of these very favorable results the commission decided on diminishing the weight of the stutzer. For further experiments, therefore, two new stutzers were fabricated after dimensions given by them; one with a tige breech-pin without a chamber, the other without tige and with a chamber. The cartridge was to be substituted for the powder-horn, and the loading with patching preserved, as it also appeared probable that the tige did not effect the filling of the grooves fully and with certainty.

For further investigation on these points, the commission again assembled in 1848, and tried the following rifles:

1. Both the stutzers, fabricated in 1847, according to the views of the commission, with a caliber corresponding to a round ball weighing twenty-four to the pound, Swiss, (322 grains.)
2. An American rifle, with balls fifty-seven to the pound, (135 grains.)
3. An Austrian chamber rifle, with balls fifteen to the pound, (488 grains.)
4. A stutzer from Appenzell, a modification of the American system, with balls sixty to the pound, (129 grains.)
5. A similar one from Aargau, with balls forty-eight to the pound, (161 grains.)
6. A stutzer from Vaud, the ball conical, and thirty-one to the pound, (249 grains.)
7. The Wild Jäger rifle of Würtemburg.
8. As the commission had convinced itself, in the progress of the experiments, of the inferior value of the American rifle—a stutzer barrel fabricated for the purpose, with a caliber smaller than the two first-named models, the ball for which had two belts and weighed thirty-one to the pound, (274 grains.)

In these experiments, too, the great accuracy of the pointed ball was manifest, even in the smaller calibers, especially the American rifle.

The commission at the same time made the important observation that the elongated ball loses much less of its initial velocity than the spherical ball, whence its trajectory is much flatter, and its dangerous field much greater. These conclusions are diametrically opposed to those derived from experiments in Sweden in the same year, where it was said that the pointed ball requires a greater elevation for the same distance than the round ball, making the trajectory more curved, and the dangerous field less.

The commission were averse to the introduction of the tige in connection with the prescribed method of loading with a patch; since, in this case, there is less need of spreading the ball into the grooves, as it is already sufficiently confined to its place by the patch. As to the other advantage of the tige—the preventing of the ball from being driven down on the powder—that was at least as effectually secured by the shoulder on the rammer as practiced in Wild's system. The latter method was, therefore, recommended by the commission.

At 400 paces, 328 yards, all the arms tried, with the exception of the Austrian chambered rifle, which was somewhat behind, gave eighty per cent. hits at a target eight feet square. At 600 paces, 492 yards, the hits were seventy per cent., except with the Wild rifle, which gave only twenty-six per cent. At 700 and 800 paces, 574 and 656 yards, only the stutzers, numbers one and eight, and the American, gave good results, which, at 900 paces, 738 yards, declined to fifty per cent. Except the rifle of Wild and the Austrian chambered rifle all fired pointed balls.

At 200 paces, 163¼ yards, the penetration was tried on sheet-iron plates, in which the stutzers, numbers one and eight, proved themselves the best, the execution of the American being small. At 400 and 500 paces, 330 and 410 yards, the fire of the pointed balls on fir plank was still effective, the stutzers just named penetrating through three inch boards, and the American through two. The round balls had no effect. The bullets of an infantry musket had no greater force at 200 paces than the pointed ball, with one half the charge, had at 500 paces.

In consequence of these favorable results the commission decided on the adoption of stutzers, number one and eight, with balls of twenty-eight to the pound, (275 grains;) and for further trial and actual service the same models were distributed to the several cantons.

The many opinions expressed *pro* and *con* on the subject caused the commission to be reassembled in 1849, as well for further proof of their own models as for the trial of new ones sent in by some of the cantons.

These arms were:

1. The approved federal stutzer, number eight of 1848, with balls twenty-eight to the pound, part with two grooves, part with one groove.

2. A pattern from Zurich, with balls thirty-nine to the pound, (188 grains,) with one groove.

3. A pattern from Thurgau, with balls thirty-two to the pound, (174 grains,) with a drift to load with.

4. Two stutzers, from Lucerne, one of which differed from the federal model, chiefly in having a smaller inclination to the grooves, which diminished twist turned out to be injurious in the sequel, and the other had a caliber between that of the federal stutzer and that of the one from Zurich; one turn of the grooves occurred in three and a half feet, and there were three balls of different length of cylinder, each with three "cannelures."

5. A stutzer from Zug, with balls thirty-seven to the pound, 208 grains, with three "cannelures."

6. Three stutzers of Colonel Bruderer, two with calibers larger than the one before submitted by him—the number four of 1848—the third of the caliber of the aforesaid American rifle, with a turn in three feet and two inches.

7. A stutzer of Major Noblet, with one turn in six feet, which did not approve itself in this respect, the ball having too small a rotation.

The commission having been prevented by the weather from continuing its experiments, reassembled in March, 1850. Meantime Colonel Wurstemberg, president of the commission, had occupied himself in perfecting improved balls for stutzers two and three, which had a common caliber of 0.407 inch. These balls proved themselves in succeeding experiments highly successful. The charge for them was sixty-two grains, and they weighed thirty to the pound. Finally a new barrel was arranged for the Luzerne stutzer, number four, with a caliber of 0.413 inch, and a twist of three feet, which, with the Wurstemberg ball, weighing 213 grains, and the charge of 62 grains, gave such remarkable results, that the commission were unanimously in favor of adopting this new stutzer with the ball in question. It was accordingly designated by the War Department as the model for the new arms with which the federal riflemen were to be supplied.*

As to accuracy, this model, in 1850, gave the following results. Out of 100 rounds, the number of hits were:

At 200 paces, 164 yards, target nearly 8 feet square, 100.
At 200 paces, 164 yards, target nearly 4 feet square, 100.
At 200 paces, 164 yards, target nearly 2 feet square, 100.
At 400 paces, 328 yards, the number of hits was the same.
At 600 paces, 492 yards, target nearly 4 by 6 feet, 97; strong wind.
At 600 paces, 492 yards, target nearly 8 feet high, 100; strong wind.
At 800 paces, 656 yards, target nearly 8 feet square, 100.
At 800 paces, 656 yards, target nearly 4 by 6 feet, 78; and without wind, 90.
At 1,000 paces, 820 yards, target nearly 10 by 13 feet, 100.
At 1,000 paces, 820 yards, target nearly 8 feet square, 96.
At 1,000 paces, 820 yards, target nearly 4 by 6 feet, 66.

With a wind, these latter figures were 92, 86, 58.

The rest of the stutzers tried with the new pointed ball approached more or less nearly to these results; but not so the stutzer and a very light ball. Here, again, it was eminently manifest in practice, that the heavy ball, with equal caliber and charge, is more effective than the light one.

Still more striking is the difference between the cylindro-conical and the spherical ball. The regulation stutzer of Bern, for example, with its round ball of 324 grains, firing 100 rounds, made the following hits:

At 200 paces, 164 yards, at a target nearly 8 feet square, 100.
At 200 paces, 164 yards, at a target nearly 4 feet square, 100.
At 200 paces, 164 yards, at a target nearly 2 feet square, 85.
At 400 paces, 328 yards, at a target nearly 8 feet square, 87.
At 400 paces, 328 yards, at a target nearly 4 feet square, 60.
At 400 paces, 328 yards, at a target nearly 2 feet square, 20.
At 600 paces, 492 yards, at a target nearly 8 feet square, 40.
At 600 paces, 492 yards, at a target nearly 4 by 6 feet, 30.

At still greater distances the results were entirely without value, while the same stutzer, with the cylindro-conical ball, at 600 paces, gave 83 to 100 hits.

A comparison of these results shows that the superiority of the pointed over the round ball was more than double, and it became still more marked with a high wind.

The commission, in their report, say, in reference to the range: "The effective range of the

---

* At the instance of Colonel Wurstemberg the patches used with the stutzer will doubtless soon be abandoned, for various reasons, and will be replaced by a mixture of tallow and wax; at the same time a slight alteration in the fore part of the stutzer ball is also in contemplation. These alterations allowed 380 rounds to be fired from a stutzer, at a temperature of thirty degrees Reaumer, in the space of two days, with the ordinary (not always unobjectionable) powder, without once wiping or washing the barrel, and rendering the loading of the last shot as easy as that of the first.

round ball does not exceed 600 paces, whilst that of the pointed ball extends as far as the eye of the marksman can distinguish his object; beyond which the proper use of small arms ceases."

This stutzer model confirmed the important observation previously made as to the flatter trajectory of the pointed ball. The greatest height of the trajectory for a range of 600 paces, (492 yards,) with the new model, was 8½ feet; whilst that of the round ball, at the same distance, was 17¾ to 18¾ feet; according to which the height of the trajectory of the one is more than double that of the other. (Fig. 117.)

These experiments further showed, quite as clearly, that when the ball is driven into the grooves without a patch, as in the Austrian chambered and Sardinian sharp-shooting rifles, it causes diminution of symmetry and accuracy. The elevations required for the different distances with the stutzers were:

For 400 paces, (328 yards,) 35'; 600 paces, (492 yards,) 1° 3'; 800 paces, (656 yards,) 1° 38'; 1,000 paces, (820 yards,) 2° 9'.

The penetration of these arms was as follows:

At 800 paces, the ball traversed five inch fir boards; at 1,000 paces, three of the same, and stuck in the fourth; while at 500 paces the American rifle penetrated only three boards, and the Wild rifle only one board.

The French tige rifle of 1846, according to practice at St. Omer, traversed five poplar boards 0.862 inch thick, at 800 paces, (656 yards,) the total thickness of which was 4.25 inches; while, as we have seen above, the ball of the federal stutzer of the model of 1850, at the same distance and with nearly the same charge—the charge of the French being 4½ grammes, and that of the latter 4 grammes—penetrated 5.908 inches.

It is true that poplar is more spongy than fir, but the greater thickness penetrated fully counterbalances this difference. If, now, we contrast the weight of the French ball with that of the stutzer—the first, (733 grains,) being nearly three times that of the latter, (256 grains)—the greater force of impact of the latter becomes apparent.

According to the experiments lately made in Prussia and Denmark, which established that a ball which penetrates an inch board will disable a man, while to pass through him it must penetrate four of the same kind, we may regard the penetration of the stutzer for the distances before given as entirely satisfactory.

At the experiments which are here detailed, over 120 shots could be fired in succession without inconvenience from the dirt, which must be ascribed to the patch and the somewhat shallow and rounded grooves.

The lock of the new stutzer has but one notch in the tumbler, the general opinion being that no middle notch is necessary with the percussion lock, since the hammer, when let down, covers the cone, and consequently, the vent, which was not the case with the flint lock, where the cock, when let down, threw back the battery and uncovered the pan.

RIFLED INFANTRY ARMS.

Initial velocity of the ball.

With the Belgian musket—Weight of ball, 416.61 grains; weight of charge, 146.56 grains musket powder = 448.75 yards.
With the French musket—Weight of ball, 416.61 grains; weight of charge, 140.97 grains musket powder = 491.75 yards.
With the Belgian tige rifle—Weight of ball, 740.69 grains; weight of charge, 61.79 grains fine powder = 337.96 yards.
With the French tige rifle—Weight of ball, 732.16 grains; weight of charge, 69.43 grains fine powder = 341.12 yards.
With the Belgian Minié musket—Weight of ball, 540.05 grains; weight of charge, 77.15 grains fine powder = 313.24 yards.

The *recoil*, expressed in terms of the initial velocity, that a ball would have which was animated with the quantity of motion the recoil imparts to the gun is, for the Belgian musket, 682 yards; for the tige gun, 406½ yards; for the Minié gun, 376½ yards.

According to recent experiments in Switzerland, made by Colonel Wurstenburg, with the assistance of a dynamometer, the mean recoil of ten shots with the following arm is:

The Minié gun, with ball & culot	46.31 pounds.
The French percussion musket	46.31 pounds.
The French carbine, for the chasseurs à pied	45.10 pounds.
The Enfield-Pritchett rifle	39.49 pounds.
The federal Jäger rifle	35.09 pounds.
The federal regulation stutzer, (according to the weight of the ball)	33.44 pounds. / 34.76 pounds.

TABLE I.

Experiments made at the National Armory in Belgium to compare the fusil de munition, the carabine à tige, and the fusil Minié.

www.ingramcontent.com/pod-product-compliance
Lightning Source LLC
Chambersburg PA
CBHW020801230426
43666CB00007B/791